THE CELTS

STORY

THE CELTS

A HISTORY

DÁITHÍ Ó HÓGÁIN

The Collins Press

Published in 2002 by
The Collins Press
West Link Park
Doughcloyne
Wilton
Cork

Reprinted 2006

Published in Britain by The Boydell Press
The Boydell Press is an imprint of Boydell and Brewer Ltd
PO Box 9, Woodbridge, Suffolk IP12 3DF, UK
ISBN: 1-0 85115 920

British Library Cataloguing in Publication Data
Ó hÓgáin, Dáithi
The Celts: A history
1. The Celts
I. Title
936.4

ISBN-10 1905172206
ISBN-13 978-1905172206

Typesetting and design: Stuart Coughlan at edit+

Cover photographs:
Front: Bronze head of th[...] [Musé]e des Antiquités
Nationales, Saint-Germ[...]
Back: Roman copy of a s[...] [w]arrior, mid-third
century BC. Now in Mu[...]

CONTENTS

And the tall men
and the swordsmen
and the horsemen,
where are they?

- W.B. Yeats

do Chaitríona, dom chlann, agus dom chairde

LIST OF PLATES

The publishers would like to thank the following who have kindly given permission to reproduce the illustrations listed above.
Cover, back, 3, 6, 7, courtesy of AKG, London, photos; Erich Lessing; 1 courtesy of The Society of Antiquaries of London; 2 courtesy of Landesdenkmalampt, Baden-Württemberg, Stuttgart; 4 courtesy of Muzeul National de Istorie a Romãnieie, Bucharest; 5 courtesy of Nationalmuseet, Copenhagen; 9 courtesy of the Ashmolean Museum, Oxford; 8, 11, 14, 15 courtesy of BSK, Dublin, photos; Brian Kelly; 12, 13 courtesy of the British Museum, London, photos; Peter A. Clayton; 16 courtesy of the National Museum of Scotland, Edinburgh; 17 courtesy of the National Library of Wales, Aberystwyth; 18 courtesy of Trinity College Library, Dublin.

LIST OF MAPS

Preface

The Celts were one of the most important population groups in ancient Europe, and this is a general survey of their military fortunes. The power of the Celtic peoples expanded greatly for some centuries, and then contracted to an even greater degree, so that their civilisation almost disappeared. Only in the west did their culture survive. For the early history of the Celts we are almost totally dependent on Greek and Latin literature, supplemented by information gleaned from archaeological studies. Since the Greeks and Romans were in conflict with the Celts, the accounts which have come down to us are almost all of a hostile character, and this should be borne in mind. If independent accounts of their early history were available from the Celts themselves, the picture would surely be altered to no small extent. As it is, our only approach can be to present the available information in systematic form, and to attempt to analyse it in order to get as accurate an understanding as possible of the situation. From the sixth century in Ireland, and from Wales soon afterwards, native Celtic literary sources do become available, and these are collated with other data in continuing the story to the medieval period, with which the book concludes.

This trip through the greater part of 2,000 years is in many ways a sad and tragic one, but it is an essential component of the overall story of Europe, and provides a vista on an aspect of European heritage which is not widely known. The description is as specific as circumstances allow, with an attempt to follow a chronological pattern. Where these only are available, names of Celtic personages and places are given in the forms attested by the Greek and Latin writers, forms which do not always accord exactly with the pronunciation used by the Celts themselves. The symbol * indicates forms of words which are not directly attested, but which have been reconstructed from comparative linguistics.

Dáithí Ó hÓgáin,
I SAMHRADH NA BLIANA 2002

1

ORIGIN AND CULTURE OF THE CELTS

Archaeological remains provide our only clues to the peoples who inhabited the Europe of several thousands of years ago, and to the kinds of lives which they led. As the Stone Age drew to a conclusion towards the end of the third millennium BC, a variety of population groups inhabited that large area, representing what must have been a range of different languages and cultures. The spread and contraction of these populations was influenced not least by new influxes of peoples from the east, and the most notable of these must have been the speakers of dialects which scholars term 'Indo-European' – that is, dialects of a foundation language which originated somewhere on the southern border of Europe and Asia and was spreading eastwards and south-eastwards into Asia and westwards into Europe.

Their most developed groups were the Hittite empire in Asia Minor, and the Minoan-Mycenaean civilisation of the Aegean which developed into the Greek culture. From these the use of bronze spread gradually into all areas of Europe and, as the power of the two peoples declined towards the end of the second millennium BC, the archaeological record shows the growth in wealth and prestige of further newcomers into other parts of Europe. The dialects spoken by these various groups were also Indo-European, developing in time into languages such as Dacian and Thracian west of the Black Sea, Slavic and Baltic in the northeast,

Germanic towards the North Sea, and Italic and Illyrian towards the Mediterranean and the Adriatic. All of these were settling among earlier indigenous populations and – though less numerous – were gradually extending their power and influence over them.

Beginnings

One of the indigenous populations are known to archaeologists as the 'Tumulus People', domiciled in the area immediately north of the Alps, and so called from the impressive barrows which they built over their dead leaders. In a broad area to the north of these again were the 'Urnfield People', who cremated their dead and placed the bones in urns in flat cemeteries. This cremation culture coincided with the advance of eastern groups into the centre of the Continent, and from there to the south and the west. These movements, indeed, appear to have been synonymous with the spread of Indo-European dialects, and the strong suggestion therefore is that the most influential element among the Urnfielders spoke these dialects.

Around the year 1,000 BC the Tumulus and Urnfield cultures joined in the Danube Basin, giving rise to strong groupings of communities in that whole region. A particularly powerful amalgam soon came to the fore in the western part of the region, speaking the Indo-European dialect which may be termed 'proto-Celtic'. These must have established themselves by military supremacy, but it is unlikely that they were originally the majority population in the centre of Europe. That these original Celts were a warlike people is evidenced by the number of weapons, particularly swords, which they buried with their dead; and this probably accounts for their name also. Comparative linguistics indicate that the designation 'Celt' comes from an Indo-European root *kel* (meaning 'to strike'). The Greek writer Pausanius, apparently quoting Hieronymus of Cardia who lived in the fourth century BC, states that 'originally they were called Celtoi, both by themselves and by all other peoples'.

The basic meaning of the term Celts therefore appears to have been 'warriors', and was probably used by themselves as a laudatory term reflecting their success in overcoming other peoples and spreading their power. That success was largely the result of the widespread use of the horse, which gave the early Celts a great advantage in both trading and fighting. In the eighth and seventh centuries BC they expanded into territories with a much wider radius than their original homeland.

Groups of them spread their range further through what is now southern Germany and western Austria, and others penetrated into the border region between modern Switzerland and France. Once they settled in an area, they lost no time in establishing themselves firmly there. Their military concerns, for instance, are reflected by the large amount of hill forts constructed and maintained by them. These fortifications must have been intended more for maintaining power over local subjects than for security against attack by marauding strangers.

Some of the attitudes of these early Celts can be learned from their burials. Combinations of bronze cremation urns with bronze swords represent the burials of chieftains, reflecting their warrior ambitions, while the remains of four-wheeled wagons and fine pottery would indicate a belief in a journey to be undertaken to the afterlife. This complex is most clearly represented in a grave chamber at Hart an der Alz in Upper Bavaria, dating from the tenth century BC. Non-cremated burials within large tumuli soon came to the fore as a special distinction for very powerful lords, and by the eighth century BC weapons of iron began to appear.

The most celebrated Celtic burials were discovered at Hallstatt, situated by a lakeside to the south-west of modern Salzburg in Austria. Large-scale salt-mining took place there, and as a result Hallstatt became the most important trading centre north of the Alps. This economic wealth was undoubtedly reflected in political power and cultural influence, and as a result Hallstatt-type burials became the standard in the area of southern Germany and western Bohemia in the seventh and sixth centuries BC. In these burials, the body is not burnt, but lies on a wagon – often within a specially constructed wooden chamber. The dead leader is furnished with iron swords and spears, as well as pottery, cups, knives, and joints of beef and pork. The latter items show that it was believed that he would continue to feast in the afterlife, as in this world. There are indications, indeed, that the ceremonies attending the interment of a chieftain included a funerary feast at the tumulus.

The increasing centralisation of power within strong kindred groups is indicated by multiple burials in tumuli at this time. These had elaborate grave goods, including women's ornaments. Reflecting their hierarchical type of society, the tumuli of these great early Celtic chieftains were often surrounded by single graves of warriors, each warrior buried with his long sword. We are dependent solely on archaeological data for the early centuries of Celtic culture, but it is clear that the power of these warlords extended along the valley of the upper Danube from the bend of the Rhine through Swabia, Bavaria, and northern Austria, and into much of Bohemia. The eastern Celts were dominant initially, for a series of great hill forts bears witness to their strength in that broad region. These include the Heuneburg, south of modern Hundersingen in Swabia; the Hohenasperg, north of modern Stuttgart; and several others of comparable importance in Switzerland.

The centre of gravity was, however, shifting gradually from the east to the west, which culminated a hundred years later in the situation whereby Herodotus could refer to 'the country of the Celtoi' as the area where the Danube rises. This shift was largely due to the decreased room for ambition in one quarter and the increased room in the other. The growth of Scythian power had pushed more Dacian and Thracian peoples into the Hungarian plains, while the resurgence of Greek and Macedonian power left the Illyrians with no alternative but to withstand Celtic pressure at all costs. In real terms, this meant that the Celts had far less hope of development eastwards than towards the territories in western Europe which were more weakly defended. These territories were inhabited by various Indo-European groups which had earlier settled there and by long-established pre-Indo-European peoples.

Another important factor was the improvement of trade routes in the west. Items found with the burials provide evidence of an increase in the importation of prestige goods from the Mediterranean cultures. Bronze weapons, as well as helmets and leg armour from Greece, were in high demand among the Celts. These were mostly imported through the Greek colony, which had been established at Massalia (Marseilles) around 630 BC, before the arrival of the Celts in that immediate area. Elaborate pottery was also acquired from the Massaliots, as well as beaked flagons of high quality and other bronze utensils from the Etruscans in Italy. Along with such ware, the most significant import was wine, which was used for aristocratic feasts. Commerce over the Alpine passes flourished, and for their part the Celts traded cattle, slaves, and apparently also gold – which was readily available to the most powerful families from alluvial deposits on the banks of the Rhine, the Danube and the Otava.

Wider expansion

Land-hunger and competition caused various pushes by powerful groups of Celts all along their western flank. One of the most significant pushes was in a north-westerly direction, along the Rhine, by a group, or conglomeration of groups, which occupied both sides of that river at the confluence of the Moselle some time in the early seventh century BC. They were powerful enough to dominate the indigenous peoples, displacing some and assimilating others.

The migration of these Celts was an extension of the old Hallstatt culture, and they extended their power over a substantial area, stretching from the Rhine almost to the Seine. They were led by a number of dominant families, who invested a great deal in their prestige and in their status as conquerors, as shown by their elaborate dwellings and burial sites. That these aristocracies, in certain circumstances, aggrandised some of their leading womenfolk as well as their menfolk, is clear from a notable burial from the western verge of their territory, at Vix, near Châtillon-sur-Seine in Burgundy, dating to just before 500 BC. The burial was of a woman of about 35 years old, perhaps a priestess, within a large tumulus. Her body was laid out on a wagon, with a golden diadem on her head, and the grave included also a finely-engraved bronze vessel of Greek origin, as well as bracelets and brooches.

Further south, since the seventh century BC, other ambitious Celtic groups were pushing south-westwards across the river Rhône, encountering an Indo-European group of the Italic branch, the Ligurians, who were already settled in that region and whose archaeological remains exhibit many aspects similar to those of the old Urnfield culture. Seizing territory from them, and no doubt assimilating large sections of them, the newcomers spread into wide areas of eastern and central France. A particularly strong group – the ancestors of the Cubi – occupied territory between the Rhône and the Loire, in the modern French département of Berry. Other groups were crossing the Rhône further south and were pushing the Ligurian tribes towards the Mediterranean. Principal among the newcomers to these southern territories were the ancestors of the Arverni ('superior ones'), who came to predominate over smaller incoming groups in the whole region stretching as far west as the river Garonne.

At an early stage – possibly in or about the same time – some of the Ligurians had crossed the Pyrenees and mingled with the indigenous peoples of north-western Spain. Celtic advances through Ligurian territory brought them as far as the Riviera, where they mingled with the Ligurians, forming tribes which were afterwards known by Celtic names such as Cavari ('giants') and Salluvii ('coastal dwellers'). Some Celts may even have crossed the Pyrenees at this time, but if so they are likely to have done so as a constituent part of the Ligurian sphere of influence.

Important developments were, meanwhile, taking place among the Celts living around the source of the Danube. Iron had been available since the ninth century BC or earlier, and the use of it for weapons had gradually increased. It gave a distinct advantage to its possessors, and it is accepted that the Germanic peoples in the north borrowed their word for iron from the Celtic *isarnon* (meaning 'hard metal'). Large iron-working centres were established between the Alps and the Danube, and these produced – in addition to weapons – a wide variety of tools which greatly increased their technical capacity. There was an increase also in the use of gold and silver for artistic decoration. From the sixth century BC a whole range of new designs, both aesthetic and functional, were developing, as the Celts of that area learned from other peoples and possessed their own master smiths and workshops. This is known as the 'La Tène' era, from the discovery of a large collection of such products at a village of that name on the shores of Lake Neuchâtel in western Switzerland.

Increasing power, wealth and efficiency were thus the hallmarks of the La Tène people. These cultural advances had their own importance, not only in terms of prestige, but also in terms of power politics. For instance, whereas ordinary four-wheeled wagons had been in general use for a long time, an increased use of bronze and iron parts, added to rich decorations, now adorned special wagons for ceremonial use. To render travel and transport more convenient, iron tyres were affixed to the wheels of wagons, and eventually the fast two-wheeled chariots for use in fighting were developed. This kind of chariot – probably patterned on such vehicles used by the Etruscans of north-west Italy – gradually displaced the older vehicles in the burials of chieftains, thus showing its importance to the new élite of leaders.

The La Tène chieftains belonged to the region around the sources of the Rhine and the Danube, reaching as far as the Alps, and they grew particularly rich through having control of the waterways and thus of trade. From that region, their power was spread directly by improved techniques of fighting, and indirectly by their prestige and cultural influence. One notable development in spoken Celtic is likely to have had its origin in the dominant position of this La Tène culture – the sound shift from the voiceless labiovelar kw to the bilabial plosive p. As the technically more advanced La Tène Celts began to extend their influence over a wide area, such pronunciation would have been considered fashionable and would have spread. The older pronunciation – as we shall see – continued in the form of the plosive velar k among Celtic groups who did not come under the immediate influence of the expanding La Tène culture.

Power and competition

In this strongly competitive atmosphere, the balance of power between various kings and chieftains would have fluctuated somewhat, but the Hallstattian chiefdoms had grown top-heavy and their self-indulgent aristocratic families lacked the ability to sustain severe pressure from without. The archaeological record shows a cultural break at the beginning of the fifth century BC to the west of the Rhine, indicating that the displacement of these chiefdoms by La Tène newcomers in that region was largely the result of military conquest. This is the type of development to be expected, not just along the Rhine but eastwards also for some distance along the Danube, for the great migrations from the sixth century BC onwards were carried out by La Tène groups or by groups in which the La Tène element was predominant. The great fortress of Heuneburg, overlooking the Danube, was in fact repeatedly destroyed by fire in the later fifth century BC.

Later writers in Latin describe a situation which must have originated in traditions preserved by the Celts themselves. According to Livy, two very enterprising princes, brothers called Belovesus and Segovesus, who did not themselves possess kingdoms, were sent to 'settle in whatever locality which the gods should by augury assign to them'. It would appear from this that large-scale migrations were regarded by the Celts as ritual acts. The name Belovesus meant 'slaying-knower', and Segovesus meant 'victory-knower', and although these may not have been real historical characters, such prestigious titles would reflect a mythical memory of great leaders.

We read that 'to Segovesus the Hercynian forest was assigned by the oracle, to Belovesus the gods marked out a much more cheering route into Italy'. In other words, the gods preferred that Segovesus should move with his followers towards central Europe, and the more promising prospect of the Po valley was allotted to Belovesus. Not much detail of value can be garnered from such a legendary account. There is a ring of truth, nevertheless, to the statements that these 'two enterprising youths' were allowed to 'take along with them as great a number of men as they pleased, so that no nation might be able to obstruct them in their progress'. A rapid increase in population would have speeded up the movement of ambitious young men away from their native surroundings in order to carve out a new destiny for themselves. In reality, the migrations, which were mythologised in the persons of Belovesus and Segovesus, must have begun in the sixth century BC and continued for well over a hundred years.

This continued movement involved powerful groups radiating out from their homeland north of the Alps in all directions. The tradition of Belovesus going to Italy is probably an echo of how some groups ventured southwards, crossing the Alps through the Gotthard and Bernard passes and dominating the Golasecca culture along the river Adda. Inscriptions in that area, which begin at that time, are written in the Celtic dialect of a people known as Lepontii. These inscriptions reveal little concerning the Lepontic culture, but they show the sound shift of the ancient labiovelar kw to p, thus indicating that this linguistic development was already common north of the Alps. The mixed Celtic-Golaseccan population was subjected by the Etruscans in the early fifth century BC, but the Lepontic dialect flourished in the area for many centuries more.

The most important thrust of all by La Tène migrants was northwards, along the east bank of the Rhine by the selfsame route taken a century earlier by their Hallstatt predecessors. These new and more advanced migrants from the Danube Basin turned westwards and crossed the Rhine midway up the river, skirted the Vosges mountains to the north, and were soon in possession of large swathes of territory. They must have brought with them substantial parts of the population from the Middle Rhine, which enabled them to displace some of the earlier Celts from that region and establish large centres of occupation on the Moselle and the Marne. Being in control of waterways which linked the far north-west of Europe to the rich south, they benefited greatly from trade, and were accordingly enabled to increase their importance and influence in the whole Celtic world.

Thus the earlier Celtic settlers in the region – who must have still retained the labiovelar kw sound in their speech – were largely displaced. Some of them were pushed towards the west – most notably the Senones, whose name may be taken to mean either 'old inhabitants' or 'worshippers of Senos' – 'the ancient one', i.e., the ancestor-deity. Most of the Senones founded a new settlement on the banks of the Yonne, where their centre was Agedincum (now Sens), but many of them broke up into smaller groups and spread into several parts of Gaul. A related group, the *Quariti (later known as Parisii) – whose name meant 'effective ones' or worshippers of the 'effective' deity – were pushed northwards along the Seine, on which they eventually established their centre of Lutecia (now Paris).

Others were pushed to the southeast, such as the Sequani (called after the name of that same river, 'Sequana'), and their relatives the Helvetii ('much-land possessors') who remained in Alsace for several generations before re-crossing the Rhine long after the great Celtic migrations had ceased. All of these peoples were, of course, in time assimilated to the generally prevailing La Tène culture, but the burial custom of the Sequani and Helvetii continued some older Hallstatt-type traits, such as the use of single tumuli rather than the newer cemeteries. In the north, the original Celts had little choice but to seek new territories and thus began to spread westwards and towards the Channel. Their descendants would probably have included the major tribe of Aulerci ('exiles'), whose name can be taken to reflect a dislocation from their original home. A dispersal is also echoed by the designations of Aulerci subgroups – Cenomani ('far removed ones'), Sagii ('seekers') and Diablintes ('untiring ones').

The migration attributed in legend to Segovesus must, in fact, have occurred some generations later than the others. The Celtic power had been weakening in the east in the sixth century BC, and thus the Segovesus migration may encompass the memories of different events, such as a push eastwards by Celts of the upper Danube to colonise that area in their own interests. These movements were spearheaded by the group which became known as Bogii or Boii ('attackers'), who penetrated into the areas controlled by the earlier Hallstatt-type chiefdoms in Bohemia, establishing their dominance over both these and non-Celtic groups. Other tribes, supported by the Boii, took over a large area of territory north-east of the Alps from the Raeti, a people related to the Venetians, a northern Italic population. As they spread their settlements over a still wider region, approaching the Hungarian plain, these La Tène Celts would have encountered further indigenous peoples in the area to the east of the Alps, Illyrian tribes such as the Dardanians and Pannonians, and finally Dacians as they approached the Carpathian Mountains.

The kingship of Ambicatus

The name 'Galatae' was sometimes given by the classical writers to the Celts – especially to those in the east. This was a native Celtic term for warriors, being based on the word gal- ('ability' or 'valour'). The Romans, however, tended to call the Celts by a corruption of this name viz. 'Galli', which slang-form came into increasingly wider usage.

The designation Galli (represented in English as 'Gauls') was in most common usage with regard to the Celtic tribes in the territories of modern-day France and in adjacent areas. This huge region of western Europe was thus known in Latin as Gallia (anglicised as 'Gaul'). The La Tène settlers on the Moselle and Marne were initially the most powerful of the Gauls, with the centre of gravity gradually shifting to those on the Marne. The culture of the Moselle settlers, which flourished at the juncture of that river and the Rhine, was in decline by the end of the fifth century BC; and soon after most of their territory was seized by the Belgae, another Celtic people who had joined in the general spirit of ambition and adventure and were extending their power northwards.

These Belgae must have originated in central Germany, in the general vicinity of the rivers Tauber and Main. They seem to have sprung from warrior cults which had grown up in the vacuum created by the waning of the old Hallstatt chiefdoms. All indications are that the earliest of the Belgae, whose name meant 'furious ones', were less concerned with stability than with adventure. Some of the warriors who led them may even have been descendants of the peripheral Hallstatt chieftains of that area, young men with no inheritance to sustain them but buoyed up by their own fighting qualities. As a developing group, the culture of the Belgae was primitive by comparison with their Celtic cousins – practicing for example cremation and urn burial rather than the elaborate inhumation in tumuli – but they gradually absorbed the dialect and customs of their more influential neighbours. It is very likely that these Belgae were associates of, and perhaps even connected with, the great Volcae tribe which inhabited Bavaria and adjacent areas of southern Germany.

The territories of the Moselle Celts fell to the Belgae, although some of their descendants maintained their identity as separate tribes, most notably the Mediomatrici. This tribal name meant 'between the mothers' – a reference to the rivers of that area and to the goddesses associated with them. Their capital was Divodurum ('divine stronghold', now Metz), and they had another important town on the Meuse called Verodunum (now Verdun). Several other descendants of the Moselle Celts survived deeper in Belgic territory, on both sides of the river Sambre and in the forest of Ardennes – the Treveri, Ceutrones and Eburones seem to have been of that basic stock.

The social system of the Marne Celts, on the other hand, proved more stable. Perhaps strengthened by some survivors of the collapse on the Moselle, these settlers on the Marne gradually attained a dominant position in the whole region, as is clear from their massive *oppidum* called Latisco on Mont Lassois at the source of the Seine. Many of the tribes listed several centuries later in that general region must have descended from the La Tène newcomers, probably indeed from their leading families. Principal among these tribes were the Lingones and the Aedui. The Lingones ('leapers' or 'energetic ones') remained on the Marne, and their centre was the origin of modern Langres. The Aedui derived their name from Aedos, 'fiery one' (a designation of the ancestor or sun deity). They were the most powerful group in all that area, and they extended their power south-westwards. Their chief centre was the great hill fort of Bibracte, meaning 'beaver-place' (now Mont-Beuvray, west of Autun).

The dominance of the Marne chieftains did not last for more than a generation or two, however. Other Celts who had settled beyond the Loire were adopting the La Tène culture and were increasing in strength and influence. Most notable of these were the Cubi, who established a powerful centre which they called Avaricum (modern Bourges). The ascent of this group was attributed by tradition to the leadership qualities of a great king of theirs called Ambicatus. Such was the prestige of this king that he became known to legendary lore as the archetype of a successful ruler, rich and courageous, whose reign was blessed with extremely abundant harvests. This is an echo of an ancient Celtic belief that prosperity attended the rule of a successful king who embodied the ritual quality of 'truth'.

In more realistic terms, the name Ambicatus signified 'he who turns battles', indicating how successful he was in asserting the cause of his tribe in arms and in forcefully advancing their interests. The tribal name Cubi meant 'victors', and they extended their territory until it embraced the whole of central Gaul between the rivers Loire and Vienne. The wealth of this area included particularly rich deposits of iron ore, which was mined extensively by the Cubi and which contributed significantly to the rapid growth of their power. It is probable that Ambicatus was the first to use the title 'Biturix', meaning 'world-king', a reference to the Celtic world which demonstrates that there was still at the time a concept of a single Celtic culture, even though the various power-centres were in effect independent of each other.

An attempt to find a chronology for the reign of Ambicatus would indicate that he flourished around the middle of the fifth century BC. The actual territories held by his tribe must have expanded considerably as a result of his campaigns, by which he achieved a dominant role over neighbouring groups. His career would appear to testify to how old style 'Hallstattian' aggrandisement and centralised rule could be success-fully combined with innovative La Tène technology and efficient man-agement of resources. As a result, his 'world-kingship' meant command of a wide confederacy, of various origins, which included all the major tribes in central Gaul – the Aedui, Lingones and Senones to the east, the Aulerci to the north, and the Arverni to the south. The major extension of the direct rule of Ambicatus' Cubi would appear to have been towards the southwest, for a section of them made their headquarters at Burdigala (now Bordeaux) where they became known as Vivisci.

This latter was derived from the name used for that area by the Ligurians, who had for some centuries been ensconced in southern France and northern Spain, but were now under increased pressure from the Celts. The pressure also effected those Celts who had long been settled in the southwest, and whose culture had been little affected by La Tène fash-ions. There are indeed several indications that it caused significant popu-lation movements among these peoples, such as the Turones and the Lemovices, groups of whom either began or speeded up a trend of Celtic migration across the Garonne into Aquitania. In that region, they encoun-tered Ligurian tribes and then some indigenous non-Indo-European peo-ples such as Basques and Iberians; and, as a result, a mixed culture developed in the south-west of Gaul – the Celtic language and social system being generally dominant in the areas settled by them.

This Celtic influence soon spread through the Pyrenees, and sec-tions of these groups continued their trek by crossing the mountains at some point near to the western coast. Penetrating into the Iberian Peninsula, they passed through Basque territories and put pressure on tribes further to the west and south – Cantabrians, Asturians and Lusitanians, who were largely descended from earlier Indo-European set-tlers. The Celtic incomers established themselves in strong hill forts, which they constructed over a widening area in the centre of the Peninsula and, gradually, in other scattered areas beyond. The usual des-ignation used by them for a hill fort was the Celtic word *briga*, and from the frequent occurrence of this word in toponymics it is clear that the Celtic language came to be widely spoken in these areas. It is probably in reference to these Celtic newcomers that the historian Thucydides cites Alcibiades as proposing to the Spartans, during the Sicilian war in 415 BC, to go to enlist Iberian mercenaries 'and others who are recognised to be the most warlike of the barbarians now there'.

Livy states that the population of Gaul grew so rapidly that, by the time that Ambicatus was an old man, he decided to instruct some of his people to relieve the strain of overcrowding by seeking new settlements far away. Livy states that the migration which followed was regarded as a ritual act, an attitude which would also have characterised the earlier migrations from the original homeland north of the Alps. The practical reason, a population explosion, was of course a repetition of what the Celts had experienced on those earlier occasions. Thus, in later tradition, the situations became confused, and Ambicatus was anachronistically connected with the two legendary brothers Belovesus and Segovesus. Livy and other Latin authors report the belief that the two were sons of Ambicatus' sister, and that it was Ambicatus himself who instructed them to go in search of conquests.

As is clear, however, the migration recommended by Ambicatus was a later and distinct affair. According to Livy, it involved surplus populations from Gaulish tribes in central and eastern areas of France such as from the Arverni, the Senones, the Aedui, and the Aulerci. Although this seems to be a rationalisation by Livy based on the names of the Celtic tribes later attested in northern Italy, it probably echoes the truth, as these would have been the elements most dangerous to Cubi hegemony. It therefore made sense for Ambicatus to urge young warriors to depart from these tribes, and his urging probably combined encouragement with veiled threats. The Gauls had long been aware, through trade contacts and through the Lepontic Celts on the southern side of the Alps, of the riches of Italy, and so that southward direction was the recommended one. If Livy is correct in putting this down to the end of Ambicatus' career, it would appear that this particular migration southwards along the Rhône valley began in the middle of the fifth century BC.

The Celts in the islands

The first written report on the actual geography of western Europe concerns a voyage by Himilco, who sailed around part of the Atlantic coast, shortly before the year 530 BC. He was a Carthaginian, who had been commissioned by the Greek colony at Marseilles to explore the sea routes for them as far as the city of Tartessos (in the vicinity of the Gulf of Cadiz). There his crew were told that some sailors of the Tartessians – an ancient people with a thriving culture in the south of Spain – had actually travelled north along the Atlantic coast, and that one of them had left an account of this. Himilco's actual report was in Greek and, although it is lost, allusions from it were included in a Latin poem written by one Avienus many centuries later. Not all of the references in Avienus' poem are necessarily from Himilco, of course, but even in this unsatisfactory form the text gives a few insights into prehistory.

The image of western Europe given in it is much condensed. It is clear that France was taken to be much shorter from south to north than it really is, the English Channel being considered a virtual continuation of the Bay of Biscay, which in turn was treated as almost synonymous with the Atlantic coast of Spain. The islands beyond (including Britain, whose product of tin is mentioned) are referred to in the text as the 'Oestrymnides', and the area of Brittany and western France in general is called 'Oestrymnis'. A hint at ongoing conquest and displacement of peoples may be given by the reference to how the people of Oestrymnis tilled the soil of their country, but 'after many years a serpent made the cultivators flee'. A definite reference to such displacement occurs in a passage on the Ligurians, whose land is said to be 'tenantless now, and wasted long by bands of Celts and by many a bloody foray'. This could be a confused memory of how the Celts, in their expansion, had pushed the Ligurians from some territory inhabited by them in central France.

The position vis-à-vis Britain and Ireland at the time is more difficult to decipher from the text. Avienus calls Britain 'the broad isle of the Albiones', and the following reference is strikingly accurate:

> Other coasts some distance off, braving the north wind's frosty blast, tower over the waters with their mighty cliffs – twin cliffs they are, with their rich soil clothed in spreading sward, stretching to where in the turbid western sea the Rhine is hidden ...

The reference is obviously to the Cliffs of Dover. Latin speakers considered that these shining cliffs had given their ancient name to the island – *Albiu, which they took to mean 'white place'. Albiu was, however, a long-established Celtic designation for the island, with the simple meaning 'land' or 'country'. Similarly with Ireland, which Avienus refers to as being 'peopled thickly by the Hierni' – this denomination was derived from an old Celtic word *Éveriju, meaning 'land' or 'soil'. The Greeks took the name of the island as Hivera, which in their own language they equated with *hiera*, with a meaning of 'sacred isle'; and thus Avienus refers to the prosperity of Ireland, which lay 'rich in green sward amid the waves'.

In all probability, the two islands were given these names, 'Albiu' and 'Éveriju', by Celts on the Continent and, even if they were not in Himilco's original account, there is every reason to believe that they were in the version of the voyage given by Eratosthenes in the third century BC. Pytheas of Marseilles, who visited Britain about 325 BC, may already have been acquainted with the toponymics, but he collectively called the countries the 'Prettanik' islands. This was derived from the population name Pritani ('those who paint themselves'), by which the whole island of Britain came to be known. The new name indicates that a significant part of the island was at that time under the control of the people who bore it, and these must have been Celts. The designation Pritani itself would appear to have been first applied to the inhabitants of the island by continental Celts.

Some such Pritani must have been in Britain since the sixth century BC, and they would have had some iron implements in addition to the more customary bronze. From lists of British tribes given several centuries later, it is likely that these included the ancestors of such as the Venicones, Selgovae, Corionototae, and Dumnonii. By the following century, more had arrived – including probably the ancestors of the Ordovices and Cornovii. The most important migration to Britain, however, seems to have been a direct result of the spread northwards through Gaul of the 'world' power of the Cubi. Pressure was being exerted on the various tribes of Aulerci who had moved into this area of northern France. One of these tribes, known as Eburovices ('yew-conquerors'), were established near to the mouth of the Seine, and it is apparent that a large number of them crossed the Channel in the early part of the fourth century BC.

Such a strong incursion into Britain would have pushed some of the earlier Celtic groups there towards the north, and others would have been bypassed by the newcomers in their progression northwards. It is therefore likely that these Eburovices were the migrants who, in time, became known as Brigantes ('high ones'). The new name may have been derived initially from the Pennine Range, around which they eventually settled, but they soon reinterpreted it in the light of *Briganti* ('the highest one'), a common designation for the Celtic mother-goddess. The name which they gave to their chief settlement, Eburacon (modern York), echoes the original tribal-name Eburovices. To judge by nomenclature, a significant group of their relatives, the Cenomani, seem also to have crossed to Britain, becoming known as Cenimagni or Iceni; as did a force of *Quariti (i.e. Parisii), who became known in their new surroundings both as Coritani and Parisi.

The old kw phoneme was usual in the speech of the Celtic inhabitants of Britain at that time, as indeed it may still have been usual in the speech of these particular incoming groups. Regarding the Coritani or Parisi, there is clear evidence in their new east Yorkshire territory from the fourth century BC of burial custom introduced from northern France, where the Parisii were in fact neighbours of the Eburovices. Though none of the Celtic arrivals in Britain to this date appear to have had a fully developed La Tène culture, they brought with them much more iron weapons and tools than were heretofore in use in Britain. Concerning Ireland, archaeological evidence suggests that scattered groups of warriors with improved bronze weapons had been landing there from Britain since the fifth century BC, but these probably were peoples displaced from Britain by the incoming Celts. The full impact of Celtic culture was not felt in that western island for another century or so.

To sum up, the habitat of the Celts was expanding rapidly at this time, on a broad sward of central Europe from the eastern Alps as far as the Atlantic in the west, into the Iberian peninsula in the south and into Britain in the north. The expansion of the Germanic peoples southwards from the North Sea was, however, beginning to set a frontier in the vicinity of the river Main, and far to the east the Illyrian, Dacian and Thracian peoples presented a similar barrier. Further advances may have been made in two fringe areas of the Celtic world, as appears from copied fragments – if these are accurate – of the work of the Greek traveller and writer Hecataeus of Miletus, who wrote in the early fifth century BC. One reference is to Narbon (Narbonne) as 'a market and city of the Celts', and the other is to 'Nyrax, a Celtic city', by which is probably intended Noreia (now Neumarkt in Steiermark). These references would mean that Celtic groups had penetrated to the shores of the Mediterranean in the Ligurian south-east of France, and deep into Illyrian territory at the south-eastern edge of the Alps.

The fantastic strangers

The basic social structure of Celtic society was tribal, with a particular territory under the control of a tribe which held it by armed power and, when necessary, by negotiation and arrangements with stronger neighbours. Although the Celts in general tended to consider themselves to be descended from the same divine ancestor, individual tribes could vary and elaborate this so as to underline their own particular identity. There are several indications that the tracing of genealogy was important, both as a means of defining the tribe and of establishing the respective status of the members. The social structures must have varied somewhat from tribe to tribe, but the general division was into three classes – the nobility, the common people, and the bondmen or slaves. The latter seem to have consisted generally of captives taken in war, and included individuals of both Celtic and non-Celtic origin. All three classes, and the gradations of them, were linked together by an elaborate system of clientage, and there was a degree of social mobility between them.

The regions of Europe inhabited by the Celts were largely forested, but means of communication were good, with navigable rivers and an improving system of roads. The forests provided timber for construction, as well as game such as deer and wild boar. Economic pursuits were mostly agricultural, large amounts of cattle and sheep being raised and wheat, barley and flax grown extensively. Essentially a rural people, the Celtic population was spread throughout their various territories, often grouped together in small hamlets. The tribal centres – to which the Romans later applied the term *oppida* – were places of public assembly and trade and usually had highways to and from them. Tradesmen and merchants congregated there, animals and goods were bought and sold, and various social and religious observances took place. The location and design of these *oppida* varied greatly. Many were situated on high ground, but others were on flat land; and whereas some had elaborate defences others had little or none. The usual type of defence consisted of timber palisades, but some oppida had substantial stone walls.

Lack of intimate knowledge of the Celts and of their society caused the early Greek writers to make some extraordinary statements about them. To these writers, the Celts were a celebrated but puzzling race, concerning whom garbled and sensationalised accounts could be gained from traders and mariners. Thus, the great dramatist Aeschylus used the name Hyperboreans (Uperboreoi, 'far-northerners') for them, and his contemporary Hellanicus claimed that they were a very just people who ate acorns and other fruit rather than meat!

As late as the fourth century BC, Ephorus could claim that the Celts were 'very careful to avoid growing fat or big bellied' and that 'if any young man exceeds the measure of a certain girdle he is fined'. Tall tales circulating among the Greeks were not all so complimentary to the

Celts. The celebrated philosopher Aristotle, at the same period, made extravagant references to them, praising them for their courage, but expressed the opinion that in this they are rash to the point of madness. He further claimed that they plunged their newborn children into a cold stream, clothed only in a light wrapper, in order to make them healthy. This may have been a misunderstanding by him of some form of baptism ritual, echoes of which are found in later druidic tradition.

Aristotle was quite dubious concerning the sexual mores of the Celts, claiming that they 'openly approve of connexion with the male'. This charge seems to result from a misunderstanding of the social informality of the Celts as opposed to the cultured manners of the Greeks. It was repeated in dramatic terms several centuries later by Posidonius:

> Although their wives are beautiful, they pay very little attention to them, but rather have a strange passion for the embraces of males. Their custom is to sleep on the ground upon the skins of wild animals and to wallow among bedfellows on each side. The strangest thing of all is that, without a thought of keeping up proper appearances, they carelessly yield their virginity to others; and this they regard not as a disgrace, but rather think themselves slighted when someone refuses to accept their freely offered favours.

To such writers, indeed, the Celts could be portrayed as the opposite of the civilised Greeks in whatever way was opportune to mention. In this vein, Aristotle's teacher Plato wrote of the Celts as one of those warlike peoples who contrasted with the abstemious Greeks in drinking wine to the point of 'downright drunkenness'. There may of course be some truth behind this, as there definitely seems to be behind Aristotle's own statement that the Celts were perturbed by 'neither earthquakes nor waves'. This was apparently a proverbial expression used by the Celts themselves in boasting of their courage, and it gave rise to other traditions about them.

Ephorus, for instance, claimed that the Celts, as an exercise of their intrepidity, allowed their houses to be washed away by flood tides and were satisfied to rebuild later, and that 'a greater number of them perish by water than by war'. Later texts refer to 'the Celts, who take up arms against the waves of the sea', and to how they resist the tides with their swords in their hands till they perish in the waters, 'in order that they may not seem to fear death by taking the precaution to flee'. Such a portrayal, though inaccurate, may have derived from some real occurrence, such as a report of an inundation of land held by the Celts, possibly in the Netherlands.

The heroic society

Rumours aside, the courage and ferocity of the Celts in battle can hardly be doubted, and this led to great demand for their warriors as mercenaries in the armies of other nationalities. The classical writers are copious on the topic, and Posidonius could declare that the whole Celtic race was 'madly fond of war, high spirited and quick to battle'. He went on:

> When they are stirred up they assemble in their bands for battle, quite openly and without forethought, so that they are easily handled by those who desire to outwit them; for at any time or place on whatever pretext you stir them up, you will have them ready to face danger, even if they have nothing on their side but their own strength and courage ... Their strength depends on their mighty bodies, and on their numbers.

This Posidonius was writing in the beginning of the first century BC, and his work survives only in fragments cited by later writers. He undoubtedly had a good knowledge of the Celts of his own time, and there are indications that several of his comments are based on views which had long been held by the Greeks concerning these people. Apparently drawing on Posidonius, the Sicilian writer Diodorus a generation or two later had this to say of their armoury and weaponry:

> Their armour includes man-sized shields, decorated in individual fashion. Some of these have projecting bronze animals of fine workmanship which serve for defence as well as decoration. On their heads they wear bronze helmets which have large projecting figures, giving the appearance of enormous stature to the wearer. In some cases horns form one piece with the helmet, while in other cases it is relief figures of the foreparts of birds or quadrupeds. Their trumpets also are of a peculiar barbaric kind – when they blow into them they produce a harsh sound which suits the tumult of war. Some have iron breastplates of chain-mail, while others fight naked, and for them the breastplate provided by nature suffices. Instead of the short sword

they carry long swords held by iron or bronze chains and hanging along their right flank. Some wear gold plated or silver plated belts around their tunics. The spears which they brandish in battle, and which they call lanciae, have iron heads a cubit or more in length and a little less than two palms in breadth. Their swords are as long as the javelins of other peoples, and their javelins have points longer than swords. Some of their javelins are forged with a straight head, while some are spiral with breaks throughout their entire length, so that the blow not only cuts but also tears the flesh, and the recovery of the spear tears open the wound.

Concerning the physical appearance of the Celts, several ancient authors refer to them as being tall in stature, and Diodorus adds that their skin was 'very moist and white'. The more romantic description is given by Virgil in his *Aeneid*: 'Golden is their hair and golden their garments, they gleam in striped cloaks, and their milk-white necks are encircled with gold.' Their hair was generally blonde, but they also used artificial means to attain this colour. 'They continually wash their hair with lime and draw it back from the forehead to the crown and to the nape of the neck'. Some shaved their beards, while others cultivated a short beard. The nobles shaved their cheeks but let a moustache grow freely so that it covered the mouth, 'and so when they are eating, the moustache becomes entangled in the food, and when they are drinking the liquid passes, as it were, through a sort of strainer'. Regarding their clothing, Diodorus states:

> They accumulate large quantities of gold and make use of it for per-sonal ornament, not only the women but also the men. For they wear bracelets on wrists and arms, and around their necks thick rings of solid gold, and they wear also fine finger-rings and even golden tunics ... They wear a striking kind of clothing – tunics dyed in var-ious colours, and trousers which they call by the name of bracae, and they wear striped cloaks, fastened with buckles, thick in winter and light in summer, picked out with a variegated small check pattern.

Posidonius was fascinated by the eating habits of the Celts. He claimed that they strewed the ground with the skins of wolves or dogs, and sat on these – without any chairs – when dining. The food was served on low wooden tables, and consisted of some loaves and boiled or roasted meat. 'They partake of this in a clean but leonine fashion, raising up whole limbs in both hands and biting off the meat, while any part which is hard to tear off they cut with a small dagger which hangs attached to their sword-sheath in its own scabbard.' Their youngest grown-up children, both boys and girls, tended to them at table. Beside them were blazing charcoal hearths, with cauldrons and spits containing large joints of meat. Those who lived beside a river or sea ate baked fish, with salt, vinegar and cummin. They concocted drinks out of barley and honey and cummin, and when they became drunk they fell into 'a stupor or a maniacal state'.

Posidonius mentions a striking feature of their culture, the heroic feast presided over by a king or chieftain. We have seen how this royal feasting was reflected in their ancient burials, and here we have a description of the ceremonial in real life:

> When a large number dine together they sit around in a circle with the most influential man in the centre, like the leader of a chorus – whether he surpasses the others in skill at war, or in nobility of family, or in wealth. Beside him sits the host, and next on either side the others in order of distinction. Their shieldmen stand behind them, while their spearmen are situated in a circle on the opposite side and feast in common with their leaders. The servers bear around the drink in terracotta or silver jars like spouted cups. The trenchers on which they serve the food are also of these materials, while with others they are made of bronze or are woven or wooden baskets.

More dramatic scenes of action sometimes followed, if these sources are to be credited, for when feasting these Celtic warriors were wont to be moved by chance remarks to wordy disputes, and the irritations could increase to the point of fighting. This was regarded as the result of an ancient ritual concerning precedence:

> In former times, when the hindquarters were served up, the bravest hero took the thigh piece, and if another man claimed it they stood up and fought in single combat to the death.

As a form of military drill, the Celts also had the custom of engaging in mock-battles. Posidonius describes this as 'mutual thrust and parry', but states that wounds were sometimes inflicted and that the irritation caused by this could lead even to the slaying of the opponent unless the bystanders held them back. Several reports represent the Celts as engaging in duels, and their fighting ideals were expressed in the most committed form in actual war, in which they considered it a glory to die and a disgrace to survive without victory. They regarded it as the utmost disgrace to desert their leader, and after the fall of a leader they retired from a battle. The bodies of those slain in battle were often left to the carrion crows to devour, in the belief that in this way they were taken by the deities. The war-goddess, or perhaps more accurately the mother-goddess in her war mien, was believed by them to appear in the form of such a bird.

The classical writers stress that the Celts were generous by disposition, and were wont to invite strangers to their feasts, and only after the meal did they enquire after their identity or business. Julius Caesar, apparently quoting Posidonius, states that 'violation of guest-friendship they regard as impious – strangers who have visited them for whatever reason they protect from injury and hold sacred, and every man's house lies open and his food is shared with them'. Caesar also would have us believe that factionalism was general among the Celts, and that leaders of such factions had the right of final decision in all matters concerning their followers. The faction leaders would not tolerate their clients being oppressed or defrauded for, if they did, they would lose their own influence and position. The reason, Caesar says, why 'this institution was established of old' was to ensure that 'no common man should lack aid against one more powerful'.

A stress is also put on co-operation among the Celts in the account given by another writer, Strabo, in his discussion of the attitude to war among them. He attributes a straightforward and slightly naïve character to them, and claims that 'they assemble in large numbers on slight provocation, being ever ready to sympathise with the anger of a neighbour who thinks he has been wronged'. This surely was a misunderstanding by Strabo of traditions binding tribes and families together. Another comment of his makes it clear, however, that social authority could be rather fluid in such situations: 'Most of their governments used to be aristocratic, and in ancient times they used to elect one leader annually, and in the same way one man was declared general by the people to lead in war'. This should probably be taken to mean that the king, although overall ruler, was assisted by an administrator or adjudicator, and that military affairs were delegated to a war leader.

Another ancient practice of the Celts is referred to by Julius Caesar, who seems here again to have been quoting Posidonius:

In peacetime they have no public magistrate, but the regional and village chieftains give legal judgements to their people and seek solutions to their disputes. Brigandage outside the state territory brings no disgrace, and they assert that it is pursued in order to exercise their young men and save them from idleness. When a chieftain in council says that he will lead a foray and asks for followers, those who approve of the man and his project rise to support him and promise their help, and are applauded by the assembly. Those who fail to keep their promise are looked on as deserters and traitors, and they are henceforth trusted in nothing.

This passage refers to the custom according to which young men learned the trade of a warrior by living outside of normal social rules and surviving on their skill and strength in raiding other groups. It is attested as a custom among many ancient peoples, including the early Greeks and Germans, and it is clear from this passage that it was a recognised aspect of early Celtic society also.

Religious tradition

Pytheas was an accomplished mariner and explorer, who in the late fourth century BC sailed from Marseilles around the Spanish coast, and then northwards by France to Britain, and perhaps even further. Notwithstanding this, he felt it safe to portray the Celts as an exotic people of the imagination like the Hyperboreans. Though his comments on these strange denizens of the northwest cannot be trusted, Pytheas may nevertheless at times have been echoing truths, as when he declares that they used to point out to him where the sun sleeps.

The ancient Greeks, from Homer onwards, spoke of an otherworld island in the west, situated where the sun goes down. They knew it as Elysion or Erytheia, and it was thought to exist somewhere west of the Gates of Gibraltar. It was thought of, among other things, as a sepulchral island on which stood the pillars of Hercules or the pillars of Cronus. It could be somewhere near Cadiz, a region rich in megalithic tombs, or off the western coast of France. There is evidence that the Celts had the same notion, and it may be that this influenced the Greek characterisation of Ireland in the west as 'the sacred isle'.

To the Celts themselves, however, such an island belonged to the otherworld, and they believed that the spirits of the dead went there with the setting sun. Plutarch, in the first century AD, using information which he had from a traveller, describes how the Britons believed that an other-world lord reigns in slumber over an island off the coast. Boatmen were awakened at night by a knock on their door, and were required to row the spirits of the dead to the island. It may well be, then, that the Celts were trying to explain to Pytheas that the otherworld lies on a sunlit island in the western sea, and that this island was the abode of their divine ancestor. The Graeco-Sicilian writer Timaeus, who lived in the fourth and third centuries BC, recorded that there was a tradition among the Celts that the gods came to them from the ocean.

Two centuries later, the Roman scholar Timagenes reported some interesting items of druidic teaching – these include the proposition that part of the population of Gaul was indigenous, but that some of the people had originally come from 'outlying islands and territories beyond the Rhine'. That is, from areas far to the west, and in this Timagenes would appear to be confusing historical lore with religious teaching. The population of Gaul – as of the Celtic territories generally – must have been descended both from earlier peoples and from the Celts who had migrated there. On the other hand, the image of the Celtic incomers has been confused with the religious belief that all the Celts had come from a mythical ancestor synonymous with the sun. Timagenes seems in fact to expose the religious source immediately after this passage, when he stresses that the druids 'were uplifted by searchings into secret and sublime things, and with grand contempt for mortal lot they professed the immortality of the soul'.

Reports of this kind relevant to the religious beliefs of the Celts led the imaginations of classical writers to run riot concerning strange islands inhabited by even stranger people in the Celtic mist. For instance, Artemidorus, towards the end of the second century BC refers to 'an island near Britain' where sacrifices were offered to goddesses. With less restraint a century later, Strabo wrote that there was a small island in the ocean, outside the mouth of the Loire, which was inhabited by women who performed Bacchic rites and made ritual sacrifices to the gods:

> No man is permitted to land on the island; and when the women desire to have intercourse with the other sex, they cross the sea, and afterwards return again. They have a custom of once a year unroofing the whole of the temple, and roofing it again the same day before sunset, each one bringing some of the materials. If any one lets her

burden fall, she is torn to pieces by the others, and her limbs carried around the temple with wild shouts, which they never cease until their rage is exhausted. It always happens that some one drops her burden, and is thus sacrificed.

It may be that Strabo – or his source – had heard something concerning worship of deities by women in the north-western Celtic area, but the portrayal of the raging women with psychotic behaviour are typical of 'savages' as seen through 'civilised' eyes.

Such rumours were also known to Pomponius Mela who, a generation later again, describes an island called Sena 'opposite to the shores of the Ossismii' (i.e. between Britain and north-west France). This, he says, was famed for its oracle of a Celtic god, to whose cult nine maiden-priestesses were devoted. The priestesses were known as *Senae*, and were said to be 'gifted with remarkable intelligence'. It was believed that 'they can raise up the waves of the sea and the winds with their songs, that they can assume the shape of any animal they choose, that they can cure complaints that to others are incurable, and that they know and predict the future'. This reads curiously parallel to the later accounts of Celtic druids, who were reputed to chant magical poems which controlled the waters, to go abroad in the form of different animals, to cure ailments, and to prophesy. It is apparent that Pytheas had heard something of such wise men of the Celts, and also accounts of druidesses with similar functions, and that he confused these with the Greek legend of Circe, who lived with her nymphs on the island of Ea and could command the winds, change men into the shape of beasts, and foretell the future.

Whatever the exact nature of the belief in question among the Celts themselves, it surely was a reflection of the otherworld island in the west rather than a reference to a real place. Its name, Sena, was based on the adjective *sen-* (meaning 'ancient'), and the god who resided on such an island was but another instance of the divine ancestor from whom the Celts fancied themselves to be descended. It appears, however, that Pomponius' report has confused such lore with another ancient cultic idea of the Celts – that of the water-goddess. There is plenty of evidence for such goddesses among the Celts, who tended to give female names to their rivers. The Danube itself appears to be synonymous with an Indo-European water-goddess, who was known as *Dánuv to the Celts and was regarded as a mother-goddess. Similarly, the name of the river Marne comes from the Celtic *Matrona* (literally 'exalted mother'); while various rivers in the Celtic world bore the name *Deva* ('goddess'). Pomponius' source may, in fact, have concerned a goddess cult in the late centuries BC, far to the west, concerning the Shannon (originally *Sena*, 'the ancient lady'), the longest river in Ireland.

Rivers were thought of as being a principal fertilising aspect of the land-goddess, who was the source of food and sustenance and to whom various designations were given. These designations appear to have varied from group to group and from locality to locality, but included such as *Briganti* ('the highest one'), *Damona* ('the divine cow'), *Epona* ('the divine mare'), and *Nantosuelta* ('the flowing stream'). There was a widespread tendency also to associate wells and springs with goddesses, for these coincided very well with the ideas of sustenance and healing being given by the earth-mother. Goddesses were naturally often paired with male deities, and the import of this would appear to be the coupling of the male sky with the female earth so as to ensure fruitfulness.

The basic name for the male sun-deity among the Celts must have been *dago-Devos ('the good god'), the second part of whose name is the Celtic version of the general Indo-European sky-god *Deiwos. Among other male-deities, who apparently were derivations of this same being, were Taranis ('the thunderer'), Sucellus ('the striker'), Ekwomaros or Epomaros ('the great horseman'), Cernunnos ('the horned one') and Lugus ('the swearer'). It is most likely that such names, and accordingly the imagery associated with them, originally referred to specific functions of the deity such as the production of rain for the crops, the development of fertility in herds, and the guaranteeing of social and commercial contracts.

That the sun was the ultimate father and the earth the ultimate mother of the people was a doctrine of the wise men of the Celts. It is clear from the classical writers that they divided these learned men of theirs into three grades, a member of each grade being known respectively as *bardos*, *vátis*, and *druis*. The *bardi* were 'singers and poets', the *vátes* were 'interpreters of sacrifice', and the *druides* were experts in 'the science of nature'. We may assume, however, that this was a somewhat pedagogic division, and that in practice the functions were often combined in one individual practitioner. There is evidence that another term was also in use for such a wise man or religious leader, namely *velitos*, meaning literally a 'seer'.

The most prestigious title was *druis* (from an original *dru-wid-is, meaning 'strong-knowledge-possessor'). These druids were entrusted with arbitration in both individual and public disputes, and were thought to mediate between their societies and the mysterious powers of destiny, being 'learned in the divine nature and, so to say, familiar with it'. In other words, they inherited the shamanic function from a more primitive stage of culture. It is difficult to speculate on the stages by which the rather spontaneous office of a mediator with the spirit world developed into a more formalised learned figure, but all indications are that by the fifth or fourth century BC the druids had some form of standardised training and systematic dogma – while still retaining the aura of mystery. The druidess (*dryas*) was also an important figure in Celtic social life, but, from the available evidence, it would appear that formal learning was less stressed in the context of druidesses and that spontaneous prophecy was their specialty.

Such practitioners of the sacred played a leading part in political matters, and the appointment of a king would depend in no small degree on the support of a druid. The ancient idea was that a king functioned as a substitute for the ancestral deity as director of his people, in effect becoming the 'husband' of the earth-goddess. A significant story was told by Aristotle in the fourth century BC concerning the first arrival of the Greek colonists at Marseilles some generations earlier. According to this, Nannus, king of the Segobriges at that place, was holding a feast at which his daughter Petta would select a husband from among assembled suitors by offering a drink to one of them. The newcomers were invited to the feast, and Petta gave the special drink to the Greek leader Euxenus, thereby becoming his wife. This can be seen as an early example of the Celtic conceit that the land-goddess, symbolised by a drink, becomes the mate of a new king at the time of his inauguration. The name 'Petta' meant 'a portion [of land]', and it would therefore appear that the Greeks of Marseilles were using the conceit to justify their seizure of territory in that area.

The story itself is anachronistic, for at the time of the foundation of Marseilles the Ligurians, rather than Celts, inhabited that area. It would have made sense in Aristotle's time, however, for Segobriges would appear to be an alternative name for the Segusiavi, who by then controlled a wide area just north of Marseilles. The Greeks of that colony were rich and influential – one writer reports that the Celts of the vicinity learned improved agricultural techniques from them and how to encircle their towns with walls for defence. Hostilities, indeed, must have become increasingly common in this region from the later sixth century BC onwards, as the Celts extended their power in the direction of the Greek colony. This pressure on Marseilles would have come not only directly from the north, but also from Narbonne and other Celtic settlements to the south-west of the colony, where the Celts were mingling with the native Ligurians and ensconcing themselves.

It is evident that the protective role of the earth-goddess, and the role of a king as substitute for the male-deity, were upheld by druidic teaching. The rationale was that, if the king was fulfilling his function properly, the tribe would enjoy good fortune – success in their dealings with other tribes, social well-being, and agricultural wealth. Conversely, when bad fortune struck persistently, doubts would be cast on the suitability of the reigning king and he was in danger of removal from his office. It is significant that tradition constantly associates druids with influence over the elements, particularly in the context of the crops and the harvest. All of this means that the druid was simultaneously at the centre of the social order and in control of the intermediate zone which connected the king to the tribal deities.

The classical accounts describe the Celts as being much given to superstition, which would entail among other things the attribution of supernatural powers to the druidic class. Thus we read of how they carefully obeyed the druids and poets, and that these men had influence not only over friends but over enemies as well. 'For oftentimes, as armies approach each other in line of battle with their swords drawn and their spears raised for the charge, these men come forth between them and stop the conflict, as though they had spellbound some kinds of wild animals'. This is surely a dramatised version of the situation, but it is clear from the sentiment that rhetorics, sacredly pronounced by their druids and seers, were generally understood to have magical power.

Since our most detailed sources describing the Celts date from the first century BC onwards, and merely echo aspects of their culture at earlier periods, it is difficult to apply a chronology to the development of their beliefs and mythology. One has no means of knowing precisely how druidic teaching varied from generation to generation and from place to place, but certain basic assumptions can be made. For instance, the connecting of sky and earth in the imagery of father and mother must have lain at the basis of the Celts' mythic understanding of themselves as a people. For the druids, it underpinned a dualistic tendency in their reasoning. This tendency assured that when it came to explaining the relationship between the actual world and the otherworld, the idea of two complimentary opposites had special appeal.

This would explain also the special veneration which the druids had for trees and why their assemblies were often at a location such as a forest clearing called *nemeton*. This word meant 'sky-place', presumably because of the illusion that the trees climbed upwards and therefore united the sky to the earth. Writing in the second century AD, Maximus of Tyre reports that 'the Celts revere Zeus, and the Celtic image of Zeus is a tall oak'. By 'Zeus', he must have been referring to the father-deity of the sky Devos or dago-Devos, and this is borne out by later Irish tradition which revered certain great trees as giving mystical shelter to particular tribes.

As we have seen, some antiquity must attach to the tradition reported most fully by Caesar, i.e. that the druids maintained that all their people were descended from one divine ancestor. 'For this reason,' he says, 'they count periods of time not by the number of days but by the number of nights; and in reckoning birthdays and the new moon and new year their unit of reckoning is the night followed by the day'. This implies a definite connection between the darkness of night and the ancestral lord. It also makes it clear that time was computed by how the sun absented itself from the world of the living and descended into the realm inhabited by the dead ancestors. This is, in fact, a development from the belief – widespread in archaic Europe – that the sun, when sinking in the west, entered the underworld each night to abide there with the dead.

Knowledge of time was not the only abstract knowledge which was believed to come from the otherworld. A Greek writer from the second century BC, Nicander, affirmed that the Celts 'spend the night near the tombs of their famous men', and this custom is echoed by later lore from Ireland and Wales of druids and other wise men acquiring knowledge in the vicinity of burial tumuli. Inspiration was accordingly understood as light which emanated from darkness, and the alternating nature of light and darkness was thus expressed as a paradox that reconciled the living with the dead. Celtic deities with names indicating brightness would have an obvious function in this type of belief. Most notable of these is the name Vindos ('illumination'), a divine appellation reflected in names of various tribes and places. Such a deity, sometimes called Vindonnos ('he who is illuminating and exalted'), seems to have been especially claimed by the druids as a patron of their profession.

The druids taught that life is continuous, even after death, and Strabo states that 'it is for this reason that they burn or bury, with their dead, things appropriate to them in life'. Furthermore, we read that 'in times past they even used to defer the completion of business and the payment of debts until their arrival in another world. Indeed, there were some of them who flung themselves willingly on the funeral piles of their relatives in order to share the new life with them.' Again, 'it is said that they lend to each other sums that are repayable in the next world, so firmly are they convinced that the souls of men are immortal'. Clearly, the afterlife was not generally understood as a sad and dreary place, but rather as a new and valuable sphere of existence.

This is borne out by Lucan, in a hostile address to the druids, claiming that 'you tell us that the same spirit has a body again elsewhere'. He goes on: 'It is you who say that the shades of the dead seek not the silent land of Erebus and the pale halls of Pluto; rather, you tell us that the same spirit has a body again elsewhere, and that death – if what you sing is true – is but the midpoint of a long life!' Caesar, drawing on Posidonius, underlines a practical purpose for this belief: 'They are chiefly anxious to have men believe that souls do not suffer death, but after death pass from one body to another; and they regard this as the strongest incentive to valour, since the fear of death is disregarded.' This is why, according to Diodorus Siculus, the Celts were wont to resort to fighting on the least provocation, 'regarding their lives as naught'.

The classical authors claim that the Celts were hot-tempered and very jealous of their honour, and it would be natural for them to consider the social and spiritual realms as reflecting each other. Thus, it is no sur-prise to read classical writers such as Posidonius comment that 'the Celts have in their company, in war as well as in peace, companions whom they call parasites. These men pronounce their praises before the whole assembly, and before each of the chieftains in turn as they listen. Their entertainers are called bards – these are poets who deliver eulogies in song'. Using information from the same Posidonius, another writer states that the bards of the Celts sang 'sometimes a eulogy and sometimes a satire'. Such references accord well with the ancient belief among European peoples that praise uttered by a poet or rhetorician has a salutory effect on its subject, whereas satire has a destructive effect. This belief seems to have survived with particular vigour among the Celts, whom the same writer accuses of being 'boasters and threateners and given to self-dramatisation'.

2

THE CELTS IN ITALY

From the beginning of the fourth century BC, droves of Celts were crossing the Alps and descending into the Valley of the Po. The classical writers give as reason for these invasions a desire to possess the riches of Italy, in particular the wine, for which the Celts had acquired a strong taste. Pliny the Elder gives a rather symbolic setting to this when he tells a story of how a skilled craftsman of the Celtic tribe of Helvetii named Helico had sojourned for a while in Rome and, on his return home, whetted the appetites of his fellows with 'some dried figs and grapes and some samples of oil and wine'. This caused them to wish to possess such fine food even by means of war if necessary. Such an anecdote was, of course, an over-simplification of the motives of a foreign and rather strange race.

Livy, while claiming also that the Celts were attracted south by 'the delicious fruits and especially the wine', gives an even more personal reason for these initial Celtic incursions. It concerns a nobleman of the Etruscan city of Clusium (now Chiusi) called Arruns, whose wife had been seduced by his protégé, a young man of powerful connections on whom it was difficult to gain revenge. To attain his purpose, therefore, Arruns decided to seek help from the Celts, and sent wine to them in order to entice them to cross the Alps and attack Clusium. Dionysus of Halicarnassus, who also tells this story, has Arruns going in person and introducing the Gauls to both wine and olives. The Gauls were extremely impressed, for they had hitherto 'used for wine a foul-smelling liquor made from barley rotted in water, and for oil stale lard which was disgusting both in smell and taste'.

Multiple incursions and settlements

Whatever was the nature of the contacts between the Celts and the Etruscan nobleman, a change in the political balance of the area would have been a more rational cause, and a more realistic temptation for the Celts. The power of the Etruscans, who had dominated the area for centuries, was in decline, and this tempted foreign adventurers. Celtic influences on some of the peoples of northern Italy can be discerned in the archaeological record for some time previously, and indeed the Lepontic Celts had been settled on the southern slopes of the Alps for over a century. It is therefore clear that those groups who now began to cross the Alps in large numbers already had good knowledge of the region into which they were descending.

The population explosion and resultant instability, which had led Ambicatus to syphon off young warriors from his Gaulish confederacy, had caused large numbers to move southwards along the valley of the Rhône. That tribes in their entirety were not involved in these movements is obvious from the fact that those with identical group names continued to play a leading role in northern and central Gaul. What actually happened was that sections of these groups, led by young ambitious warriors, had decided to risk their fortunes by migrating. As the Etruscan power declined, leaving the Ligurian and other Italic peoples of the region without the necessary defence to withstand large-scale Celtic influxes, such periodic migrations would have grown bolder, eventually developing into permanent and uncontested settlements.

The first of the invasion forces to arrive was a large group of the Insubres, who belonged to the powerful Aedui people. The legendary claim that these were led by the young prince Belovesus can hardly be sustained, but it can be accepted that this, and several other incursions into Italy, resulted from the movement which had been initiated by Ambicatus in central Gaul. Livy states, no doubt with good reason, that they comprised 'an immense force of horse and foot', and that sections from other tribes were also included. He goes on to claim that, on reaching the Alps, they hestitated to survey the mountains and ponder a

way through these great heights. While thus engaged, Livy claims that
news came that the Greeks of Marseilles were being attacked by the
Salluvii, the Celto-Ligurian tribe of that area. We read that their leader
('Belovesus') felt honour bound to go to the assistance of the Massaliots.
This tradition indicates that the migrant Insubres and their supporters
crossed the Alps from the western side.

We know that the Celts of that area were threatening Marseilles at
the time, and it would appear that Livy's sources had preserved some
memory of hostility between the tribes of south-eastern Gaul and the
force passing through their territory. A story relating to the period was
told in the lost work of the Gaulish historian Trogus Pompeius. According
to this, a tribal king called Catumandus was selected by a broad Celtic
alliance to lead them in an attack on Marseilles. While besieging the city,
he saw in a dream a woman with a fearsome expression who told him that
she was a goddess. During a truce, he visited the temple of Minerva in
Marseilles and saw a statue of the same goddess there. Realising that the
gods favoured the Massaliots, he offered a golden torque to the goddess
and made peace with the city. It is possible that this story relates to the
conundrum in which the Segusiavi, Salluvii, and allied tribes found
themselves when the migrant horde led by the Insubres appeared on the
verges of their territory, thus distracting them from their intended attack
on Marseilles.

Livy states emphatically that, in crossing the Alps, the Insubres
went through the Torino pass and that, on entering northern Italy, they
defeated an Etruscan tribe, the Tuscani, in a battle near the river Ticino.
He further states that, on finding that the name Insubres had already been
attached to the surrounding countryside, they took this as a good omen
and founded a settlement there, which they called Mediolanum (literally
'middle plain', now Milan). This makes good sense, for the invaders were
settling in the area where the Lepontic dialect of Celtic was being spoken.
They would therefore have encountered people there who would have
been acquainted with the names of several Celtic tribes, and would
presumably have understood the meaning of the tribal name Insubres.
The name meant 'holm-dwellers', from their home territory between the
tributaries of the river Saône, which sense was replicated by their new
situation on the confluence of the Adda and the Po. Moreover, the
Lepontic people probably regarded the newcomers as friendly cousins
who were freeing them from Etruscan overlordship.

Soon after, some Cenomani (who were a branch of the Aulerci) crossed by the same pass, under a leader called Elitovios. Livy claims that this incursion enjoyed the good will of Belovesus, which can probably be read as an indication that they were welcomed by both the earlier Lepontii and the more recently arrived Insubres. The Cenomani settled on both sides of the river Oglio, establishing as their chief centres Tridentum (now Trent), Brixia (now Brescia) and Bergomum (now Bergamo). Livy states that they were followed by groups of Libui and Salluvii. The Libui or Libici were in fact a sub-tribe of the Salluvii, who had been finding the Greek colony at Marseilles a great stumbling-block to expanding their territory. It would appear that these, and other small groups from the south-east of Gaul, followed on when they perceived the easy progress of the earlier invaders. They settled in areas held by the Ligurians, in the northwest between the Ticino and the Po, and had Rigomagus (now Trino) as a centre.

Livy next mentions what must have been a very large group of invaders, the Boii. These Boii came from a different direction, to the north-east of the Alps, where they had already seized much territory from the indigenous Raetian tribes. They probably made their way down the Brenner Pass, and their presence shows that there was more to the Celtic invasions of Italy than the migrations instigated by Ambicatus. Italy had obviously come to appeal to the Celts in general as a promising hunting-ground, and the most adventurous of them were determined to move in. Finding all the country occupied by their fellow Celts, Livy claims that the Boii crossed the Po on rafts and drove the Etruscans and Umbrians before them as far as the Apennine mountains. They occupied the rich lands south of the Po, as far as the river Reno, and established centres at Mutina (now Modena) and Bononia (now Bologna).

There would seem to have been a certain sense of common purpose among the various Celts who invaded the north of Italy. For instance, a migration of Lingones, from the area around the source of the Rhône, crossed the path of the Boii and settled to the east of them, on the Adriatic. Finally, a numerous group of Senones descended on Italy and, passing by the other Celtic settlements, pushed as far along the coast as Ancona. They established the centre which the Romans later called Sena Gallica (now Senigallia). The Senones were one of the most numerous tribes in Gaul, and they moved about quite a bit, but it is likely that these migrants had come all the way from the banks of the Yonne, towards the north of Gaul. The Lingones and Senones may have made their way across the Alps through the St Gothard Pass, but ultimately they came from the same region of Gaul as most of the Celtic invaders of Italy. Like the Cenomani, they seem to have originated among the old Hallstattian Celts of Gaul.

Polybius, who wrote a century earlier than Livy, also has the Celts first entering from the western Alps, but he – apparently with less historical accuracy – claims that the Laevi and Libici (branches of the Salluvii) were the first of these tribes to settle on the southern side of the Alps. His account echoes the description of Livy regarding the Torino pass as the path of entry by having them occupy the area near the source of the Po. After them, states Polybius, came 'the largest tribe of all', the Insubres; and then the Cenomani, who moved south along the bank of the river. Further south, in the Apennine district, the Anares (probably a mixture of Celts and Ligurians) settled, and to the east of them the Boii. Polybius agrees that the Lingones settled on the Adriatic, and that the Senones went even further south along that coastline.

The Celtic invaders were sufficiently established in northern Italy for them to seize and destroy an 'exceptionally wealthy town' called Melpum in 396 BC. This would seem to have been an Etruscan settlement (now Melzo) on the northern bank of the Po. The Latin writer Cornelius Nepos claims that Melpum was taken by a combination of Insubres, Boii and Senones on the very same day as the celebrated Roman leader Camillus captured the huge Etruscan centre of Veii, about 300km to the south. This was the culmination of a long war between the Romans and Etruscans, a war which had concentrated Etruscan attention on the southern end of their territories and had thus facilitated the Celtic expansion to the north. It was now only a matter of time before these two land-hungry groups, Celts and Romans, came face to face with each other.

The demographic map of northern Italy was changing rapidly. The power of the Etruscans in the region was considerably reduced, and local Italic peoples – Ligurians, Raetians, Picenes and Umbrians – found their territories being cramped by large new settlements. The Celts definitely assumed a dominant role in the wide area of the Po Valley, taking over from the other peoples, for there is archaeological evidence that some of the places which they occupied had already been settlements or towns before they arrived. They did not, however, completely displace the earlier inhabitants. Many of these natives were either subjected or assimilated, while others retreated to upland areas, leaving the better land to the ominous newcomers. Polybius describes the Ligurians, Etruscans, and Umbrians as continuing to occupy the slopes of the Apennines over a wide area. He also gives an interesting description of the way of life of the Celtic intruders:

> They lived in open villages, without any permanent buildings. As they made their bed of straw or leaves, and fed on meat, and followed no pursuits but those of war and agriculture, they lived simple lives without being acquainted with any science or art whatever. Each man's property, moreover, consisted in cattle and gold; as they were the only things that could easily be carried with them when they wandered from place to place and changed their dwellings as fancy directed. They put a high esteem, however, on friendship: for the man who had the largest number of clients or companions in his wanderings was looked upon as the most formidable and powerful member of the tribe. In the early days of their settlement, they did not merely subdue the territory which they occupied, but rendered also many of the neighbouring peoples subject to them, overawing them by their audacity.

Within the first decade of the fourth century BC then, Celtic tribes had spread their dominance over most of the countryside between the Alps and the Apennines. This region was afterwards known to the Romans as Gallia Cisalpina ('Gaul on this side of the Alps').

The sacking of Rome

The dominance of ambitious Celts in northern Italy, and such a rapid change in the power structure of so large an area, could hardly be expected to bring stability. Thus, when the Senones in the year 391 BC began to threaten the Etruscan city of Clusium (Chiusi, on the southern side of the Apennines) a chain of events began which would bring them into confrontation with the emerging superpower in central Italy, the city of Rome.

The inhabitants of Clusium had refused to give support to their fellow Etruscans, the Veii, in the recent war with the Romans, and now in their hour of need they looked for repayment of the debt from the Romans. A delegation sent by them to the Roman Senate was refused immediate military support, but three sons of Fabius Ambustus were sent as ambassadors to the Senones. The Romans intended to secure the Senones as allies, but their ambassadors made it clear that the armed force of Rome would be available if Clusium were attacked. Somewhat angered by this, the Senones replied that they would keep the peace only if the Clusines ceded some territory to them. If this were refused, they said, 'we shall fight, while you are still here, so that you may report to those at home how far the Celts surpass all other men in courage!'

The Roman ambassadors chided the Senones, demanding to know what right the invaders had in the area, and the Senones replied that they carried their right in their swords, and that 'everything belonged to the brave'. The meeting broke up, and both sides prepared for battle. When battle was joined, the Roman ambassadors exceeded their function by participating on the side of the Clusines. During the fighting, a Celtic chief charged right at the Etruscan standards. Seeing this, one of the ambassadors ran his spear through him, slew him, and was in the act of despoiling his body when he was recognised by the other Celts. Shocked by this intervention, the Celts withdrew in sullen anger, uttering threats against the Romans. Some were in favour of an immediate advance on Rome, but the older men persuaded them to send a complaint to the Senate instead. No satisfaction was given, and instead of being repimanded, the Roman ambassadors were actually honoured by the Senate for the role they had played.

The Celts took this as a prelude to outright war, and undoubtedly the Senones were reinforced at this time by strong contingents from the other tribes in Cisalpine Gaul. Some time must have been spent in making preparations for the impending struggle, but Livy prefers to imagine the gathering Celtic forces as acting out of impetuosity. He claims that 'as a nation they cannot control their passions' and so, burning with rage, they seized their standards and a massive army of them set out without delay for Rome. 'Horses and men, spread far and wide, covered an immense tract of country – wherever they went they made it understood by loud shouts that they were going to Rome'. In 388 BC, they met the Roman army about seventeen km from the city, where the Allia river flows into the Tiber. Livy states that 'their hideous howls and discordant clamour filled everything with dreadful noise'. Their leader was one Brennos and he, very astutely, attacked the Roman reserves first, and when these broke before his charge the whole Roman force was seized with panic and took to flight. The date of this great defeat, 18 July, was forever remembered by the Romans as an *infaustus dies* ('unlucky day').

Astonished at their easy victory, and fearing a ruse, the Celts did not immediately follow the fleeing Romans, but soon began to despoil the dead and, as their custom was, 'to pile up the arms in heaps'. They then resumed their march on Rome, which they reached before sunset and found the gates open and no force protecting the city. The Roman soldiers who had got safely home made frantic preparations to defend the hill of the Capitol, while all night long the cautious Celts circled around the walls of the city uttering wild war-cries. As morning dawned, the Celtic army entered the city, and found the aging patricians sitting in their full regalia. A Celtic warrior, half in jest and half with wonder, began to stroke the beard of one of these patricians, and was immediately struck on the head by the old man with his ivory staff. The Celts in fury then slaughtered all the patricians and set to burning parts of the city. A different report is more flattering, claiming that a Roman priest called Caeso Fabius descended from the Capitol to perform a religious duty, and that the Celts allowed him through their ranks, either from religious awe or out of respect for his bravery.

After several days of burning and plunder, the invaders decided to make an assault on the remaining Roman forces in the Capitol. Raising their battle cries and locking their shields together over their heads, they advanced to the attack, but the Romans rushed on them from the top of the hill and drove them back down. The Celts then decided on a blockade, but this delay allowed the Romans who had fled to Veii to reassemble, and these were joined by support groups from other parts of Latium. Another attempt by the Celts to take the Capitol failed – according to legend this was under cover of darkness, but the sacred geese warned the Roman defenders and the attack was again repulsed. One report has it that the Celts found a large amount of wine in Rome and that they so indulged in this novelty that 'drunkenness proved their undoing'. Livy states that famine and malaria began to play havoc with their army, unaccustomed to prolonged fighting in so warm a climate, so that in the end they had to pile the bodies of their dead in heaps and burn them indiscrimately at a place which became known as the *Busta Gallica* ('Celtic Pyres').

Feeling all this increasing pressure, coming so quickly upon their initial successes, the Celts were disheartened and agreed to a parley. Their leader Brennos met with the Roman Tribune Quintus Sulpicius, and it was agreed that the Romans would pay a ransom of 1,000 pounds in gold. This was probably understood as compensation for the slaying of the Celtic chief by the Roman ambassador, which had precipitated the war. Livy claims that the Celts were despicably mean in the discussion and that they tried to cheat at the weighing of the gold. When the tribune protested, Brennos threw his sword into the scale, exclaiming 'Woe to the vanquished!' He then agreed to withdraw from Rome and its immediate area, a miscalculation which would have disastrous effects on the Celtic peoples in the long haul of history.

The ancient historians reckoned the number of Celtic warriors engaged in the battle of the Allia at 30,000 men, and this gives an indication of the magnitude of their settlements in the north of Italy. We can surmise that the total population of all the tribes together, including women and children, amounted to hundreds of thousands.

The Romans rally

After their advance was stopped at Rome, the Celts did not pursue their advantage further. It is difficult to decipher the exact reasons for this, but Polybius claims that 'a circumstance intervened which recalled them home, namely, an invasion of their territory by the Veneti'. This, he says, hastened their coming to terms with the Romans and their vacation of the city. The Veneti were a long-established Italic people in the eastern Alps and around the Gulf of Venice, and it is indicative of their strength at the time that the Celtic intruders had left most of their territory intact. Nor were the Veneti the only threat in the north, for the Etruscan empire had been heavily dented by the hordes of Celts, and it is likely that pressure on the new settlements continued from that quarter.

Polybius also states that the Celts, after their attack on Rome, fell into difficulties of their own making. Those who had established themselves in the valley of the Po were being harassed by their cousins on the northern side of the Alps, who were 'comparing their own barren districts with the rich land occupied by the others'. Furthermore, the arrival of reinforcements for their armies from these northern areas must have been as much a disadvantage as an advantage, for such mercenaries had to be paid off in land and in wealth. Disunity of this kind caused the Celts to concentrate their attention on their northern bases as much as it contributed to raiding southwards. Sporadic raiding did continue against the weakened Romans, some such adventures well to the south of Rome, but the assault was not renewed in a comprehensive way for at least a generation. Even then, the only major undertaking seems to have been the seizing of a large amount of plunder as far south as Alba in Latium in or about the year 367 BC.

The later Roman historians were anxious to disguise the fact that, in this period, the Celts had military superiority in Italy. They therefore invented a campaign of resistance by the famous Roman General Camillus, who they claimed returned from exile during the siege of Rome and renewed the war, routing the Celts from the city. Both Livy and Plutarch describe Brennos retreating from Rome and regrouping his army eight miles to the southeast on the road to Gabii. There Camillus made a sudden attack on the Celtic camp and scored a final great victory. There may indeed have been a memory of a battle at that place between Celts and Romans, but it is obvious that in this case the writers were drawing on fictional sources. They **even** have **Camillus confronting** Brennos at the **counting of the ransom and not allowing the** payment. According to **Plutarch,** Camillus ordered **the** Gauls to take their weights and scales and **depart** without the gold, for 'it was customary with the Romans to deliver **their** country with iron, not with gold'!

Besides strengthening military morale and serving feelings of Roman patriotism, there was a further purpose to such stories – that of family propaganda – for Roman arisocrats of later centuries found it expedient to invent accounts of how illustrious ancestors of theirs had saved the city in times of need. In one such account, Livy has a large Celtic force encamping on the river Anio and threatening Rome in 361 BC. We read that the Roman Dictator Titus Quinctius marched out of the city with a large army, and camped on the opposite side of the river. Then a Celt of enormous size, in multicoloured dress and painted armour inlaid with gold, came to the bridge over the Anio and shouted out a challenge to the bravest man in Rome to fight him in single combat. A young Roman nobleman called Titus Manlius volunteered to take up the challenge. On seeing a much smaller man than himself come forward, the Celt stuck out his tongue in mockery. When they came to close quarters, the Celt slashed at Manlius with his great sword, but to no effect, and the Roman stabbed at him with his shorter sword and slew him. He seized the torque from the corpse of the Celt and put it on his own neck, thus earning the nick-name 'Torquatus'. The whole Celtic army was much disheartened by this, and next night they raised their camp and withdrew to Campania.

Livy goes on to describe how the Celts forged an alliance with the Tiburtines and continued the war until the following year, when they were defeated within sight of Rome itself by a new dictator, Quintus Servilius Ahala. The Celtic survivors fled to the city of Tibur, where they were welcomed and given refuge, while the Romans were too occupied with their struggles against other Italic peoples to pursue their advantage.

Again, in 358 BC, a Celtic force advanced as far as Praeneste, but were repulsed by a Roman army under Gaius Sulpicius. They were driven with great slaughter into the mountains and woods, and Livy claims that the Romans collected from their spoils a considerable quantity of gold. A much larger incursion into Roman territory occurred seven years later, and near Alba the Celts were encountered by a strong Roman army which occupied the higher ground. Attacking 'with wild shouts', the Celts tried to charge uphill in the face of a torrent of javelins and spears, but their charge was broken. Thinking that they had already gained victory, the Romans descended to the plain, but were confronted by a fresh troop of Celtic warriors. Here the Romans showed their superior tactical skill, and Livy says that the Celts broke ranks 'for lack of proper command or leadership', and retreated in total disarray to the distant hills.

Yet again, in the winter of 349 BC, they are described as coming down from the Apennine heights, 'being unable to withstand the severity of the winter weather', and – without much regard for strategy – fighting an indecisive battle with Greek pirates who were ravaging the coast off Rome. Eventually, they were encountered by a Roman army of nearly 40,000 men under Furius Camillus, son of the famous general of the same name. Realising that the Celts lived off plunder, Camillus embarked on a policy of preventing individual raids rather than engaging in all-out confrontation. For the purpose of protecting the whole area against such sudden attacks, he set up a large camp as headquarters in the Pomptine district.

Livy cannot refrain from telling another dramatic anecdote here. He relates how a huge and heavily-armed Celt approached the Roman camp, demanded silence by striking his shield with his spear, and then through an interpreter issued a challenge to single combat. A young tribune called Marcus Valerius took the field. As he faced the Celtic warrior, a raven suddenly alighted on the helmet of Valerius, and joined with its beak and claws in the attack on the Celt. Bewildered and half-blinded, the warrior was slain by Valerius, and the raven then flew off towards the east. Both sides took this as a sign of divine intervention on behalf of the Romans, who proceeded to attack the Celts when the latter went to recover their fallen warrior. This, we read, developed into a general mêlée, and then into an outright battle, from which the Celts turned and fled towards Apulia and the sea. Camillus is quoted as shouting to his men to 'cut down the Gaulish hordes around their fallen leader!'

Despite these stories of glorious Roman victories, Livy himself admits that raiding for plunder rather than war for conquest was the Celts' purpose. We can accept that several of such raids were repulsed by the Romans, but others must have been largely successful. Indeed, regarding the events of the year 349 - 348 BC, instead of the great Roman victory in the dual battles described by Livy, Polybius states that the Romans got intelligence of an advance by 'a great force' of Celts and, mustering their allies, they marched forth in eagerness to fight a decisive battle. 'The Galatae were dismayed at their approach, and besides weakened by internal feuds, retreated homewards as soon as night fell, with all the appearance of a regular flight.' A later source claims that the Romans allowed the Celts to withdraw without hindrance, and that their path of retreat became known thereafter as *Gallica* ('the Gaulish Way'). It seems clear, at any rate, that the Celts were too cautious to risk a disastrous defeat, and were shrewd enough to see that there was no great plunder to be had on that occasion.

There is even more reason to doubt the inevitable victory of Roman champions in single combat. The nickname Torquatus given to Manlius and his descendants points to some tradition of him overcoming a well-caparisoned Celtic warrior and seizing the *torcus* from his neck, but the circumstances of that individual struggle were hardly as strategic and symbolic as presented by Livy. It is indeed clear from both classical and native Celtic sources that the Celts had a custom, when two armies were drawn up in opposition to each area, for a champion from either side to engage in single combat as a prelude to the general battle. Diodorus Siculus, for instance, drew the following description of Celtic battle custom from the work of Posidonius: 'When the armies are drawn up in battle-array they are wont to advance before the battle-line and to challenge the bravest of their opponents to single combat, at the same time brandishing before them their arms so as to terrify their foe. And, when someone accepts their challenge to battle, they loudly recite the deeds of valour of their ancestors and proclaim their own valorous quality, at the same time abusing and making little of their opponent and generally attempting to rob him beforehand of his fighting spirit.' This was the type of Celtic practice of which Livy had heard, and which he or his sources turned to the propaganda advantage of the Romans.

The episode of the crow must spring from a similar Celtic tradition. The raven or carrion crow – which haunts the battlefield waiting to prey on the carnage – had long been a symbol of war for the Celts, and indeed such a bird was represented on the helmets of some of their leading warriors for a long time. The image was assimilated to that of the war-goddess, which was the form taken by the land-goddess on behalf of her adherents in time of strife. She was known as Catubodua ('battle-rave-ness'), a designation which survived with the very same meaning in later Irish tradition as Cathbhadhbh or Badhbh Chatha. Livy's claim that Celtic armies were demoralised by defeat of their champions in single combat accords with the order which he attributes to the younger Camillus to cut down the Gauls 'around their fallen leader'. This also rings true to Celtic tradition, for Irish sources state that 'battle is discontinued after the loss of a lord'.

The great defeat

Two major failings of Celtic armies are accurately pinpointed by Livy, their lack of overall planning and their quarrelsomeness and disunity. Polybius agrees with this, for – in describing the situation at the beginning of the third century BC – he shows how their internal tensions and their short-sightedness caused increasing problems for them.

He relates how the Celts in Italy were alarmed by a threatening movement of the Transalpine tribes, and tried to divert a new invading horde by presents and by appeals to their ties of kindred. Eventually, they had no alternative but to recommend a new attack on Rome, which would allow the newcomers full scope for their enthusiasm, and the Cisalpine Celts themselves offered to join in the expedition. They furthermore enlisted the support of an Etruscan army, and in the resulting raid on Roman territories in 299 BC they took a great quantity of booty. 'But when they got home, they quarrelled over the division of the spoil, and in the end destroyed most of it, as well as the best of their own force. This is the way of the Galatae when they have appropriated their neighbours' property, and it mostly arises from brutish drunkenness and intemperate feeling.'

A logical strategy for the Celts in these wars would have been to forge close military links with the other peoples of northern and central Italy, whose interests were also being threatened by the Romans. They were very slow to realise the wisdom of this, however, and in the year 296 BC only joined a combined force of Etruscans, Samnites and Umbrians after much coaxing by the others. The Romans were alarmed at this devel-opment for – as Livy says – the Celts were 'a race born to the clash of arms, fierce not only by nature but moreover by their hatred of the Roman people' and 'what was most dreaded at Rome was a Gaulish rising'. They

had good reason for this fear, for in the following year the Senones surrounded and wiped out a whole legion at Clusium. The Roman consuls,
Fabius and Decius, who were hastening to that place, got the first inkling
of what had happened when they caught sight of Celtic horsemen 'carrying
heads on their horses' breasts and fixed on their spears, singing their
usual song of triumph'.

The plan was to destroy all the legions by a combined force of
Celts and Samnites taking the field against the advancing Romans, while
the Etruscans and Umbrians were to attack the large Roman base-camp at
Sentinum. Three traitors from the combined camp at Clusium, however,
kept the Romans informed of all plans, and the latter decided to draw the
attention of the Etruscans and Umbrians away by ravaging their lands. A
large force undertook this work of destruction, and the Etruscans and
Umbrians had no alternative but to go and defend their people. Then the
Romans pressed the combined force of Celts and Samnites into a confrontation near Clusium. As the opposing armies drew up to face each
other, Livy relates that a wolf chased a hind down from the mountains
and onto the plain between them. The hind raced towards the Celts, but
the surprised wolf headed for the Roman lines, where it was let through
with great acclamation. They took this as a portent, for the wolf was
sacred to Mars, the Roman god of war.

The numbers on both sides were enormous. Livy mentions as an
exaggeration a report that the combined Celts and Samnites had over
500,000 infantry, with 46,000 cavalry and 1,000 chariots, but even a third
of such a force would have been massive. The Romans had four full
legions. The Celts were on the right wing of their side, and the Samnites
on the left, and Livy remarks that if the Etruscan army had been there it
would have meant certain defeat for the Romans. As it was, the fighting
was ferocious, lasting all day long without any advantage to either side.
The Roman Commander Fabius decided to remain on the defensive and
to hold his lines for as long as possible, knowing that the Celts were very
fierce and determined on their first onslaught but tended to tire and to
succumb to the heat as time wore on. The other commander, Decius, however, was more impetuous, and he launched his cavalry with full vigour
onto the Celtic lines. They broke through the Celtic cavalry and set upon
the infantry, but suddenly they were alarmed by a style of fighting which
they had never before encountered. The Celts, standing up in their chariots, and hurling their weapons, bore down on them with a fearful
clamour of hooves and wheels.

Decius' cavalry was seized with panic and fled through the lines of their own infantry. Then the Celts came at them, wreaking havoc in all directions. Decius realised that he had almost lost the battle and, solemnly dedicating himself to the gods, rode his horse right into the Celtic mass, where he was cut down. The Celts crowded exultantly around his body, flinging their javelins in all directions 'as if they had lost their wits'. The patient and resourceful Fabius, however, was determined to turn disaster into victory. Perceiving that the madness of war was upon the Celts, he sent reinforcements over to the weakened Roman flank, encouraging them to renew the attack.

The Celts stood in close formation with their shields overlapping in front of them, and the slaughter continued there in stalemate. Meanwhile, Fabius pushed the Samnites over towards their Celtic allies and, judging that his opponents were beginning to show signs of fatigue, he collected all his reserve troops, chased the Samnites through the Celtic lines, and then ordered a new attack on the rear of the Celts. Eventually the Celtic formation broke, and the Romans had prevailed. The Celts and Samnites lost 25,000 dead and 8,000 captured, while Roman losses totalled nearly 8,000. It took the Romans a long time to locate the body of the Consul Decius, for he had been buried under a mound of Celtic corpses.

That many got away, however, is clear from what Polybius has to say about this battle. The Romans, having killed a large number of Celts and Samnites, 'forced the survivors to retreat in hot haste, each to his own land'. The Samnites were able to continue the war for several years more; and, as for the Celts, within ten years their powerful southern tribe, the Senones, were besieging the town of Arretium (now Arezzo). Polybius describes how the Romans went to the assistance of the town 'and were beaten in an engagement under its walls'. The Roman Praetor Lucius was killed in this battle and many Roman prisoners taken.

The new praetor Manlius Curius felt constrained to send ambassadors to the Senones to treat for the prisoners. The new Senones leader was Britomaris, whose father had been slain at Sentinum. He was in no mood to relent and – perhaps in recollection of the treachery of Roman ambassadors to the Celts a century before – ordered the slaying of these envoys. Their bodies were cut into pieces and scattered in the fields, in accordance with the Celtic belief that this treatment of offenders brought good luck to the crops. The furious Romans then sent another army to the area, and in a pitched battle in 283 BC they cut the army of the Senones to pieces. Britomaris was captured and tortured to death.

The surviving Senones were expelled from most of their territory, and Roman colonies were planted at Sena Gallica, north of Ancona, and further north still at Ariminum (now Rimini) – the first ever in Celtic lands. The Romans boasted that their consul, Livius Drusus, recovered from the Senones the 1,000 pounds of gold which had been paid in the ransoming of Rome itself 100 years before. Some accounts state that all the adult males of the Senones were slain by the Romans, and the captured women and children sold into slavery.

Frightened by these events, the other front line Celtic people, the Boii, called up their men, made an alliance with the Etruscans, and gave battle to the Romans near the small lake of Vadimo (now Bassano, close to the Tiber between Volsinii and Falerii). The Etruscans lost half of their army there, while scarcely any of the Boii army escaped. As a result, the Boii were facing extinction in the area, and in the following year found it necessary to enlist all of their young men who had just come of age in order to withstand the Romans. But they were defeated again, and had to surrender and accept Roman settlements on their lands. For a whole generation and more, the Celts of Cisalpine Gaul had no choice but to accept Roman dictates and continuing evictions.

The tidal wave of expansion into Italy had been in surge for over a century, but it had finally been turned and, instead of the Celts making encroachments onto Roman territory, it was the Romans who were beginning to encroach on the hard won soil of the Po Valley. Italy had proved, and would further prove, to be a precarious adventure for the Celts, but it was not the only stage on which their ambitions could be played out. Territories much further away from the homeland were also beckoning and, by this time, Celtic warriors were making dramatic progress in these.

3

THRUST TO THE EAST

According to tradition, the area of the Hercynian forest had anciently been assigned by the expanding Celts to Segovesus and his followers. This great ancient forest stretched eastwards from the Celtic territories in southern Germany and Switzerland, and the newcomers proved to be daunting warriors who made rapid progress. The legendary account must refer to the sweeping campaign carried out eastwards by the Boii and allied tribes in the late fifth and early fourth centuries BC, accompanied by and followed by other smaller groups. They assimilated the earlier proto-Celtic chiefdoms in Bohemia and northern Austria, and opened the way for the migration of other groups from north of the Alps. The most important of these migrations was spearheaded by a very powerful Celtic tribe, the Volcae from central Germany, who advanced to the north of the Boii and then set out on an eventful trek which brought them still further east.

Advance through the Balkans

The historian Trogus Pompeius, writing in the first century BC, drama-tised this thrust to the east by claiming that Segovesus and his followers were 'guided by birds, for the Celts are pre-eminent in the art of augury'. It is believed that Trogus, who was himself a Celt from Gaul, was using native sources, and it is indeed probable that migrators were reassured at the start of their expeditions by signs and prophecies. The advances eastwards did, at any rate, meet with singular success. The Dacians stood in the way of the Volcae but failed to prevent them. To their south, the Boii continued to take fresh terrains under their sway, pushing into Illyrian territory and reaching the northern Balkans within a few years.

As the nation nearest to the Celts on their south-eastern flank, the Illyrians had borne the brunt of Celtic ambitions for some time. It is apparent, for instance, that the old Hallstatt chiefdoms of Austria had penetrated into Illyrian territory in the eastern Alps, had taken control of the area around the river Drava and had established a centre which they called Noreia there. It is of interest that the Celts did not intrude upon the territory of the Venetians or of the Istrians, the Italic tribes who inhabited both sides of the Gulf of Venice. Illyria was considered a softer and more worthwhile target. A vignette illustrating Celtic guile in their dealings with an Illyrian people, the Ardiaci, who lived just south of the Istri, is given by the Greek writer Theopompus in the fourth century BC. Being aware of the Illyrians' taste for fine food, the Celts 'prepared a very sumptuous banquet in their tents for all the soldiers, and mixed with the food an herb of intoxicating properties which strongly purged their bowels'. It would appear that the Celts prepared this feast in their own encampment, and then allowed the Illyrians to seize the camp and partake of it. The result was dramatic, for Theopompus states that, while in this helpless state, many of the Illyrians were captured and slain by the Celts, while others 'unable to endure the workings of their stomachs, threw themselves into the rivers'.

This account is, of course, fanciful, but it symbolises Celtic ambitions towards power in that whole area. These ambitions were increased greatly when the Boii came to dominate most of the region which now comprises eastern Austria. In addition to their prowess as warriors, the Boii and their allies benefited from instability in the region. The Illyrians were at war with the Macedonians, a factor which left their western flank quite vulnerable. The course of that war was varied. In the year 393 BC the Illyrians forced the Macedonians to pay them tribute, and in 359 BC they slew the Macedonian king Perdiccas in battle. Before they could devote their attention to the Celtic intruders, however, the Illyrians faced a new crisis. The Macedonians unexpectedly recovered from their setback and, under the leadership of Perdiccas' brother Philip, drove the Illyrians from their territory. After many successes, Philip was assassinated in 336

BC by one of his bodyguards. The assassin was a Macedonian, but the weapon used was a Celtic dagger.

The accession to power in 335 BC of Philip's son, Alexander the Great, sounded a death knell for the Illyrian empire. While Alexander was embarking on his campaign against the Thracians in the area of the eastern Danube, the Celts felt themselves ready for further incursions into the lands of the Dacians and, more ominously, into the lands of the Illyrians along the Adriatic. It was at this time that their ambassadors appeared at the court of Alexander. Ptolemy son of Lagus, who was a lieutenant of Alexander, gives an anecdote concerning these Celtic ambassadors. When they arrived, seeking a treaty of goodwill and friendship, they were cordially received and, while drinking, were asked by Alexander what they feared most of all – expecting, of course, that they would diplomatically say that they feared him. However, they replied that they feared no man, but that 'they were worried lest the sky might perhaps fall on top of them'.

This was a proverbial expression common among the ancient Celts, but in the context of Alexander's high opinion of himself it caused some unease. One version of this anecdote has the Celtic envoys adding a diplomatic note to their bravado, by having them say that 'they valued above everything the friendship of so great a man as he'. Another version may be more illustrative of their real mentality when it states that they made the unexpected reply in full awareness that they 'lived far away in lands difficult of access, and had perceived that Alexander's expedition at that time was destined for other parts'. Their attitude left a wry taste in the mouth of the great conqueror, for 'having addressed them as friends and made them allies he dismissed them, and afterwards expressed his opinion that the Celts were braggarts'.The Celt s were no fools, however, and must have been pleased to have formalised a convergence of interest which had existed for some time. It suited Alexander that these new-comers were keeping the Illyrians occupied, and the presence of further Celtic envoys when Alexander was in Babylon twelve years later shows that the arrangements lasted.

These Celts are reported to have settled along the Ionian Gulf, which shows that they had progressed southwards by the flank of the strong Venetians and had taken over part of modern Slovenia. To go further at that time would have incurred the hostility of Alexander, but after his death in the year 323 BC they were once more on the move. In the year 310 BC, under the leadership of Molistomos, they drove the Illyrians before them, and the Macedonian king Cassander felt obliged to intervene and take the Illyrians under his protection. This, however, had little effect on the Celts, who within some years had reached as far as Bulgaria. There, in 298 BC, a large body of them clashed with Cassander's army on the slopes of Mount Haemos. Cassander triumphed, but further afield the Celts were still advancing, and a second large body – under the leadership of Cambaules – marched on Thrace. The power of the Thracians had been reduced by the Macedonians, and now much of the area fell into Celtic hands. Many placenames of that area in ancient times bear witness to the presence of Celtic strongholds, presiding over what must have been a large majority of indigenous inhabitants.

The Boii and the Volcae were the most adventurous of all the Celtic peoples. They seem to have worked in co-operation with each other from early times, establishing a network of communities in the wide area running all along the foothills of the northern Alps, and later along the Danube and into the Hungarian plain. The Boii (originally Bogii, 'strikers'), have left their name on Bohemia, but their settlements spread over a vastly greater area to the east and south. Strong groups of them played a leading part in the invasions of Italy and Thrace, and they provided security for smaller groups of neighbouring Celts in times of threat to their recently acquired territories. The strongholds of the Boii included Boiodurum (now Passau-Innstadt), Juvavum (now Salzburg), Gabromagus (now Windischgarsten), and the celebrated hill fort called Vindobona (now Vienna), which seems to have been dedicated to the deity Vindos ('the bright one'). The Volcae (literally 'wolves', meaning raiding warriors) had a comparable migratory record. Branches of them moved to southern Gaul in one direction, while others spread their power in the opposite direction as far as the Carpathian mountains, where they left their name on the region of Walachia in modern Romania. Some of the Volcae came to be known as Tectosages (Celtic Textosages, meaning 'wealth-seekers'), a pseudonym which suited their migratory record.

A contemporary Greek writer described how the terror of the Celtic name was so great in the east that 'kings, even before they were attacked, bought peace with large sums of money'. Finally, weakened by divisions and internal fighting over the succession to Cassander, Macedonia itself came under threat. The followers of Cambaules, flushed with victory and greedy for more booty, decided to try their luck further. At their continual instigation, a great force of warriors – both on foot and mounted – assembled and, after some deliberation, their leaders decided to divide into three sections. Thus, in the year 281 BC, three armies of Celts moved southwards. The eastern army was led by Cerethrios, and was to attack the Thracians and the Triballi. The central army was under the dual command of Brennos and Acichorios, and was to attack Paeonia. The western army, led by a chieftain who is known to us by the nickname Bolgios, had the most daunting task, that of attacking the Macedonians and their new Illyrian allies. This campaign threatened to make the Celts the most powerful people in all the Balkan Peninsula.

The advance of Bolgios was towards the territory ruled by Ptolemy, the Macedonian king. This Ptolemy was notorious for his treachery and cruelty, and had been only a year and a half in the kingship after a chequered career. When his earlier intrigues in Egypt failed, he had fled to the Syrian court, where he was given refuge and protection by King Seleucus I. Seleucus was one of the generals of Alexander, who after the death of the great leader had fought each other for different parts of his empire, and, by a stroke of good fortune, he had managed to add the kingship of Macedonia to his realm when Ptolemy arrived at his court. Ptolemy, however, assassinated his protector, and through further murders and internecine strife established himself on the Macedonian throne. From his violent and unpredictable nature, he bore the nickname 'Ceraunos', which meant 'thunderbolt'. With a large Celtic army advancing on his territory, he failed to appreciate the gravity of the situation and – according to Greek writers – behaved like a boastful lunatic.

Celtic emissaries were sent to Ptolemy's court, offering peace if he wished to purchase it. Taking this as a sign that the Celts wished to avoid fighting, Ptolemy boasted that they were afraid of him and demanded that they gift up their arms to him and surrender their chieftains as hostages. On hearing news of this, the Celtic leaders broke out into laughter, remarking that 'he would soon see whether they had offered peace for his sake or for theirs'. One report is that Ptolemy actually slew the envoys, thus enraging the Celtic forces further, and then rashly marched out to give battle. The Celts won a resounding victory and decimated the Macedonian army. Ptolemy himself was thrown from his elephant, and the Celtic warriors tore his body to pieces and fixed his head on a lance.

It may be that the Celtic leader got his own nickname from this actual event, for Bolgios was the Celtic equivalent of the Greek Ceraunos, a thunderbolt. After this dramatic success in 279 BC, his army could well claim that he was the real thunderbolt, a designation which moreover was often used for their own god of war. Panic now gripped all of Macedonia, and the gates of the cities were shut, but a minor chief called Sosthenes gathered together the remnants of the Macedonian army and began a guerrilla campaign against the forces of Bolgios. This caused the Celts to cease their advance and, satisfied with the booty which they had gained, they returned to their base to plan further raids.

Meanwhile, the army of Cerethrios was penetrating further south and east and, pushing as far as the Maritsa river in present-day Bulgaria, proceeded from there across the Rodopi Mountains to Thessaly. Brennos had reached the borders of Greece and, when he heard that Bolgios had

Below:
The expansion of Celtic peoples from the sixth to the third century BC.

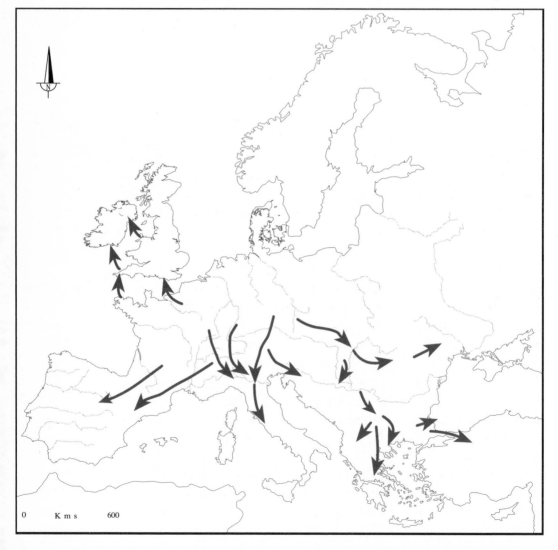

K m s   0   600

not pursued the campaign through Macedonia, he decided to direct his own army there. As he was laying waste the whole Macedonian countryside, Brennos encountered the forces led by Sosthenes and defeated them. The Celts now began to plunder not only human settlements but religious temples as well; and Brennos is reputed to have jested that 'the gods being rich ought to be generous to men'.

Invasion of Greece

It is apparent that most of the Celtic leaders in these campaigns, and probably much of their fighting force also, belonged to the Boii and Volcae. Brennos himself, the most daring of the leaders, was described as of the Tolistoboii, one of the most enterprising groups among the Boii. He now took the initiative by arranging private meetings with other Celtic leaders and calling public assemblies, all the time advocating a massive expedition into Greece. He pointed out to the various Celtic chieftains that Greece, though a very wealthy country, was in a weak military position, and he tempted their greed by reminding them of the immense treasures of gold and silver to be had there.

Brennos was celebrated for his astuteness and wile. According to a later story, he introduced Greek captives before a full assembly of Celtic chiefs. The captives were weak and puny in body, their heads were shaven, and they were clad in filthy tattered clothes. Beside these he placed the strongest and most handsome of his own warriors, fully dressed for war. The point which he wished to make, of course, was that the task of overcoming the Greeks would be an easy one, and his fellow-chiefs were thus easily persuaded.

By such astute diplomacy and manoeuvering in the year 278 BC, Brennos put together a huge army in the northern Balkans – one report claims that it exceeded 150,000 foot and 20,000 horse, while another is perhaps more accurate when it puts the total number at 50,000. With this force, and accompanied again by his lieutenant Acichorios, Brennos headed south for Delphi. A later Greek writer, Pausanius, with an excess of exuberance, states that the actual cavalry strength was over 62,000. He nevertheless gives an interesting explanation in this context of the fighting tactic which the Celts called *trimarcisia* ('feat of three horsemen'):

> The servants remained in the rear, close at hand; if a trooper had his horse killed, the servant brought him a fresh mount; if the trooper

himself were slain, the man mounted his master's horse; and if this man too fell, the third servant in turn took his place in the fight. If the master were wounded, one of the servants conveyed him to the camp while the other took his place in the ranks.

The successes of the Celts had been rapid, but they had been gained at a diplomatic price, and this became particularly evident in the Greek campaign. The Greeks had observed that the payment of tribute had not protected the Macedonians, Thracians, Paeonians, and Thessalians from devastation. Reasoning that it would not protect them either, they determined to oppose the invaders to the death. The Celts soon found that in this case they were facing a far more formidable foe than heretofore, and one comparable to Rome which their kinsmen were facing in the great peninsula to the west of them.

When the army of Brennos entered Greece, they met with no opposition for a while, and advanced towards the pass of Thermopylae, through which entry could be gained from Thessaly into the centre of Greece. The Greeks were determined to defend this narrow pass, not only because of its strategic, but also because of its cultural, importance to them. For it was there that, two centuries before, 300 brave Spartans had held at bay an immense army under King Xerxes of Persia, reputed to have numbered several millions. Now again Greece was threatened by an army of invasion at Thermopylae, and contingents from several of the Greek states rallied to the defence. The full Greek force was probably about 40,000 strong, and was under the command of the Athenian Callippus.

Learning that Brennos' army had reached Magnesia, they sent a force of 1,000 chosen footsoldiers and a company of horse to the river Sperchius to impede their approach. They accordingly destroyed all the bridges and encamped on the opposite bank. Brennos, however, had foreseen this, and so sent 10,000 tall men downriver by night. This would appear to have been Brennos' own personal troop, for the Greek writers – while remarking that 'the Celts as a race are far taller than any other people' – claim that his company 'was composed of the tallest and bravest' of the army. These crossed the river at a broad point, some of them swimming, others wading across, and others using their shields as rafts. When the Greek force on the river bank realised what had happened, they fell back to rejoin their own body.

Brennos lost no time in having new bridges built over the

Sperchius, so that his whole army could cross. He ravaged the country-side, but left the city of Heraclea untouched in his haste to reach Thermopylae. On being informed by deserters that the Greek force was very small by comparison with his own, he offered battle at sunrise on the following day. The Greeks advanced to the pass silently and in close order, and the Celts soon discovered that the pass was so narrow, and the ground so slippery and rocky there that their cavalry was useless to them in the battle. They also found themselves at a disadvantage with regard to armour, for the Greeks were well-clad while the Celts' only defence was provided by the shield. Hieronymus of Cardia describes the way in which the Celts fought in this battle:

> They rushed on their enemy with the rage and fury and blind courage of a wild beast. Hacked with swords and axes, and pierced with darts and javelins, their fury only died with life itself. Indeed, some even plucked out the weapons that struck them and hurled them back at the Greeks, or used them in hand-to-hand fighting.

Meanwhile, the Greek fleet came as close to the shore as possible, at the rear of the Celts, and raked them with all kinds of missiles and arrows. Before long the Celts – caught between the assaults from front and rear and confined on the narrow ground – grew tired and frustrated, and their leaders ordered a retreat. Their losses continued as they withdrew, some of them being trampled and others pushed into the mud and water. As in Italy, they had proved to be no match for a well-organised, disciplined, well-equipped, and tactful fighting force. Only 40 of the Greeks were killed in the battle, whereas the Celtic losses ran into thousands. It is reported that the Greeks buried their own dead and despoiled the corpses of the enemy, whereas the Celts made no effort to bury theirs but left them to be devoured by wild beasts and birds. This was attributed to a wish to strike fear into the Greeks by their callous indifference, but the real reason may have been a religious one, for – as we have seen earlier – the carrion crow was a representative of the war-goddess to the Celts.

It is obvious that the battle of Thermopylae was by no means a decisive one, and by Brennos it was regarded as no more than a tempo-rary setback. Six days after the battle, a detachment from the Celtic army began to ascend Mount Oeta by a narrow path from the city of Heraclea. Their objective was the ruins of Trachis, where there was a sanctuary of Athena rich in votive offerings. They were intercepted, however, by the garrison from Heraclea, under the leadership of Telesarchus. In the ensuing battle, Telesarchus was slain, but his men managed to repulse the Celts and to save the shrine. This second defeat dampened the spirit of the Celts further, but Brennos – who was a skilled strategist – determined to persist.

He thought of a plan to draw away from the main Greek force the Aetolians, who numbered something in the region of 10,000 fighting men. The plan was to invade and lay waste the whole of Aetolia, and for this purpose Brennos is claimed to have selected 40,000 foot and 800 horse, and to have placed them under the command of Orestorios and Combutis. The force crossed back over the river Sperchius and passed through Thessaly and on to the town of Callium in Aetolia, which they attacked with a terrible ferocity. Reports began to come back to the Greeks of the wholesale murder of the menfolk in Aetolia, of the rape of women, and even of cannibalism by the Celts. The Aetolian army quickly set out for their homeland, where they were joined by the frantic inhabitants of the towns which had not yet fallen. A force of Patreans from Achaea also came to support them.

As the Celts under Orestorios and Combutis were returning from their destruction of Callium, they were waylaid by this combined Aetolian and Patrean army. The Patreans made a frontal assault on them, and managed to withstand the fierce counter-attack by the Celts. Meanwhile, the Aetolians lined the whole road and kept up a barrage of missiles against the Celts, who had only their shields for protection. Groups of the Celts tried to pursue their tormentors but, failing to catch up with them, were met with renewed attacks on their return to the road. They were harassed all the way back to Thermopylae, and it is reported that less than half of them reached Brennos' camp safely.

Brennos now determined on a new plan, to cross Mount Oeta – not by the steep path through Trachis but by a less precipitous one through the territory of the Aenianes. In order to rid themselves of the Celts, the inhabitants of Heraclea as well as the Aenianes offered to guide him. So Brennos set out on this path with a reported 40,000 of his men, leaving the remainder of his force in camp under the command of Acichorios, with orders to attack the Greeks as soon as Brennos himself had got to their rear. The Phocians, one of the Greek peoples most renowned for valour, had been posted on the pass to block this advance, but it chanced that on that day a thick mist was on the mountain so that they did not see the Celts until they were almost upon them. The Phocians were overpowered and driven from the pass, and the way was now clear for Brennos. Some of the Phocians, however, managed to get word of what was happening to the main Greek force, which was transported by sea away from Thermopylae and out of the trap.

Noticing that the Greek army had escaped him, Brennos did not even wait to rejoin forces with Acichorios, but headed straight for Delphi. The terrified inhabitants of that city fled to their celebrated oracle, which reassured them of their safety in the impending danger. The Phocians and Aetolians mustered at Delphi, preparing for a last stand and, fired by their example and courage, the Greek army – though somewhat depleted in numbers – began to reassemble there. In order to build up the confidence of the Greeks, and for strategic reasons, a strong party of Aetolians went to impede the army of Acichorios, which was trying to rejoin that of Brennos. Acichorios had left part of his force at Heraclea to guard the spoils there, and the Aetolians hung on the rear of his marching force, capturing his baggage and cutting off the men in charge of it.

Brennos himself, meanwhile, had reached Delphi and was being confronted there by the main body of the Greeks. The Greek authors report that Apollo, the god of the oracle, gave the message through his priestess: 'I will defend my own!' One account has the priestess writhing on her chair and saying with a raging voice that Apollo and 'white virgins' would protect the site. Brennos laughed at the idea that the gods could appear in human shape, but the Greek historians were keen to expose him as a sacriligious and helpless mortal who tempted fate. So we read that, when the battle was begun, the god Apollo immediately showed signs of his hostility to Brennos. The ground under the Celtic army began to tremble violently, and then thunder and lightning broke out over their heads. Flashes from heaven struck into the middle of them, striking individuals down and setting fire to the shields and clothes of others.

It was also said that phantoms of great Greek heroes of the past appeared before the Celts, and as night fell it snowed hard. The Greeks interpreted the snowflakes driven into the faces of the Celts as the 'white virgins' mentioned by the oracle, and to add to the effect of the blizzard great boulders began to slip down from Mount Parnassus on top of the invaders. Much of this is no doubt poetic elaboration, and the disturbances of earth and sky would seem to be an echo from the Celts' own proverb – discussed earlier – that they feared nothing, unless the sky were to fall upon them and the earth open underneath them. Their position, though, was in reality serious. At break of day the main body of Greeks advanced from Delphi directly towards them. As the surprised Celts came to terms with this, they were attacked from the rear by the Phocians, who descended the steep slopes of Parnassus through the snow. Caught in the crossfire, the Celts fought bravely, and particularly the bodyguard of Brennos, whom the Greeks described as 'the finest and bravest men of them all'. Brennos was wounded and carried helpless off the field, and the loss of their leader in this way so disheartened his army that they determined on a general retreat.

They continued their retreat until nightfall, when they encamped as best they could. The Greek authors claim that they were struck by the fears inspired by Pan – in the evening some of them imagined the sounds of a hostile army approaching and the hoofbeats of horses charging at them, and this panic spread gradually throughout the whole army. In the darkness they began to mistake each other for Greeks, and in this way fighting broke out among themselves. Observing this from a distance, the Phocians renewed their pressure, and we read that, in addition to the loss of 6,000 men in the battle the day before, the Celts lost a further 10,000 in their frantic retreat. The Phocians saw to it that no supplies were available in the path of the retreating army, so that hunger also set in, causing the deaths of thousands more. The Athenians and Boeotians joined in the pursuit, hanging on the flanks of the Celtic army, ambushing sections of them and cutting off stragglers.

Acichorios managed to join forces with Brennos at Heraclea, but by now the strength of the whole Celtic army had been so reduced as to be a mere shadow of its former self. Although his wounds were not of a fatal character, Brennos felt shamed and disgraced at his failure. He called his army together, and advised them to kill all the wounded and to burn their wagons so that they could return home unburdened. He also advised them to make Acichorios their leader, and then committed suicide – probably with a sword, but one source claims by drinking undiluted wine. Acichorius had him buried, and then slew thousands of their incapacitated dependents, before setting out for home by the same route that they had come. Eventually, the retreating Celts reached the river Sperchius, and after crossing this they were further attacked by the Thessalians and Malians, who wished to avenge former wrongs. Their tormented journey continued northwards, until they reached relatively safe surroundings among their own people who had settled in Thrace.

The Greeks were elated at the turn of events, and much relieved, and the victory was celebrated at Delphi every four years afterwards with a festival of salvation called the *Soteria*. Brennos too was long remembered, with a mixture of repulsion and admiration. Because of his looting of temples, he became the archetypal committer of sacrilege, yet he was regarded as a handsome and brave man whose tragic mistake was to interfere with the god Apollo, a deity which it was believed had dealt him three wounds in the battle. Apollo and the other supernatural forces at Delphi were in effect the guardian spirits of the treasures there, and it was logical that they would align themselves against Brennos when he attempted to seize these treasures. Little is known of Brennos himself, but he obviously was a charismatic leader and he may have been named after the other great Celtic warlord of a century before in Italy.

Extension of Celtic power

The losses sustained by the Celts in the Greek campaign had been atrocious, but their power in eastern Europe was by no means at an end. The classical writers bear witness to the fact that they restabilised their power base in the home territories and held onto much of their conquests in adjacent territories. They even managed to expand their power in the only direction left open to them, further eastwards. In this the major factor must have been the availability of large troops of warriors after the failed expedition to Greece, for there was no means of demobilising these warriors without some other hope of conquest. The historical records show that, within a short time after the debacle at Delphi, such troops of Celtic warriors were seizing more land in eastern Thrace and planning to go even further afield.

The Volcae were much weakened by the eastern wars, but the groups of them which had settled in Carpathia were probably less effected than those nearer to the theatre of hostilities. When reinforced by the survivors of the Greek campaign, they were willing to join with groups of Boii and others in a new adventure in Asia Minor, while yet more Celts poured in their rear into Thrace. In all of these developments, the Boii remained a bulwark, for their territories were extensive and in most cases long settled by them. Client groups of theirs along their northern flank included the Vindelici on the Bavarian plateau, whose name indicates that they were devotees of the same deity as that of the Boii, Vindos. On the southern side of the Danube, and into the eastern Alps, Venetic peoples such as the Raeti, Carpi, and Carni occupied a wide area, but they were being increasingly influenced by the Celts.

Eastwards again, reaching to the Carpathian mountains, were the Celtic Aravisci ('nearby friendly ones'), a name which may have been given to them by the Boii. In the highlands to the north of the Aravisci were the Osi ('high-dwellers'), while the Cotini (perhaps more correctly Cottini, 'old tribesmen') were settled in Galicia and in scattered groups beyond the Carpathian Mountains. These drove Germanic tribes such as the Bastarnae and Sciri before them, and established important *oppida* along the river Dniester, such as Carrodunum, Maetonium, Vibantavarium, and Eractum. The Osi and Cotini probably were branches of the Volcae, and from the end of the fourth century BC they and kindred groups had settled among the Dacians – no doubt in isolated but sturdy groups – almost as far as the Black Sea.

The Cotensii, who must have been of the same tribe as the Cotini, had as their centre Ramadava, on the river which became known as the Ramna. This placename, the first half of it Celtic (*rama*, 'rowing') and the second half Dacian (*dava*, 'town'), symbolises the bilingual situation into which these far Celtic outposts set themselves. The furthest reach of the Celts is instanced by an attack made by a raiding party of them in the third century BC on the Grecian settlement of Olbia (near Odessa) at the most northern point of the Black Sea. The attack, which failed, was carried out in midwinter and with the assistance of a Germanic tribe called Sciri. Several Celtic *oppida* were in fact established at the mouths of the Danube – such as Arrubium, Noviodunum, and Aliobrix – and Plutarch even mentions Celtic settlements as far east as the Sea of Azov. It is interesting to note that these Celtic warriors did not advance south along the coast of the Black Sea in order to make contact with their cousins who were intruding into southern Thrace. The strong Greek cities along that coast were obviously a bulwark against such a development and, as it was, the Celtic settlers at the mouths of the Danube must have been greatly outnumbered by local peoples and soon assimilated.

In the northern Balkans, new formations of Celtic peoples resulted from their general push eastwards, reinforced by warriors returning from the failed expedition to Greece. These fused together in order to hold on to whatever possible of their gains, and managed to stabilise their position as the dominant element among the more numerous local populations of Thracians and Illyrians. The most powerful such new group of mixed Celts was the Scordisci. They were sprung from those who, on their return from Greece under their leader Bathanatos, had settled at the confluence of the Danube and the Sava. Their name was taken from

Mount Scordus (now the Shar-Dagh range), and they founded an important fortress which they called Singidunum (the origin of Belgrade). The Scordisci were fine metalworkers, and it was probably they who first developed an indigenous Celtic coinage, which was in silver and based on Macedonian designs. Their influence was strong in the whole surrounding region, in particular to their southwest where – between them and the Adriatic – the strong Illyrian tribe called Iapodes lived. Sections of that tribe became bilingual, and some of them seem even to have replaced their own language with Celtic.

The Taurisci were settled in the south-eastern Alps and were known from the name of Mount Taurus in that area. They were probably an amalgam of Celtic peoples native to this area since the time of the Hallstatt chieftains, who had combined with various smaller Celtic and groups of Veneti and Illyrians in the foothills of the Alps. They divided themselves into Ambidrava (those astride the river Drava) and Ambisonti (those astride the river Isonta, now the Salzach). Their principal centres were Noreia (now Neumarkt in Steiermark) and Virunum (now Magdalensburg, near Klagenfurt). Due to the iron mining in that area, great success was enjoyed by these centres in trade and commerce with the Balkans and even with Italy, and the lowland Taurisci gradually grew in power and became largely separate from their mountain relatives. Thus the inhabitants of this eastern area became known collectively – from the placename Noreia – as Norici, and the territory under their control as Noricum.

Undaunted by the defeats in Greece, the Scordisci determined to expand their power eastwards, and Comontorios, who had been an officer in the army of Brennos, conquered a large part of Thrace and established a Celtic kingdom in the south-east of that region. In reality, this must have consisted of a dominant class of Celtic warriors lording it over the local Thracians. They made Tylis (apparently modern Tulovo, near Stara Zagora) their capital, and from there carried out raids for tribute against the Byzantines, as a result of which they gained the reputation of preferring to steal gold rather than to mine it. The first such attacks were carried out by Comontorios, and his forces were bought off at an enormous cost of thousands of gold pieces. Eventually the Byzantines agreed to pay a yearly tribute of 80 talents in return for security.

Intrusion into Asia Minor
The Celts in eastern Europe were usually called Galati by the Greeks and

Romans. One writer states that the Galati were at that time so numerous that they began to swarm into Asia. This is, of course, an exaggeration, but it is clear that, with their defeat in the southern Balkans, their eyes inevitably turned eastwards again. In the year 278 BC, we read that 'most of the Galati' crossed to Asia Minor in ships and plundered its coast.

The Roman historian Livy claims that the Celts who went to Asia Minor had departed from the army of Brennos in the Balkans due to a disagreement with him. He states that about 20,000 men, under the leadership of Lonorios and Lutarios, left Brennos before he set out to attack Delphi, and instead went through Thrace to Byzantium. This report seems to be a confusion arising from the complicated series of expansions undertaken by the Celts between the years 281 BC and 278 BC. It may be that, when Brennos tried to bring together the majority of the Celtic fighters for his invasion of Greece, some who had been involved in Cerethrios' campaign to Thessaly had opted rather to pursue their fortunes in an eastern direction. These would later have been joined in Thrace by remnants of Brennos' army, and the combined force would have undertaken the crossing to Asia.

It is clear, at any rate, that groups of Volcae and Boii were to the forefront in this venture and, to judge by their continuing success, their total number must have far exceeded the 20,000 attributed to them by Livy. That writer goes on to state that, having gained control of the coast of Propontis and having imposed tribute on the towns of that area, the Galati were tempted by reports of the riches of Asia. Seizing more territory, they went down to the Hellespont, from where they sent messengers to Antipator, king of Cilicia, who controlled the coast. While waiting for a reply, dissension arose between the two leaders, and Lonorios returned to Byzantium with the larger part of their forces. Lutarios seized some ships from Antipator's delegates and ferried his men in batches across the Hellespont into Asia Minor. Shortly afterwards, Lonorios crossed from Byzantium, having obtained the assistance of the king of Bithynia, Nicomedes.

The two forces then rejoined, and acted as clients in Nicomedes' war against his rival Ziboietes. Nicomedes was successful, largely due to the help of the Celts, but these were dangerous hirelings and proved difficult to satisfy. Disregarding Nicomedes, they advanced further into Asia Minor, receiving tribute from all whom they encountered. The peoples of regions such as Pontus, Paphlagonia, Cappadocia, and Pergamon were weakened by continuous wars, and were in no position to oppose

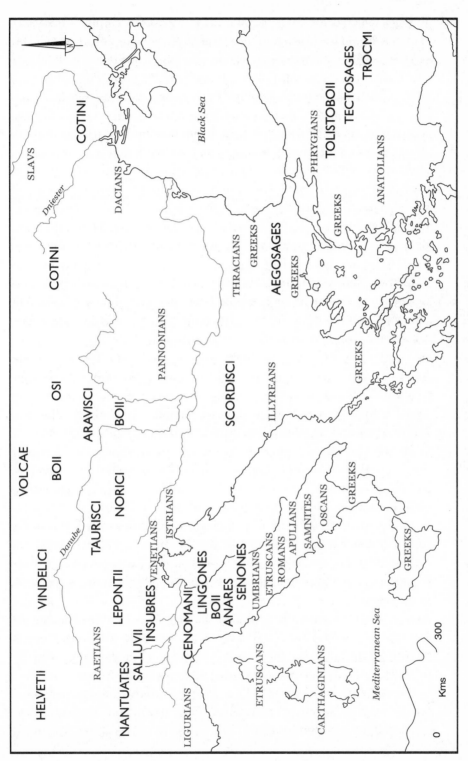

Above: Celtic groups on the Danube, in Italy, and in the east during the third century BC. The Celtic peoples are marked in black, others peoples in grey.

invaders who, even though badly armed, had such a warlike reputation. An inscription from the city of Priene states that they robbed the sanctuaries, burned farmhouses, and so terrorised the people that nobody dared to oppose them. They threatened major cities like Troy, Ephesus, and Celaenae. Greek legend had it that the people of Themisonion were directed to caverns for safety from the Celts by the gods Heracles, Hermes, and Apollo; and that three virgins of Miletus had committed suicide to avoid being molested by the fearsome raiders.

Other people's wars
There was another sequel to the failed invasion of Greece in the year 277 BC, and again the Celts were the losers. When he had embarked on his great campaign, Brennos had left a force of 15,000 foot and 3,000 horse to guard the Celts' own frontier at Pannonia (the Hungarian Plain). Left leaderless, these embarked on military adventures of their own, winning battles against the Getae and Triballi, both Thracian peoples. They then decided to plunder Macedonia once more, but an able soldier, Antigonus Gonatas, was returning from the east to take over the kingship of his country. It is reported that the Celts sent emissaries to this Antigonus, with the usual offer of peace in return for money, but with the hidden intent of spying on both his wealth and his military strength. The wily Antigonus invited the emissaries to a banquet, and made much show of his wealth and pretended weakness. Inevitably, his camp was soon after raided by the Celts, but he had foreseen all of this and had concealed his army in a neighbouring wood. The army attacked and slaughtered the raiders as they departed with their plunder.

Antigonus was, in fact, engaged in a power struggle which extended through much of the east Mediterranean area, and in this the Romans were increasingly involved. After Rome had stabilised the situation in northern Italy by repelling the Celtic raids, and then forming settlements in the southernmost territories of Cisalpine Gaul, she was turning her attentions to the south of Italy, where the Greeks had long been ensconced and which for them was known as Magna Graeca. When the city of Tarentum was threatened by the Romans, the Greeks of that area called on a famous general named Pyrrhus to come to their assistance.

This Pyrrhus had been king of Macedonia and was now king of Epirus. In the year 280 BC he landed on the south-eastern coast of Italy with an army of 25,000 men and twenty elephants, and soon after routed a much larger Roman army near Heraclea. Marching north to Apulia, he persuaded the Celts of that area to join him, and at Asculum (now Ascoli) he clashed with another large Roman army and defeated it also. His own losses in this battle were, however, so high that he commented afterwards 'another such victory and we are lost!' Abandoning his campaign in Italy, he left for Sicily to support the Greek cities there against the Carthaginians, but returned again four years later and raised a new army in Italy comprising Samnites, Greeks, Celts, and others. After his defeat by the Romans at Beneventum, he finally returned to Macedonia, in an attempt to regain his kingdom there from the incumbent Antigonus Gonatas.

Having defeated the Celtic invaders of his country, Antigonus had enlisted many of them as mercenaries, and these were led by Cerethrios, probably the same man who had been one of the leaders of the Celtic invasion of Greece a few years before. Antigonus even lent a contingent of 4,000 Celtic mercenaries to King Ptolemy II of Egypt, who was at war with his half-brother Magas in 277-276 BC. Ptolemy won his war, but the Celtic corps mutinied against him and attempted to seize his treasures. He besieged them on an uncultivated island in the river Nile, where some of them starved and the rest appear to have committed ritual suicide. Ptolemy was so overjoyed at this success that he had a Gallic shield printed on his coins and had a great monument constructed which depicted decapitated Celtic warriors. Undeterred by his experience of these hired fighters, he and his successors had more Celts in their employ in later years.

On his return to Macedonia, Pyrrhus was joined by a number of Celtic mercenaries and later by some Macedonians. In 274 BC, he made a surprise attack on the army of Antigonus at the entrance to a narrow defile, causing so much confusion that the elephants of Antigonus were hemmed in and their drivers surrendered. The strong contingent of Celts in Antigonus' army fought bravely but most of them were slaughtered in the fierce fighting, and soon after the rest of the army surrendered to Pyrrhus. After the battle, Pyrrhus remarked that of all his successes this victory over the Celts was 'the one which added most to his fame'. In commemoration of the victory, he had the long shields of the Celts dedicated to the goddess Athena at a Macedonian sanctuary, while the round shields of the Macedonians themselves were dedicated to Zeus.

Pyrrhus then captured the city of Aegae and garrisoned it with his Celtic troops. The historian Plutarch described what happened then: 'As a race the Celts have an insatiable appetite for money, and they now dug up the tombs of the rulers of Macedonia who are buried there, plundering the treasure and scattering the bones without respect.' Plutarch adds that Pyrrhus refrained from punishing the mercenaries for doing this because he was afraid of them. He lost support through this and other indiscretions and, still supported by his Celtic mercenaries, he was killed in an attack on Sparta in 272 BC – after which Antigonus regained the Macedonian throne. Antigonus continued to oppose the Celtic raiders, and in 271 BC he inflicted another major defeat on them, but he also continued to employ their warriors as mercenaries. In the year 265 BC, the Celts who had been stationed by him in the city of Megara, in the east of Corinth, mutinied because of poor pay. The mutiny was suppressed by Antigonus, and all of the rebels were put to death.

The Galati in the east

The Celtic newcomers into Asia Minor must have been heavily outnumbered by the local Phrygian and Greek populations. Within a few decades they had established themselves firmly in the area in the centre of that landmass which came to be known from their name as Galatia, and they kept together in dense groups in order to guarantee their safety and extend their control. They built several fortresses on heights, from which the Galati leaders gave protection to the commoners of their tribes and governed the older native peoples. The Roman writer Pliny describes how each of the three Galati tribes were subdivided into four branches, which he regarded as 'tetrarchies'. The reality must have been that – as with Celtic peoples elsewhere – each branch had designated specific functions to its king, its judge and its war-leader. A streamlined organisation was indeed necessary, for resentment against them simmered among, not only the indigenous peoples, but among neighbouring potentates.

Antiochus I, the king of Syria, was particularly displeased with the presence and the demands of the Galati. In the year 275 BC, he met them in battle at an unknown location – probably in the area of Ionia in the west of Asia Minor – and threw his sixteen elephants into the fray against the cavalry and chariots of the Galati. Terrified by the sight of such strange and huge animals approaching them, the horses of the Galati took fright and careered backwards through the Galati ranks, with the scythed chariots causing particular havoc. The infantry of the Galati were thus in effect under attack from their own cavalry and chariots, and the elephants finished off the general slaughter, trampling, tossing and piercing the foe.

It was easy for the army of Antiochus to finish off the rout, with the majority of the Galati warriors either slain or captured, and only a small number escaping to the mountains. As a result of this victory, Antiochus gained the Greek title Soter (meaning 'saviour').

After the defeat of Antiochus in 261 BC at Sardis by his officer, Philetarus, the founder of the kingdom of Pergamon, the ambitions of the Galati began to grow again. In 246 BC they went so far as to intervene in a dynastic dispute between the Syrian King Seleucus II and his brother Antiochus Hierax. The latter engaged them as mercenaries to do most of his fighting and, in an attempt to counter this, Seleucus confronted them in a major battle at Ancyra. The Galati defeated him, and as a result Hierax found himself the most powerful ruler in all of Asia Minor. Buoyed up by success, the Galati continued in their customary practices, gaining an unenviable reputation for pillage, for slaughter, and for ferocity. Particularly odious were the moneys collected by them through blackmail and the ransoms which they demanded for people whom they kidnapped – these levies were aptly known as *Galatica* ('Celt-money'). The Pergamon king, Philetarus, resisted their demands and defeated them in battle on the issue, but his nephew and successor Eumenes decided that payment was a safer policy and thus gave credence to it as a system of taxation.

The patience of many rulers in Asia Minor was, however, running out. In 241 BC a new man ascended to the kingship of Pergamon, Attalus the young brother of Eumenes, and he was in no mood to kowtow to plunderers. He refused to pay the tribute and, when the Galati came in force to menace his kingdom in 240 BC, he met them with his army near the source of the river Caice and inflicted a stunning defeat on them. A later story claims that the Galati had a plan to scatter all their gold and silver on the battlefield, so that Attalus' soldiers would delay to collect it up and thus allow them to escape. Whatever plan they had did not work, however, and two-thirds of the Galati warriors were slain. Like Antiochus a generation before, Attalus was as a result of this victory hailed as a 'saviour'. To celebrate his victory, he had great monuments erected at Pergamon and other places, depicting images of his army defeating the Galati.

Eight years later, the Tolistoboii tribe thought to avenge their defeat by a raid on Pergamon, but they were met and routed by Attalus close to the city. Alarmed at the growing power of Attalus, the patron of the Galati, Hierax, planned a campaign against him, and to this end turned again to the Galati as allies. They proved unreliable, however, deserting him before a crucial battle and leaving him to suffer several defeats at the hands of Attalus. In 228 BC, Hierax fled to Thrace, where he was slain in an encounter with Celtic marauders.

As a result of these setbacks, the Galati were, in effect, confined to the area which came to be known from their name as Galatia, in central Turkey. There were three tribes of them, between which their territory was divided. The Tolistoboii were in the area around modern Eskisehir, with centres at Gordion, Blucion, and Peïon. They were also known as Tolistoagii – this probably was a nickname meaning 'treasure-demanders', used originally for the groups of Boii who had led the invasion of Greece. The Tectosages were to the northeast, where they captured the ancient city of Ancyra (modern Ankara), probably with the assistance of Mithradates I, king of Pontus, and made their capital there. The Trogmi were east again in the mountainous Kirikalle area, with a capital at Tavion. Regarding their governmental structure, the ancient Greek geographer Strabo states that each of the three tribes were divided into four 'tetrarchies'. Their full council, including these twelve chieftains, amounted to 300 persons, and they all assembled periodically at a place called 'Drynemeton'. This is probably a corruption of *dru-nemeton* ('very sacred place'), a place-name with many parallels throughout the Celtic world, and the custom of assembling at one central shrine to decide on public affairs was later known also in Celtic Gaul and Ireland.

In Asia Minor – as in the Alps and southern Gaul – the Volcae (Tectosages) and the Boii are thus found in association with each other, and there may indeed be a functional connection between the names of the three Galatian tribes – Tectosages ('wealth-seekers'), Trogmi ('poor people') and Tolistoboii (perhaps 'increasing Boii'). We may speculate that the Galati preserved an ancient Celtic ritual by which the sharing out of treasure symbolised the relationships between different groups. Accordingly, at Drynemeton or another such assembly, the leaders of the three groups could have had the ritual titles 'Tectosagis', 'Tolistos', and 'Trogos' respectively. Strabo seems to support this by stating that the Trogmi and Tolistoboii got their names from their chieftains.

The Greek writer Phylarchus in the third century BC gives an account of one great ritual display of wealth in Galatia. According to this, a chieftain called Ariamnes announced that he would give a year-long feast to all the Galati. He divided the country by marking out specific distances on the roads, and at these points he had banqueting halls erected from poles, straw and wicker-work. Each hall had space for hundreds of men. Great cauldrons were commissioned from artisans, and in these all kinds of meat were cooked, to be consumed with great jars of wine. It is clear that these Celts of Asia Minor had, within a few generations, settled down to a reasonably stable existence, and had brought their culture with them, adapting it to the new environment. Their numbers must have been continually increasing, probably due to new influxes of Celtic migrants from Thrace.

The Galati mingled with the native Phrygian people of that area, and although they were very much the masters the Celtic elements did not always predominate in that mix. For instance, at Pessinus (now Ballihisar, near Sivrihisar) they encountered the strong Phrygian cult of Agdistis, mother of the gods, to whom a temple adorned with marble was dedicated. Despite being within the territory held by the Galati, Pessinus, with its indigenous ritual, remained more or less an independent centre, and the Galati seem to have found this easy to accept as it echoed the Celtic devotion to a mother-goddess. At Ancyra itself, indeed, the same cult persisted and in time came to be subscribed to by Galati leaders. That is not to say, however, that the Galati conformed socially to the agricultural lifestyle of the indigenous people in their area. They remained quite cynical, leaving the heavy agricultural work to the natives, and even developing a trade in supplying such natives as slaves to foreign markets, while themselves following mostly military pursuits. Like the Celts in other areas, they soon gained a fearsome reputation as hired soldiers in wars between foreign rulers.

Short-lived Celtic power in Thrace

Despite its initial success in levying tribute on the Byzantine cities to its east, the Celtic kingdom of Tylis does not seem to have enjoyed much stability. Though doubtlessly reinforced by new migrations from along the Danube, Tylis seems to have been little more than a halfway house for Celts in search of new prospects in Asia Minor. Thracian chieftains proved themselves strong enough to withstand any further push by the Celts towards the river Marica to the south, and the cities on the Black Sea began also to resist. In or about the year 250 BC, one of these cities, Apollonia (now Sozopol), was attacked by the Thracian Celts. A sister-city far to the north, Histria (now Navodari), sent a detachment of soldiers by ship down along the coast to the relief. The soldiers were commanded by an able officer, Callicrates, and the Celts were forced to withdraw.

It is clear that the true competence of these eastern Celts lay in raiding and piecemeal fighting. Noting this, the rulers in Asia Minor invited other Celts into their realms as mercenaries, but not always with benign results. For example, the son and successor of the Syrian king Seleucus II, who had been defeated in battle by the Celts, was not free from their pernicious influence. This King, Seleucus III, planned to counter the growing power of Attalus but, as he advanced with a large army in 223 BC, he was assassinated by one of his own mercenaries, a Celt named Apotouros.

His brother and successor, Antiochus III, was not deterred by this experience, but continued to keep a large contingent of Celtic mercenaries in his army. In his war against Molon, satrap of Media, in the year 220 BC, he had a troop belonging to the Celtic tribe Rhigosages, who were imported by him from eastern Europe, probably from Thrace. Three years later, he suffered defeat at the hands of an Egyptian army led by Ptolemy IV in a huge battle at Rafah on the southern border of Palestine. In that battle, the opposing armies both had bands of Celtic mercenaries from Thrace in their ranks.

Attalus himself hired a large force of mercenaries from the Aegosages ('combat-seekers'), another Thracian Celtic tribe, and used them in his wars against the Aeolians, Lydians and Phrygians. He was disappointed with their performance, however, for they disliked the hardship of the long marches and 'despised all authority', moreover bringing their wives and children in wagons with them wherever they went. When these Celts were on the march in September 218 BC, an eclipse of the moon occurred, and they claimed that it was a bad omen and refused to go on. Attalus therefore had little choice but to allow them to return to where they had crossed into Asia, and he settled them around the Hellespont. Notwithstanding this, these Aegosages soon after rebelled and besieged the city of Troy. The siege was raised, and the Aegosages withdrew to Bithynia, where they continued to plunder until defeated by the army of the king of that region, Prusias I, at Arisba. Prusias massacred all of their warriors on the battlefield, and then slew nearly all their women and children in their camp. In describing this action the historian Polybius remarks that it was 'a signal warning for future generations against barbarians from Europe being too ready to cross into Asia'.

Regarding the Greek cities in the west of Asia Minor and along the western coast of the Black Sea, Polybius claims that these continued to pay their 'Byzantine tribute' to the Celts until the reign of Cavaros as Celtic king of Thrace. There is little doubt but that Polybius is here exaggerating the power of the Thracian Celts, and that the payment of any such tribute would have been sporadic and intermittent. Polybius further states that, in order to raise the money to pay, the Byzantines put a tax on ships sailing into the Pontus and that this was the cause of a war between them and the Rhodians in 220 BC. The ancient historian seems here to be confusing the tribute paid to the Celts with an unrelated effort to raise finances by the Byzantines. The confusion may have arisen from the fact that Cavaros acted as an intermediary and negotiated a treaty to end this war.

This Cavaros (whose name was titular and meant 'the huge warrior') was described by Polybius as being 'of a truly royal and high minded disposition'. The same writer adds, however, that he was corrupted by a flatterer from Chalcedon called Sostratus, and it was apparently advice from that source which led Cavaros into increasing taxes on the native Thracians in his territory. This was a foolish move, for the neighbouring Thracian chieftains had been recovering their strength for some decades, and those under Celtic control felt confident enough to revolt in 212 BC. In the ensuing fighting, Cavaros was killed and the Celtic kingdom of Thrace was destroyed in 193 BC. This left the Galati in Asia Minor completely isolated from their fellow Celts in the heart of Europe.

4

CELTIBERIA AND CISALPINE GAUL

The Greek writer Xenophon describes how Dionysius of Sicily, in assisting his allies in the Peloponnesian War of 369-368 BC, employed Celts and Iberians as mercenaries. About 2,000 of these, along with about 50 horsemen, were sent to assist the Spartans against the Thebans, and they proved very effective. From the account given of their fighting tactics, this small contingent of mounted warriors would appear to have been of the same stock as the infantry.

The practice was to scatter these mercenaries among the rest of the army, from which positions they would make sudden charges on horseback against the Thebans, throw their javelins, and then dash away, turning around abruptly to throw more javelins. They would dismount and rest regularly, and when threatened would leap onto their horses and retreat. They would lead pursuers far from their own lines, and then wreak havoc on them by a shower of javelins. In this way they could control the entire movements of the opposing army during a battle, proving themselves to be of great strategic importance. Plato, however, was not as complimentary as Xenophon, and complained that the Celts and Iberians were given to drunkenness, an attribute which he probably noticed while he was at the court of the same Dionysius.

The Iberian Peninsula

It is probable that some of Dionysus' mercenaries were recruited from Cisalpine Gaul, but most of them seem to have been from Iberia. These would have been representative of the generally mixed population of central Iberia at the time, for Celtic groups had for centuries been settling there among earlier local peoples. There are indications that these Celtiberians were well accustomed to the mercenary way of life, and that – as well as gradually encroaching upon lands to the west and south of the peninsula – many of them also served as hired fighters for the native peoples long settled there, such as the Vascones (Basques), Iberians, and Tartessians, as well as the Ligurians who had preceded the Celts into northern Spain.

Most of the original Celtiberians were descended from Gaulish groups – such as the Turones and Lemovices – who had reached the Iberian Peninsula by the early fifth century BC. These had passed over the western Pyrenees, and from there had spread into the centre of modern Spain. Their influence soon extended into much of the west of the peninsula, their language being adopted in whole or in part by some indigenous tribes, particularly by the Lusitani. Although their influence was much less in the east of the peninsula, the Celtic warriors seem to have worked in conjunction with the Greek settlements along the eastern coast there, against the Carthaginians who were long ensconced in the south and were attempting to extend their conquests northwards. This would explain why the Greek writer Ephorus, around the year 340 BC, stated that the Celts were 'great admirers of the Greeks'. It is apparent that a significant new Celtic element was added soon after, the result of new groups crossing the Pyrenees on that eastern side. Many of these seem to have belonged to the great Volcae tribe, sections of which had moved west from their original home in Bavaria, skirting the Alps and moving down the Rhône valley.

As a result of this movement, the Volcae had several strong settlements just north of the Pyrenees, and it may be that reports of gains in this fertile area attracted further migratory groups of Celts from east of the Rhine. When coming within reach of the Mediterranean, and finding some unexpected crowding there, the newcomers would have cast greedy eyes further south. There were flourishing trade contacts between the Greek coastal towns from Marseilles to Sagunto, through which the Celts learned of the rich mines in the peninsula producing silver, gold, iron, copper and lead. Gathering momentum and strength, but stoutly resisted by the Greeks and Iberians in the east, these latest Celtic arrivals would have – in their thrust southwards – skirted the territories of the earlier Celtiberians, and would have mingled with some of them.

It can be taken for granted that the origins of many of the Celtiberian tribes are indicated by the names which they bore. For instance, in the north-west of the peninsula were the people known as the Callaeici. Although this was an Iberian name, they were much influenced by Celtic incomers, so much so that in time their name was corrupted to Gallaeici, from which the toponymic Galicia derives. Their chief centres were given Celtic names, such as Brigantium ('high place' now La Coruña) and Caladunum ('strong fortress', now Calahorra). The most important of the Celtic intruders who remained in this region bore old Gaulish names, albeit in somewhat altered form, such as the Lemavi (or Limici), Lucenses, and Turoli. Some tribes in the region, such as the Querquerni and the Equaesi, were known by Gaulish names which preserve the kw consonant of original Celtic. This shows that they had been in the peninsula before the general change of this old labiovelar to p in Gaul, and indeed the Iberian Celtic inscriptions dating from the third and second centuries BC indicate this also.

Further east – in the whole area of Saragossa around the confluence of the rivers Jalón and Ebro – were a population to whom the Latin writers often referred specifically as 'Celtiberi'. The word would appear not to have originally indicated Celts who had settled in Iberia, for there were many such groups, but was rather a co-ordinate compound meaning people of mixed Celtic and Iberian background and culture. This can be said, of course, of most if not all of the people of Celtic origin in the peninsula, but the fact that these groups were particularly identified as 'Celtiberi' suggests that the mixture was more comprehensive in their case. Diodorus Siculus explains the name as follows: 'In ancient times, these two peoples – the Iberians and the Celts – kept warring among themselves over the land, but when later they solved their differences and settled upon the land together, and when they went further and agreed to intermarriage with each other, on account of such an intermixing the two peoples received the appellation.' This was also the opinion of Lucan, who described the Celtiberi as 'Celts, emigrants from an ancient tribe of Gaul, who added their name to that of the Iberi'.

These 'Celtiberi' consisted of tribes otherwise known as Galli, Lusones, and Turolenses. Their presence is echoed by the placenames Gállego and Teruel, and they – like the groups bearing similar or identical names in Galicia – were descended from the initial Gaulish incursions into Iberia. The most important centres of the 'Celtiberi' were Contrebia (now Botorrita), Nertobriga (now Calatorao), Bilbilis (now Calatayud), and Segeda (now Belmonte). To the east of them, on the northern bank of the Ebro, were the Ilergetes, who were sometimes referred to as Celtiberi and who probably also had a strong Celtic element in their makeup.

To the west and south of the Celtiberi, and also strongly linked with them, were the Pelendones, the Belli and the Titti. These three tribal names seem to have been Iberian rather than Celtic, even though Celtic toponymics were common in their territories. The Pelendones had as their centre the massive hill fort of Numantia (now Garray); the Belli were to their southeast, as far as the river Jalón, with a centre at Arcobriga (now Arcos); and the Titti were on the southern side of the Jalón, with a centre at Segobriga (now Cabeza del Griego). Bordering on these tribes to the west were the Arevaci, occupying a large area which stretched as far as the river Areva (now the Zapardiel). They took their name in Celticised form from that Lusitanian river name, and their centre was Segontia (now Sigüenza). Both Pliny and Strabo, in fact, describe them as Celtiberi, and Strabo says that they were the most powerful group among that people.

Their neighbours and allies were the Vaccaei, who inhabited the area between the rivers Duero and Tormes, with a centre at Cauca (now Coca). These Vaccaei were one of the most numerous and powerful tribes in the whole region. A late report claims that they took their name from 'the town of Vacca in the vicinity of the Pyrenees'. It may rather have been that the town took its name from them, but either way the connection would indicate that they had moved southwards at an early date. This increases the probability that they were largely of Celtic descent, and the fact that they often acted in consort with the Celtiberi would support the theory. The name may even be derived from the Celtic word *vacos*, meaning a 'slayer', and they were indeed celebrated fighters. Diodorus Siculus refers to a custom among them which would suggest that their society was largely an egalitarian one: 'This tribe each year divides among its members the land which it tills and, making the fruits the property of all, they measure out his portion to each man, and for any cultivators who have appropriated some part for themselves they have decreed the penalty of death.'

In the western part of the Ebro valley were the Turmogidi and the Nerviones, both names also apparently Celtic. In that area also were the Berones, whose centre was Varia (now Varea, near Logroño). Strabo states specifically that these Berones 'had their origin in the Celtic expedition' – they may perhaps have originally been the same as the Eburones, who were situated far to the south, on the western bank of the Guadiana. In the far northwest (around Cabo de Fisterra) were a people called simply Celtici, and Strabo makes a curious reference to a small tribe inhabiting the area between them and the sea at Cabo de Fisterra. These were the Artabri, whom he says are 'at the present day denominated the Arotrebae'. This latter designation is Celtic, meaning 'inhabiters of a large territory', and the change may reflect the corruption of an original Iberian tribal name.

Strabo further states that relatives of the Celtici had gone far south and settled on the banks of the Guadiana. He relates an interesting story of them: 'They say that these, together with the Turduli, having undertaken an expedition thither, quarrelled after they had crossed the river Lima and that, as well as this disagreement, their leader also died, and so they remained scattered there.' The Turduli were a Tartessian people from the extreme south of the peninsula, and the legend may contain some memory of competition between them and the Celtic newcomers in the area. This group of Celtici, at any rate, were – with the Eburones – the most southerly of all Celtic settlers, and their centre was the hill fort which they called Mirobriga (now Santiago de Cacém, near Lisbon).

With regard to descendants of Celts who entered the peninsula from the east, the nomenclature also provides echoes of origin. These intruders would have belonged to tribes to the north-east of the Pyrenees, such as the Segusiavi, Salluvii and Volcae. In view of the latter having made a powerful thrust towards the Riviera in the late fourth century BC, it is not surprising to find names of places and population groups reflecting those of the Celtic world east of the Rhine and in the valley of the Rhône. Just south of the Pyrenees on this eastern side were the Volciani, whose name appears to be a variant of the Volcae themselves. Further south, between the Celtiberi and the Mediterranean, were the Edetani, an Iberian tribe, but with some Celtic admixture, as is clear from the fact that a district in their territory was called Suessetania. This recalls the tribal name of the Suessiones on the Rhine.

Further south again were the Olcades and the Oretani, who were apparently a mixture of Iberian and Phoenician peoples but who also had a Celtic element in their makeup. Both tribal names were Celtic – Olcades meaning 'plain-dwellers' and Oretani meaning 'highlanders' – and, interestingly, a sub-tribe of the Oretani was later known to Pliny as Germani.

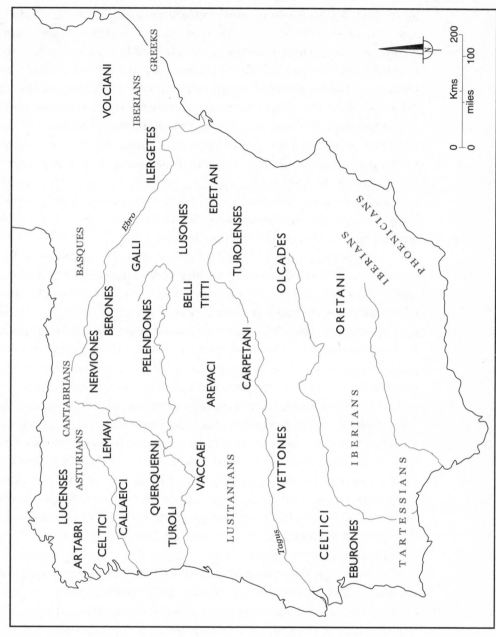

Right: Celtic and partly Celtic tribes of the Iberian Peninsula (in black, other peoples in grey)

If this is not a reference to German mercenaries serving with the Romans in the Oretanian territory, it could indicate that some Celts with origins on the Rhine had penetrated into this area centuries before. A reported city of the Celtiberians, called Belgida – if the name be accurate – would be further suggestive of Celtic culture being transplanted from the region of the Rhine; and, finally, mention can be made of the fact that a chieftain of the Celtiberians, killed fighting against the Romans in eastern Spain in 213 BC, was called Moenicaptus. This is a Latinised form of a name meaning 'slave of the Main', a titular dedication to a deity and of a type for which there is other evidence among the Celts. The deity in question here was synonymous with the river Main in Germany, and the name suggests that even after some generations had passed the cultus of the original homeland had not been forgotten.

As is clear from ancient Celtic toponymics in their territories, some of the most powerful tribes in the centre of the peninsula also had substantial Celtic infusions. These included not only the Lusitani, but their easterly neighbours of Iberian origin along the river Tagus, the Vettones and the Carpetani. The Celtic culture, however influential when expressed militarily such as in names of hill forts, must have been a minority one among these peoples. A remark made by Pliny is significant in this context: 'That the Celtici came from the Celtiberi of Lusitania is proved by their religion, their language and the names of their towns.' He was referring to the Celtici of the Guadiana, who were to the south of the Lusitani. Their basic stock was the Celtici of the northwest, on the far side of the Lusitanian territory. By confusing these northern Celtici with the Celtiberi of the Ebro valley, Pliny reveals that different Celtic groups in the peninsula were not as clearly distinguishable from each other as the ancient authors would generally have us believe. The remark also under-lines the fact that the Lusitani were on particularly close terms with the Celts of their region.

In the second century BC, the writer Posidonius gave a colourful account of the Celtic tribes in the peninsula, in which he seems to have been referring especially to the groups known as 'Celtiberi'. His account survives through the works of other writers, such as Strabo and Diodorus Siculus. They wore, he said, black clothes, hairy like goatskin. Some had shields of the lightly-coloured Celtic type, and others had a round shield of the kind more familiar in the Greek world. About their shins and calves they wound greaves made of hair, and on their heads they wore bronze helmets adorned with purple crests. Their swords were two edged, shorter than the Celtic great ones, and wrought from excellent iron. They were accustomed to bury a piece of iron in the ground until the softer layers of the metal were rusted away, and they then forged the harder part of the metal into a sword. They also had dirks, a span in length, which they used for fighting at close quarters.

The Iberian Celts, according to Posidonius, were impulsive and brave, and like the Celts of other areas they mixed infantry and cavalry in their war troops. 'They have some cavalry interspersed among the foot soldiers, and the horses are trained to traverse the mountains and to sink down on their knees at the word of command, in case of necessity.' The horses of Celtiberia, according to him, were spotted rather than all black but, strangely, they tended to lose that colour when they were brought into western Spain. In battle, a warrior would first fight on horseback and, having defeated his mounted opponents, would descend and fight against the infantry on foot. Polybius also was impressed with their fighting ability. He claims that, when their infantry were hard pressed, the cavalry would dismount and go to their assistance, pegging the reins of their horses to the ground. So well trained were the horses that they remained obediently in that spot until the riders returned. He further praised the Celtiberian swords, which were of excellent steel and were strong, pointed and double edged.

These people, according to Posidonius, were cruel towards enemies and towards malefactors, but they rivalled each other in hospitality. They were accustomed, indeed, to entreat any strangers who came among them to take lodgings in their homes, and those who were good hosts were 'spoken of with approval and regarded as beloved of the gods'. They loved to eat meat, and for drink they purchased wine from merchants and mixed it with honey. However, Posidonius claimed that, like the other Iberians, they were lazy and indifferent to hygiene – sleeping on the ground and using stale urine to wash themselves and to clean their teeth.

Strabo has a curious description of religious practices among some of the Iberian Celts and adjacent tribes: 'Some say that the Callaeci are atheists, but that the Celtiberi and their neighbours to the north sacrifice to a nameless god, at every full moon, at night, in front of their doors, with the whole family passing the night in dancing and festivities'. If this is based on genuine report, it may refer to the celebration of the Celtic festival of the harvest, which in Gaul was dedicated to the god of commerce, Lugus. This deity, who was patron of both the harvest and of crafts, is in fact invoked in Celtiberian inscriptions. One of these refers to a 'procession through the fields' in his honour, and another is a dedication to him by a guild of shoemakers. There is also evidence from the region for the cults of other Celtic deities such as the mother-goddess and the god of horned animals called Cernunnos, as well as for the usual Celtic custom of associating deities with rivers and mountains. The name Deivoréks ('divine king'), referred to in one inscription, may have belonged to an ordinary person, but it reflects that of the Celtic father-god.

The major power with which the Celtiberians came into conflict was Carthage. This was a strong north African city, which from the seventh century BC had been extending its power greatly. Carthaginian colonies were established in the Mediterranean on the islands of Corsica, Sardinia, and Sicily, and towns were seized and fortified as strongholds all along the southern Iberian coast. Themselves a Phoenician people, the Carthaginians engaged mercenaries from different parts of the Mediterranean, including Spartans, Ligurians, and Celtiberians, and – in order to bolster their struggles against the Greeks – made several treaties with Rome. The situation whereby the Carthaginians depended so heavily on mercenaries, however, proved to be risky and unstable, as events in the course of the third century BC were to show.

Between Rome and Carthage

Meanwhile, in Sicily, events were taking shape which would involve the Celts in a much bigger way in the struggles of others. There the Romans began to challenge the control by the Carthaginians of most of the island, and they manoeuvered a war against the latter which began in 264 BC and lasted for 23 years. The Romans gained several initial victories but, after an invasion of north Africa, they were disastrously defeated by the Carthaginian army which was led by a Spartan mercenary called Xanthippus. Confining their efforts to Sicily itself thereafter, the Romans won several victories on land and sea and eventually forced the Carthaginians to vacate the island. Thus ended the First Punic War in 241 BC.

Most of the fighters in the Carthaginian army in Sicily had been Celtiberian mercenaries, and their reputation was not good. Polybius states that they had committed treachery against their own people and had been expelled from Iberia, but the Carthaginians had taken them on board and posted them as a garrison in Agrigentum (now Girgenti). A dispute over pay gave them the opportunity to plunder that city, following on which they were posted to the Carthaginian force under the command of Hamilcar Barca on the steep slopes of Mount Eryx (now Giuliano). The Carthaginians were besieging the Roman fortress on the summit, but were in turn being besieged by a Roman force at the foot of the mountain. Disliking this assignment, about 800 of the Celtiberian mercenaries lost no time in deserting to the Romans. As soon as the war was over, the Romans put these on board ship and forbade them to land in Italy. The renegades were eventually accepted at Epirus in Greece, but within a few years they deserted their new employers and betrayed that city to the Illyrians.

After peace was concluded in Sicily, the Carthaginian leaders Hamilcar Barca and Gisgo arranged to transport the remainder of their mercenaries from that island back to Africa. Gisgo planned to bring them over in groups, so that each group could be paid off and sent to their own country before they could cause trouble at Carthage. In an attempt to spare money, however, the government at Carthage did not dismiss the various detachments as they landed but detained all the mercenaries together in the hope that they would accept less than their full pay.

This was an ill-judged policy, for the mercenaries grew restless and began to commit depredations in the city. They were ordered to withdraw in one great mass to the town of Sicca. When a further attempt was made to decrease the payment due to them, the mercenaries revolted. They consisted principally of Celtiberians, Ligurians, Balearics and Greeks. Buoyed by their exploits against the Roman legions in Sicily, they advanced on Carthage, and Polybius states that 'not only was it impossible for the Carthaginians to face them in battle, but it would be difficult to find any nation in the world who could'. The Carthaginians made many more promises, but by this stage the mercenaries could not be placated.

Their leaders were a runaway Roman slave called Spendius with a force of mixed nationalities totalling 6,000 men, a Libyan soldier called Matho, and a Celt called Autaritos with 2,000 of his nationality. Their plan was to conduct their campaign from the slopes of the mountains, where the Carthaginians could not use their elephants and heavy armaments. Thus began 'the truceless war', which lasted for 40 months, with atrocious acts of cruelty on both sides. The rebels, whose tactics were successful for a long time, seized many towns and were joined by a huge force of Libyans, who wished to assert their country's independence from the oppression of Carthage. The Carthaginian forces were led initially by Hanno, but after repeated failures on his part he was replaced by Hamilcar Barca, whose desperation was so great that he abandoned Sardinia to the Romans in return for their neutrality.

A superb tactician, Hamilcar managed to lure the rebel army onto the plains and defeated them in several battles. In these dire straits, Polybius describes a speech given by the Celtic leader Autaritos, an experienced soldier who had learned the Phoenician language and therefore could communicate very effectively with all the rebel army. He spoke strongly against any compromise, and recommended that all the Carthaginian prisoners be slain. Eventually Hamilcar contrived to trap the rebel army near the city of Carthage itself and, with supplies cut off, the rebels were reduced to cannibalism in order to survive. Spendius, Autaritos and some other leaders went to discuss a surrender with Hamilcar, but they were treacherously seized on his orders and crucified on the city walls in full view of their own army. The rebellion soon after collapsed.

The Carthaginian general now turned his attention to the Iberian Peninsula, where the emboldened Celts had begun to threaten the Carthaginian colonies. He crossed over in 237 BC, at the head of a formidable army, and accompanied by his son, the nine-year-old Hannibal. By a combination of war and diplomacy, Hamilcar extended the power of the Carthaginians from Cadiz and Tartessos over all the southern half of the peninsula. As he advanced northwards in 229 BC, he clashed with the Celtiberians, who were in league with the Greek cities of the eastern coast. The Celtiberian leaders were Istolatios and his brother, and their forces far outnumbered those of Hamilcar, but they were cut to pieces by the Carthaginians. The new Celtiberian leader was Indortes, who reputedly gathered a force of 50,000 warriors, but this force again was easily scattered and he himself captured and crucified on the orders of Hamilcar.

Hamilcar then founded a new city called Acra Leucê (now Alicante), where he placed the greater part of his army and elephants in winter-quarters while he himself went on to attack the town of Helicê (now Ilici), south-west of there. The king of the semi-Celtic Oretani came to him at Helicê, apparently as an ally. It was, however, a trap, and Hamilcar soon found himself being attacked. He attempted flight, but was overtaken by the Oretani and plunged his horse into a river which was in flood in order to deflect the attention of his pursuers. He was drowned, but most of his troops managed to escape to Acra Leucê with his young sons, Hannibal and Hasdrubal.

Hamilcar Barca was succeeded by his son-in-law, another Hasdrubal, who set sail from Carthage immediately. Arriving at Acra Leucê with an army of 50,000 infantry, 6,000 cavalry, and 200 elephants, he immediately undertook a war against the Oretani. He slew all those who had been involved in the defeat of Hamilcar Barca and seized all the towns of the region. Intending to bring all of Iberia under his control, he married an Iberian princess and founded the city of Cartagena at the south-eastern corner of Spain. This was a port of great strategic importance, as it faced Carthage itself across the sea. The Romans now began to notice that the Carthaginians had been using Spain to rebuild their power, but felt unable to counteract this for the moment due to a new threat which was being posed in Italy itself. This was from the Celts of Cisalpine Gaul, from whom a fresh campaign against Rome was imminent. The wily Romans therefore made a treaty with Hasdrubal, according to which the Carthaginian army undertook not to cross the river Ebro. This, in effect, left almost the whole of the Iberian Peninsula in the sphere of influence of Carthage.

Huge battles in Italy

After their terrible struggles against the Romans, the Celts had been comparatively quiet in their areas of northern Italy for 45 years. They made the best of the situation, and their economic life began to revive, as evidenced by the development of their own coinage based on the drachmas minted at Marseilles. A new generation was, however, now growing up which – according to Polybius – was 'absolutely without experience of suffering or peril'. Some young chieftains made contact with their relatives on the other side of the Alps, inviting them to come and join them in a new war against the Romans. Such a force of Transalpine Celts advanced south as far as Ariminum (now Rimini) in the year 236 BC, and threatened the Roman colony there, but the local Celtic population resented their presence.

The Boii killed their own leaders Atis and Galatos, who were in sympathy with the newcomers, and as a result fighting broke out between the two parties of Celts, with great mutual slaughter. The Romans, who had dispatched a legion to the area, looked on in relief as the danger to themselves thus receded. Five years later, the Romans carved up the territory of the Senones among their own settlers, and the Celts began to fear that Rome no longer made war on them only for the sake of supremacy, but with a view to their total destruction. The Boii were the most concerned, for their territories were next in line.

In the year 231 BC, the two largest Celtic tribes, the Insubres and

Boii, made a compact and sent invitations to a dramatic new company of Celts who were converging in the western Alps and near the river Rhône. These were the Gaesatae ('javelin-men'), an emerging band of professional fighters drawn from different tribes. Their organisation was probably based on a young warriors' cult which developed into a large force prepared for fighting expeditions. The leaders of the Gaesatae were Concolitanos and Aneroestes. The Insubres and the Boii pointed out to these leaders what great treasures could be had at Rome, and encouraged them by referring to how their own ancestors had once seized that great city. They found ready listeners, and as a result Polybius states that 'on no occasion has that district of Gaul sent out so large a force or one composed of men so distinguished in battle'.

Aware of what was happening, the alarmed Romans were making frantic preparations for the coming storm, even before the Gaesatae had yet left their home bases. In describing this crisis, the historian Plutarch expressed the opinion that the Romans feared the Celts more than any other enemy, since the Celts were the only people to have captured their city. He states that 'never before nor since were so many thousands of Romans called upon to bear arms at once' and he describes how, in their terror, the Romans resorted to gross superstition. According to directions on how to avert disaster which they read in their Sibylline books, they buried alive a Greek man and woman, and a Gaulish man and woman, at the cattlemarket in Rome. To add to the consternation, inauspicious omens were seen – a river ran red as if with blood and three moons were reported to have been seen at Ariminum, in the area which the Romans had some years before seized from the Senones and which was now being threatened by the Boii. The Boii were supported by a force of Taurisci who had crossed the Alps from the east for the campaign.

Finally, in the year 225 BC, the Gaesatae took the initiative. They gathered their forces and crossed the Alps into Italy, where they joined up with their Insubres and Boii hosts. By this time, however, the Romans had persuaded the Venetians in the northeast and the Celtic Cenomani into an alliance with themselves, so that the advancing Celtic army had to leave part of their forces behind them to protect their territories from these. The Romans called up all their available forces, and support from other peoples of central Italy who were alarmed at the approach of so large a foreign army. The Celtic force numbered in all 50,000 foot and 20,000 cavalry and chariots, and it headed towards Ariminum. There the Roman army awaited them, led by the Consul, Lucius Paullus Aemilius. He had under his command four legions, numbering over 20,000 men, with well over 100,000 allies and support troops, and with hundreds of thousands more spread out from there all the way to Rome.

The Celts entered Etruria without opposition, and decided to march directly on Rome itself. Reaching the city of Clusium, they got news that a large Roman force was approaching, so they encamped there. At nightfall, they lit their campfires and retired under the cover of darkness, leaving their cavalry to give the impression that they had not moved. The Romans were duped and, when they saw the cavalry departing, they presumed that the whole Celtic army was in flight. However, the Celts were awaiting them at a town called Faesulae (now Fiesole), where they ambushed them. The Romans lost 6,000 men in the fighting and were forced to seek refuge on a hilltop. The Celts besieged them there, but a huge Roman army under Lucius Aemilius hastened to the relief. Realising what was happening, the Celtic leader Aneroestes recommended a retreat to their own territories, since they were too encumbered by the great amount of booty they had taken and could return presently in greater preparation to face the Romans. Accordingly, the Celtic army broke up their camp at daybreak and retreated north along the seacoast of Etruria.

The Roman army of Paullus hung upon their rear as the Celts retreated. All went well for the latter until their advance guard encountered another Roman army, under the command of Gaius Atilius, which had crossed from Sardinia and was marching south from Pisa. Gaius encamped his army on a hill near Telamon and, when they observed that they were caught between two Roman armies, the surprised Celts decided to make a stand there. They deployed their infantry to face in both directions, with the Boii and their Taurisci allies opposing Atilius in front, and the Gaesatae and the Insubres defending the rear against Aemilius. They stationed their wagons and chariots at the fore of each front, and placed their booty under guard on a neighbouring hillock.

Polybius describes the appearance of their army thus: 'The Insubres and Boii wore their trousers and light cloaks, but the Gaesatae had discarded these garments owing to their proud confidence in themselves, and stood naked, with nothing but their weapons, in front of the whole army.' He explains this Gaesatae behaviour as caused by the fact that the ground was overgrown with brambles which would catch in their clothes and impede them. There is no doubt but that fighting stark naked gave more agility to these young warriors, but they probably also intended to make use of a widespread superstition that ritual nudity was sacred and gave magical protection. Another reason for the tactic undoubtedly was that, by their apparent craziness, they could strike extra fear into the foe. Indeed, like other ancient peoples, the Celts had a strong belief that war fury gave extra strength to men engaged in combat.

The initial fighting was against the army of Atilius for possession of the hill, around which the Celtic and Roman cavalries were fighting a pitched battle. Atilius himself was slain, and his head was brought as a trophy to the Celtic commanders. After a bitter struggle, however, the Roman cavalry prevailed, and the respective infantries now closed on each other. The Celts, between the two Roman armies, were in a danger-ously congested situation, but it could be turned to advantage given the ferocity of their fighters. The Romans, according to Polybius, 'were terri-fied by the fine order of the Celtic host and the dreadful din, for there were innumerable trumpeters and horn-blowers and, as the whole army were shouting their war-cries at the same time, there was such a tumult of noise that it seemed that not only the trumpets and the warriors but all the surrounding countryside had got a voice and had caught up the cry.' This description echoes the purpose of the Celts, who had a belief that the ele-ments themselves could be harnessed to events taking place on the human level.

The appearance and the gestures of the Gaesatae added greatly to the terror felt by the Romans. These naked warriors were 'all in the prime of life, and finely built men, and all in the leading companies, richly adorned with gold torques and armlets'. The Roman soldiers, however, were not overwhelmed by the antics of the Gaesatae, and probably had less respect than expected for ideas of sacred nudity. As the Gaesatae advanced to throw their javelins, their bodies – unprotected but for their shields – were easily targetted by the Roman missiles, until in final desper-ation they rushed madly on the enemy, only to be cut down mercilessly. They were replaced in the onslaught by Insubres, Boii and Taurisci fighters, and despite terrible losses these more conventional warriors kept up a hand-to-hand combat with the Romans for a long time.

Having lost the initiative through the defeat of the Gaesatae, the Celts were at a great disadvantage, for their shields were much smaller than those of the Romans and their swords were serviceable only for cutting and not for thrusting. When the Roman cavalry launched a fierce attack from the higher ground on their flank, the Celtic cavalry was put to flight, and the infantry was left unprotected from that quarter. Finally the Celtic ranks broke completely, with about 40,000 slain, and at least 10,000 taken prisoner. Among those captured was Concolitanos, while Aneroestes escaped with a few followers and then committed suicide. The Celts had lost their last great battle in Italy and, soon after, the Romans undertook the inevitable invasion of the lands of the Boii, pillaging and destroying as they went. The prisoners were paraded through the streets of Rome to celebrate the triumph, and the Celtic standards and golden torques were sent to adorn the Capitol.

After the battle of Telamon, the Romans decided to pursue their advantage, and in the following year they organised a campaign to take control of the whole valley of the Po. Their armies were now led by the consuls Quintus Fulvius and Titus Manlius. The Boii were forced to submit, but continuous heavy rains and an outbreak of an epidemic in the Roman army prevented any further action that year. The Romans did not delay long in pursuing their ambitions, however, for in 223 BC they again invaded Celtic territory – this time under the consuls Publius Furius and Gaius Flaminius. Having secured the assistance of two local Celtic tribes, the Anares and the Cenomani, they returned to the attack on the Insubres. Mustering a substantial force – though the Roman reports of 50,000 men must be a great exaggeration – the chieftains of the Insubres determined on a last stand on the banks of the Po. The Romans, cautious at the prospect of fighting in strange territory against a large force, and suspicious that their Celtic allies might change sides, sent these allies first across the river into the attack. They then crossed the river themselves, destroying the bridges behind them.

Polybius says that the Roman leaders had noted the age-old vulnerability of the Celts in prolonged struggle, and that their swords were easily bent and needed to be reshaped against the ground by the foot in the heat of battle. The Romans thus instructed their men to first use their javelins, and then resort to their swords before the Celts had repaired their own. In the ensuing battle, the Insubres slashed with their swords, 'which is the peculiar and only stroke of the Celts, as their swords have no points'. With their backs to the river, the Romans used their own swords to great effect on the breasts and faces of their opponents, and gained a decisive victory.

In the following year, the Celts of Italy sued for peace, and the Roman Senate was inclined to grant this, but the new consuls, Claudius Marcellus and Gnaeus Cornelius, stirred up the people against these proposals. Marcellus was a tough military man, and was reputed to be an expert at single combat. Realising that Rome could not be placated, the

Celts in desperation sent requests for new Gaesatae from Transalpine Gaul, and they managed to hire a large number of these. The mercenaries were led by one Viridomaros, who called himself 'son of the Rhine'. The Romans besieged a town called Acerrae between the Po and the Alps, and the Insubres – unable to lift the siege – crossed the Po in retaliation and laid siege to the town of Clastidium (now Schiattezzo) in the territory of the Anares, who were in alliance with the Romans. Marcellus set out with a cavalry force to relieve this siege, and the Insubres advanced to intercept him.

The Insubres were far superior in numbers, and when the two forces drew close to each other, they launched a furious attack, accompanied by blood-curdling shouts. Marcellus prepared for a cavalry charge, but his horse shied away from all the din and bolted backwards. He reined the horse in and wheeled it about, pretending that he was merely performing a sun-wise turn as the Romans were wont to do in their religious rites. The Celtic leader, Viridomaros, now noticed Marcellus, and rode directly towards him, brandishing a lance. Viridomaros was wearing beautiful armour, embossed with silver and gold which made it glitter like lightning. Marcellus, with his own lance, rode straight for him, hurling him from his horse and slaying him while on the ground. The Roman cavalry then put the Celtic horsemen to flight and savaged their accompanying infantry. Marcellus took the armour of the dead leader and later ritually offered it to the gods in Rome.

Following the defeat at Clastidium, the Insubres retired to Mediolanum (Milan), their stronghold. Gnaeus Cornelius brought his army there to besiege them, but he was attacked from the rear, and many of his soldiers were put to flight. Marcellus came to his assistance, however, and in the counter-attack the main body of the Insubres was defeated and their fortress taken. The leaders of the Insubres had no choice but to surrender, and soon afterwards most of the Celts were expelled from the valley of the Po into the foothills of the Alps to the north and into the Apennines to the west. Polybius states that the Celts lost because all their decisions had been governed 'by the heat of passion rather than by cool calculation'.

Hannibal's campaign

The Romans, now unchallenged masters of Italy, could at last turn their attention to countering Carthaginian ambitions in Spain. Events suddenly took an unexpected turn there, for in the year 221 BC Hasdrubal was assassinated in his dwelling at night by a Celtiberian captive whose master he had executed. The assassin was seized immediately and put to death with hideous tortures, but he showed no sign either of fear or remorse. Livy states that 'even under torture the expression on his face never changed, and one could imagine that triumph had so far subdued his pain that he was actually smiling'.

The man appointed to succeed Hasdrubal as chief commander of all the armies of Carthage was Hamilcar's son Hannibal, who was 24 years old and had served as commander of the cavalry in Spain for some years. Like his predecessor, he married a local girl, Imilce, from the town of Castulo (now Cazlona, south of Linares, on the Guadalquivir). This town belonged to the Oretani and, although Imilce's name was not Celtic, some of her relatives may have been. Hannibal immediately began an attempt to subjugate the whole peninsula by capturing by assault Althea, the city of the Olcades. In the following summer he began a campaign against the Vaccaei, and – though he had a large army and about 40 elephants – he had some difficulty in seizing their cities of Salmantica and Arbucala. On his return march to Cartagena, he was attacked by the Carpetani, who were incited by warriors of the Olcades and Vaccaei who had survived the previous sieges. Hannibal astutely retreated until he had crossed the river Tagus, and then turned to give battle. As the combined Iberian and Celtic warriors came out of the water, they were attacked by the Carthaginian cavalry, and those who reached the bank were trampled by the elephants. Then Hannibal ordered a counter-attack and his cavalry re-crossed the river and put the enemy forces to flight.

Being now master of all the territory south of the river Ebro, Hannibal directed his attentions to the city of Saguntum (now Sagunto) on the eastern coast. This was a Graeco-Latin colony and was in alliance with Rome. Hannibal had long been preparing for a conclusive contest with Rome, and intended to provoke a quarrel between the Saguntines and the neighbouring Iberian tribes, such as the Turdetani, which would give him a pretext to attack Saguntum. The tactic worked and, much to the alarm of the Romans, he began the attack on Saguntum in 219 BC and took it with great slaughter eight months later. The Roman Senate immediately declared war on Carthage, and so the Second Punic War had begun. In this great struggle between the two giants of the ancient world, the Celts were by no means an insignificant factor, and both sides made strenuous efforts to gain their support.

Envoys were immediately dispatched by the Roman Senate to

Spain, in the hope of bringing the various peoples of that area into an alliance with them. They met with little success, however. They were ordered off by the Volciani with the assertion that Rome's word could not be trusted. The envoys then approached the Celts of Transalpine Gaul, asking them to resist the Carthaginians if Hannibal were to bring his army through their territory to attack Italy. The envoys were alarmed at the sight of these Celts attending the council in full armour, as was their custom. The Roman request was met with roars of laughter and derision by the young warriors present, and again the envoys were dismissed with reminders of how the Romans were expelling and oppressing 'men of their nation' in Italy. The only support which the envoys got was from the Greek colonists at Marseilles, who informed them that Hannibal had already won most of the Celts over to his side.

In the spring of the year 218 BC Hannibal made his move. Leaving his brother Hasdrubal to hold Spain with troops from north Africa, he crossed the river Ebro with a force of 90,000 foot, 20,000 horse, and 37 elephants. He was careful to send delegates ahead with promises and bribes to guarantee safe passage through the various Celtic territories. Reaching the Pyrenees, he left a force of 10,000 men to guard the passes there, for he mistrusted the independent spirit of the Celtic peoples. He encountered his first major problem after crossing the Pyrenees, for the Celts of that area became alarmed by the approach of so large an army, and a number of them assembled in arms at Ruscino (Rousillon) to oppose him. Hannibal above all else wished to avoid a delay, and so he invited their leaders to his camp and won their approval with protestations of friendship and with gifts.

In Italy, the Boii heard of the passage of Hannibal through Transalpine Gaul, and they encouraged their Insubres neighbours to join them once again in a revolt against Rome. They immediately attacked two new Roman settlements which had been made at Placentia (Piacenza) and Cremona, in their territories, and drove the settlers and the Roman officials headlong before them to the city of Mutina (Modena), which they then blockaded. They next invited the Roman officials to negotiations at their camp outside Mutina, and then seized them as hostages. A relief force under Lucius Manlius was twice ambushed in the woods by the Celts and badly mauled. Over 1,000 Romans were slain in these encounters, and the remainder struggled on to Tannetum, near the Po, where they fortified a position with the help of some Celts from Brescia. The Roman Senate, foreseeing a Celtic uprising to coincide with Hannibal's approach, sent

Gaius Atilius with a whole legion and 5,000 allies to the area, and the Celts wisely abandoned both sieges and retired further north.

Meanwhile, Cornelius Scipio was dispatched from Rome with a large naval force to Marseilles to impede the progress of Hannibal. Scipio sent out a party of 300 cavalry, with local guides and a pro-Roman Celtic contingent, to reconnoitre. They discovered that Hannibal had come as far as the territory of the Volcae (the region around Toulouse), and that most of the Volcae had decided to resist him and with this purpose had withdrawn to the eastern side of the river Rhône. Some of the Volcae and other neighbouring tribes, however, took the opposite view in their eagerness to be rid of him and his large army as soon as possible. These latter assembled a large number of boats, canoes and rafts to bring the Carthaginians across the river. Foreseeing what was going to happen on the far side, Hannibal secretly sent one of his senior officers with a force of Celtiberians to make a crossing further north and to descend at the rear of the Volcae. As the Carthaginian army crossed the river, the Volcae warriors came to the opposite bank to oppose them 'howling and chanting as their custom was, shaking their shields above their heads and brandishing their spears', but they were surprised to hear the shouts of Hannibal's other men behind them. They stood their ground for a while, yet soon had no choice but to force their way out of the trap as best they could and disperse.

Hannibal was pleased with the outcome, but was not yet decided whether to engage Cornelius' army or to head straight for Italy. He was persuaded by a delegation of Boii, who came to him under their chieftain, Magulus, promising to act as his guides and allies. Anxious to have the Carthaginian army in Italy in order to counter Roman threats against their territory, the Boii insisted that in order to gain victory he needed to head for there immediately with his full strength. Determined, therefore, not to be hindered by the Roman forces assembled at Marseilles, Hannibal turned north and proceeded quickly along the Rhône valley, passing without hindrance through the territories of the Celtic tribes known as Tricastini, Vocontii and Tricorii.

He crossed the Drôme with some difficulty, for it had an unstable stony bed and was in flood. The area almost enclosed between the Rhône, the Drôme and the Isère was known as 'the island', and produced much corn. This neighbourhood was inhabited by the Allobroges, one of the strongest and most numerous of the Celtic tribes. It happened, at that time, that two brothers were contending for the kingship of the Allobroges. One of these, Brancos, was already king, and had the support of the tribal council and elders, but the younger brother had the support of the ambitious young nobles. Hannibal was invited to arbitrate on the issue, and he astutely ruled in favour of the stronger of the two, Brancos. In return, Brancos gave provisions and suitable clothing to the Carthaginian army.

Hannibal did not delay and, turning east, soon reached the foothills of the Alps. As he approached the high mountains, he found the precipices held against him by the tribesmen of that area. These seem to have comprised Celtic tribes of the western Alps such as the Everones and Caturiges, as well as the Celto-Ligurian Graioceli and Salluvii. Because their language was very similar to that of his own Celtic guides, Hannibal used these guides to infiltrate them and to listen to their deliberations. The guides discovered for him that by night most of the tribesmen were wont to disperse to their homes. Giving the impression that his army had camped, therefore, he went with a force of light infantry up the mountains under the cover of dark, through the territory of the Quariates (now Queyras), a sub-tribe of the Caturiges. He soon cleared the pass, and gained the higher ground.

On the return next day of the full force of tribesmen, they found the Carthaginian army ascending through the pass. The tribesmen, who were used to the terrain and therefore very surefooted, swarmed down upon the huge army, creating a terrible din. The Carthaginian horses in particular were driven wild by the war-cries and the javelins, and several of these plunged over the cliffs, bringing many men with them. Seeing this, Hannibal descended from his own higher position and, with one charge, put the tribesmen to flight. The Carthaginians then seized the village of these tribesmen, and took all their cattle and grain. It is not clear why these mountain tribes put up such a determined resistance to Hannibal's army passing through the Alps. They must indeed have been alarmed by the approach of such a large army, which had already overpowered the Volcae of the area and which was foraging widely. They probably saw in Hannibal's strategy also the inherent threat of the extension of the power of the Allobroges into the mountains, and in the long-term feared being caught in the centre of the theatre of hostilities between the Carthaginians and Romans.

Moving on through the mountains, Hannibal met with the elders from other villages, who came to him 'with branches and garlands' as signs of friendship, and offering cattle and hostages to him. This was a trick, and Hannibal was not deceived, though he pretended to be. As he had suspected, his army was attacked in a high mountain pass a few days later. Again from above, the tribesmen struck at his front and rear, rolling rocks down from the heights, and then leaping into the fray throwing missiles. In trying to protect his rear, which had not yet entered the pass, Hannibal found himself cut off overnight from the bulk of his army, but next day he managed to make a juncture again between the divided forces. His army got through, but sustained further losses in driving the enemy away. From that on across the Alps, the raids made by local tribesmen were for purposes of plunder only, harassing the front and rear of the Carthaginian army and attacking stragglers in particular. These local groups hestitated to launch any more large-scale attacks on the huge army, and they were especially frightened by the prospect of Hannibal's elephants, a kind of animal they had never seen before.

Finally, as the winter snow began to fall, Hannibal and his army caught sight of Italy, and they descended the Alps with great hardship. The Roman consul, Cornelius Scipio, whom Hannibal had eluded in Marseilles, came to oppose him, having taken over the troops of Manlius and Atilius who were still reeling from their recent battles with the Boii and Insubres. Hannibal, for his part, was quick to seize upon the dissatisfaction of the Cisalpine Gauls, for his arrival in Italy coincided with the outbreak of hositilies between the Taurini people of Liguria and the Insubres. As soon as his Carthaginian army had recovered from the deprivations of their Alpine crossing, he attacked and took by storm the chief town of the Taurini (modern Turin), and would have secured the Insubres as allies but for the rapid Roman advance.

Many of the Insubres were forced to serve in the Roman army, while the others withdrew to comparative safety. Nevertheless, Hannibal continued his attempts to attract various Celtic tribes of Italy to his side, instructing his foraging parties to refrain from taking property from them in particular. The Carthaginian and Roman armies met at the river Ticino, which flows from the Alps into the Po. As he prepared his army for the battle, Hannibal kindled the ferocity of his own troops by a display which showed his true feelings of superiority towards the natives.

Some Celtic prisoners had been captured in the Alpine fighting, and had been subjected to great hardships – having been flogged mercilessly, half-starved, and kept in heavy chains. Hannibal now had these men brought forward in the full view of his whole army, and had prizes exhibited. The prizes included 'some suits of Gaulish armour, such as are worn by their kings when they engage in single combat', as well as some horses and military cloaks. 'He then asked these young prisoners which of them were willing to fight with each other on the condition of the conqueror taking these prizes and the defeated escaping all his present miseries through death'. Lots were arranged to select those who would contend in the combats. The young prisoners behaved in a truly heroic manner, answering loudly that they would all fight, and 'each one prayed the gods that he might be one of those to draw the lots'. When the combats were over, the surviving captives congratulated the ones who had fallen no less than the victors, 'as having been freed from many terrible sufferings, which they themselves remained to endure'. Hannibal then made a homily of this frightful scene, encouraging his soldiers to fight the Romans with the same sense of desperation as the prisoners had fought each other.

In the ensuing battle, the Carthaginian army triumphed, inflicting heavy casualties on that of Scipio, who retreated in haste to the other side of the river. Most of Hannibal's losses in this battle consisted of his Celtic allies, almost 1,000 of them; but as a result of his victory, many more Celts from the vicinity came to him, offering to join his force and bringing provisions. He received them cordially, and proceeded quickly to Placentia, where he besieged the army of Scipio. There another group of Celts took a hand in affairs. This group consisted of over 2,000 who had been conscripted into Scipio's army, and they now slew the sentries at the Roman camp and deserted to Hannibal. He welcomed them, and sent them off to their own communities to incite their people against the Romans.

Most of the Celts, however, remained cautious still, earning the indignation of Hannibal, who stated – with more guile than honesty – that it was the Celts themselves who had invited him into Italy to liberate them. Eventually he lost his patience and ordered that the whole district as far as the Po be pillaged. In desperation, the Celts appealed to the Romans for help, but Scipio was lukewarm in his response, for a weakened Celtic population was suitable to his interests. The other and recently arrived Roman consul, Sempronius, however, considered that this was a good way to secure the loyalty of the Celts, and he engaged the Carthaginian raiders and repulsed them. In his preparations for a clash with Hannibal, Sempronius used spies from among the Celts for – as Livy states – 'it was safer to use Gauls in this capacity, as they were serving in both camps'.

Hannibal and Sempronius clashed on the river Trebia on a snowy day, and during the course of the battle Hannibal turned his elephants against the Cenomani, the only large-scale Celtic group which was in the Roman army. The Cenomani, who were on the left flank, broke and fled, causing consternation among the Romans, who now had no way out but to go straight through the centre of the Carthaginian army. At that centre, with the African troops, were Celtic contingents; and the Romans sustained heavy losses in getting through and were lucky not to have lost their entire army.

The Carthaginian army now headed south through Etruria, enduring terrible hardships because of the bad weather and the lack of proper provisions. Those to suffer most were the Celtic allies, whom Hannibal distrusted and regarded as being lazy and impetuous, and who were unused to such long marches in difficult terrain. They became restless, and would have deserted but for the fact that the African cavalry watched them closely from behind. It is reported that Hannibal himself feared that the Celts were plotting to assassinate him, and that he took to wearing various disguises as a precaution. He frequently changed his clothes and his hairstyle and, according to one account, this caused some disconcertment even to those who recognised him. 'When the Gauls saw him moving amongst their people now as an old man, then as a young man, and again as a middle-aged man, and continually changing from one to the other, they were astonished and thought that he partook of the divine nature.'

Other successes for the Carthaginians followed, the most dramatic being at Lake Trasimene, where the new Consul Flaminius walked straight into a trap set by Hannibal. In the ferocious fighting, a horseman of the Insubres, called Ducarios, recognised Flaminius and charged straight at his personal bodyguard. Shouting that Flaminius was a destroyer of his nation, Ducarius swore to 'offer him as a sacrifce to the ghosts of our people who were foully slain!' He cut down the armour-bearer who tried to stop him, and then drove his lance through the body of Flaminius himself. He would have stripped the corpse, but was prevented from doing so by Roman shields. Soon after the death of their leader, the Roman army turned and fled, 15,000 of them being slain.

Rome was now in a state of terror as Hannibal advanced swiftly through Umbria and scored his famous victory over a huge Roman army at Cannae. In that battle, his left flank consisted of Gaulish and Celtiberian cavalry, and at the forefront of the centre he had positioned infantry drawn from the same peoples. The Gauls, who were naked to the waist, had long swords for slashing; while the Celtiberians, clad in white tunics bordered with purple, had shorter swords for stabbing. As soon as hostilities began, the Celtic horsemen on the flank dashed at the Romans, grappled man-to-man at close quarters and, dismounting from their horses, continued to fight on foot. The superior numbers of the Romans began to prevail, however, and then the Celts at the centre took the main brunt of the Roman assault, being slaughtered in their thousands, and serving Hannibal's master plan to bring the Roman legions into a position where he could outflank and surround them.

One report claims that Hannibal, at the commencement of the battle, used 500 of his Celtiberian mercenaries in a sophisticated trick. These Celtiberians left their lines, pretending to desert, and were welcomed by the Romans, but then at the opportune moment they caused havoc in the Roman rear. Facing furious attacks from Hannibal's cavalry and infantry on all sides, the Romans rallied for a while, but when their generals Aemilius and Servilius fell they were seized with despair and tried desperately to escape. Their army was cut to pieces, almost 50,000 of them being slain in the few hours which the battle lasted. Most of the losses on the Carthaginian side were Celts, over 4,000 of them.

The victory at Cannae should have sounded the death knell of the Roman Empire, but Hannibal allowed total victory to slip from his grasp. Although he clearly had the upper hand in Italy, he was over-cautious and postponed a direct march on Rome itself. He thus allowed the enemy to reorganise, which they did with great precision according to the advice of the celebrated Quintus Fabius. Within a few weeks Hannibal had lost the initiative, and the Romans henceforth were able to contend with him on equal terms.

In that same year of confusion, 216 BC, the Boii took their opportunity, for when a Roman army of 25,000 men under Postumius Albinus tried to enter Italy from the Adriatic coast, these Celts lay in wait for them in the forest which they called Litana. They had the trees by the roadside almost cut through at the base and, as soon as the legions of Albinus marched by, they knocked the trees over on top of them. Then the Boii jumped in among the terrified soldiers and slew them with swords. The body of Albinus himself was stripped, and his head was cut off and brought by the Boii to their temple along with the rest of the spoils. They decorated the skull with gold, and used it as a holy vessel. This accords with the Celtic custom of honouring the heads of fallen enemies, a practice described by Diodorus Siculus, quoting Posidonius, as follows:

They cut off the heads of enemies slain in battle and attach them to the necks of their horses. They hand over these bloody spoils to their servants to carry off as booty, while striking up a paean and singing a song of victory, and they nail them up as first fruits upon their houses ... They embalm in cedar oil the heads of the most distinguished enemies, and preserve them carefully in a chest, and display them with pride to strangers – saying that for this head one of their ancestors, or a man's father, or the man himself, refused the offer of a large sum of money. They say that some of them boast that they refused the weight of the head in gold.

The destruction of Albinus' army caused alarm in Rome, with the one great fear of a combined Celtic and Carthaginian assault appearing to materialise. The Celtic resurgence had come too late, however, for Hannibal was beginning to encounter difficulties further south. He held on for several years in the hope that his brother Hasdrubal would bring another army from Spain over the Alps into Italy. Things had not gone so well for the Carthaginians in Spain, where the Romans were gaining more success in enticing the Celtiberians over to their side. Helped by the Greek colony at Marseilles, a Roman army was ferried by sea to Spain in 217 BC, and these advanced as far south as the Ebro. In the same year a large group of Celtiberians went into an alliance with the commander of this Roman army, Gnaeus Scipio, and took three towns from the Carthaginians. They then engaged Hasdrubal himself and, fighting magnificently, slew 1,500 of his men and took 4,000 prisoner.

While Hasdrubal was thus engaged in fighting the Celtiberians, a second Roman fleet landed, under the command of Publius Scipio, brother of Gnaeus. Soon after, an event of major diplomatic importance occurred. Before his departure, Hannibal had been given the sons of many Celtiberian leaders as hostages and these were being held in Saguntum, but they were now handed back to their parents by an Iberian named Abilyx, who was trusted by the Carthaginians but who had entered into communion with the Romans. This development brought more of the Celtiberians over onto the Roman side, so that they were now to be found in almost equal numbers in the armies of both superpowers. In 213 BC, the Romans gained an important victory south-west of Saguntum against a Carthaginian force which consisted mostly of Celts. The latter lost almost 8,000 men, and two of their chieftains, called Moenicaptos and Vismaros, were slain. The Romans collected a huge amount of golden collars and bracelets from the fallen Celtic warriors.

The attachment of the Celtiberians to the Carthaginian side weakened as a result, and many of them went over to the Romans, who offered them the same conditions of pay as the Carthaginians had. These were reputedly the first true mercenaries ever employed by the Romans. A group of their noblemen were afterwards sent over to Italy, to try to induce the Spanish auxiliaries in Hannibal's army to desert. The Celtiberian mercenaries proved just as untrustworthy to the Romans as to their previous employers, however, for Hannibal's brother Hasdrubal made secret contact with their leaders and bribed them to desert. When a large force of them left the camp of Gnaeus Scipio, they were asked by the Romans where they were going, and they replied that a local war in Celtiberia required their presence!

The Romans soon took Saguntum itself, and wreaked vengeance on the Turdetani tribe, who had started the war, by selling most of them into slavery. Though the two Scipios were slain in separate engagements soon after, the Roman successes continued when Publius Scipio's son, named after his father, was given command. Finally, in the year 210 BC, Cartagena itself fell, and the young Scipio was quick to release the Iberian hostages held there, thus gaining the support of more of the natives of the peninsula. One diplomatic incident was particularly effective. Among a number of natives captured by Scipio was the intended bride of a young Celtiberian chieftain. The young man, Aluccios, went to seek her release, as did her parents who offered a large sum of gold to ransom her. Scipio released the girl unharmed, and gave the gold as a dowry to Aluccios. The young Celtiberian chieftain was filled with gratitude, and soon after raised from among his people a brigade of 1,400 cavalry to support the Romans.

At long last, in the year 207 BC, Hasdrubal succeeded in getting his army north and crossed the Alps without difficulty. In Italy, he was joined by large groups of Celts and Ligurians. Overall, the Carthaginian position was still strong, for as well as the two armies now in Italy they had three large armies in the Iberian Peninsula, with which they managed to keep the Roman forces tied down there. A new commander, Hanno, was sent over from Carthage, and he recruited and armed about 9,000 young men of the Celtiberians to join his own troops, but the Romans sent an army under Marcus Silanus to engage them. The armies met on rough ground, which hindered the rapid skirmishing tactics of the Celtiberians, and most of these raw recruits were butchered in hand-to-hand fighting.

Hanno himself was captured, but the whole Carthaginian cavalry and much of their infantry escaped. The Celtiberian survivors scattered in the woods and then returned to their homes.

Meanwhile, from the north of Italy, Hasdrubal tried to make contact with his brother Hannibal, whose army was far to the south. The messengers, four Celtic and two Numidian horsemen, were captured by the Romans, and under threat of torture they revealed the Carthaginian disposition and plans. The Roman Consul Claudius Nero immediately set out to intercept Hasdrubal and trapped him in a pincer movement at the river Metaro, near Senigallia. Hasdrubal placed his Celts on the left wing of his army, directly facing the Roman commander, 'because he thought the Romans were afraid of them'. The fighting continued from before dawn until midday, and Hasdrubal's elephants ran amuck in the terrible confusion. Hundreds of the Celts were captured and many others took to flight, and in the climax of the battle Hasdrubal himself was slain. The slaughter was atrocious, but a large number of Celts and Ligurians scrambled away to safety.

Celts defenceless

The Celtiberians and their neighbours still had hopes of asserting their independence from both Carthage and Rome, a fact well illustrated by the career of the king of the Ilergetes, Indibilis, whose name was Celtic and who was described by the historian Diodorus Siculus as a Celtiberian. Though elderly, Indibilis and his brother Mandonius followed an astute policy in dealing with the two massive foreign forces. He had been deposed from his kingship by the Romans, but was restored to power by the Carthaginians, and became a close ally of them. In the year 211 BC, however, he broke with the Carthaginians, when the latter had demanded a large sum of money. The wives and daughters of the Ilergetes' leaders, who were held as hostages by the Carthaginians, were in imminent danger, but after the fall of Cartagena these hostages came into the possession of Scipio, who treated them well. This prompted Indibilis and Mandonius to go over to the Roman side in 207 BC.

Two years later, they considered that they had an opportunity to break with the Romans also, and they got support towards this objective from other tribes. Their hopes for success were increased when dissatisfaction spread among Scipios's army. Scipio, however, soon quelled the mutiny and within a fortnight he had crossed the Ebro and surrounded and defeated the Celtiberian forces. The Celtiberians sustained heavy losses, Indibilis was killed and Mandonius was handed over to the Romans as the price of peace. The tribute on all the tribes who had participated was doubled, and the Romans in addition requisitioned a huge amount of corn and other products.

More and more of the Celtiberians continued to go over to the Romans, and an episode in the year 206 BC shows how close to Roman interests they had become. It happened that the Roman commander, the younger Publius Scipio, was staging a public festival at Cartagena in honour of his father and uncle, who had been killed six years before. Many Celtiberians volunteered to take part in a gladiatorial show, some of them being sent by their chieftains to show their valour and others simply enjoying the excitement of fighting. Some others also used the occasion to settle old rivalries, and among these were two cousins who were contending for a chieftainship in the Iberian town of Ibe (now Ibi, south of Valencia). The older of the two, called Corbis, by his skill easily mastered the strength of the younger man, Orsua, and slew him.

Meanwhile, the great war was coming to a close, and the Romans landed a strong force in Africa in 204 BC and began to attack Carthage itself. The Carthaginian forces were in hasty retreat, but they were rallied and greatly heartened by the arrival from Spain of a 4,000-strong force of Celtiberians, who had been newly recruited. Following on this, Hasdrubal, son of Gisgo, prepared his army to oppose the Romans near Carthage, placing these Celtiberians at the centre of his formation. In the ensuing battle, the African forces took to flight, but the Celtiberians held their ground until they were completely surrounded. They surrendered, and the Roman Commander Publius Scipio massacred them all. Hannibal's great adventure had now turned into a trap of his own making, and with disaster facing him on all sides he was recalled from Italy to save Carthage. In the final battle of the war, at Zama, he arranged his Celtic troops in the centre once more, along with the other mercenaries, directly behind the elephants. The Romans slowly pushed them backwards, and soon the battle developed into a mass slaughter, from which Hannibal himself barely escaped with his life.

In retrospect, it can be seen that if the Celts of Italy had postponed their great contest with the Romans for a few years until the Second Punic War began, they would almost definitely have won. It was impossible for them to have such foresight, however, for the re-emergence of faraway Carthage as a superpower had come quite suddenly, and even then its attack on Rome through the Alps was unexpected. Equally unexpected, as it transpired, were the dogged persistence of the Romans and their victory over their great African rivals. As the second century BC dawned, the balance of power had changed dramatically. Hannibal had come and gone, and Rome was now mistress on both sides of the Mediterranean. Much of north Africa, an increasing slice of the Greek colonies, and the Iberian Peninsula itself was under her hegemony. She reigned supreme in Italy, with the Celts on the defensive all along the Po Valley. The ancient sack of Rome had been duly avenged, and Cisalpine Gaul had been savaged by Roman armies for more than a century, but it was not to stop there.

5

WIDESPREAD TUMULT AND DISASTER

Despite the setbacks in Italy, and the increasing uncertainty in other areas, the peak of Celtic power, based on the achievements of varied and far-spread groups, had been reached by the third century BC. The picture was, however, steadily changing, partly due to conflicts between the Celts themselves but mostly due to the growth of Rome as the superpower on the Mediterranean.

Migrations to Britain and Ireland
The Cubi had dominated the whole area of central Gaul for a long time and their dynasty retained the title 'Biturix' claimed by their great king Ambicatus. From this the dynasty, and the tribe of Cubi themselves, became known as Bituriges ('world-kings'). From the beginning of the fourth century BC, however, their power waned and then went into rapid decline, due no doubt to the increasing influence of more southern groups such as the Aedui.

This left something of a vacuum in northern Gaul, and it would appear that it was the initial circumstance which tempted the Belgic Celts to extend their territories northwards through the broad coastal area along the Channel. Pushing westwards, some groups of them seem even to have crossed the Seine and made inroads into the territories of the various groups of Aulerci, who had been weakened for some generations by pressure from the Bituriges. Other smaller groups seem to have gone even further – to the north-western coast of modern France – for there are indications that the tribes known as Aremorici ('those by the sea') in this area were partly Belgic in origin. Within a generation or two, however, new circumstances caused the increasing sphere of influence of the Belgae to contract somewhat.

The growing strength of the Aedui in the southeast is indicated by the spread of their septs. The Insubres had branched off early, but another section of them carved out a considerable territory directly to the east of the main tribe. These settled along the banks of the river Arar (now the Saône), thus becoming known as the Ambiarari ('those around the Arar') or, in shortened form, Ambarri. The Aedui directed their ambitions northwards also. A significant branch of them, known as Carnutes ('people of the horned deity') established themselves in a strategic area west of the river Seine, with Autricum (now Chartres) as their capital and Cenabum (now Orléans) as their commercial centre. So great was the impact of the Carnutes in that northern region that they soon felt emboldened to claim that their new territory was 'the centre of all Gaul'. No doubt they attempted, with a large degree of success, to impress this point upon the Belgae, the main bulk of whom accordingly were pushed back eastwards across the Seine. Other Belgae groups, who through the shifting borders found themselves isolated in the west, had little choice but to migrate further afield.

An interesting case in point is that of the 'Catuellauni' (*recte* *Catuvellauni*, meaning 'battle-superiors'), a tribe who were reduced from a position of considerable power all along the banks of the Seine. Sections of them seem to have been dispersed into various parts of their original territory, becoming known by such designations as Veliocasses, Baiocasses, Viducasses, Tricasses and Vadicasses. The likelihood is that these names belonged to different family branches of the Catuvellauni, being based on those of a set of legendary ancestors called Casses ('handsome ones'). One section made a very significant move, some time towards the end of the third century BC, when they migrated across the Channel to Britain. There they retained the more martial designation of Catuvellauni, and brought many of the earlier inhabitants under their control. From their centre at Verulamium (now St Alban's), they soon became the most powerful population group in all of southern Britain.

Other Belgic tribes were also crossing the Channel. The most significant, apart from the Catuvellauni, were the Trinovantes, who may have been a branch of the Viromandui from the banks of the Oise. These established themselves at Camulodunum (now Colchester) in the south-east of Britain. The Catuvellauni soon proved to be quite unfriendly neighbours to these fellow Belgae, as indeed they did to earlier Celtic settlers. Peoples such as the Brigantes, Iceni, and Parisi stood firm to the north, but the pressure on some of the longest established Celtic groups must have resulted in further but smaller migrations.

In Ireland, the ancient population stock seems not to have been greatly changed by immigrants, and one must therefore postulate the entry of small but compact bands of warriors from the fifth century BC onwards, and reaching its high-point in the third century. Ireland was not thickly populated, and so it would have been easy for such bands – hungry for new land and perhaps regarding their migration as a sacred act – to dominate the areas where they settled. Their offspring with native Irish women would have been in an even more dominant position socially, perpetuating the Celtic language as the symbol of success and prestige, and so Ireland would have gradually but inevitably become Celticised. The incomers, being part of the knock-on effect from changes in Britain, spoke the older form of the Celtic language (that with the labiovelar kw).

The lack of contemporaneous sources means that we have no clear idea of the identities of these early Celtic groups in Ireland, but all indications are that the Celts of Britain used the general term Iverni for them and for the indigenous non-Celtic peoples alike. The Iverni in reality must have been a fusion of both, but from the third century BC, the Celtic or Celticised elements were dominant among them. In Ireland itself, the various groups were known by different names, most prominent being the Vinducati, Soborgii, Darinii and Uluti towards the north, the Ceuleni and Aucii on the east coast, the Gamarnates in the west, and the Autinii and Veldobri in the south.

The Iverni, by gaining possession of the major hill forts and burial sites of the country, expropriated the prestige of these places and perpetuated their cults in Celtic guise. One of the most important of the ritual hilltop sites was in the rich plain watered by the river Boyne, and commanded a wide view of the north midlands. This was taken over by a group of Iverni, apparently the Lugunii, whose name indicates that they were devotees of the god Lugus. It was given the Celtic name Temoria, meaning 'spectacle' (later Teamhair, or Tara in County Meath).

A strong challenge to the Iverni tribes, however, soon presented itself in the form of a new amalgam of peoples in the broad area of the southern midlands. Again, this force may have been composed mostly of the population indigenous to that area, but it seems to have been headed by a band of warriors belonging to the Brigantes who had crossed the Irish Sea in search of new lands to settle. The group became known as *Leiquni ('[spear]casters'), a name which in time came to be reinterpreted as *Lagini ('lance-men'). By the beginning of the second century BC they had gained control of the great hill fort which was later known as Ailinn (in modern County Kildare) and had established it as their cultic centre. The Lagini seem to have coalesced at an early date with another group of incomers called *Gaiso-lingi ('javelin-jumpers'), and together they extended their power over most of the south-eastern quarter of Ireland, reaching as far as the river Shannon in the west and Wexford in the south. Some Ivernian tribes managed to preserve their identity in that region, but they were pushed to the poorer lands or to the borders, where they became known as the 'marginal peoples'.

All of these developments were occurring in the isolated and lightly populated islands in the north-west, however. In the east and south of Europe – where the most dramatic spread of Celtic power and influence had taken place – the fortunes of the Celts were on the wane, and everywhere this was due to the Romans.

Defeat of Cisalpine Gaul

The first half of the second century BC saw developments which greatly altered the political map of the known world, and the Celts were the greatest losers. The Boii continued to resist in Italy. In 200 BC they surrounded a large detachment of Roman soldiers who were cutting the corn near the fortified town of Mutilum (in the vicinity of modern Cesena), and in the ensuing fighting 7,000 Roman soldiers along with their leader Gaius Ampius were slain.

The fighting spread, and even the Cenomani, who had been allies of Rome in Hannibal's war, soon found that they were to get little thanks for their efforts. The Romans valued their own colonists more than erstwhile allies, and the continuing confiscation of Celtic lands in Cisalpine Gaul caused these same Cenomani to join forces with the Boii and the Insubres. The combined Celtic force numbered up to 40,000 and was aided and directed by a Carthaginian officer called Hamilcar whom

Hannibal had left in Gaul. They attacked and sacked the Roman colony at Placentia, and then crossed the Po, with the intention of attacking Cremona, where the colonists quickly barricaded themselves. A large Roman force arrived to relieve the siege, and soon after they routed the Celts with great slaughter. Livy claims that more than 35,000 Celts were killed or captured, and Hamilcar himself was slain, as well as three Celtic leaders.

The Boii, Insubres, and Cenomani continued to work in tandem, and there was a lull in the fighting for some time. Preparations at Rome for an all-out invasion of the Celtic territories three years later, however, caused the united forces to split up in order to protect their respective areas. So, in 197 BC, the Consul Gaius Cornelius led a large army northwards along the eastern coast to attack the Insubres and Cenomani, whose forces were concentrated on the banks of the river Mincio, while his fellow Consul Quintus Minucius led another army further west against the Boii. Cornelius succeeded in persuading the Cenomani to return to their Roman allegiance, and then attacked the Insubres, who were defeated with the loss of many thousands of their men. Hearing of this defeat, the Boii forces broke up, each man concerned to defend his own property as best he could from the rampaging army of Minucius.

The Roman armies moved at will throughout the Celtic territories, but in the following year the Boii hit back. A Roman army under the Consul Claudius Marcellus (whose father had defeated the Insubres at the battle of Clastidium) was constructing a road through their territory, and the Chieftain Corolamos attacked them with a large force. About 3,000 Romans, including several officers, were slain. Marcellus held the camp with most of his legionaries, however, and some days later he led these men in an attack on a concentration of Celtic warriors in the region of the Comum (now Como). These were Insubres who, despite their defeats, were still resisting. In furious fighting, the Roman cavalry broke the Insubres lines, putting them to flight and slaying a large number of them. According to Livy, 87 standards were taken in this engagement, along with hundreds of wagons and much treasure. A necklace of great weight, which was among the booty taken by the Romans, was taken to the Capitol in Rome and presented there as a gift to the god Jupiter.

The territory of the Boii was laid waste by the Romans as far as the town of Bononia, causing the women, children, and other dependents of the Boii to retreat into the northern forests. After the surrender of Bononia, the Roman army turned west to attack the Ligurians, who were also in rebellion. Many of the Boii warriors followed the legions by secret tracks, hoping to set up an ambush but, when no opportunity offered itself, they crossed the Po in boats to ravage the lands of the Celto-Ligurian tribes, the Laevi and Libici, who were in alliance with Rome. As they were returning to their own people with the plunder they had taken, they unexpectedly clashed with the Romans on the borders of the Ligurian territory. In fierce fighting, the Boii force was cut down almost to a man, and Livy remarks that in this battle the Romans 'fought more for bloodlust than for triumph'.

A further attempt was made by the Boii to retrieve their fortunes in 194 BC when, under their leader Dorulatos, they crossed the Po to arouse the Insubres to revolt, but they were overcome by the Romans in a pitched battle, and thousands were slain. Following this, the Consul Tiberius Sempronius took his legions into the territory of the Boii, but the new Celtic leader Boiorix determined to stop them and attacked the Roman camp. The legions tried to break out through the gate of the camp, but in a great crush of shields and bodies the position was stalemate. Then another group of the Boii burst into the camp from the opposite side, killing hundreds of the Romans and some of their commanders. The Romans rallied, and fierce fighting continued until midday. Finally, over-come by heat and thirst, the Boii withdrew, and the Romans sounded the retreat. Some of the Romans went in pursuit of the Boii, who turned and cut them to pieces. Finally, both forces drew off, and the Boii retreated into the interior of their territory. They had lost about 11,000 men, and the Romans almost half that number.

Undaunted, the Boii were again in the field the following year, this time in alliance with the Ligurians, who were resisting renewed Roman pressure on their lands in north-west Italy. This time they were more cautious, backing away from a Roman army under Lucius Cornelius which was plundering their territory. All the countryside was burned and looted by the Romans, and the Boii waited for their opportunity for an ambush. They got it as the Romans returned to Liguria through a defile near Mutina (modern Modena), but their plan was noticed and the Romans were prepared. The Boii put the Roman front line to flight, but fresh Roman troops were introduced, bringing stalemate to the fighting. The sun blazed overhead, scorching the Boii warriors who found the excessive heat debilitating, but they stood their ground in dense forma-tion, propping each other up as they fell. A ferocious cavalry charge by the Romans broke their lines. The Boii leaders tried to stop the disintegration, striking the backs of their terrified men with spear-shafts, but they failed to prevent a precipitate flight. The Roman cavalry cut down the terrified warriors as they fled, killing 14,000 of them and taking over 1,000 prisoners. The Celts had taken their toll of the enemy also in this battle, for the Romans lost no less than 5,000 men, including some leading officers.

Towards the end of the same year, the Ligurians blocked a Roman army as it was going through a narrow pass in the border country of the Ligurians and Celts. The commander tried to turn his army back the way they had come, but they found themselves hemmed in at the rear by a force of Celts. In these wars, the Romans had the service of Numidian cavalry which had formerly been to the fore in Hannibal's army. These Numidians now offered to relieve the situation by breaking through the Celts and going to ravage their land. The Celts were taken off guard by the pathetic appearance of the Numidians, who were poorly armed and riding scrawny, ungainly horses, and who moreover appeared to have lost control of their mounts as they approached. Drawing near, however, the Numidians changed abruptly, suddenly spurring their horses into a fierce charge, and by this ruse they broke their way through. They immediately set to burning and slaughtering all over the surrounding countryside, and the Celts had no choice but to abandon their position, each man racing to protect his own family.

In this type of fighting in their own lands, the Celts were at a great disadvantage, for the Roman armies had no scruples concerning the wholesale slaughter of villagers and destruction of the countryside. The Boii made efforts to negotiate a surrender, but this was rejected, and one recorded episode shows the savagery of the Roman attitude towards them. It so happened that a nobleman of the Boii went with his sons to the camp of the Consul Lucius Quinctius Flaminius, imploring the protection of the Roman people. The consul was partying with a boy-prostitute, and he enquired of the boy if he would like to see a man being killed. The boy nodded, and straight away Flaminius drew his sword and slew the unfortunate nobleman.

The Ligurians were defeated by the army of the Proconsul Quintus Minucius in 191 BC. Incessant warfare had greatly reduced the Boii, and soon after Publius Scipio – the conqueror of Hannibal – inflicted a crushing defeat on them. Details of this battle are lacking, but it was claimed to have been the greatest triumph ever gained over the Boii by any Roman commander, with half of their 50,000 warriors slain, leaving little of their fighting force intact apart from boys and old men. They had no choice but to surrender and give hostages, after which Scipio confiscated half of their remaining lands. A great procession of triumph was held in Rome, in which prisoners, arms, standards, captured horses, and booty of all kinds, were paraded through the streets in Celtic wagons. Also on display were 1,471 golden necklaces, 247 pounds weight of gold, and 2,340 pounds of silver, much of which was in the form of beautifully wrought Celtic vessels.

From this on, the Romans strictly controlled the Celts of Cisalpine Gaul, which they renamed 'Gallia Togata' (i.e., Celtdom where the Roman toga must be worn). The Boii lost their three great centres, which were turned into Roman colonies – Bononia in 189 BC, Mutina and Parma in 183 BC. In the latter year, a small group of Carni, a people of Venetic origin but now strongly under Celtic influence, came down from the Alps and settled on the Adriatic coast. They were ordered back by the Roman army, and the Roman Senate declared the Alps to be the northern border of Italy and decreed that no more Celts should cross it. Even the Cenomani, who had been allied to the Romans, were threatened. They were forcibly disarmed by Furius Crassipes, but had the weapons conditionally returned by the Consul Aemilius Lepidus.

Everywhere, Roman interest prevailed. By 178 BC, Celtic warriors from the eastern Alps were being enlisted into the Roman armies which were attacking Istria and Illyria. A further futile rising by the Cisalpine Gauls and Ligurians was crushed in 175 BC, after which the Roman Senate proclaimed a three-day thanksgiving and the sacrifice of 40 victims.

Defeat of eastern Celts

Having involved themselves on the side of the Greek states against the Macedonians, the Romans had already begun to concentrate their attention on conquests in the east. In this, their main obstacle was the humane and enlightened King Antiochus III of Syria, who had many of the Galatian Celts as mercenaries in his army and who had given refuge to Hannibal in his court. In the year 191 BC, Antiochus crossed to Greece in support of the Macedonians, but he was defeated by the Romans a year later at the battle of Magnesia. This gave Rome the opportunity to intervene in Asia Minor, and in the summer of 189 BC they sent an army under the command of Marcus Fulvius against the Aetolians, the result of which was the surrender of several cities to them and an acceptance of their role as superpower in Asia Minor.

In that same summer, another Roman army, under Gnaeus

Manlius Vulso, had established itself at Ephesus, and was undertaking a campaign against the Galati. Addressing the soldiers, Manlius excused his aggression by saying that these Celts had supported Antiochus and, moreover, 'that they were by nature so ungovernable' that their power must be broken. Manlius was joined in his task by an army led by Attalus, brother of the king of Pergamon, Eumenes II – both of these being sons of the old enemy of the Galati, Attalus I. The combined armies advanced in triumph north-eastwards through Asia Minor, plundering and laying heavy tribute on all the peoples in their way, until they reached Phrygia on the frontier of the territory of the Tolistoboii. 'This was the enemy with whom the Romans had now to fight,' states Livy, 'an enemy very terrifying to all the people of that region'.

Manlius, according to the Roman historian Livy, again rhetorically addressed his soldiers, calling the Celts 'a fierce nation' and stating that they ranked highest of all the peoples of Asia Minor in their reputation for war. He went on: 'Their tall physique, their flowing red hair, their huge shields and enormous swords, along with their songs as they go into battle, their howling and leaping, and the fearful din of arms as they bang their shields according to some kind of ancestral custom – all these things are designed to terrify!' Then Livy has Manlius give a long lecture on the history of the Celts in Italy – which we may regard as Livy's own composition, or at the very least a great elaboration on what Manlius would have said.

According to this, Manlius spoke of how the Romans alone had never feared the Celts but had repeatedly defeated them in battle. Then he compared the Galati to wild animals, whose fathers and grandfathers had been 'driven from their land by the barrenness of the soil' and had made their way through Illyricum, Pannonia and Thrace, being 'hardened and made savage by all their misfortunes'. In Asia Minor, however, they had been tamed and softened by the rich lifestyle there. So the celebrated 'Celtic frenzy' in battle should not be feared, and Manlius here gives the typical Roman strategic assessment of Celtic warriors:

> This has been learned from experience – that if you withstand the first charge, into which they hurl themselves with blazing passion and blind rage, their limbs become slack with sweat and weariness, their weapons waver in their hands. They are flabby in body, flabby in resolve when their passion subsides, and they are laid low by sun, dust, and thirst, so that you need not even use weapons against them then.

Despite his confident attitude, Manlius took care to contact one of the Galatian leaders, Eposognatos, who had refused to support Antiochus against the Romans. Eposognatos was one of the leading men of the Tolistoboii, and he concluded a treaty of friendship with Manlius, who then proceeded to encamp near Cuballum, a stronghold of the Tolistoboii at the loop of the river Sakarya (in the centre of modern Turkey). A sudden attack was made on the camp by Galatian cavalry, which retreated after inflicting some casualties on the Romans. Next day Manlius moved about 50 km northwards to Gordion, on the banks of the Sakarya, where Eposognatos contacted him with news that he had failed to get the other leaders of the Galati to join his alliance with the Romans. The vast bulk of the Tolistoboii under their chieftain Ortiago was moving to Mount Olympus (halfway between Gordion and Ancyra), and they were bringing their families and herds with them in the hope of resisting the Roman army from that position. It was later reported that the Tectosages, under Combilomaros, had gone to fortify themselves to the east of Ancyra on Mount Magaba (also known as Mordiacum); and that the Trogmi, having left their dependents with these Tectosages, were going with their chieftain Gaulotos to join the Tolistoboii.

Confident that the Romans would be sufficiently weakened by the ascent of the steep and freezing Mount Olympus, the Tolistoboii threw a ditch and other defensive works around the summit. For his part, Manlius encamped within five miles of the mountain, making sure that he had a sufficient amount of missiles and javelins to undertake an assault. He then went with Attalus and 400 cavalrymen to reconnoitre, but was attacked by the Galatian cavalry and put to flight. Some days later he set out again to reconnoitre, this time with his whole force, and discovered a route running to the summit. He decided that the main prong of his attack would be from there. Accordingly, he sent two smaller contingents by more difficult routes and, leaving his cavalry and elephants on level ground at the foot of the mountain, he commenced the ascent with his main infantry force. The Galati, suspecting an assault only from the facile path, sent about 4,000 warriors to occupy a hill there.

This hill was the first objective of the Romans' advance. They discharged volleys of missiles, arrows and javelins at the Galati, who were equipped only for fighting at close quarters with swords. The frustrated Galati had only stones to throw back, while they were struck by a mass of missiles. They fought naked, and with their shields not large enough to cover their bodies. The sight of the gashes, and of the red and blackened blood flowing from their white bodies, was horrible, but they attempted to cut the javelins and arrows from their own flesh, imagining that the terrible wounds brought them greater glory. They rushed madly at the Romans, who used their short swords with deadly effect at close range. Most of this Galatian force was slaughtered, and the remainder raced back up the mountain to their women and children, who were in a state of absolute panic. As the main body of the Romans advanced, the two other contingents joined them, and the whole force prepared to attack the summit.

The Galati had taken up position in front of their final rampart near the summit, and they were overwhelmed by missiles of all kinds before being driven back behind the rampart. Then the Romans unleashed a torrent of missiles right into the Galatian camp, where men, women, and children thronged about. The Romans knew by the shouting of the warriors and the wailing of the women and children, that the missiles were having deadly effect; and soon the legionaries burst into the camp itself. The whole crowd of the Galati took to flight, running headlong down the steep mountain slopes, and being massacred by the pursuing Romans as they went. Manlius ordered his men to kill as many as possible of the fugitives, and those fortunate enough to reach the foot of the mountains encountered the Roman cavalry, who wrought further havoc on them. In all, about 10,000 people were slain, and about 30,000 were taken prisoner.

Manlius now set out to destroy the Tectosages, and after a three-day march he reached Ancyra (modern Ankara), about fifteen km from their fortifications on Mount Magaba. He had brought a huge number of captives with him, among whom was Chiomara, wife of the Tolistoboii chieftain Ortiago. She was a very beautiful woman, and the centurion in charge of her detachment tried to seduce her and, failing this, raped her. Greed was added to his lust, for the centurion then offered her freedom to Chiomara in return for a large ransom in gold. Desiring to keep knowledge of this from his soldiers, he made arrangements secretly to bring her to an appointed place outside the camp and to trade her to her own people for the gold. Chiomara accepted this arrangement, but when they reached the place and the gold was being paid out by her people, she ordered them in her own language to 'draw their swords and kill the centurion as he was weighing his money'. They cut his throat and decapitated him, and Chiomara wrapped his head in her garment and brought it to her husband. She threw it at his feet, explaining to him that 'there is only one man alive who has partaken of my bed!'

Meanwhile, the Tectosages sent envoys to Manlius offering peace, and a meeting was arranged halfway between the Roman camp at Ancyra and the Galatian camp on Mount Magaba. Manlius went to the rendezvous, accompanied by 500 cavalry, but found no one there. The same envoys turned up again at the Roman camp, explaining that their chieftains could not come on account of a religious obstacle, but that they would send delegates to another meeting. After further procrastination, Manlius realised that the Galati were playing for time in order to get their dependents and valuables away from the area. Finally, they ambushed the consul with a large force of cavalry as he was proceeding to a meeting. They routed his strong bodyguard, and would have captured him if a force of Roman foragers had not come to his rescue. Most of the Galatian ambushers were put to death by the Romans for their breach of faith.

The Romans, burning with anger at this episode, prepared for an all-out assault on Mount Magaba. A reputed 50,000 fighters of the Tectosages and Trogmi prepared for the defence, but the legionaries – using the same tactics as at Mount Olympus – routed them. Thousands of the Galati were slain, but most of the Roman soldiers stopped at their camp, attracted by the huge amount of plunder there. This allowed the greater part by far of the Galati to escape, and these later sued for peace and agreed to send envoys to discuss surrender. Manlius was confident that his conquest was complete, and realised that winter was approaching and that he would soon be isolated in the coldness of the mountains. He was therefore in a hurry to return to Ephesus, and directed the Tectosages and Trogmi to send the envoys to him there. The Romans were by now in control of all of Asia Minor, and the Galati – having lost their independence – were much reduced. Many of them were in slavery, and those who remained in their own lands were placed under the rule of Rome's ally, King Eumenes II of Pergamon.

Despite all this, they made a remarkable recovery. First of all, the Tolistoboii leader, Ortagio, strove to unite the three tribes and so assert their independence. Polybius describes Ortagio thus: 'He possessed many qualities, which he owed to his natural gifts and to acquired experience. He was generous and magnanimous, affable and prudent in dealing with people and – what matters most among the Galati – he was brave and skilled in the affairs of war.' He managed to forge an alliance with King Prusias of Bithynia and King Pharnaces of Pontus against Eumenes, and this arrangement looked promising for a while. Ortagio seems to have died by 181 BC, and the Galati were led by the chieftains Cassignatos and Gaisatorix, who committed themselves to the cause of Pharnaces. The king of Pontus, however, arrogantly assumed total control over the Galati and garrisoned their territory with his own army.

Shocked by the cruelty of Pharnaces, Cassignatos and Gaisatorix sent messengers to Eumenes in 180 BC offering to change sides. Eumenes somewhat sceptically accepted the offer and, strengthened by the new alliance, the Galati succeeded within a year in driving Pharnaces out of their territories. They then joined with Eumenes and the Romans in the war against King Philip of Macedonia who, in fact, had a large number of Thracian Celts in his army. Philip intended to recruit onto his side a large force of Bastarnae, a Germanic tribe from north of the Danube who had been heavily influenced by the Celts. Livy refers to the likelihood that these Bastarnae would have been joined by the Scordisci, 'for they were not greatly different in language or culture'. After the death of Philip in 179 BC, his son Perseus lost the support of this strong Germanic-Celtic alliance by refusing to pay them the fee they demanded.

The Galatian leader Cassignatos was killed in a cavalry engagement during this war in 171 BC, and three years later a force of 1,000 Galatian cavalry was attacked by the Macedonians as they attempted to sail from Asia Minor. They attempted to land on the island of Chios, but were wiped out. The eastern Celts were by this time reduced to being agents of greater powers. For example, while large numbers of Thracian Celts were arriving in Macedonia to strengthen the army of Perseus, the Galati were in the Roman camp and even a Celtic leader, from beyond the Alps, Balanos, was promising aid to the Romans.

The Galati soon found themselves on the horns of a dilemma for, after the defeat of the Macedonians in the autumn of 168 BC, they were so pressurised by their erstwhile ally Eumenes of Pergamon that they forged a new alliance with Prusias of Bithynia against him. In 167 BC, under the chieftain Advertas, they overran Pergamon and almost overthrew Eumenes. The Galati behaved with customary savagery in this campaign, taking many prisoners. They crowned the youngest and most handsome of these with garlands and offered them as human sacrifices to the gods, while the rest they shot to death with arrows. The Romans intervened to resolve the issue and, two years later, it was agreed that the Galati should withdraw from Pergamon but that Eumenes should accept their independence. Henceforth, the Galati, in common with all the peoples of the Balkans and Asia Minor, were dependent on the Roman Senate as ultimate arbiter in their territorial and other disputes.

In the general expansion of their power, the ambitions of the Romans were not only directed towards the eastern Mediterranean region but also inland towards the north. A foretaste of what was to come was provided in 171 BC when a Roman army under Gaius Cassius Longinus, returning from a campaign in Macedonia, marched through the territory of the Scordisci and other Celtic groups in the eastern Alps. They ravaged the area and dragged thousands of people away as slaves, causing such outrage that the local tribes sent delegations to the Roman Senate to complain. The delegations included the brother of Cincibilos, king of the Norici. The Roman Senate seized this diplomatic opportunity, promising amends when they had investigated the case and sending envoys bearing gifts to the aggrieved Celts. Cincibilos and his brother were each given a caparisoned horse and a finely wrought golden necklace, as well as five silver vessels.

This does not seem to have been the first attempt by the Romans to forge links with the Norici. Indeed, the Celtic contingent in the Roman army attacking Istria in 183 BC had been led by Catmelos, probably the brother of Cincibilos who later negotiated with the Senate; while Balanos who offered his help to the Romans' war effort in Macedonia may well have been the son of Cincibilos. Friendly relations, based on trade, between the kingdom of Noricum and the Romans lasted for several generations. Events were, however, moving inexorably towards massive change in the territories around the Danube, and the Romans had got into position to effect this by spreading their power along the Adriatic. In 175 BC they had taken advantage of civil disturbances in Venetia to crush the longstanding independence of that people, and four years later they had seized Istria. After the fall of Macedonia, and when the Illyrian King Gentius surrendered in 167 BC, the Romans were in total control of southeastern Europe and poised for the final uprooting of the Danubian Celts.

Conquest and reduction of Celtiberians

The ending of the Second Punic War had not brought peace to Iberia. The Romans, taking the place of the Carthaginians as overlords, divided the whole peninsula into two regions – which they called 'Hispania Citerior' (Hither Spain) and 'Hispania Ulterior' (Further Spain) – and proceeded to levy taxes on all the peoples there.

This led in 197 BC to an uprising in Hither Spain by the Turdetani

– neighbours and close associates of the Celtiberians – and they routed a
Roman army under the Proconsul Gaius Sempronius, slaying many officers
including Sempronius himself. After a defeat near their town of Turda, the
Turdetani continued the struggle and hired 10,000 fighters of the
Celtiberians for this purpose. The disaffection spread, and the Romans
began to disarm the Iberians, stating blandly that this was for their own
protection from the hazards of war. In 195 BC, the writer and notoriously
severe Consul Marcus Porcius Cato was sent by sea to pacify the peninsula.
Equipped with two legions, 15,000 Latin allies, 800 cavalry and twenty
warships, Cato encountered little difficulty in eastern Spain, capturing a
large number of towns and seizing the rich silver and gold mines of the
region. He then turned south in order to subdue the Turdetani.

Cato began this campaign by trying to buy off the Celtiberian
mercenaries – one report is that they demanded 200 talents as the price of
their support, and that he saw no choice in the matter but to agree and to
offer them safe passage to their homelands in the Meseta. Thus weakened,
the Turdetani proved no match for Cato's army, and before the end of the
year they were completely overcome. Now on a firm footing, Cato determined to avenge the humiliating deal which he had been forced to strike
with the Celtiberians, and so he turned his army northwards. He captured
the Celtiberian town of Segontia (now Sigüenza), and then marched up
the Ebro valley, forcing several tribes of the area to surrender to him and
to knock down the defensive walls of their towns. He brought his army to
the massive hill fort of Numantia (near modern Garray), but his plans for
further conquests did not materialise, for he was removed soon afterwards
at the instigation of his rival Publius Scipio.

Sporadic fighting continued in the Iberian Peninsula for several
years, with Scipio conquering more and more territory. Once Cato had
departed, the Celtiberians returned to the road of rebellion, and in the
winter of 193 BC a combined force of Vaccaei, Vettones, and 'Celtiberi' was
defeated near the town of Toletum (Toledo) by Gaius Flaminius. Their
king, Hilernus, was captured, and things were quiet for a while. A Roman
plan to bring thousands of settlers to the peninsula caused great anxiety
among the Celtiberians, however, and in 181 BC they mustered a huge
force – about 35,000 men – to oppose the Roman Proconsul Quintus
Fulvius Flaccus. At the beginning of spring in that year, the two armies
were within a few miles of each other near the town of Aebura (now
Talavera). The Celtiberians drew up their line halfway between the two
camps, on a level plain, while the Romans remained in their fortified camp.

For four days the positions remained so, until the Romans suddenly sent a force by night to a hill at the rear of the Celtiberians, while another force marched straight towards them from the front. The cavalry and infantry of the Celtiberians advanced to meet the latter force. When they had thus proceeded far from their camp, the Romans on the hill attacked the camp and set it on fire. The two armies had come into contact, and the fighting had begun, when the Celtiberians noticed what had happened. They wavered for a short while between returning to save the camp or continuing the battle, and this was enough to give the advantage to the Romans. After a stubborn fight, the Celtiberians were surrounded, over 20,000 of them were killed and almost 5,000 captured, as well as 500 horses. The Romans lost almost 4,000 men.

The Romans followed up this victory by advancing towards the Celtic town of Contrebia (modern Botorrita, near Saragossa), which surrendered. A Celtiberian force, which had been delayed by heavy rain and floods, came to the assistance of the town, not knowing what had happened. Seeing no signs of Romans there, they approached in disarray and without any precautions. Suddenly the Romans sallied forth, and again the Celtiberians were routed, with thousands slain. The survivors returned to their homes and villages, while Flaccus took his legions throughout the whole countryside, plundering as they went. As he took fortress after fortress, the great majority of the Celtiberians surrendered to him.

Having cowed the defeated Celtiberians by parading his large army through their territories, Flaccus in the following spring began to ravage the lands of the tribes of the interior, who had not yet surrendered. In retaliation these tribes ambushed his legions at the Manlian Pass, in the Sistema Berico mountains where the Celtic Berones had their territory. The fighting was fierce, and the Celtiberians used a wedge formation to try to break the Roman lines. Flaccus ordered his cavalry to give their heads to the horses in order to give more force to their attack on the wedge. The tactic succeeded, and the Celtiberians were put to flight with great slaughter. Their warriors were cut down by the pursuing Romans all along the pass, about 17,000 being slain and 3,700 captured along with 600 horses.

In 179 BC the two praetors Sempronius Gracchus and Postumius Albinus undertook to finally crush the Vaccaei and 'Celtiberi', and it is reported that in their campaign they destroyed no fewer than 300 fortresses. On one occasion, when he was besieging the Celtiberian town of Certina, Gracchus had an experience which brought home to him the differences in attitude between the Celts and the Romans. A deputation came to him from the town, saying that they intended to fight and seeking his permission to go and consult with their people in the countryside. Gracchus and his officers were amazed at this old-world heroic attitude to war, but permission was granted. The envoys returned from their business a few days later, and since it was midday they demanded a drink before they spoke. Then they demanded a second drink, much to the amusement of the Roman bystanders, and finally enquired of the Romans by what means they intended to take the town. Gracchus replied that he would do so by relying on his army, which was of exceptional quality, and he had his soldiers paraded before them in order to impress the truth of this on them. The envoys departed, and soon after the town surrendered.

These envoys had gone to consult with a Celtiberian force which was encamped at the town of Alce (modern Alcázar), and Gracchus lost no time in going there. He had his men engage in several minor actions against that force, to give them false confidence and thereby to draw them gradually out of their camp. Finally, he made a mock attack on the Celtiberians, instructing his men to retreat towards their own camp as if under strong pressure. The ruse succeeded, for the whole Celtiberian force rushed headlong into the Roman camp, only to find themselves confronted by a far superior force. The Celtiberian camp was taken, and 9,000 of them slain, to the loss of 109 on the Roman side. After this battle, Gracchus ordered his troops to devastate Celtiberia. They took a huge amount of plunder, as well as many noblemen as prisoners. Among these was the Celtiberian Chieftain Thurrus, regarded by the Romans as the most influential man in Spain. Thurrus agreed to change sides, on the condition that his life and that of his children should be spared, and he afterwards served successfully as a Roman army officer.

When the stronghold of Ergavica fell to the Romans, the power of the Celtiberians was almost at an end, but they made one last effort. In the Chaunus mountains (near modern Complega), they fought a pitched battle with the legions of Gracchus, which lasted from daybreak to the sixth hour, with great losses on both sides. The Romans were reeling from this surprise result, but with characteristic resilience they returned to harass the Celtiberian camp next day. On the third day, the Celtiberians emerged from their camp, but were defeated by the Romans with the loss of over 20,000 men. The enormous losses suffered by the Celtiberians in this whole war meant that they were in no position to assert their power or even their rights from that on. Gracchus' word was law, and he set about dismantling the whole social structure of Celtiberia by establishing

Roman towns in their lands and by encouraging Celtiberian warriors to enlist in the Roman army.

He did, however, introduce a more reasonable taxation system, and his stern combination of conquest and diplomacy resulted in twenty years more or less free of fighting. There were a few exceptions, such as when, a few years after his departure, in 174 BC, the Celtiberians made a surprise attack on the camp of the new praetor Appius Claudius. The attack was unsuccessful, with the natives again losing thousands of men, but the fact that it was attempted in itself shows both the relief at the departure of so ruthless a Roman leader and also the abiding hope of the Celtiberians that they could one day muster a force which would expel the Romans.

They tried again in 153 BC, when two of their tribes, the Belli and Titti, joined a revolt of the Lusitani. They began by adding to the fortifications of Segeda (modern Seges), which was in breach of the treaty with Gracchus. The rebels had a charismatic leader called Salendicos, who brandished a silver spear and claimed that it had been sent to him from heaven. He prophesied victory for his people, and his courage matched his vision, for he tried to assassinate the consul. Entering the camp by night, he managed to get near the consul's tent before he was speared to death by a sentinel. The Romans were so alarmed at the situation that they brought the date of the New Year forward from 15th March to 1st January, an alteration which became the basis for the Calendar which is still in use today. This was in order to facilitate the appointment of a new consul specifically for the task of suppressing the revolt.

The new consul – Fulvius Nobilior – soon set out with an army of 30,000 men, with ten elephants and a force of Numidian cavalry in support. He destroyed the town of Segeda, but the inhabitants had already fled to join their compatriots in the great hill fort of Numantia (to the north of modern Garray in Soria). This fortress was originally the capital of the Pelendones, and had developed into a small city with an elaborate network of streets. By this time it had come into the possesssion of their southern neighbours, the Arevaci, and was being used as a kind of general headquarters by all the Celtiberian tribes of the region. In expectation of a Roman attack, the Celtiberians chose Ambro and Leuco as their leaders.

Nobilior now besieged that fortress, and the defenders showered rocks onto the attackers. One of the elephants was struck, and it caused the others to panic. Many of the soldiers were trampled and, seeing the confusion, the Celtiberians surged down from the hill fort and put the whole Roman force to flight. Soon after, they appointed a new leader, called Caros, who had a high reputation for military skill. Three days after his election, he placed 20,000 horse and 5,000 foot in ambush in a dense forest and attacked the Roman army as it passed by. The Celtiberians scored a great victory, with 6,000 of the Romans slain. Caros led a pursuit of the fleeing soldiers, but he was counter-attacked by the Roman cavalry who were guarding the baggage. In the ensuing struggle, thousands of his men were slain, and he himself – although 'performing prodigies of valour' – also fell.

The fighting was savage and continuous, and the Romans – who wished for one large engagement in which they could inflict a telling defeat on the Celtiberians – began to speak of it despairingly as 'the fiery war'. In 152 BC Nobilior was succeeded as governor of Hither Spain by Claudius Marcellus, whose father and grandfather of the same name had fought successfully against the Cisalpine Gauls. Marcellus without delay besieged Ocilis, a town of the Nertobriges i.e. the Lusones who lived at the hill fort of Nertobriga near Saragossa. Fearing defeat, the Nertobriges sent a delegate 'who wore a wolf's skin instead of bearing a herald's staff, and begged forgiveness'. Marcellus replied that he would not grant this unless all the Arevaci, Belli, and Titti would ask for it together. Accordingly, when Marcellus besieged the fortress of Numantia, the new Arevaci Leader Litenno came out of the fortress and held a conference with him. Marcellus warned that a tough Roman commander, Lucius Licinius Lucullus, was being sent to reduce the Celtiberians and their allies, and as a result Litenno surrendered to him on behalf of all the tribes.

Marcellus had saved the 'Celtiberi' from the brutality of Lucullus, who began his campaign in 151 BC by massacring the Vaccaei in northern Spain. He then moved south to join the governor of Further Spain, Servius Sulpicius Galba, in the war against the semi-Celtic Lusitani, who had inflicted a heavy defeat on Galba. Soon after, Lucullus and Galba caught the Lusitani in a pincer movement, and they surrendered. Galba pretended to be lenient, but then treacherously surrounded the Lusitani and sent in soldiers to slaughter them 'as they lamented and invoked the names of the gods and the pledges which they had received'. In these and other massacres, Galba mercilessly slew 9,000 of the Lusitani, and sold 20,000 into slavery.

One of the survivors of the massacres was a young man with the Celtic name of Viriatos. He came from near the Atlantic and had started life as a shepherd and hunter on the mountains. Noted for his extraordinary strength, speed, and agility, his reputation for bravery and endurance was so great among the Lusitani that they chose him as their leader in the hope that he would reverse their fortunes. A skilled horseman and swordsman, Viriatos soon showed his talent and resourcefulness, luring the Romans into ambushes, and bringing fire and sword to all their possessions on both banks of the Ebro and Tagus. He was held in honour and affection by his followers on account of his unselfishness and his fair-handed attitude to the spoils of war, which he always divided according to merit.

Viriatos was a master of strategic deception, and had superb knowledge of the terrain, which enabled him to disperse his forces and reassemble them at will. He defeated Roman armies under various generals, but his most celebrated triumph was gained over Caius Vetilius at Tribola in 147 BC, south of Osuna in the extreme south of the Peninsula. Here he feigned flight, thereby leading the Romans into a dense watery thicket, where they were ambushed and 10,000 of them were slain. Vetilius himself was captured, and Viriatos killed him with a sword. After these victories, Viriatos erected – in the mountains of Lusitania – trophies adorned with robes and fasces taken from the Roman commanders.

He suffered a setback when his army was scattered at Urso in 144 BC by the Consul Fabius Maximus Aemilianus. To relieve Roman pressure on the Lusitani, Viriatos then persuaded the Celtiberian tribes of Arevaci, Belli and Titti, to join his revolt. In response, the Consul Quintus Caecilius Metellus was sent to attack Celtiberia with a large army, and he took the hill forts of Nertobriga (now Calatorao), Centrobriga (now Ricla) and Contrebia (now Botorrita). His successor as consul, Quintus Pompeius Aulus, attacked Numantia two years later, but his forces were routed by the 8,000 Celtiberian defenders there. After further setbacks, Aulus agreed to a peace treaty, but soon after he broke the treaty and began hostilities again.

A new Roman army, with elephants and cavalry, was sent from Africa in 142 BC to crush the Lusitanian revolt. It was under the command of the Consul Fabius Maximus Servilianus, and he put the army of Viriatos to flight near Itucca. Viriatos quickly rallied his forces, however, and counter-attacked, driving the Romans back to the safety of the town. He then retired to his own territory to rebuild his forces, and soon after he trapped the army of Servilianus against a cliff at Erisana (now Azuagia). Servilianus was forced to agree to a treaty, according to which the territory occupied by the Lusitani was to be left under their control and Viriatos was to be recognised as 'a friend of the Roman nation'. The outraged

Roman Senate had no choice but to ratify the treaty, but they were determined to find a way around it.

Thus, in 140 BC, the brother of Servilianus, Servilius Caepio, was sent to Spain with a strong army, and he drove Viriatos' forces back into Lusitania. In the following year, Caepio attacked the Vettones and Callaeici, neighbours and allies of the Lusitani to the east and north, thus cutting off supplies to the rebel forces. In these straits, Viriatos offered fresh negotiations, which Caepio pretended to accept. Viriatos sent three of his most trusted friends, Audax, Ditalco, and Minuvius, to negotiate, but Caepio bribed them to assassinate their leader. Soon after, while Viriatos was sleeping, these three stabbed him in the throat and slew him. The Roman writer Florus says that, in this way, although overcome, Viriatos gained 'the glory of seeming to have been invincible by any other means'. The respects paid to him by his followers are described thus by the historian Appian:

> They arranged the body of Viriatos in splendid garments and burned it on a lofty funeral pile. Many sacrifices were offered for him. The infantry and cavalry ran in troops around him, in armour, singing his praises in barbarian fashion, and they all sat around the pyre until the fire had gone out. When the obsequies were ended, thay held contests in swordsmanship at his tomb.

The leadership of the Lusitani passed to Tautalos, but the Romans now clearly had the upper hand, and Tautalos and his army surrendered soon after and were resettled on new land by Caepio. The 'Celtiberi', however, continued to resist. In 138 BC, a large Roman army under the General Caius Mancinus besieged Numantia but, failing to take it and running short of supplies, decided to evacuate by night. The Celtiberians rushed out from their fort to attack the retreating Romans, and the fighting turned into a rout, with thousands of Romans surrendering. Mancinus made a truce with the Celtiberians, but this was rejected by the Roman Senate, who were livid that he allowed his army of 30,000 soldiers to be defeated by a force of 4,000. On his own request, the disgraced Mancinus was handed over to the Celtiberians, naked and with his hands tied behind his back , but they – probably realising that he had acted in good faith – refused to take him as a prisoner.

The Romans sent one of their best commanders, Cornelius Scipio Aemilianus (adopted son of the celebrated Publius Scipio) with 60,000 men to pursue the war. He began to lay waste the plains of the Arevaci and Vaccaei, destroying the food of these tribes and spreading fire and slaughter everywhere. Then he laid siege to the great hill fortress of Numantia, capital of the Arevaci, where large numbers of Celtiberians had gathered for refuge under the leadership of Avaros. Scipio surrounded the town with ballistas and catapults, and several attempts by Avaros' men to dislodge the Romans from their positions failed. These attacks were fierce, and accompanied by great commotion and trumpet blowing, but the besiegers held firm. As the siege dragged on, one report claims that the defenders began to throw all caution to the wind and gorged themselves with half-raw meat and beer before rushing out in the hope of a final battle. This failed, and in another sally a large number of them were slain by the Romans.

Finally the defenders began to run out of supplies, and a chieftain named Rhetogenes Caraunios was chosen to attempt to break through the Roman lines with a few men. This small group slipped out of Numantia under cover of darkness, slew the Roman sentries, and scaled the siege works with a folding ladder. Reaching a neighbouring hill fort, Rhetogenes appealed to those Arevaci who lived there to come to the assistance of Avaros, but they had gone into alliance with the Romans and refused. At Lutia (now Cantalucia) 400 young men agreed to join Rhetogenes, but the older and more cautious citizens of that town sent word of what was happening to Scipio. He immediately sent a legion to besiege Lutia, and under threat of massacre the town surrendered. Scipio had the young rebels paraded before him and ordered their right hands to be cut off.

Meanwhile, the besieged Celtiberians at Numantia were being reduced to starvation and even cannibalism. Rumour spread that Avaros and his family had made a secret deal with the Romans, and as a result he was assassinated and the defenders surrendered. The Latin writer Appian – drawing on a lost account by Polybius – describes their state:

First of all, those who wished to do so killed themselves in various ways. Then the rest went out on the third day to the appointed place, a strange and shocking spectacle. Their bodies were foul, their hair and nails long, and they were smeared with filth. They smelt most horribly, and the clothes which they wore were likewise squalid and emitted an equally foul odour. For these reasons they appeared pitiable to their enemies, but at the same time there was something fearful in the expression of their eyes – an expression of anger, pain and weariness, and the awareness of having eaten human flesh.

Fifty warriors Scipio selected to grace his triumphant march through Rome, and the rest were sold into slavery, while the great hill fort of Numantia itself was burned and razed to the ground. The Roman writer Florus could not refrain from expressing his admiration for the bravery of the defenders. In their extremity, he said, the women had cut the saddlegirths of their husband's horses so that they would not flee. 'Peace be to the ashes of the bravest of all cities ... a city which protected its allies with honour and withstood, with its own force and for so long a period, a people with the strength of the whole world.'

Such noble sentiments were not, however, typical of Roman attitudes towards the Celtiberians. For the next 50 years these people were brutally held down by Roman commanders, and various minor rebellions were crushed without mercy. As Europe underwent vast changes in the final century before Christ, Celtiberian independence was a thing of the past, and the Celtic language and culture in the peninsula began to disappear along with most of the other languages and cultures in the increasingly Latinised south-west corner of the Continent.

6

CLASHES WITH ROMANS, GERMANS, DACIANS

As the second century BC drew to a close, the western half of Europe had taken on the ethnic configuration which was to be known in the era of written history. Most of modern Switzerland, France and Belgium, as well as significant parts of modern Germany and Holland, were inhabited by the Gaulish Celts. The population movements which would alter all of this were, however, already beginning. The Germanic tribes from the broad region bordering on the eastern North Sea and the western Baltic Sea were extending their settlements southwards into Gaulish areas, while in the south the Romans had gained control of all of Italy and Spain and were looking further afield for conquest.

Initial Roman attacks on Gaul
The Romans referred to the whole region which comprises modern Switzerland and France as Gallia Transalpina ('Gaul beyond the Alps'). They had had experience for some time of several of the tribes who inhabited that vast region, and no doubt their intelligence concerning them was good. These Gauls were powerful and had a quite sophisticated social system. Their trading system was developed over a wide area, and – following on the example of their Cisalpine cousins – several tribes began to mint their own coins, using motifs which were heavily influenced by

Massaliot and Etruscan models. Around the same time they also acquired writing from the Greeks of Marseilles and began to produce inscriptions on stone and metal. These Gaulish inscriptions, which continued for several centuries, consisted of funereal, dedicatory and magical texts, and even some calendrical and poetic material. There are also indications that among them the absolute rule of kings was giving way to rule by assembly of the nobles.

The Aedui, who occupied the modern French department of Saône-et-Loire, had been dominant in Gaul for some time. From the end

of the third century BC they were losing their leading position, but were still a force to be reckoned with. Their centre was the hill fort of Bibracte ('beaver-place', now Mont-Beuvray, west of Autun), and they had several kindred groups and allies. Important peoples who had grown out of them were the Carnutes on the Seine, the Ambarri on the Sâone, and the Insubres also on the Sâone and in Italy. As well as these, they had several client peoples – including the Mandubii ('tramplers') on their northern border; the Brannovices ('frenzied conquerors'), a branch of the Aulerci, between the Loire and the upper Yonne; and the Segusiavi ('victorious ones'), whose celebrated fortress was called Lugudunum (now Lyon) after the deity Lugus.

To the north of the Aedui – in the modern department of Haute-Marne – were the Lingones ('springers'), whose centre is now called Langres. Like the Insubres, a branch of these had settled in Italy. Between the Saône and the Jura were the Sequani, who had come from the basin of the Seine, and had the name of that river (Sequana, i.e., 'spouting lady') attached to them. Their chief centre was Vesontio (now Besançon). Several small groups lay to the south of these Sequani. The Vertacorii inhabited the plateau between the Isère and Drac rivers, the Segovellauni were on the western bank of the Rhône, while the Tricastini had their centre at Senomagus ('old market', now Senos). The Vocontii (meaning 'twenty septs') inhabited the mountainous area to the east of these.

The Celtic groups in the extreme south were strongly mixed with the Ligurians, who had been the first Indo-European inhabitants of the region. The two most numerous of such groups were the Cavari and the Salluvii (also written as 'Salassi' or 'Salyes'). The Cavari ('giants') were in the modern department of Vaucluse, and had the towns of Arausio (now Orange), Avenio (now Avignon) and Cabellio (now Cavaillon). A branch of these Cavari, called Memini, had the town of Carpentorate ('chariot course', now Carpentras). The Salluvii ('seacoast dwellers') were along the banks of the Durance, and their territories – as their name suggests – reached as far as the Mediterranean. They were to the north and west of the strong Greek colony of Marseilles, and – as we have seen – a strong branch of them was settled in the Alps. To their west again, stretching to the Pyrenees, were groups of Volcae who had penetrated into that area from north of the Alps in the late fourth century BC. There were three groups of these Volcae – one, using their favourite pseudonym Tectosages, were at Toulouse, enjoying the wealth offered by the extensive goldmines there; another called Arecomici ('proximate allies') were at

Nîme; and another, mixed with local Ligurians at Narbonne, were called
Atacini (perhaps Atecingi, 'great warriors').

One very important tribe in the south-eastern region, with whom
the Romans knew they would have to contend, were the Allobroges, who
had welcomed Hannibal a few generations before. These inhabited a vast
area encompassed by the modern departments of Savoy and Dauphiné
as well as the adjacent parts of south-western Switzerland. Their chief
centres were Vienna on the Rhône (now Vienne) and Genava (now
Geneva). The name Allobroges meant 'those from another territory', and
indicates that they were remembered as having migrated to this area from
some distant part. They had probably come from between the Danube
and the Rhine, following on other tribes who had moved westwards since
the sixth and fifth centuries BC. The most noted of these migrants westwards must have been the ancestors of the Arverni, to whom the
Allobroges were allied.

The Arverni ('superior ones') were in the Rhône valley and in a
broad area to the west of that, and their name reflects the fact that they
had for some generations been the leading Celtic group in that whole
region. This they achieved by raiding the territories of the Aedui, thus
weakening their foremost rivals. The modern department of Auvergne
preserves their name, and their principal centre was Gergovia (modern
Gergovie). By the beginning of the second century BC, the Arverni were
the most powerful tribe in all of Gaul. They had several client peoples,
including the Vellavi ('superior ones') on their southern flank, and the
Gabali ('capturers') further south again in the Cévennes. On their western
flank they had as clients the Ruteni ('red ones', referring to battle), and the
Cadurci ('battle-boars'), whose capital – called Divona ('the goddess',
now Cahors) – enjoyed great prestige.

After the conquest of the Iberian Peninsula, and with the
Carthaginian threat removed, Rome was in a position to extend its influence
permanently north-west of the Alps, and an occasion for this presented
itself in the year 154 BC when the Salluvii launched an attack on
Marseilles. The assault was repulsed by the Massaliotes with the help of
Roman troops, but the Salluvii returned to the attack in 125 BC, and now
the Romans offered – under guise of protection – to control all the territory
held by this Greek colony, which stretched from Cisalpine Gaul along the
coast to Marseilles. This was accepted, and the consuls Fulvius Flaccus
and Sextius Calvinus defeated and slaughtered the Salluvii in battle. The
Romans sold large numbers of the survivors into slavery; but the king of

the Salluvii, Toutomotulos, and some others of their leaders fled north-wards to take refuge with the powerful Allobroges.

At this time of crisis the king of the Arverni was Bituitis, son of the former king Lovernios (literally 'the fox'). Lovernios had been famed for his lavishness, as is clear from a near-contemporary account of him:

> In an attempt to win popular favour he rode in a chariot over the plains, distributing gold and silver to the tens of thousands of Celts who followed him. Moreover, he made a square enclosure one and a half miles each way, within which he filled vats with expensive liquor, and prepared so great a quantity of food that for many days all who wished could enter and enjoy the prepared feast, it being served without a break by the attendants. And when at length he fixed a day for the ending of the feast, a Celtic poet, who arrived too late, met Lovernios and composed a song magnifying his greatness and regret-ting his own late arrival. Lovernios was very pleased, and asked for a bag of gold and threw it to the poet who ran beside his chariot. The poet picked it up and sang another song, saying that the very tracks made by his chariot on the earth gave gold and largesse to mankind.

The Romans were, of course, very anxious to reduce and loot a kingdom which had such a reputation for wealth, and they used the issue of the Salluvii refugees as a pretext for launching an all-out campaign against both the Allobroges and Arverni. Two strong armies were accord-ingly sent northwards in 121 BC, under Cnaeus Domitius Ahenobarbus and Quintus Fabius Maximus. In an attempt to avoid conflict, the Arvernian king, Bituitis, sent an ambassador to Domitius as he passed with his legions through the territory of the Salluvii. The historian Appian states that the ambassador was arrayed magnificently and followed by attendants and hounds, 'as the barbarians of this region use dogs also as bodyguards'. A musician was also in the train, singing the praises of Bituitis, but the ambassador's efforts were of no avail.

The Romans were determined to pursue their advantage, and their two armies, having joined, clashed with a large force of Arvernian warriors at Vindalium (now Vedene, where the river Sorgue flows into the Rhône). Bituitis – flamboyant like his father – was a conspicuous figure in the battle as he wore variegated armour and drove a silver chariot. It is reported that he was surprised that the Romans did not have as large a force as his and that he boasted that they would 'hardly suffice to feed the dogs which he had in his army'. When the fighting began, however, his warriors were dispirited by the sight of elephants in the Roman army, 'which matched the fierceness of these people', and the Arverni were routed. Bituitis had many boats chained together so as to ferry his men across the Rhône, and in their haste to retreat the chains broke, causing as many to be drowned as were slain. One Roman report put the total Gaulish force in the battle at over 100,000, but this was undoubtedly much exaggerated, as another account puts the number of dead at 20,000 with 3,000 captured.

The initiative had now passed to the Romans, and they acted quickly. While Fabius ravaged the territory of the Allobroges, Ahenobarbus rode ceremonially through the conquered territory on an elephant and forced other tribes of the area, such as the Helvetii and the section of the Volcae Tectosages who inhabited Toulouse, to conclude treaties of 'friendship' with Rome. Bituitis, who had survived the battle of Vindalium, also offered to make peace with Rome, stating that he wished to deal with the Roman Senate in person. Once he arrived in Italy, however, he and his son Congentiatos were detained by the Romans as virtual prisoners. It would appear that Congentiatos later made a deal with the Romans and that he was in fact the 'Contoniatus' appointed by them as king over the Arverni.

These events, the breaking of the power of the Allobroges and the Arverni, were followed by the capitulation of the remaining Celtic peoples with territories immediately to the north and west of the Alps. These included the Caturiges ('battle kings'), who had the strong fortresses of Eburodunum (now Ebrun) and Brigantio (now Briançon). These may have come originally from central Gaul, for a section of them, the Quariates, had a designation cognate with that of the Parisii in that region. Other Alpine peoples who now found themselves under Roman sway were the Ceutrones ('foresters'), and smaller groups such as the Veragri, Uberi, Sedunes, and Everones. The Romans showed how ruthlessly they would deal with any opposition when, in 118 BC, the Consul Quintus Marcius attacked an unnamed Celtic tribe who were settled at the foot of the Alps. The later writer Orosius reports that, when surrounded, these Celts committed mass suicide, and that 'no one survived, not even a little child, by his love of life to endure slavery'.

The Romans celebrated their first triumph in Transalpine Gaul by founding a colony at Narbonne and naming the whole area as the 'provincia' of 'Gallia Narbonensis', from which comes the designation

Provence. They also built a great road stretching all the way from Genoa to there, and further along the eastern coast of Spain as far as Cartagena. Celtic and other peoples inhabiting that whole area soon came to terms with the new arrangements, and had little choice but to offer themselves as allies to the new superpower. Among these were the powerful Aedui, and this particular alliance gave the Romans a hand in affairs at the very heart of Celtic territory.

Germanic attack on Italy

Before the Romans could extend their power further, however, a new threat emerged from the north. The Cimbri and Teutones were Germanic peoples who had originated in the area of the North Sea and had been encroaching on Celtic territories for some time. During the course of their expansion, these people – and particularly the Cimbri – seem to have absorbed a good deal of Celtic influence, so that many of their recorded leaders were known by Celtic or Celticised names. The Romans were confused as to their exact identity, and sometimes equated them with the more northerly Celts.

The reality, however, was that the Celtic peoples in southern Germany and northern Austria were being pressurised by the Cimbri. When the thrust of the Cimbri brought them westwards as far as the Rhine and southwards as far as the Danube, the inhabitants of these areas thought an alliance with them preferable to destruction at their hands. Some of these Celtic peoples were quite powerful in their own right, such as the Taurisci, in the area of Mount Taurus, who had held firm in that area after their expansion eastwards had been halted by the Greeks and Thracians.

More directly in the line of the Germanic advance were the Helvetii, who had resided on both sides of the Rhine, but who had been pushed southwards to the area between the Jura and Lake Constance, where their main forts were Aventicum (modern Avenches) and Vindonissa (modern Windisch). Their principal dependent tribes were the Rauraci and the Tigurini. The Rauraci, who once inhabited the Ruhr Valley, had been moving southwards due to Germanic pressure for a long time, and they had settled at the bend of the Rhine, with Basilea (now Basel) as their main town. The Tigurini ('claimers'), a very numerous tribe, had also come from the north – probably from the area along the river Main – and were particularly willing to join in the Cimbri advance and turn it to their own benefit. Others dependent on the Helvetii were the Tulingi and Latobrigi. These seem to have been branches of the very influential and far-flung people, the Volcae.

Reference has already been made to the parallelism in the fortunes of the Volcae and another celebrated people, the Boii, throughout much of Celtic history. Sections of both peoples had joined together in the great Celtic push into eastern Europe and Asia Minor, and other sections of them made their way westwards, skirting the southern borders of Gaul and settling at various locations. In this way, the Volcae groups provided a significant Celtic bulwark between Marseilles and the Pyrenees, but a small group of Boii had continued on almost as far west as Arcachon on the Atlantic coast. When the Volcae and Boii decided willy-nilly to join with the overwhelming force of Cimbri, these settlements in the extreme south of Gaul were to prove of some value in the war against the Romans.

The Romans had for some time been trying to gain a foothold in the Celtic territories along the eastern Danube, especially because of the rich mineral deposits there. They established a colony at Aquileia in 169 BC and, from this, they began to interfere in the affairs of Macedonia, which they subdued and turned into a Roman province by the middle of the second century BC. Thereafter the Romans felt ready to extend their power into Celtic parts of the region, using as a pretext the continuous raiding activities of the Scordisci, against whom they fought several battles. Gold was discovered in the territory of the Taurisci around 140 BC and, after Italians who had joined the gold rush were expelled, Roman forces were sent into the area in 129 BC and again in 115 BC.

These Roman expeditions were successful but, before they could follow up their advantage, the Scordisci scored a victory over the Consul Gaius Porcius in the year 114 BC and began to push southwards towards the Adriatic. The Roman writer, Florus, claims that, on this campaign, the cruelty of the Scordisci knew no bounds – 'they offered human blood to the gods, they drank from men's skulls'. Such descriptions probably reflect the cult of heads among the Celts, but the imagery is conveniently out of context. A similar denigration is instanced by Appian's jibe that Illyria got its name from Illyrios, son of the one-eyed giant of Greek mythology, Polyphemos, and his wife Galatea. The two brothers of Illyrios were called Celtus and Galas, according to this parody on the mixed populations of eastern Celts and Illyrians. The fighting ability of the Scordisci, at any rate, alarmed the Romans, and to add to their discomfiture there were reports of alliances between the Germanic invaders and various Celtic groups in the region. An army under the Consul Papirius Carbo in 113 BC was sent to oppose these, but the Roman legions met with a large force of combined Cimbri and Celts near Noreia (modern Neumarkt in Steiermark), and were soundly defeated.

Roman alarm soon developed into despair, for a further build-up of combined Cimbric and Celtic forces was taking place at the other end of the Alps. In the year 111 BC the Cimbri resumed their advance westwards, into the Rhône Valley, and began to threaten the province of Gallia Narbonensis. The Roman governor of the province, Junius Silanus, refused their offers of negotiation and attacked them, but his army was routed. The Cimbri, under Claodicus, were now joined by the Teutones under their leader Teutoboduos (probably a Celticised form of the Germanic Theudabadus), and by Celtic tribes of the area. The Tectosages also rebelled and laid siege to the Roman garrison at Toulouse in 107 BC. They were joined by a strong body of Tigurini who had reached the area. To counter this, the Romans sent two new armies into Gaul, under the consuls Lucius Cassius Longinus and Servilius Caepio (son and namesake of the general who had encompassed the death of Viriatos in Iberia).

Longinus chased the Tigurini northwest through the Garonne Valley as far as the territory of the Nitiobroges. These were the most powerful Celtic group in that area, as is clear from their name, which meant 'owners of territory'. No doubt encouraged and assisted by these, the young leader of the Tigurini, Divico, decided to make a stand near the capital of the Nitiobroges, which was called Aginnum (now Agen). The Romans were defeated, and Longinus himself was slain. When they agreed to give hostages and to surrender half their possessions, the Roman survivors were sent under the yoke and then allowed to go unharmed.

Meanwhile, the army of Caepio managed to relieve the siege of Toulouse and inflicted a defeat on the Tectosages, who surrendered. Their leader, Copillos, was captured soon afterwards. Caepio, knowing that the Gauls were accustomed to load their temples with offerings, committed the sacriligious act of seizing a huge amount of gold there. Caepio tried to keep the treasure for himself, but was later accused with purloining it from the Roman State. He was dispossessed of his property by the Romans, imprisoned, and ended his days in misfortune, thus giving rise to 'the gold of Tolosa' as a proverbial expression to indicate ill luck. Some accounts claim that he took it from a sacred lake near Toulouse, and that it was treasure which had been taken from Delphi almost 200 years before. According to the legend, some of the Tectosages, after the failure of the invasion of Greece, had travelled to Toulouse and settled there. A pestilence came upon them, and they could only recover by following the advice of their wise men to throw the gold and the silver into the lake.

The treasure which Caepio seized is, however, unlikely to have originated at Delphi. It must rather have been the result of ritual deposits made regularly there, from which that lake got its name Tolosa (referring to it 'filling' or 'increasing' with the treasure). The fact that the Tectosages ('wealth-seekers') had settled there, and that some members of the same tribe had taken part in the invasion of Greece almost two centuries before, would easily have caused the belief to develop that the treasure in that particular lake had come from Delphi. Cultural connections, or the memory of such, may well have survived between some Celtic tribes of the same stock in the east and the west. At the beginning of the second century BC, the Greek colony of Lampsacus in Asia Minor wrote to the Greek colony at Marseilles seeking letters of introduction to the Tolistoboii. Marseilles was of course neighbouring on the Volcae Tectosages of Toulouse, and the Tolistoboii and Tectosages were the leading Celtic groups in Asia Minor. The name Tectosages ('wealth-seekers') would indeed suggest that these groups had treasure-lore as part of their tribal cultus, and they themselves may have given the name 'Tolosa' to the lake.

Caepio's victory at Toulouse proved to be a hollow one, for within two years another Roman army was wiped out at Orange, and a combined force of Cimbri and Teutones then proceeded to cross the Pyrenees and enter Spain. They met with stout resistance there from the Roman garrisons, helped by Celtiberian tribes who had no welcome for more strangers in search of land. The invaders soon returned from Spain and joined their main force which was now threatening Italy itself. In 102 BC it was only with great difficulty that the Cimbri were prevented from going through the Brenner Pass by a large Roman army. Soon after, the Teutones were defeated with great slaughter by the Consul Gaius Marius as they attempted to enter Italy from the direction of Gallia Narbonensis. A few surviving horsemen took refuge with the Celtic Sequani, but the Sequani were forced by the Romans to hand them over for execution.

Finally, in 101 BC, the Cimbri broke through into Italy with an enormous force, and the advancing horde was confronted by the Romans under Marius near Vercellae, between Milan and Turin. It was a very hot day, and the adroit Marius had his soldiers advance through the dust and haze. To the consternation of the Cimbri, the Romans suddenly charged upon them from the east, with their helmets seeming to be on fire from the shining of the sun's rays. In a ferocious struggle, the Cimbri were defeated, and it is reported that no less than 60,000 of their fighters were killed. The leader of the Cimbri fell in this battle, fighting furiously and slaying many of his opponents. The Roman writers give his name as Boiorix, a Celticised form of the Germanic Baiarikas which was probably the variant used by his Celtic followers. The Roman writers claimed that the women and children, who had been brought with them in wagons by the Cimbri, then proceeded to commit suicide, but we can be sure that the Romans themselves had a hand in the indiscriminate slaughter which followed.

The Romans continued to strengthen their grip on the new province of Gallia Narbonensis beyond the Alps, causing concern among the peoples of that area that wholesale confiscation of their lands was in prospect. The Aedui themselves were oscillating between their feud with the Arverni and fear of their new Roman 'protectors', and lesser peoples felt far more vulnerable. The Allobroges and Volcae in particular had recent experience of Roman cupidity, and the Salluvii must have regarded themselves as a prime target, in view of their record and of the rapid erosion of their territory which was going on before their eyes. A forlorn attempt at rebellion by them in the year 90 BC was rapidly put down by a Roman army under the Praetor Gaius Caecilius. The way was now open for expansion of the Roman power into the vast territories of the Gauls to the north.

In the east, too, the Romans had their revenge. Successive consuls campaigned against the Scordisci, driving them northeastwards through the mountains. Minucius Rufus inflicted a disastrous defeat on them in 108 BC, after which large numbers of Scordisci warriors were captured. They were treated savagely – Florus states that 'cruelties by fire and sword were inflicted on them' and that 'nothing seemed more horrid to these barbarians than that they should be left with their hands cut off, and be obliged to live and survive their sufferings'. Finally, in 88 BC, the remainder of the Scordisci were defeated by Lucius Scipio Asiagenus and driven across the Danube. Many of their surviving fighting men became mercenaries in the army of Mithradates the Great, king of Pontus, in his unsuccessful campaign against the Romans in Macedonia.

The power of the Cimbri and Teutones had been broken even more abruptly than it had arisen, and the Celts had been completely overthrown in the Balkans. As a result of all these battles, moreover, a huge number of captives had been taken by the legions, and this swelled the slave population of Rome. Many of the slaves who joined the revolt of the gladiator Spartacus in 73 BC were Cimbri, Teutones, and Celts. Spartacus himself was a Thracian and two of his generals, Crixos and Cenomaros, had Celtic names. Indeed, during his revolt, Spartacus got large numbers of recruits from Cisalpine Gaul and, when he was defeated two years later by a huge Roman army under Marcus Licinius Crassus, the thousands of his men who were crucified between Capua and Rome must have included many Celtic warriors who had risked all in his daring adventure for freedom.

Contraction and struggle

Everywhere it was the Roman power which was now crucial to the Celts, and their history was being re-shaped in the context of struggles which were developing within the Roman world itself. The first such power struggle was between Gaius Marius and another famous general, Lucius Cornelius Sulla. Marius represented the popular party and Sulla the nobility. The struggle continued for 30 years and outlasted the deaths of both leaders, and many of the leading figures used the Celtic world as their stamping ground and arena for gaining credit at home.

Iberia was a clear instance, to which, in 83 BC, a governor, Quintus Sertorius – who belonged to the popular party in Rome – was assigned. In the following year Sulla had appointed himself dictator, and Sertorius joined the Lusitani in a revolt. Many of the other leading tribes flocked to his support, including the Arevaci, Vaccaei, Vettones and most of the 'Celtiberi'. Those who did not support him soon felt the force of his wrath – he besieged the Lusones at Contrebia in the winter of 77 BC and reduced that city after 44 days. He then in the spring captured Vareia, the city of the Berones. Although a brilliant strategist, Sertorius was also something of a charlatan, and he inspired religious awe in his Iberian supporters by claiming that his pet white fawn was an intermediary between himself and the gods. He succeeded in holding most of Spain against the Roman armies sent there, including one led by the celebrated Pompeius Cneus (Pompey) in 76 BC, but was assassinated four years later by his lieutenant Perperna.

Far to the east, the situation of the Celts in Asia Minor was somewhat different. Through the second century BC they increasingly brought the prestigious cultic sites under their control. We read that, towards the end of that century, a beautiful Galatian woman called Camma was hereditary priestess of a temple of the divine mother (probably that at Pessinus), and that she was in fact the wife of a Galatian chieftain called Sinatos. He was murdered by Sinorix, leader of the Tolistoboii, who lusted after Camma, and she devised a plot to avenge her dead husband. She offered to marry Sinorix in the temple, and as part of the ceremony asked him to share a drink with her. The drink was poisoned, and in this way she brought about his death as well as her own.

In a broader political context, the Galatian state survived, but only through a strategic dependence on Roman power. All of this was threatened with the accession to power of Mithradates VI ('the Great') as king of Pontus, to the north of Galatia and bordering on the Black Sea. He built up a large army, and seized large parts of the neighbouring kingdoms of Colchis, Paphlagonia and Bithynia. Goaded by an attack on Pontic territory, Mithradates declared war on the Romans in 88 BC. His forces immediately overran Phrygia, Cappadocia, Galatia and Pergamon. Seizing the Roman province in the west of Asia Minor, he had all the Italians massacred there. He then sent a large army to Greece, but it was utterly routed by the Romans at Chaeronea in 86 BC.

After this, Mithradates began desperately to replenish his forces with recruits from Asia Minor, forcibly enlisting large numbers of young men from all the regions. Knowing that the Galati had already provided troops for the Roman army and suspecting that their nobles would create difficulties for him, he summoned these leaders to confer with him at Pergamon in 86 BC and then treacherously put them to death, along with their wives and children. It is reported that some of these he seized by stratagem, and others by treacherously slaying them at a banquet. One account has it that he ordered the mass executions after discovering that a Galatian chieftain called Poredix was plotting to assassinate him. He then confiscated the property of the Galati, placed garrisons in their towns, and appointed one of his officers, Eumachus, as a satrap over them. Only three of the Galatian nobility escaped the purges, and one of these was Deïotaros, son of the poisoned Sinorix. Deïotaros was an enterprising young man, and he managed to take many Galatian warriors with him onto the Roman side.

The armies of Mithradates were defeated in several battles by the Romans led by Sulla in Greece and by Fimbria in Asia Minor, and in 84 BC, he had to sue for peace. He agreed to abandon the territories he had occupied and to pay an indemnity, but the Romans continued to intimidate him, and fighting was renewed in 74 BC. In the following year Deïotaros, serving under Lucullus, drove one of Mithradates' armies eastwards out of Phrygia – this victory must have been particularly satisfying to the Galati, for that army was led by Eumachus, who had over a decade before been imposed as the satrap over them. When Mithradates himself was defeated by Lucullus at Cabeira in 72 BC, he was almost captured in his flight into Armenia by a troop of Lucullus' Galatian horsemen. Dazzled by the immense riches to be had in the place, the horsemen turned aside from the pursuit to loot the pack of a mule, which was laden with gold and silver.

Mithradates managed to rally his forces once more, and he recovered many of his possessions in Pontus and Armenia, but he suffered a final defeat at the hands of the famous Roman general Pompey, after which he was deposed by the rebellion of his own son in 64 BC. He tried to commit suicide by poison, but he had so inured himself by taking antidotes over the years that the poison would not work. He then asked the assistance of one of his Celtic officers, called Bitocos, saying 'I have profited much from your right arm against my enemies – I shall profit from it most of all if you will kill me!' Bitocos, who was greatly moved by this, did as was requested of him.

Here, as earlier in the Macedonian War, the position of the Galati contrasted with that of other Celtic groups, who favoured the enemies of Rome. Many of the Galati were forced by Mithradates the Great to serve in his armies, but the popular support was with Deïotaros. Bitocos, the officer loyal to Mithradates, probably belonged to the Illyrian Celts, and it is interesting to note that Mithradates himself seems to have been aware of the possibility of enlisting more general Celtic support. This had led the Pontic king to seek alliances with Sertorius and his Celtiberian followers in 75 BC and with the Cisalpine Gauls in 64 BC.

There was, of course, little which the Celts remaining in Cisalpine Gaul could do, and Transalpine Gaul was at the same time being seized with a panic of insecurity. This derived largely from the Roman threat, which was giving rise to civil wars between the inhabitants of that region. The Aedui had begun to challenge the weakened Arverni and their allies the Sequani, and around 71 BC these two latter tribes had brought in some Germanic mercenaries to assist them. The result was that the king of the Germanic Suebi, Ariovistus, got a foothold among the Sequani, who came more and more under his control. He occupied all their towns, and began to settle large numbers of Germans in their territory.

The Aedui mustered as many of their neighbours as they could, and spearheaded the resistance against Ariovistus. In 61 BC, however, Ariovistus scored a massive victory over a united force of several Celtic tribes at Admagetobriga (in Alsace), after which he began to penetrate further into the Celtic territories in Switzerland and eastern France. He now demanded as hostages the children of Gaulish leaders, and began to issue commands to these leaders at will. Refusal to obey his commands resulted in torture or death. The Aedui, whom he saw as the major stumbling block to his ambitions, had lost many of their best warriors and virtually the whole of their national council. In their hour of desperation, one of the leaders of the Aedui, Diviciacus, went to Rome requesting aid against the Germans, reminding them of the alliance contracted two generations before and promising that his tribe would be loyal to the Roman interest. The wolf was at the door, and Celtic Gaul was beginning to doubt its own resources for survival.

This was clearly exemplified by a more localised crisis. In 63 BC a delegation of Allobroges leaders had gone to Rome to complain to the Senate about how Roman governors were plundering their tribe. These complaints were not addressed, and two years later in desperation the Allobroges attacked the fountainhead of their oppression, the Roman province of Gallia Narbonensis. In retaliation, the Roman governor of the province, Gaius Pomptinus, sent an army under Manlius Lentinus to ravage their lands. One of their oppida, at Valence, was besieged, but the local Allobroges population came to the support of that town and the Romans were driven away. Lentinus continued to plunder the area, but the chieftain Catugnatos gathered a large force of his people and brought them across the river Isère. Lentinus prepared ambushes for them in the forest to the west of the river, but he was counter-ambushed by Catugnatos, and his army would have been wiped out but for a sudden storm which arose and hindered the attack, thus allowing the Romans to escape. Lentinus next besieged the town of Solonium (now probably La Sone). Catugnatos arrived with his men to raise the siege, but they in turn were surrounded by a large army led by the governor Pomptinus. The bulk of the Allobroges warriors were captured, but Catugnatos got away.

The year 60 BC was momentous for the Celts, not least because of the appointment as consul at Rome of a young man who already had had some experience of Celtic peoples but who was destined to be their greatest enemy. This was Caius Julius Caesar, who was connected by marriage to Marius, and therefore belonged to the same party as

Sertorius. Caesar, however, was far more ambitious and destined for a far more successful career. He had served as quaestor in Further Spain in 68 BC, but this tour of duty disappointed him since it offered no opportunity for glory, and he soon returned to Italy. There he flung himself headlong into the factionalism between various groups who were contending for power.

His political skills became clear when a conspiracy was discovered at Rome by the orator Cicero in 63 BC, at the very time that the Allobroges delegation was in the city. The conspiracy was organised by a Roman nobleman, Sergius Catilina, who planned to assassinate the upper-class senators and confiscate their wealth. Catilina contacted the Allobrogian envoys and, on hearing of their determination to be rid of the rapacity of the Romans, he enlisted them into his group. Feeling insecure in the confines of Rome and its internal squabbles, however, the Allobroges decided that it would be safer for them to inform Cicero, and this they did. Cicero quickly used them as agents to gain more information on the conspiracy, and thus had Catilina and his followers arrested. Suspicion of involvement in the conspiracy fell on Caesar also, but he had so ingratiated himself with the people by lavish games and entertainments that he survived.

He finally extricated himself from danger by gaining the governorship of Further Spain in 62 BC. This appointment was given to him specifically in order to counteract the Lusitani, who had embarked on another series of raids on Roman settlements in the peninsula. Caesar was determined to use the opportunity to further his political ambitions at home, and also to gain enough wealth to clear the massive debts which he had incurred. An anecdote of his journey to Spain illustrates the manner in which he intended to use the Celts. Passing through a miserable little Alpine village, his companions remarked that people in that place were as ambitious as those in any other place, whereupon Caesar answered that he himself would prefer to be 'the first man here than the second in Rome'. Eager for glory and to emulate the achievements of other Roman commanders, he won several battles against the Lusitani and established his authority as far as the Atlantic. He then sailed up along the coast and took the Celtic city of the Callaeici, Brigantium (modern La Coruña), in the north.

Disaster was also looming for the Celts along the Danube, where another powerful enemy had come to the fore. This was the king of the Dacians, Boerebistas, who succeeded in uniting his own people with their kindred Getae and Boeri into one kingdom. In 60 BC, the same year that Caesar was appointed consul at Rome, Boerebistas began to put pressure on the Celtic tribes of the Danubian basin. He had a huge army – reported to have numbered 200,000 men – which he first used to scatter those remnants of the Scordisci which had survived the Roman genocide some decades before. Then he advanced against the Taurisci and Boii, gaining his most notable success near to the river Tisza in Hungary, where he routed the forces of the Boii king Critasiros. The latter were pursued as far as the west bank of the Danube, leaving their former territories to be described as 'the desert of the Boii'. In a vain effort to stabilise their position, the retreating Boii attacked the Celtic city of Noreia, which looked to their Roman allies for assistance. The attack failed, and many of the Boii, with smaller dependent groups, escaped through Bohemia into the original Celtic homeland north of the Alps.

The Celts in their homeland were thus coming under pressure from three sides at once – from Germanic tribes in the north, from the reviving Dacians in the east, and from the Romans in the south. The latter threat, in the guise of Caesar, was to be the most devastating of all.

7

THE DESTRUCTION OF GAUL

In Rome, the new consul Julius Caesar courted the friendship of the two other leading figures, Crassus and Pompey, although these two were rivals. The end result was a general reconciliation of the three men, and the establishment in 59 BC of a triumvirate by which they ruled the Empire together. Caesar next achieved two of his principal purposes – one was the reduction of the power of Cicero, and the other was having himself put in charge of the Roman province of Gaul for five years. This latter office he intended as a springboard to total power in Rome.

There was turmoil in the whole Transalpine region, where the Boii and others from the east had been thrown back upon the incumbent peoples, such as the Celto-Venetian tribe of Raeti and the Celtic Nantuates ('valley-people') and Latobrigi ('hillside-people'); where the Helvetii had similarly been pushed from the north; and where the Arverni and Allobroges were still trying to recover from the earlier crushing defeat by the Romans. It was into this vortex of contracted territory, tribal rivalry, and general frustration, that Caesar entered.

Attack on southern Gaul
The Helvetii were situated between the river Rhine, the Jura mountains, and Lake Geneva, and they wished to migrate to an area which would be

safer from German attacks. Their leading chieftain, Orgetorix, had for years been planning to make room by extirpating the Roman influence from Transalpine Gaul, and to this purpose he had cemented agreements with Casticos, son of the former king of the Sequani to the west, and with Dumnorix, a chieftain of the Aedui and brother of their pro-Roman king Diviciacos. To cement the alliance, Orgetorix gave his daughter in marriage to Dumnorix.

The Helvetii, under their aging King Divico, lacked a strong central leadership, and other nobles of the tribe suspected that Orgetorix intended to grab supreme power for himself. When they learned of his dealings with Casticos and Dumnorix they summoned him to stand trial for his life, but Orgetorix arrived for his trial accompanied by 10,000 followers, thereby aborting any proceedings against him. Civil war was imminent among the Helvetii, but soon after Orgetorix was found dead. Suicide was claimed to have been the cause of death, but assassination would appear more likely. His policies, however, had become very popular, and in 58 BC, the Helvetii en masse decided to migrate southwards through the Roman province of Gallia Narbonensis.

Caesar immediately began to muster a large army in the neighbourhood of Geneva, and had the bridge over the river Rhône destroyed. The Helvetii appealed to him to allow them to pass peacefully through the Roman province, but he delayed an answer as he built up his army. In reality, he had no intention of acceding to the request, and in his own war commentary he makes it clear that he thirsted after vengeance for the defeat inflicted by the Tigurini on the Romans at Agen almost 50 years before. He fortified the banks of the Rhône, and then forbade the Helvetii to cross. Some of them attempted to do so, but were driven back by the Roman soldiers. Now Dumnorix the Aeduan made representations to the Sequani to allow the Helvetii to pass through their territory. Dumnorix (whose name meant 'earth-king'), was a generous and popular man, endowed with great courage and diplomatic skill, and he secured an agreement between these two tribes and an exchange of hostages to guarantee it.

Although the intended passage did not touch on the Roman province, Caesar chose to regard it as a threat. Not only did it provide a pretext for him to get more deeply involved in Gaulish affairs, but he was also disturbed by the revolutionary activities of Dumnorix and by the fact that many slaves were escaping from the Romans to join the Gauls. Caesar therefore raised two new legions in Italy, bringing his total to six legions, and rushed to the scene. Attacking the final group in the Helvetii migration, the Tigurini, as they crossed the river Saône, he slaughtered many of them. Immediately, the elderly Helvetian king, Divico, went in person to offer peace. Divico said that they were willing to settle only in a region which would please Caesar, but warned that if they were forced into war they might destroy his army for 'they had learned from their fathers and ancestors to fight like brave men and not to rely on trickery or stratagem'. Taking this as a hint at the defeat which Divico as leader of the Tigurini had long ago inflicted on the Romans, Caesar answered haughtily and demanded hostages. Divico replied that the Helvetii were accustomed to accept hostages, but not to give them, and he departed.

The Helvetii raised their camp and continued their journey. Caesar followed them closely for a fortnight with his cavalry and legions. The forces under his command would have numbered upwards of 30,000 men, the majority of them well-trained and experienced soldiers. Finally, near the Aeduan centre of Bibracte, the two armies came to grips. The Helvetii formed a phalanx, but in the fighting their spears were so long that they began to hinder each other. They began to retreat towards the hill fort there, and the pursuing Romans were suddenly attacked on their right flank by thousands of Boii and Tulingi. The fighting lasted from midday until night, and finally the Celts left the field. Caesar had captured a son and daughter of Orgetorix, but a huge number of Celtic warriors had survived the battle. These marched for three days through the territory of the Lingones and, finally, reduced by hunger and harassed by the Romans and their allies, they surrendered.

Caesar states that he was presented with some lists, written in Greek characters, which the Helvetii had made of the numbers involved in the attempted migration. According to these lists – which recorded men, women, and children – the Helvetii had numbered 263,000 people, supplemented by 36,000 Tulingi, 14,000 Latobrigi, 23,000 Rauraci, and 32,000 Boii. Of this host, 92,000 had been men capable of bearing arms. After the surrender, a subgroup of the Helvetii, called Verbigeni, numbering 6,000 men, slipped away, hoping to escape to Germanic territory; but Caesar issued threats against anybody who helped them, and as a result they were brought back. Caesar executed them all, but allowed the Helvetii and their other allies – whose number had by this stage been reduced to 110,000 people – to return home. He directed the Allobroges to supply them with food until their crops grew again, and persuaded the Aedui to accept the survivors of the Boii contingent on their territory. This leniency was dictated by Caesar's concern to maintain the Celts as a bulwark against German expansion.

His victory left Caesar in control of most of southern and central Gaul, so much so that he made arrangements to call together delegates from the tribes of all of this region in what he described as a 'general council of the Gauls'. Such a council would in fact be little more than an assembly to learn his dictates. Requiring diplomacy to cement his conquests, however, he determined to keep the façade of voluntary alliance for as long as it suited, and therefore courteously received the Gaulish leaders who came 'to offer their congratulations' on his victories. Thus did several powerful peoples and their client groups accept his overlordship. It must have been particularly pleasing for the Romans to find among these the Bituriges, whom Dumnorix had also included in his plans for a Celtic alliance, and to which end he had actually married his widowed mother to their most powerful chieftain. Memory still survived, of course, of how the Bituriges had been the leading tribe in the great Gaulish federation which had sent the Celtic invaders into Italy in the fifth century BC. Another tribe well known to the Romans from their branch in Italy were the Senones – these and their allies the Parisii in the north were now, fully though indirectly, under the control of Caesar.

Others to come for the first time within the ambit of the Romans had territories stretching as far as the Atlantic. These included the Turones ('energetic ones'), who have given their name to Tours, where their chief fortress was; the Pictones ('belligerent ones'), who had their chief town at Lemonum (now Poitiers); and the Lemovices ('elm-conquerors') whose capital was the origin of Limoges. The new Roman overlordship extended also to the Petrucorii ('four squadrons'), from whom the region of Périgord in the Dordogne derives its name, and whose capital was Vesunna (now Vésone); to the Santones ('journeyers'), who have left their name on the area of Saintonge, north of Bordeaux; and to smaller groups such as the Vasates ('pillagers') at modern Bazas and the Medulli ('mead-drinkers') on the peninsula of Médoc.

Caesar's foresight concerning the Germans proved correct, for Diviciacos soon pointed out to him that all the Gaulish tribes of the area wished to throw off the yoke of the Germanic overlord, Ariovistus, who was treating them with great cruelty. Ariovistus had, in fact, concluded a treaty with the Romans – both sides considering the defence of Noricum to be crucial as a bulwark against a possible thrust westwards by Boerebistas and his massive Dacian army. Boerebistas was, however, for the moment concentrating his efforts on the eastern borders of his kingdom, allured by the rich Greek cities of the Aegean and the Asian border. Realising that the growing power and ambition of Ariovistus posed the more immediate threat to Roman interests, Caesar quickly decided to act against him. He sent envoys demanding a meeting, but Ariovistus was in no hurry to comply. The meeting was eventually held in the area of Alsace, where their respective armies had drawn close to each other near the Sequanian capital Vesontio. Ariovistus spoke as an equal to Caesar, reminding him that they were both conquerors and suggesting that they carve up Gaul between them. Caesar was peeved at this frankness, and demanded that Ariovistus withdraw all his forces back across the Rhine.

Ariovistus and his forces were anxious to postpone the contest, having been warned by their diviners that the moon was waning and that this was an unlucky time for them. When he learned this from prisoners, Caesar pressed the issue and, soon after, the two armies clashed near modern Mülhausen. The result was a complete victory for the Romans, most of the Germans being killed and Ariovistus himself barely escaping with his life. This was not an unmixed blessing for the Celts, for Ariovistus, apart from his previous dealings with the Arverni and Sequani, had in fact some strong Celtic connections. His name seems to have been less Germanic than Celtic, comprising the elements *ario-vid-s-* ('he who foresees'), and this suggests that his native Suebi tribe had been strongly influenced by the culture of their Celtic neighbours. Indeed, he himself had learned Gaulish, and Caesar states that 'by long practice' he spoke it fluently. Furthermore, one of his two wives killed in the battle was the sister of Voccio, the Celtic king of Noricum.

Pleased with his achievements so far, Caesar left his army in winter quarters in the territory of the Sequani, and he himself returned to Italy. One issue, however, he had left unresolved. This was the relationship between the Aeduan king Diviciacos and his younger brother Dumnorix. After his experience of the war against the Helvetii and the war against the Germans, Caesar described Diviciacos as the man whom he 'trusted more than any other Gaul', yet the very brother of this man was the leading figure in the whole anti-Roman movement. During the campaign against the Helvetii, Caesar had been informed by the Aeduan, Liscos, that Dumnorix had continually been inciting the Aedui to break with the Romans. Further investigations revealed to Caesar that he had assisted the Helvetii in every way possible and had kept them informed of all the Romans' plans. As commander of the Aeduan cavalry, Dumnorix had instructed his men to flee from the Helvetii and thereby undermine morale. He had married off several female relatives to leading men in other Gaulish tribes in order to forge alliances, and he was extremely popular with the ordinary people. It was easy for him to finance his activities, for he had assumed to himself the collection of all taxes amongst the Aedui.

Caesar suggested to Diviciacos that his brother be put to death, but Diviciacos pleaded brotherly affection and also that such a course of action would alienate all of Gaul. Caesar then relented, but sent agents to watch Dumnorix's every move. Caesar was dependent on Diviciacos, and Diviciacos wished to keep his own options open in the event of the Gauls strengthening and the Romans weakening. It is clear, at any rate, that Gaulish acceptance of the Roman overlordship was still far from being complete.

Attack on the Belgae

In his winter quarters in Italy, repeated reports began to reach Caesar that the Belgae tribes to the north-east of Gaul knew that they would soon be invaded by the Romans and were preparing for war. These Belgae, with roots in the old Celtic areas of southern Germany, had developed into a loose confederation of tribes, and had been spreading for many centuries into adjacent regions of Gaul. Sections of them were settled on the shores of the North Sea, and significant groups had been crossing the sea to Britain for several generations and establishing kingdoms there. They were therefore accomplished as seafarers and traders, in addition to their military skills.

The numerous and widespread Belgic peoples had been ruled within living memory by a very powerful king of the Suessiones called Diviciacos, and his overlordship had even included the settlements in south-east Britain. In his war commentary, Caesar states that the king of the Suessiones in his own time was called Galba, 'a just and able man'. These Suessiones ('six clans') occupied most of the modern department of Aisne, and their capital was at Soissons. They had long been one of the strongest and more adventurous tribes of the Belgae. Closely related to them were the Remi ('premier ones'). It may be that – as their name indicates – these Remi were traditionally the leading group of the Belgae. They occupied the north of the modern departments of Marne and Aisne, and had as their capital Durocortorum (now Reims). Another stronghold of theirs was called after a leading Celtic deity *viz.* Lugudunum ('fortress of Lugus', now Laon).

In the north, the Menapii ('waterside-people') had an extensive population, inhabiting coastal parts of modern France, Belgium and Holland from Calais as far as the Rhine. Their territory bordered on that of the powerful Germanic tribe, the Batavi, and their chief centre was the origin of the town of Cassel, south of Dunkerque. One of their foundations was – like several other Celtic ones – known as the 'fortress' of the deity Lugus, *viz.* Lugudunum (now Leiden). Another of their towns was Noviomagus ('new market', now Nijmegen). South of the Menapii were the Nervii ('people of Nerios' – Nerios being a Celtic god whose name meant 'the strong one'). They were reputedly the bravest of all the Belgae. The territory of the Nervii covered the plain of Belgium as far as the Sambre, and the modern department of Nord in France. Their centre was Bagacum (now Bavai). A northern branch of them, next to the Menapii, were called Ambivariti, and from them comes the modern placename Antwerp.

The Ambiani ('those astride the water'), were in the modern French department of Somme. Their capital was Samarobriva ('bridge on the Samara', now Bray-sur-Somme), taking its name from that of the river. Neighbouring on them were the Viromandui ('directors of men' or 'tramplers of men'), whose centre later came to be known from their name as Vermand; and the Atrebates ('inhabitants'), whose centre was Nemetacus ('sacred place', now Arras). The Atrebates had as clients the Morini ('sea-people'), whose centre was Tarvanna (now Thérouanne) and whose chief port was Bononia (now Boulogne-sur-mer). Through this port the Belgae maintained contact with Britain.

To the west, occupying the modern French department of Oise, were the Bellovaci ('war-slayers'), whose capital was at modern Beauvais. Their name suggests that they were very effective fighters, and they had the largest population of all the Belgae. It is likely that groups emanating from them and from the Suessiones had penetrated into western France some centuries earlier. The main body of these Belgic tribes had been pushed back eastwards by the resurgent Carnutes and other peoples of central Gaul, but the ethnic distribution along the banks of the river Seine illustrates the tension which continued to exist. There the Suessiones themselves were strongly entrenched in a south-westerly direction, and clients of theirs, the Meldi ('pleasant ones'), were in the frontline, at a place which – from their tribal name – later became known as Meaux.

Another group of Belgae, the Catalauni – more correctly Catuvellauni ('battle-superiors') – were within the territory of the Senones, where they had to be content to play client to the latter. Their capital was Durocatalaunum (now Chalonge), but they would appear to have been more powerful at an earlier date and in a more northernly area. The various groups called 'Casses' are usually classified as Gauls rather than Belgae, but this may be misleading. The Baiocasses ('agile strikers') were along the Atlantic coast, their town becoming known from their name as Bayeux; and their relatives the Viducasses ('agile woodsmen') had the town of Aragenuae (now Vieux). Another people of this group, the Veliocasses or Caleti ('brave ones'), were settled on the east bank of the Seine. Their centre was Rotomagus (now Rouen), and their port was Caracotinum (now Harfleur). Such a tribal name is echoed also by the Tricasses of Troyes and the Vadicasses near Nancy. As suggested earlier it is likely that the Catuvellauni had lived to the north-west of the Seine but had been broken up into these disparate groups by the resurgent tribes of central Gaul.

In the south-east of this whole Belgic region dwelt a very powerful tribe called Treveri ('ferrymen'). These Treveri occupied the Moselle valley as far as the Rhine, and their capital was the origin of modern Trier. Archaeological data suggests that they were not in origin Belgae, but were rather descended from the Moselle Celts who had occupied that entire region in the early La Tène period. Other tribes who appear to have been descended from these older Moselle Celts were the Eburones ('yew-people'), a small but hardy group in the forest of Ardennes, and other small but not insignificant tribes in the vicinity of the river Sambre, such as the Ceutrones, Levaci, Condrusi, Caeroesi, Paemani, and Segni. Further south again were the Leuci ('bright ones'), whose territory stretched to the source of the river Meuse and to the borders of the territory of the Lingones. These Leuci, whose centre was Tullum (now Toul), may also have been a tribe of pre-Belgic origin who had come under the Belgic sway.

Caesar instructed the Senones and other Gaulish tribes bordering on the Belgae to provide him with good information concerning them, with the result that he had good intelligence regarding their confederation, the disposition of their territories, and how they interacted with their neighbours. He lost no time, but raised two further legions in Italy, and rushed back to Gaul in the spring of 57 BC. He now had eight legions and this, when auxilaries were added, would have brought the full force at his command to well over 40,000 men. The Remi immediately sent their leading men, Iccios and Andecombogios, to him, offering an alliance and hostages; but the rest of the Belgae held firm. According to information furnished by the Remi, the Belgae were mustering a huge number of warriors in preparation for the coming war. Caesar, in his war commentary, may be exaggerating somewhat when he cites these figures as amounting to almost 300,000 – including more than 60,000 from the Bellovaci, and 50,000 each from the Suessiones and Nervii.

Aware of the fighting potential of so large a host, if it could be assembled and properly prepared by the Belgae, Caesar decided on a preemptive strike against the strongest tribe. He had learned that these, the Bellovaci, were insisting on either standing alone or else being recognised as leaders in the war, and he now sent Diviciacos with his Aeduan force to raid their lands. The Belgae, however, had already concentrated most of their forces and had advanced to besiege Bibrax (modern Bievre), a town of the Remi. Here they used what Caesar described as the typical Gaulish method of laying siege – 'surrounding the whole circuit of the wall with a large number of men and showering stones at it from all sides', then locking their shields over their heads, advancing close up, and undermining the wall.

Bibrax was showered in this way with stones and javelins, and the commander of the town, Iccios, could not have held out for long if Caesar had not rushed some forces to relieve him. The attackers then set out in force towards the Roman camp. Caesar was cautious, knowing that the Belgae had a great reputation for bravery, and he had arranged trenches on each side of his camp, with redoubts and artillery. Having used his cavalry to test the enemy, he drew up his lines for battle. After a brief skirmish, he decided on one of his favourite tactics, a feint, leading the infantry back into his camp and causing the Belgae to rush triumphantly after them. Caesar counter-attacked as the pursuers waded through the river Aisne, and after a fierce struggle the Belgae withdrew. The Bellovaci were anxious to return to their own territory, which was being ravaged by the Aedui, and the general Belgic force broke up for the moment to await what the Romans would do next. Caesar sent out his legions to attack them as they dispersed on the following morning, and all day the pursuing Romans wrought havoc on the Belgae warriors.

Caesar now decided to reduce the tribes of the Belgae one by one, and this he did by taking their hill forts. The method he usually employed was to pile up earth against these strongholds and to erect towers and

Left: Plan of the burial of a Celtic chieftain within a tumulus. At Somme-Brienne, Département of Marne, France, dating from the fifth century BC.

Below: The fortress at Heuneburg in southern Germany, dating from the sixth century BC.

Top Left: Carved stone heads from a Celto-Ligurian shrine, dating from the third century BC, at Entremont, Bouche-du-Rhône, southern France.

Centre: Ceremonial Celtic helmet surmounted by a raven, dating from the third century BC (Romania).

Above: Stone Inscription from Greece, describing the attack on Delphi by the Celts and their defeat in 278 BC.

Left: Bronze relief of mounted Celtic warriors, from the Gundestrup Cauldron, dating from the first century BC (Denmark).

Right: Circle of severed heads in relief on Celtic silver horse-harness, from Manerbio, Brescia, northern Italy – dating from the first century BC.

Above: Stone Fort, Dún Aenghusa, on the Aran Islands off the west coast of Ireland dating to the first century BC.
Left: Image on a Roman coin, probably the face of Bituitis, the great Arvernian king in the second century BC.
Below Left: Face of Vercingetorix on a copy of a contemporaneous coin.

Facing Page (Top): Aerial view of Tara, the great ritual site of early Ireland.
Below (Left): Face of Carausius, pretender to the office of Roman emperor, on a contemporaneous coin
Below (Right): Face of Magnus Maximus, also an Imperial pretender, on a contemporaneous coin.

Above: Eamhain Mhacha, County Armagh, Ireland – centre of the Ulaidh kingdom.

Below Left: Stone with Celtic decoration from the first century AD at Turoe, County Galway, Ireland.

Below Right: Stone relief of a Pictish horseman with drinking horn.

Above: Folio from a manuscript of the Welsh text of the Laws of Hywel Dda, the tenth-century Welsh king.

Above: Folio from a manuscript from the eleventh century Irish text describing the deeds of Brian Bóraimhe.

catapults for the assault. The Suessiones soon surrendered at their principal hill fort, and he took hostages from them, including the sons of King Galba. Next he besieged the Bellovaci stronghold, and accepted their surrender after the intercession of Diviciacos on their behalf. The Ambiani also surrendered to him, but their neighbours the Nervii vowed not to submit to the Romans. The Nervii had a strong martial tradition, and they persuaded the Atrebates and the Viromandui to join with them in their resistance. Although they had no cavalry, they specialised in arranging obstacles such as cut saplings, hedges and briars for the horsemen of their foes. In describing the preparations made by the Nervii, Caesar refers to a precaution taken by them, of a type which must have been too frequent among the Celtic peoples being attacked by him. 'They had,' he states, 'hastily put their women, and all who were considered too young or too old to fight, into a place which marshes made inaccessible to an army.'

Some of the surrendered Belgae were giving secret information to the Nervii concerning the deployment of the Romans, especially the fact that each legion marched on its own and at a far distance from the others. Caesar got word of this information seeping through, and astutely had his legions march close together. When they encamped near the Sambre, a wide river with steep banks, they were suddenly attacked by the Nervii, who charged on foot across the river with incredible speed. The Romans were taken by surprise, and their Numidian cavalry fled, but the legions held their ground against waves of Nervii led by their commander-in-chief Boduognatus. Caesar's lieutenant Labienus, who had been at the rear with two legions accompanying the baggage, now joined the fray, and the Romans rallied.

The tide of battle turned, but the Nervii and their allies disdained to flee. Even in their desperate plight, Caesar says, they 'showed such bravery that, when their front ranks had fallen, those immediately behind stood on their prostrate bodies to fight; and when these too fell and the corpses were piled high, the survivors kept hurling javelins as though from the top of a mound, and flung back the spears intercepted by their shields'. Fighting to a finish, almost all the Nervii warriors were annihilated in that battle. Caesar claimed that their full fighting force of 60,000 men had been reduced to barely 500, while only three members of their national council of 600 elders were left.

A comparable disaster awaited a mixed tribe of that region, the Aduatuci. These were descended in the main from remnants of the Germanic and Celtic army which had fought fiercely against the Romans in the far south of Gaul in the year 105 BC. It was thus a mere generation or two since they had been settled on the river Sambre to protect the approaches to Germany. They had firmly established themselves at Aduatuca, from which they took their group name, and which place later became known by the Germanic name of Tungros (now Tongres). Their historical memory gave the Aduatuci good reason for suspecting Roman designs, and accordingly, with the menacing approach of Caesar's legions, they prepared for the expected onslaught. They organised a strong force to go to the assistance of the Nervii, but on hearing of the defeat of the latter and of the approach of the full Roman army they decided to ensconce themselves in their strongest fortress, probably the rocky stronghold at Namur.

The Romans besieged that fortress, and the Aduatuci – realising that their position was hopeless – hestitated between surrender and fighting on. Negotiations broke down, and the Romans attacked and took the fortress, despite a brave defence. Caesar claimed that the Aduatuci had tried to trick him by surrendering most of their weapons and then carrying out a sneak attack, and he acted ruthlessly towards them. The entire population of the Aduatuci at that place, numbering 53,000 people, was sold into slavery.

Attack on the west

Caesar had meanwhile sent a legion to the Atlantic seaboard in the north-west under Publius Crassus, son of the Roman General Licinius Crassus who had defeated Spartacus. Some of the tribes of the Atlantic region were of considerable importance in the Celtic polity. For instance, the Carnutes, situated west of the Seine, had been and still were a powerful people. Their territory was regarded as the centre of all Gaul, and the periodic general assembly of Gaulish druids is reported to have taken place within it – in the area between Sully and Saint-Benoit-sur-Loire.

West of them, in the modern departments of Sarthe and Mayenne, were the widespread Aulerci who had in previous centuries sent significant groups into Britain and even southwards into Italy. Their strongest group at this time were the Cenomani, whose chief town was Vindunum (now Celmans). Another section had the name Eburovices and had a settlement at Mediolanum (now Vieil-Évreux). The Sagii ('seekers'), connected with the Eburovices, occupied the major part of the modern department of Orne – they were also known as Esuvii ('people of Esus', this name indicating the divine 'lord'), and their town was known as Noviodunum ('new fortress', now Sées). Towards the banks of the Loire were the Andes or Andecavi ('great strikers'), whose chief town was later called from their name Angers. Some of these, in league with the Cenomani, had also been involved in the invasion of north Italy. Between the Andecavi and the Atlantic to the west were the Namnetes ('seizers'), whose centre was Condevincon (now Nantes). The smallest group of the Aulerci was the Diablintes, whose town was also called Noviodunum (now the village of Jublains in the north of Mayenne).

To the north of the Aulerci, in the Cotentin Peninsula of modern Normandy, were the Venelli ('tribesmen'). Their centre was Cosedia (now Coutances), and their principal port was Coriovallum (now Cherbourg). A southern branch of the Venelli were known as the Abrincatui (perhaps 'springers into battle'), from whom comes the placename Avranches. Situated in the western elbow of the Channel and the Seine were the Lexovii ('slope-people'), whose centre was Noviomagus ('new market', now Lisieux). These may have belonged to the same stock as the tribes to their west known as Aremorici or Armorici, who – the evidence suggests – derived centuries earlier from a mixture of indigenous peoples, Gauls, and Belgae. Most powerful of the Armorici were the Veneti ('clansmen'), with their centre called Darioritum ('oak-ford', now known from their name as Vannes). Another group, the Redones ('[chariot]drivers'), had as their capital Condate (now known from their name as Rennes). The people in the far northwest were known as Ossismii ('the furthest ones') – their centre was Vorgium (modern Carhaix-Plouguer).

Despite the importance of these north-western peoples, the legion under Publius Crassus had no great difficulty in obtaining their submission. There was little fighting, for these tribes knew only too well what had befallen their compatriots in other parts and they thought it the wiser option to avoid all-out war for as long as possible. They therefore gave hostages, and Caesar was content with the situation in that area for the moment. Leaving Crassus there to quarter his men among the Andecavi, he took care to quarter the other legions for the following winter in the territories he himself had recently conquered and in central Gaul. He then returned to Italy and Illyria, where he wished to inspect how the Roman method of governing other peoples was progressing. While he was there, a legion which he had left under Servius Galba to establish a permanent safe passage through the Alps was attacked and badly mauled by the Celtic mountain tribesmen of the area – the Nantuates, the Veragri ('great hunters'), and the Sedunes (perhaps Sidones, 'skilled ones'). Although the Romans succeeded in routing their attackers, killing about 10,000 of them, they had little choice but to abandon their efforts and withdraw to the safety of Provence.

Disregarding this temporary setback, Caesar considered that he had by now finally 'pacified' Gaul. This was not, however, to be, for the peoples of the northwest soon found themselves drawn into the conflict which they had sought to avoid. Publius Crassus was proving a hard taskmaster and, though food was scarce in the region, he began to commandeer provisions for his own troops. Smarting under his rule, the Venelli, Veneti and others eventually rebelled and took some Roman officers hostage, demanding the release of their own hostages in return. Caesar ordered ships to be built on the Loire, and he rejoined his troops in Gaul again in the spring of 56 BC. He appointed his lieutenant Sabinus to put down the rebellion among the Venelli, and he himself prepared for an attack on the Veneti, whom he regarded as the most powerful group in the whole region. Their navigational skill and their control of all the harbours in the area caused him particular anxiety, and he refers in his war commentary to the large fleet of strong oak-built ships which they had and which they plied between their own ports and those of Britain.

As his army advanced by land, Caesar had his new naval squadron sail up the Loire to the Atlantic and there skirt the coast towards Brittany. He attempted to take several coastal towns, but was repeatedly foiled, for even when his legions overcame the stubborn wall defences the population of these towns made their getaway by taking ship. Finally, as Caesar's new fleet approached, 220 ships of the Veneti sailed out to meet them. The two fleets clashed in Quiberon Bay, in full view of Caesar and his land troops. The Romans encountered some difficulty initially but, since the massive flat-bottomed ships of the Veneti were dependent for movement on their sails, the Romans targeted the rigging with missiles and hooks mounted on long poles so as to immobilise them. Most of the Veneti fleet was destroyed, and then Caesar reduced the hill forts of the Veneti and their allies. After their surrender he treated them mercilessly – executing their leaders and selling into slavery all of their people on whom he could lay hands. The other campaign was equally successful. Sabinus used a Gaulish double agent to instil false confidence into the Venelli, who forced their leader Viridovix to attack the Roman camp against his better judgement. The result was a disaster, a large number of the Venelli being slaughtered and most of the rest captured.

Caesar next sent Publius Crassus to reduce the peoples of the southwest. In fact, the Celtic presence beyond the Garonne was sporadic, most of the inhabitants being of Iberian stock. The stiffest opposition here was put up by a tribe of these Iberians, the Sotiates under their leader Adiatuanos, whose name was Celtic. After heavy fighting, the chief town of the Sotiates was taken and they surrendered. Crassus then set out to attack other tribes of the area, the Vocates and Tarusates. These people called on all their neighbours to support them, and even brought veterans of Sertorius' campaign in Spain to their assistance. After a fierce onslaught on their camp, the combined Celtic and Iberian forces were routed, and the remaining tribes of the area submitted.

Towards the end of the summer, Caesar himself led an attack on the Morini and Menapii, tribes of the Belgae on the shore of the North Sea who had not yet surrendered. The Morini and Menapii withdrew into the forests, creating difficulties for Caesar, and the onset of bad weather forced him to withdraw. Virtually the whole of Gaul was now in his hands, and in 55 BC he defeated large forces of the Usipetes and Tenctheri, Germanic tribes who had been pushed by the Suebi into the north-east of Gaul. He then crossed the Rhine on a short campaign, slaughtering the people and laying waste the land in Germanic areas so as to deter any future incursions. Finally, as that summer drew to a close, Caesar determined on an even more adventurous course, to cross the sea to Britain and thus to gain glory in Rome for conquests as far as the borders of the known world.

Britain targeted

Celtic groups had been settling in Britain since the early sixth century BC or thereabouts. As we have seen, the earliest of such groups would appear to have been those displaced in Gaul by the powerful peoples of the Marne and Moselle, and these were followed by sections of the Aulerci and their neighbours. Having been established in Britain, such Gaulish groups came to be known to their Continental cousins as Pritani ('painted ones'), from which designation the island got its name (later Latinised as Britannia). Some centuries later, when Belgic tribes had spread into northern Gaul, significant sections of these began to cross into Britain. The Belgae took over most of the southern British coast and large stretches of territory inland, and in time established strong kingdoms. They brought with them all the military and commercial skills which had been accumulated on the Continent, and were even developing a coinage of their own. It was these Belgic peoples in Britain with whom Caesar would now come into contact.

Definitely Belgic were the Catuvellauni of central England, at that time the most powerful people in all of Britain. They were a branch of the Catuvellauni, who had previously been powerful among the Continental Belgae, and their capital at this time seems to have been the fortress at Wheathampstead, five miles to the north-east of St Albans. The Trinovantes ('very energetic ones ') were further south, with their capital of Camulodunum (now Colchester). Finally, nearest to the Continent were tribes who represented the latest wave of Belgic settlement in Britain towards the end of the second century BC. These must have been the tribes which – as Caesar was told – had given fealty to Diviciacos, king of the Suessiones on the Continent. They included the Durotriges ('strong-hold-people'), with a capital at Durnovaria (now Dorchester); the Regnes ('stiff people' in the sense of being proud), with a centre at Noviomagus (now Chichester); and the Cantiaci ('border-people') whose centre was at Durovernum (now Canterbury). There was also a small group near the southern coast called Ancaleti, who must have been an offshoot of the Veliocasses (otherwise known as Caleti), on the opposite side of the Channel.

Caesar noted that the Belgic tribes in the south of Britain had sent reinforcements to their Continental cousins when these had been resisting him, and he now used this as a pretext to extend the war across the Channel. He already had some information on the political situation in Britain, but he wished to know more and to be better prepared before he committed his army. He had recently installed as chieftain of the Belgic tribe of Atrebates an able man called Commios, and he now sent Commios across the Channel ahead of him. The task of this envoy was supposed to be easy, for the Atrebates were well acquainted with the southern coast of Britain and may even have had a settlement there already at Calleva (now Silchester).

Caesar entrusted his envoy with the task of securing the submission of the Britons, but Commios was seized and held as a captive, apparently by Cassivellaunos, king of the Catuvellauni. This did not overly upset Caesar. Leaving some of his forces to guard the ports, he crossed in the autumn of 55 BC with two legions from the territory of the Morini, using about 80 transport boats and a number of warships. When he arrived at the British coast, he found cavalry and chariots waiting to attack him. His men had difficulty in landing, but once on shore at Walmer, just north of Dover, they routed the enemy, who soon sent envoys with Commios offering to surrender. Caesar took hostages, and they promised to bring more hostages from the interior.

The transport ships bringing Caesar's cavalry ran into foul weather, however, and had to return to the Continent. Furthermore, many of his beached ships were damaged by the storm and, on learning this, the chiefs of the Britons decided to renew hostilities. In the ensuing battle, the Britons showed their style of fighting, by driving their chariots all around the Romans while hurling javelins, and then retiring and fighting on foot. It is of interest to note that the war chariot had continued in use by the Celts of Britain long after it had grown obsolete among the Gauls. Caesar noticed the great ability of the charioteers at controlling the horses: 'They can run along the chariot pole, stand on the yoke, and get back into the chariot as quick as lightning.'

The legionaries had little experience of this particular kind of fighting, so Caesar very wisely withdrew them to camp for the moment. After several days of bad weather, however, he engaged the foe again and put them to flight. He now demanded twice as many hostages as before, saying that these should be sent after him to the Continent, and then he embarked and returned to Gaul before the weather got even worse. There he found the Morini again engaged in rebellion, and after a punitive expedition against them he quartered his legions on Belgic territory for the winter, before himself returning again to Italy.

Hostages arrived from only two of the British tribes, and so Caesar determined on a second invasion of Britain. In the spring of 54 BC, however, he found that he must first deal with the Treveri, who had refused to submit to him. Two rivals, Indutiomaros and his son-in-law Cingetorix, were contending for the leadership of that tribe, and Caesar astutely used this division for his purpose. He first accepted the surrender of Cingetorix, and as a result Indutiomaros found excuses to make peace also. Caesar took hostages from both, and then hurried on with his preparations for a crossing to Britain. He had an established practice of keeping hostages from all the major Gaulish tribes with him so as to discourage rebellion, and he now paid particular attention to the Aeduan leader Dumnorix. As we have seen, Caesar had disliked and distrusted Dumnorix from the beginning, describing him as 'a man of boundless courage, extremely popular with the masses because of his liberality, and an ardent revolutionary'.

He would, indeed, have killed Dumnorix long before but for the risk of alienating his brother Diviciacos, an ally of the Romans. It is obvious that he still feared the influence of such an able leader among the Gauls, for he now demanded that Dumnorix accompany him to Britain. The latter used several excuses – claiming that he was afraid of the sea and also that he was forbidden to leave Gaul due to religious reasons. Caesar did not relent, and so Dumnorix slipped out of the camp with some horsemen. Caesar immediately sent a detachment of cavalry after him, with orders to bring him back dead or alive. When he was surrounded, Dumnorix fought fiercely with sword in hand, and as he was cut down he continued to shout out that 'he was a free man and a citizen of a free state'.

Following on this, Caesar set sail for Britain in early July with five legions and 2,000 cavalry – a full force of nearly 30,000 men which he brought over in 600 boats. This time he had a carefree landing, but as soon as camp was set up he was attacked by cavalry and war chariots. He put these to flight, but as he advanced inland he was repeatedly attacked by the Britons, who came swooping out of the woods when least expected. These tribesmen were commanded by Cassivellaunos, the Catuvellauni king, who had been for some time attempting to enforce his authority on other tribes in the south of the island. Eventually, Cassivellaunos decided against engaging Caesar in pitched battles and kept his distance from the Roman legions as they advanced across the Thames and into his territory.

Caesar now used his old trick of divide and conquer, by restoring a young prince called Mandubracios to his tribe. This young man was the son of the former king of the Trinovantes, who had been killed by Cassivellaunos, and he had gone to the Continent to seek Caesar's protection. The ploy of rekindling old animosities between the Britons proved successful, and soon several tribes came over to Caesar's side. Advancing to the main hill fort of Cassivellaunos – probably that at Wheathampstead – he attacked it and forced the defenders to abandon it. It was, Caesar says, a typical British Celtic stronghold, in a densely wooded location and fortified with a rampart and trench.

Cassivellaunos, undeterred, called on leaders of the Cantiaci to join his efforts, and they attacked the Roman naval camp on the coast of their territory in Kent. The attack failed, and Cassivellaunos finally sent envoys to Caesar, offering peace and using Commios as an intermediary. Caesar, who was anxious to return to the Continent before winter set in, accepted the offers, on condition that Mandubracios and his Trinovantes would not be molested, that a tribute be paid annually to the Roman government, and that hostages be handed over. Cassivellaunos was glad to accept this, knowing that the Romans would soon be out of the way; and Caesar then returned to the Continent, leaving no permanent power-structure to subdue the Britons. In his war commentary, Caesar portrays himself as dictating terms to Cassivellaunos, but it is obvious that he failed to achieve his purpose in Britain, and later Celtic tradition in the island regarded Cassivellaunos as in fact the victor of the campaign.

The great Gaulish rebellion

The Gauls were soon in rebellion again. This time it was the Eburones from the forest of Ardennes between the Meuse and the Rhine, led by Ambiorix and Catuvolcos. The Eburones were encouraged by the Treveri chief Indutiomaros, whom Caesar had good reason already to distrust. Ambiorix, a skilled leader, threatened a Roman legion under Sabinus and Cotta who were encamped for the winter near his territory at Aduatuca, where the Aduatuci tribe had been extirpated by the Romans. Apparently Ambiorix had reason to believe that a similar fate lay in store for his own people. The Romans claimed that he misled the legionaries by protestations of friendship, before attacking them and slaughtering them almost to a man. At any rate, 6,000 Romans fell fighting in the battle, the greatest single defeat which Caesar's forces suffered in all of his campaigns in Gaul.

Ambiorix then set about enlisting in his cause the many tribes which had suffered grievously at Caesar's hands. A legion under the command of Quintus Tullius Cicero (brother of the famous orator) was wintering in the territory of the Nervii, and a combined force of Eburones, Nervii, and other Belgic tribes determined on an all-out attack on the camp of this legion. They had, from captives taken by them, learned Roman techniques of laying siege, such as throwing up earthworks, constructing towers, and using ballistics. After several days of fighting, a messenger got through and summoned the help of Caesar, who quickly collected as much infantry and cavalry as he could and marched to relieve the siege with two legions. He later claimed that the whole Gaulish force numbered 60,000, which would mean that his own forces were outnumbered by at least three to one. Caesar used all his experience and guile, however, receiving information from the besieged Romans through a Gaul who slipped through the enemy lines, and then giving the impression that his army was frantic and dispirited. In this way, he lured the Gaulish force into an unfavourable position, and tempted them to attack his camp. Their onslaught, when it came, was unorganised and unplanned, and Caesar ordered a sudden devastating cavalry charge which routed them.

Despite this resounding Roman success, it would appear that the great majority of Ambiorix's fighting force got away to safety, and the rebellion continued unabated. All through the winter there were disturbances, and all the Gaulish tribes – with the exceptions of the Aedui and Remi – were inclined towards revolt. With the Belgae already organised by Ambiorix, a leading man among the Senones called Acco began the same work in greater Gaul and made rapid progress among the Carnutes as well as his own tribe. Indutiomaros of the Treveri hosted a great assembly, at which he announced his intention to banish the Romans once and for all. The council of the Senones promptly dethroned Caesar's nominee Cavarinos from their kingship; and then Ambiorix, Acco, and Indutiomaros were free to combine their followers into one great host. Before this could be effected, however, the cavalry of Labienus made a surprise attack on the camp of Indutiomaros and slew him, bringing his head back to their own camp in triumph.

Caesar was so alarmed at developments that he sent for three fresh legions as reinforcements from Italy in the spring of 53 BC. Having a large army at his disposal now, he first ravaged the territories of the Nervii, forcing them to surrender. Then he called together a general parliament of the Gaulish leaders at Lutecia (now Paris), a place deliberately chosen because the Parisii were at that time his allies and their neighbours the Senones were in revolt. By this parliament he intended to replace the traditional Gaulish council which met annually in the territory of the Carnutes. Noticing that the Senones, Carnutes and Treveri did not attend, on the very first day of the proceedings he departed with his legions into the nearby territory of the Senones, cowing them into submission. The Carnutes also hurriedly submitted, whereupon Caesar returned to his parliament at Lutecia, imposed his authority on all the assembled tribal leaders there and requisitioned cavalry from them.

He next marched north against the Menapii, forcing them to submit to him for the first time. Meanwhile, Labienus, by pretending to retreat, tricked the Treveri into attacking his force before German support arrived. The Treveri were defeated, and Caesar's ally Cingetorix was restored to the kingship. Caesar then again crossed the Rhine, to ensure that promised German support for Ambiorix did not materialise. The

Germanic Suebi – who had been involved in negotiations with the Gauls – withdrew to the east of their territory, and Caesar decided not to follow but returned through the Ardennes to fight the Eburones, sending a cavalry detachment ahead to try to capture Ambiorix. The house of Ambiorix was in a wood, and the Romans came suddenly upon him. He barely escaped with his life, being placed on horseback and sent away by his loyal followers as they engaged the Romans.

Seeing no remaining chance of success, Ambiorix advised his allies to disperse, and he himself retreated to the forests with a small band of horsemen. His fellow leader of the Eburones, Catuvolcos, committed suicide by poisoning himself with the juice of a yew tree. Caesar advanced through the Eburones territory slaughtering the inhabitants and spreading famine everywhere, and several times his forces came near to capturing Ambiorix. The determined Eburones leader 'would escape by hiding in a wood or ravine, and under cover of night would make off in some new direction – escorted only by four horsemen, for to no one else did he dare entrust his life.' Caesar finally gave up the pursuit, and called a council at the Remi town of Durocortorum (modern Reims), where he reasserted his authority over the Gauls and had the Senones patriot Acco, who had inspired the revolt, put to death by flogging and beheading.

In his war commentary, Caesar would have the reader believe that his purpose was to bring stability to Gaul, but he fails to explain why the Gauls repeatedly rebelled against his rule, even being willing to invite German aid, and why his Aedui and Remi allies continued to intercede with him on behalf of defeated rebels. The general situation is nowhere more clear than in the case of the greatest revolt of all, which began at the start of 52 BC. The Gauls were livid at the treatment meted out to Acco, and resigned themselves 'to die in battle' rather than suffer 'the loss of their ancient military glory and the liberty inherited from their ancestors'. The Carnutes, at their celebrated 'centre' of Gaul, took the initial risk. Under their leader Gutuator, they called on all tribes to unite in the common cause, and 'to stack their military standards together' as was their symbolic custom. They then attacked the Roman settlers in Cenabum (modern Orléans) and slew them, and word passed quickly throughout all Gaul that the rising had begun.

The leadership was given to a young prince of the Arverni, the powerful tribe who inhabited the area west of the Cévennes mountains. He was called Vercingetorix ('great-warriors' king'), and his father Celtillus had been the most powerful chieftain in all Gaul but had been killed in internecine fighting. Vercingetorix had independently recruited to his cause young men of different areas – Caesar calls them 'beggars and outcasts' – and now that many tribes supported him he prepared for a final conflict with Rome. He was a great speaker, who could easily win the approval of Gaulish warriors, which they customarily did by cheering and clashing their weapons together. But he was also a shrewd campaigner, not prone to impetuosity like so many Celtic leaders, and proved himself a match for Caesar in strategy.

As more and more of the Gauls became involved in the rebellion, the Roman General Labienus grew suspicious of their old ally Commios, and he sent some officers under Volusenus to a sham interview with him. The plan was to assassinate him, but when Volusenus gave the signal by shaking hands with him, Commios' friends rushed to his aid and he survived the sword-thrust and escaped with a wound to his head. After this, Commios vowed never to come again into the presence of a Roman, but busied himself in trying to recruit fighters from the Germanic tribes on the Rhine to come to the assistance of the Celts. Meanwhile, Vercingetorix sent a detachment under a daring leader of the Cadurci, Lucterios, to invade the territory of the Bituriges, and the latter called on the pro-Roman Aedui for help. The Aedui sent cavalry and infantry, but these began to suspect that a trap was being prepared for them, and they turned back at the Loire, which was the border between their territory and that of the Bituriges. Their suspicions may have been well-founded, for immediately afterwards the Bituriges joined forces with the Arverni.

Lucterios followed this up by enlisting the Ruteni, Nitiobroges, and Gabali to his cause, and began to threaten the Roman Province of Gallia Narbonensis itself. To forestall an attack on this, the very basis of Roman power in Gaul, Caesar himself rushed to the territory of the Helvetii, and from there began to terrorise the Arverni. He hoped to lure Vercingetorix into open battle, but the latter chose as a diversionary tactic to attack the Boii, who were at that time in alliance with Rome. Realising that the Gaulish army was trying to extend the Roman lines, Caesar reacted by pushing into central Gaul and ravaging the territories of the Senones and the Carnutes. He captured two of their strongholds, Vellaunodunum (now Montargis) and Cenabum (now Orléans), and then proceeded to attack the Bituriges.

He soon, however, found his army being shadowed by that of Vercingetorix, determined to test his strength. After a few minor engagements, in which the Romans were successful, Vercingetorix decided on a scorched earth policy, hoping to weaken the enemy by a combination of harassment and starvation. All of the Gaulish towns in the path of the Romans were destroyed, with the exception of the splendid oppidum of Avaricum (modern Bourges), which the Bituriges prevailed on Vercingetorix to spare against his better judgement. When Caesar besieged that town, Vercingetorix encamped near to him on a hill. The Gauls, using tactics learned from the Romans, attacked Caesar's camp with rocks and torches flung from towers and platforms, but the attack failed and the Romans took the town and massacred all its inhabitants.

Vercingetorix quickly repaired his losses, calling up more recruits from the different tribes and taking special care to assemble a large number of archers. A particular boost was given to his cause by the arrival at his camp of Teutomatus, king of the Nitiobroges, with a strong force of cavalrymen and some mercenaries recruited in Acquitaine. With restored confidence, but showing more caution now, Vercingetorix decided to bide his time. As Caesar's legions set out on the march towards the great Arverni hill fort of Gergovia (modern La Roche Blanche, south of Clermont-Ferrand), he brought his army along on the opposite side of the river Allier, making sure that all the bridges were broken to prevent the Romans from crossing. Caesar hid two of his legions in a forest, and when Vercingetorix had passed on he managed to rebuild a bridge and brought his own forces across. As a result he was able to besiege Gergovia.

The Gauls had built a high wall halfway up the hillside, but Caesar feigned a build-up of his troops facing a ridge on the opposite side of the hill, thus causing Vercingetorix to bring a large number of warriors to that side in order to fortify it against a possible attack. Then Caesar unexpectedly sent a legion against the wall, which was virtually unguarded while the Nitiobroges who had been stationed there were enjoying a siesta. The legionaries crossed the wall, seizing the Nitiobroges camp and forcing Teutomatus to flee semi-clothed on a wounded horse. The bulk of the Gaulish forces, however, were soon switched to that side of the hill, and a pitched battle ensued. Almost 700 of the Romans were cut down, and the rest were driven back to their own camp on the plain. The next day, Caesar offered battle to Vercingetorix's army, but after a few cavalry skirmishes the Gauls returned to their entrenchments. Faced with stalemate, and with alarming reports reaching him from other areas, Caesar had no choice but to raise the siege.

Time was on Vercingetorix's side, for his repeated calls to the Gaulish tribes to unite as one great force for liberty were quickly bearing fruit. The young men of many tribes were bringing more and more of their people onto the side of the rebellion. The sense of a common cause among the Gauls had progressed even to the point of splitting the Aedui, whose *vergobretus* ('stern judge') Convictolitavis, declared for Vercingetorix. Some of the Aeduan rebels seized the town of Noviodunum (modern Nevers), where the Romans held all their hostages. The Roman garrison there was massacred, and the hostages transferred to the Aeduan headquarters at Bibracte. Perplexed by this, Caesar also became anxious for the welfare of his legions which were with Labienus to the north, laying waste the territory of the Senones. His anxiety was well founded, for the Bellovaci, reputedly the best fighters of all the tribes, had joined the rebellion.

With the whole of Gaul in turmoil, Vercingetorix held a great council at Bibracte, by invitation of the Aedui, and this was attended by almost all the leading tribes. There he was confirmed in command, and he explained his policy of avoiding a pitched battle and wearing down the Romans by destroying all the provisions of the countryside. 'Destroy your corn and burn your granaries,' he told them, 'and this sacrifice will make you free men forever!'

After Labienus had won an engagement in the north against the Bellovaci and Senones, he rejoined Caesar's army. Vercingetorix, undaunted, decided to extend the theatre of war still further. With the Aedui now firmly on his side, he directed them and the Segusiavi to attack the Roman garrisons in the southeast, while the Gabali, Ruteni and Cadurci were to begin the assault on the Roman stronghold of Gallia Narbonensis. In these crucial areas, the Helvetii and the Allobroges clung to their Roman allegiance, but the Helvetii were routed by the Gabali and other Arvernian allies. Caesar was worried that the whole Roman base of operations in Gaul, the Province of Gallia Narbonensis, would fall, but he also realised that to force him southwards was part of Vercingetorix's strategy. Having succeeded in recruiting a strong force of Germanic mercenaries, therefore, he decided that he was still in a sufficiently strong position to gamble on the issue.

He began to move his army southwards, giving the Gauls the impression that he was alarmed, disheartened and in retreat. Vercingetorix followed him and, considering that the Romans were trying to disguise their weakness, could not refrain from attacking them on the march. Vercingetorix told his army that the Romans were withdrawing from Gaul, but that a severe defeat should be inflicted on them so as to guarantee that they would not return. The engagement took place near modern Dijon. In it, the combined Roman and German cavalry proved more than equal to their Gaulish counterparts, and then proceeded to maul the Gaulish infantry. Having suffered heavy casualties, Vercingetorix was compelled to withdraw his forces 30 miles to the north-west, to the hill fort of Alesia (now Alise-Sainte-Reine in Burgundy). This was a stronghold of the Mandubii, a small tribe in clientage to the Aedui. Vercingetorix thought that the Gaulish forces would have the opportunity to regroup there, but Caesar was in hot pursuit and within a day had encamped his legions – numbering now about 60,000 – near to the stronghold.

The tide had turned, and – perceiving at last the real strength of the Romans – Vercingetorix felt it necessary to send his horsemen in all directions to muster more recruits. Soon his force of 80,000 warriors was being besieged by Caesar's legions, who began to construct elaborate siege works all around. The Gaulish tribes convened a great council in the territory of the Aedui, and all agreed to send a relief force to rescue Vercingetorix's army. Even Caesar's old ally Commios of the Atrebates joined in the effort. The result was – according to Caesar – that a force of 8,000 horse and 250,000 infantry set out to the relief. These numbers must be exaggerated, but the force was no doubt a considerable one.

When the army of Vercingetorix, cut off by the Roman encirclement and reduced to cannibalism for want of food, caught sight of the relief force approaching, they were overwhelmed with joy, and sent out a large cavalry detachment, interspersed with archers and infantry, to give battle to the Romans. Caesar immediately ordered his own cavalry into action. All day long the battle raged, in full view of the main Roman army and the two Gaulish armies, but in the end Caesar's German mercenaries broke the Gaulish lines. Two days later, the whole Gaulish relief force attacked the Roman camp, and Vercingetorix led his forces out of the stronghold to join the fighting. The Gauls were encumbered by all the fortifications which Caesar had erected, however, and they were again repulsed. Next day they made another mighty effort to break through the Roman fortifications, but Caesar ordered a counter-attack, and in ferocious hand-to-hand fighting the Gaulish forces finally broke and retired from the field.

The relief army dispersed soon afterwards, and Vercingetorix was again cut off within the stronghold. He spoke to his men, reminding them that he had not undertaken the war for his own benefit but for the freedom of his people. He was now willing, he said, to give himself up in order to assuage the Roman anger, and so he put on his most beautiful armour, had his horse carefully groomed, and rode out through the gates of Alesia. Approaching the seated Caesar, he rode around him on his horse, before leaping from it, stripping off his armour, and throwing himself on the ground. Dio Cassius paints a striking picture of his arrival at Caesar's camp: 'He came to him without any announcement by herald, but appeared before him suddenly as Caesar was seated on the tribunal, and threw some who were present into alarm, for he was very tall, and in his armour he was a very imposing figure.' The Romans, however, were in no mood to be generous, and Vercingetorix was taken in chains to Rome, where he was imprisoned.

Final resistance to Caesar

After the surrender of Vercingetorix and his army, Caesar gave the vast bulk of the Gaulish warriors as slaves to his own soldiers, and in the following winter he embarked on a punitive campaign against the Carnutes, who had started the revolt.

Gutuator, leader of the Carnutes, was joined in the resistance by the Bituriges and Bellovaci, and the leaders of the combined force were Commios of the Atrebates and Correos of the Bellovaci. Initially, they met with some success, overpowering the pro-Roman Remi and slaying the principal magistrate of that tribe. As Caesar approached with six legions, they prepared for battle and established their camp on the hillside at Mont St Marc, about three miles south of the river Aisne. They began to prepare a long train of wagons – which was the usual Gaulish manner of travel – in order to evacuate their dependents, but before they could effect this Caesar surrounded them on two sides and hemmed them in against the higher ground. At nightfall, they set fire to bundles of straw and sticks, creating a curtain of flame and smoke, which enabled them to retreat to a more favourable position ten miles away at Mont Ganelon. From there, they sent out parties to ambush the Romans, a tactic which proved very successful.

Eventually, Correos himself led out a group of 6,000 infantry and 1,000 horsemen, intending to ambush a force of Roman foragers, but Caesar learned of this and sent out a large legionary force for a counter ambush. Correos' men were trapped and, after a long and ferocious engagement, they were overcome and took to flight, but Correos himself disdained to flee or to surrender. Fighting fiercely, he was eventually shot dead by a Roman archer. The main body of Bellovaci and their allies surrendered soon after, claiming that Correos, 'the popular agitator', had been resonsible for the war and that he had martialled the poor against the aristocratic leaders of the Bellovaci. Caesar now attempted again to capture Ambiorix, the elusive leader of the Eburones. He ordered his legions to go to the territory of the Eburones, and to strip it of 'inhabitants, cattle, and buildings'. The genocide continued, and was soon extended to the neighbouring Treveri, but its immediate purpose failed, for Ambiorix escaped across the Rhine and was never heard of again.

The Gauls in the west had not been completely subdued. The leader of the Pictones, Duratios, had taken the Roman side, but he found himself besieged at Lemonum (now Poitiers) by a large force of Andecavi under the leadership of Dumnacos, backed by warriors from the Carnutes and other tribes. A Roman army under Caninius went to the rescue and encamped nearby, but Dumnacos turned from the siege to attack their camp. After several days of fighting, Dumnacos withdrew, but he ran into a second and much larger Roman army under Caesar's lieutenant Fabius as he attempted to cross a bridge over the Loire. In the ensuing battle, the Pictones were defeated and 12,000 were killed. Dumnacos survived and went into hiding 'in the remotest corner of Gaul'.

News soon reached the Romans of trouble in another quarter – the south – for Drappes of the Senones and Lucterios of the Cadurci were leading a small force of about 2,000 in a raid on the Roman province. These two were expert guerrilla leaders, who had harassed the Romans right through the war with their bands of escaped slaves and outlaws. Realising that a large Roman army under Caninius was on their heels, they turned towards the territory of the Cadurci and occupied the rocky stronghold of Uxellodunum (near to modern Cahors). They were besieged by Fabius there, and Lucterios began to organise bands to collect food from the surrounding countryside before they were completely surrounded. They were intercepted in this work by the Romans, however, and in two separate engagements Drappes was captured and Lucterios escaped.

Caesar had meanwhile been in the territory of the Carnutes, in an attempt to quell final resistance there. He was particularly anxious to capture the rebel leader Gutuator, and to this end he ordered the cowed and defeated Carnutes to discover the fugitive and hand him over. This they promptly did, and the Roman legionaries clamoured for revenge against the man whom they blamed for starting the rebellion. Like Acco before him, Gutuator was flogged savagely and then beheaded. His name, like those of most of the Gaulish leaders, seems to have been titular rather than personal – it probably meant 'voice-father' and was used of men with a druidical function. This leader of the Carnutes would thus appear to have had a religious office among his people, and it can be assumed that his oratory and advice had been very influential.

Caesar next proceeded to Uxellodunum to personally take command of the siege there. He regarded this as the finale of his whole campaign, and accordingly meant to leave an example of his stern rule. The Gaulish force, totally surrounded, was starved into submission and, after their surrender, Caesar had the hands cut off of all those who had borne arms. Drappes cheated the Romans of their desired vengeance by starving himself to death, while Lucterios remained free until handed over in chains by an Arvernian collaborator called Epasnactos. Determined that there should be no repeat of rebellion against his rule, Caesar garrisoned all of Gaul with soldiers. Four legions were stationed in the Belgic territories, two in the country of the Aedui, two among the Turones on the border of the Carnutes, and two among the Lemovices close to the Arvernian lands. As the year 51 BC drew to a close, he returned to the territories of the Belgae to winter there, where some sporadic resistance continued.

The Atrebates, having been crushed by the Romans, were quiescent, but the persistent Commios, at the head of a band of horsemen, continued the struggle. The Roman army in that north-eastern area was under the command of Marcus Antonius (Mark Antony) and, troubled by the continuing guerrilla campaign, he sent Commios' old enemy, the cavalry commander Volusenos, to capture him. The mounted detachments led by both men clashed, and Commios charged at Volusenos, wounding him severely in the thigh with his lance before making his getaway on a swift horse. Soon after, Commios sent word to Antony that he would give hostages and accept Roman conditions. Using his previous experiences as an excuse, however, he refused to present himself in person.

In a rare act of magnanimity, Antony accepted this condition. Having succeeded in avoiding contact with the Roman victors, Commios was taking no further chances, and – accompanied by many of his followers – he soon afterwards crossed to the relative safety of Britain. According to a legendary account, he was almost caught by the pursuing forces of Caesar but escaped by a trick. His ships were aground waiting for the tide, but he hoisted the sails, thus giving the impression that he was already under way and causing the pursuers to abandon their efforts. It may be that a branch of the Atrebates had already been settled in Britain but, at any rate, Commios was accepted as the leader of the tribe there and set up a kingdom in the area south-west of the Thames.

Caesar's ambition had come to fruition, but at a terrible cost to Gaul – Plutarch computes that 1,000 towns had been destroyed, 300 tribes had been subjected, a million captives had been taken, and a million had been killed or injured. There was one final act left in the gruesome drama. Caesar returned to Italy in 50 BC to wild jubilation. His total conquest and subjugation of Gaul was to be his springboard for the gaining of total power at home, but he soon clashed with his equally ambitious colleague Pompey. In the ensuing civil war – fought out on the broad stage of the growing Roman empire – Pompey was murdered and Caesar at last achieved his lifelong ambition. He was appointed dictator, and in the year 46 BC Vercingetorix was beheaded in Rome as part of his triumphant celebrations. Caesar was appointed dictator for life and was declared divine. He was not, however, to enjoy his absolute power for long, for in 44 BC he was stabbed to death in the Senate by a mixed cabal of friends and foes.

8

TWILIGHT OF THE CELTS

T he assassination of Caesar removed from the scene the most deadly enemy of the Celts in the west, while in the east the powerful Dacian leader Boerebistas was also assassinated soon afterwards. It was too late for the Celts, however, as mortal blows had been dealt to their power in both quarters.

Ending in the east

Before his death, Caesar had the experience of meeting one Celtic leader who was comparable to himself in deviousness. This was Deïotaros, the Tolistoboii leader in Asia Minor who came to prominence during the Roman wars against Mithradates the Great, king of Pontus. Deïotaros had every reason to cling to the Roman cause, and he was especially popular with the victorious Roman general Pompey. In the general reorganisation following on the war, Pompey decided to reduce the number of Galatian tetrarchs from the customary twelve to just three, one ruling each tribe. Thus, Deïotaros was appointed by the Romans tetrarch of the Tolistoboii and king of Galatia in 63 BC, and a part of western Armenia was added to his territory.

Five years later, his son-in-law Brogitaros, tetrarch of the Trogmi, was ratified as king of that tribe by the Romans. Deïotaros was not pleased with the influence wielded by such a rival. He was further aggravated when Brogitarios appointed a new priest to the temple at Pessinus, and he wasted no time in ejecting Brogitarios' nominee under the pretence of preserving the 'pristine sanctity' of the temple. When Brogitaros died in or about the year 50 BC, Deïotaros seized the opportunity to join the whole Trogmi tribe to his own Tolistoboii, thus increasing his power still further. Not content with being the unchallenged leader of Galatia, he presented himself as a priest-king (a status echoed by his name, which meant 'divine bull'), allotting to himself the function of reading omens for his people.

Deïotaros had an army of 12,000 foot soldiers and 2,000 horse, armed in the Roman manner, which made him one of the strongest rulers in Asia Minor. As one might expect, he fought on the side of his benefactor in the Roman civil war between Pompey and Julius Caesar, which broke out in 49 BC, but he soon found that he was backing the loser. Further misfortune struck when Pharnaces of Pontus, son of Mithradates the Great – hoping to take advantage of the inter-Roman struggle – occupied the lands of Deïotaros in Armenia and routed his army at Nicopolis.

Refusing to panic, the resourceful Galatian king decided to change his strategy. Accordingly, when Caesar, fresh from his victory over Pompey and now the most powerful man in the world, arrived in Asia Minor in 47 BC, Deïotaros met him in the dress of a suppliant. This form of diplomacy proved a success, for he was promptly ordered by the great and shrewd conqueror to resume his royal attire. Deïotaros then joined his surviving forces to those of Caesar in the campaign which resulted in the defeat of Pharnaces at Zela. He was confirmed by Caesar as king of Galatia, with his son and chosen successor Deïotaros Philopator sharing in the title. A heavy fine was imposed on him, however, and he lost his lands in Armenia. Furthermore, the tetrarchate of the Trogmi was taken from him and given to Mithradates of Pergamon. This was the son of Brogitaros' sister, Adobogiona, and was rumoured to be in fact an illegitimate child of Mithradates the Great.

The young Mithradates was slain soon afterwards in an attempt to seize the kingdom of Pontus, and in 45 BC Deïotaros sent a request to Caesar to grant the possessions of the dead man to himself. The rivals of Deïotaros wished to dethrone him, however, and another son-in-law, a leader of the Tectosages called Tarcondarios, accused him of having planned an attempt on the life of Caesar two years before on their journey together from Zela to Nicaea. The accusation was actually made by

Tarcondarios' son Castor, grandson of Deïotaros, and the case was heard by Caesar himself in Rome, with the orator Cicero defending Deïotaros. The verdict was put on hold, and the assassination of Caesar may have saved the old rogue.

He was soon restored to all his territory in Galatia by Mark Antony, in return for a massive bribe. Deïotaros then gained vengeance on Tarcondarios, slaying both him and his wife and razing their fortress at Gorbeus (now Beynam, south of Ankara) to the ground. This left Deïotaros himself as leader of all three Galatian tribes, and with tacit Roman support to boot. He changed sides again, however, in the inter-Roman tussles, supporting Caesar's assassins for a while, before returning his loyalty once more to Antony. He thus lived out a long life, dying in or about the year 39 BC. His son, Deïotaros Philopator, had pre-deceased him by a few years, and had been buried in a corbel-vaulted chamber-tomb at Karalar, about 20 miles northwest of Ankara. This place has been identified with Blucion, which was the royal seat of Deïotaros, and he himself may have been interred along with his son or in one of two other tombs found at the site.

The ambition of Deïotaros had in effect put an end to the traditional Galatian system of tetrarchies, replacing it with the centralised rule by one king with Roman support. After his death, his grandson Castor was confirmed by the Romans as king of Galatia, to which a part of Paphlagonia was added; and Deïtoaros' secretary Amyntas, whom the wily old king had appointed to lead his army after the death of his own son, was given half of the province of Cilicia, to the south of Galatia. Castor either died or was deposed within a few years, and his dominions in Paphlagonia were inherited by his son, Deïotaros Philadelphos. The kingdom of Galatia, however, was given by the Romans to Amyntas, while small principalities were created in southern Pontus for the Galatian chieftains Ateporix and Adiatorix. Amyntas continued to support Mark Antony, joining the latter's forces against Sextus, the son of Pompey, who was continuing to resist in the east. Sextus was finally seized by the cavalry of Amyntas and handed over to Antony.

When Antony was facing defeat by Octavian at Actium in 31 BC, however, both Amyntas and Deïotaros Philadelphos deserted to the side of Octavian, and as a result they retained their territories. The possessions of Amyntas, in fact, were greatly increased to include large areas of Lycaonia and Pamphylia to the south-west of Galatia. Amyntas undertook the fortification of the stronghold of Isaura in his newly-acquired mountainous region of Taurus, and started on a campaign to suppress a rebellion by the local population in 25 BC. He slew the leader of the rebellion, but was soon after captured by a trick played on him by the dead man's widow and put to death by the rebels. The Romans moved in quickly and ended the uncertainty by abolishing the Galatian kingship and turning the whole area into the Roman province of Galatia.

Octavian became the first Roman Emperor, with the title of Augustus, and a cult of his divinity was instigated by the Romans at Ankara, in the heart of Galatian territory. In place of the divine couple Agdistis and Men who had been worshipped there, a great temple was dedicated to the goddess Roma and the divine Augustus. The Romanisation continued apace, with the celebrated centre of the mother-goddess at Pessinus undergoing the same political change, and that city along with Tavion (called by the Romans Tavium) underlining the new devotion to the divine Emperor by adding the epithet 'Augusta' to their names. The Galatians had little choice but to accept this, and some even benefited by it. For instance, one Dyteutus, son of the chieftain Adiatorix who had ruled a principality in Pontus, was made high-priest of a temple at Comana in that area by the Emperor.

By this time, the power of the Celts had been completely broken in the whole land-mass of Europe and in the Middle East. Their only importance was in the realm of military service, and it is interesting to note that the famous Graeco-Egyptian queen Cleopatra had Galatian Celts in her army. After her death, Octavian gave 400 of these to the Jewish king Herod the Great, and this troop figured prominently in the funeral service for Herod in the year 4 BC.

Neither was there any Celtic revival on the Danube for, after the death of Boerebistas, the Romans moved into his territory. They now no longer needed Noricum as a buffer-state, and so in 15 BC they launched a major offensive into the eastern Alps. The pretext used was raiding by the Raeti, the Venetian tribe under Celtic influence which occupied the Alpine area between Como and Trent in the south to Lake Constance in the north. These Raeti were attacked on all sides by Roman armies under Claudius Drusus and Tiberius. They were overpowered, and all the strongest young men were deported, leaving behind only those who could offer no further resistance. Of the Norican tribes, the Ambisontes alone offered resistance, but they too were soon overcome. Noricum was annexed without opposition, and due to their acceptance of the inevitable the inhabitants were not subjected to military repression. Administration was mostly left in local hands on condition that Roman political and economic domination was secure.

Events followed a similar pattern in the western Alps, where the Celt-Ligurian tribe of Salluvii or Salassi were long settled in the sloping area between the St Bernard Pass and the Po Valley. They were a proud and independent people, who in 44 BC had forced Decius Brutus, one of the assassins of Julius Caesar, to pay them tribute of one drachma for each of his soldiers as he retreated through their territory. There were rich gold deposits in that territory, which caused the Romans to use the pretext of Salluvian banditry to attack them. Augustus sent his general Terentius Varro against them, and after their defeat in 25 BC the whole tribe was sold into slavery by public auction at the Roman settlement of Ivrea. Apart from their 8,000 men fit to bear arms, the rest of the tribe numbered 36,000 persons. Augustus then sent 3,000 Roman settlers to found a city named after him Augusta (now Aosta) in the heart of the conquered territory.

A federation of fourteen highland tribes, mostly of Ligurian extraction, had developed in the western Alps. Cottius, son of the late King Donnus, who ruled over this federation, tried for a while to stay aloof from events in his high mountain strongholds. Seeing what was happening to neighbouring peoples, however, he astutely chose the time to offer his friendship and loyalty to the emperor, and so in 13 BC he signed a treaty according to which his territory would be handed over to Rome. The six north-western tribes in the federation – the Celtic or Celticised Medulli, Ucenni, Caturiges, Brigiani, Sogionti and Ceutrones – rejected his policy. Like the other Celtic tribes to their north – the Uberi, Nantuates, Sedunes and Veragri – they offered resistance, but they were soon overcome and suffered the wrath of the Romans.

While other inhabitants of the Alps were being subjected to 'pacification' with heavy military occupation and forced enlistment into the army, Cottius himself was rewarded with Roman citizenship and the name 'Julius Cottius'. He was appointed governor of the region, in which office he served the Roman interest diligently. When Augustus visited his territory in 8 BC, Cottius welcomed him to his capital of Segusio (now Susa), and to honour the Emperor he had a splendid arch erected to span the Mont-Genèvre road. After his death, his son – also called Cottius – was even allowed the hereditary title of king by the Emperor Claudius. On the death of this second Cottius in AD 63, however, the Emperor Nero converted all of his territory into a new Roman province called Alpes Cottiae (the Cottian Alps).

In 6 BC a great monument was erected at the cost of the Roman Senate on the great road from Italy to Spain at present-day Monaco. This, topped by a bronze statue of Augustus with two prisoners at his feet, commemorated his victory in the wide sweep of the Alps from east to west. An inscription on the monument listed 45 Alpine tribes which had been conquered. It did not take long to confirm the conquests and to establish absolute Roman rule. Most of the area of modern Switzerland was united as one Roman province called Raetia. The Carni, Vindelici and Taurisci were also defeated, and by the year AD 8 the Emperor Augustus instituted an enlarged Noricum as a Roman province covering much of modern Austria. Soon after, the last remnants of the Boii north of the Danube were absorbed by the expanding Marcomanni, a Germanic people. Peoples from the east, such as the Sarmatians, were penetrating into the Hungarian plain at the same time, with the result that all vestiges of Celtic culture soon disappeared.

There was one last flicker of Celtic independence at the other end of Europe, in the Iberian Peninsula, where the Callaeici and Vaccaei found themselves embroiled in the continuing rebellions of non-Celtic tribes such as the Lusitani, Cantabri and Astures. The Emperor Augustus was keen to subjugate all the peoples in the north-west of the Peninsula, especially since there were rich gold and tin resources in the territory of the Callaeici. The war began in 29 BC, and two years later Augustus himself went to Iberia to take over the command. Attacking by land and by sea, his army took hill fort after hill fort, and eventually the north-western tribes and their Celtiberian supporters surrendered at Mons Vindius (probably the Peñas de Europa).

Having defeated the Astures in 25 BC the Romans started the final drive into Galicia. The Callaeici took refuge in a hill fort on Mons Medullius (apparently near modern Lugo), where they were besieged by the governor of Hither Spain, Antistius Vetus. The Romans built a wall over 25 km in length around the hill, intending to starve the defenders into submission, but these defenders decided instead on a mass suicide. Augustus then returned to Rome, but sporadic fighting continued until the year 19 BC, when all resistance was exhausted. During this war, the Romans treated captured fighters with extreme cruelty, selling many into slavery and cutting off the hands of others.

The triumphant Romans erected altars dedicated to the Emperor Augustus the 'pacifier', some apparently in the territory of the Celtic Artabri in the extreme north-west of the Peninsula. Cowed by these events, the other tribes of the Peninsula knew that further resistance was futile, and they began to wear the toga, symbolic of full acceptance of Roman control. Writing soon afterwards, Strabo could boast that tribes of the peninsula were even forgetting their own languages. 'A short time only is required,' he writes, 'before they will all be Romans. The very names of many of the towns at present, such as Pax Augusta amongst the Celtici, Augusta-Emerita amongst the Turdulli, Caesar-Augusta amongst the Celtiberi and certain other colonies, are proof of the change of manners of which I have spoken. Those of the Iberians who adopt new modes of life are called *togati*. Amongst their number are the Celtiberi, who formerly were regarded as the most uncivilised of them all.'

Romanisation of Gaul

The conquest of Gaul was complete, and the Roman armies had little further fighting to do in that quarter. There were sporadic rebellions by Bellovaci, Allobroges, Morini and Treveri during the twenty years or so after the departure of Caesar, but these were quickly put down. The Roman Empire could now act in whatever way it chose, and so Gallia Cisalpina ceased to be a province and was incorporated entirely into Italy. The massive Gaulish territories to the west were divided into administrative provinces for the benefit of Rome. The area between the Alps and the Pyrenees was the province of 'Gallia Narbonensis', from the Loire to the Atlantic became 'Gallia Aquitania', from the Somme and Marne to the Loire became 'Gallia Celtica' (or 'Lugdunensis'), while the whole area from there as far east as the Rhine became 'Gallia Belgica'. The Emperor Augustus personally held assizes at Narbon in 27 BC, at which a census of the latter three provinces was conducted.

Under this new Roman administration, many of the Gauls were being driven to desperation by tax-collectors. Especially notorious was a certain Licinus, a native Gaul who had been a slave of Julius Caesar but had been freed by him. Licinus had subsequently been appointed procurator of Gaul by the Emperor Augustus, and he used this position to amass a huge treasure by extortion and trickery. His audacity even went so far as to insist for his purpose that November meant 'ninth month' and December 'tenth month', and thus computed fourteen months in the year for taxes. When complaints were made against him to Augustus in 15 BC, Licinus claimed that he had collected the treasure for the service of the Romans and in order to deprive the natives of the finance they would need for a revolt. This excuse saved him, but in reality the Gauls were in no position to contemplate rebellion.

A whole new socio-economic structure was being built, the purpose of which was to completely Romanise the whole region. This followed the pattern which had earlier been applied to Iberia, i.e., the construction of a network of new roads so as to facilitate the military dominance and commercial system of the Empire, and the recruiting of the warrior class of the Celts into the Roman army. The latter aspect of the conquest was crucial, for it guaranteed the re-education of the Celts into Roman ways and correspondingly weakened all aspects of their culture and identity. For instance, the Emperor Augustus not only prohibited druidic practices to those Gauls who became 'Roman citizens', but he also had a special Roman school set up to educate the sons of Gaulish nobles at the Aeduan capital Bibracte, where a druidic school had earlier flourished. Bibracte, moreover, was itself given the new name of Augustodunum ('the fortress of Augustus', modern Autun).

The census carried out on Augustus' orders in 12 BC caused disaffection in Gaul, probably because of a Roman demand that it be linked to taxation. One report states that 'the Gauls were restive under their slavery', and Claudius Drusus, who was campaigning in the north against the Germanic tribes, moved quickly to Gallia Celtica to head off a possible revolt there. With a strong army at his disposal, he sent for the leading men among the Gaulish tribes to dedicate an altar to Augustus at Lugudunum (now Lyon). This was done on the first day of August, and the stratagem of bringing the Gaulish leaders together there was successful, for they could see no choice but to accept the overwhelming Roman power. The dedication of the altar was a deliberate expropriation and Romanisation of the ancient autumn festival which the Celts dedicated to the god Lugus. The Emperor Augustus, still living but declared divine, was now to take the place of the ancient Celtic god from whom Lugudunum ('the fortress of Lugus') got its name.

A member of the Aedui tribe, Vercondaridubnus, was appointed as priest of this new cult of Augustus. As a further expression of the cultural conquest, he was given a Roman name of the highest prestige, Gaius Julius, that of Julius Caesar himself. This displacing of native names by Roman ones, particularly in the case of leading Gauls, seems to have become general during the reign of Augustus. Romanisation, however, did not bring general ease or contentment. The imperialist exploitation continued to be resented, particularly in the case of the overwhelming taxes, and this was the cause of a rebellion which broke out in AD 21.

The rebel leaders were Julius Florus of the Treveri and Julius Sacrovir of the Aedui, an unusual alliance in view of previous history. Both were trained military men of the Roman army, and as well as appealing to their tribes they also sought support from serving Roman soldiers. First to take the field were the Turones and Andecavi, and Florus felt constrained with other Gauls to give support in their suppression. He put on a display of helping the Romans in the fighting, but kept his head uncovered, which caused suspicion that he wished to be recognised by the rebels and so spared. He then prevailed on some of the Treveri cavalry to join him in revolt, but was defeated by some of his own tribesmen sent by the Romans to oppose him. He successfully eluded pursuit for some time, and when no hope was left he took his own life.

The Aeduan Sacrovir was more successful, seizing Augustodunum. He got the support of the tribal youths who were being educated by the Romans there, arming them with whatever weapons he had managed to accumulate, and hoping to use them to gain the support of their parents and relatives. He also recruited slaves who were being trained by the Romans as gladiators in that place, and many volunteers flocked to him from among the Aedui. Soon his force amounted to 40,000, and he won the support of the Sequani, who were in turn ravaged by two Roman legions. When the Romans approached Augustodunum, they found the forces of Sacrovir drawn up on a plain to confront them, with Sacrovir himself on a splendid horse in the frontline. After fierce fighting, Sacrovir retreated to the fortress, and then with a few followers took refuge in a country house. They were surrounded, and the house set on fire, but Sacrovir and his friends took their own lives in the flaming ruins rather than surrender.

This rebellion must have been encouraged by the druids, and as a result their profession was declared illegal by the Emperor Tiberius. This decree was intended to 'put an end to the druids and that class of seers and medics', but the contemporaneous Spanish writer Pomponius Mela tells us that members of the outlawed profession continued to teach in caves and hidden forest clearings. In AD 54, the Emperor Claudius had reason to suspect the druids again, and he took firm action to abolish completely 'the barbarous and inhuman religion of the druids in Gaul'. The measures taken were rigorous. By way of illustration, Pliny describes the fate of a chieftain of the Vocontii, of southern Gaul, who had obtained Roman citizenship. This man, while attending a lawsuit in Rome, was found to have a druidic talisman on his person. The talisman, known as an 'egg', was a little ball reputedly made from emissions of serpents in summertime and collected on a particular day of the month. It was claimed by the druids to guarantee success in diplomacy and victory in the law courts. The chieftain was summarily arrested and put to death by order of Claudius.

Roman invasion of Britain

Only the islands in the west remained outside of the overbearing power of the Roman Empire, and this rankled with the Romans. Caesar's invasions of Britain had been for prestige rather than for conquest, and he left no permanent force behind him. In fact, these invasions had the opposite effect, in that the man whom he had sent to negotiate, Commios of the Atrebates, had later joined the rebellion against him in Gaul, and had finally carved out his own kingdom in the south of Britain.

It is not clear what attitude the strongest leader of these established groups, Cassivellaunos, took to Commios' arrival, but there is plenty of evidence for a rearrangement of power among the Celtic peoples of Britain in the ensuing period. Cassivellaunos had been king of the Catuvellauni, who were situated in the wide area north of the Thames, casting greedy eyes eastwards to the hill forts of Camulodunum (modern Colchester) and Verulamium (modern St Albans). These two great fortresses belonged to the Trinovantes, whom Caesar had won into his alliance, but within a generation this tribe had come under the sway of one of Cassivellaunos' successors, called Cunobelinos.

The south of Britain thrived under the hegemony of Cunobelinos, despite an initial lessening of trade across the Channel due to the Roman conquest on the far side. Various tribes began to mint their own coinage, based on that which had been in wide use among the Belgae for several generations, and soon commerce began to revive. In fact, the nobles' craze for wine and other luxury items became so great that the Romans gained increasing economic power over them. According to the geographer Strabo, the British leaders submitted so easily to heavy Roman duties on both exports and imports that, from an economic point of view, there was 'no need to garrison the island!'

The gradual extension of Cunobelinos' influence meant a displacing of other rulers. Some of these, well aware of the massive power across the sea, fled to Rome to seek assistance against him. Among such refugees was Dubnovellaunos, displaced king of the Trinovantes, and Tincommios, son and successor of Commios as king of the Atrebates, both of whom appealed to the Emperor Augustus around the year 6 BC. Others were to follow – including a son of Cunobelinos himself called Adminios who fled to the Emperor Gaius, and another son of Commios, called Verica, who fled to the Emperor Claudius. Augustus had planned an invasion of Britain, and Gaius had boasted that Adminios had handed over Britain to him, but their plans were frustrated by affairs nearer home. Claudius was equally determined, and circumstances were more favourable to the project in his time. Another invasion was imminent when Cunobelinos died in or about the year AD 40.

An invasion army of five legions, accompanied by auxiliaries – numbering over 40,000 men – set sail in AD 43, under the command of Aulus Plautius. The leaders also included Flavius Sabinus and his younger brother, the future Emperor Vespasian. They disembarked in Kent, and found no major force ranged against them until they were crossing a river – probably the Medway. Here they were opposed by the sons of Cunobelinos, Caratacos and Togodumnos. During the first day's fighting, Plautius sent some of his soldiers to swim across the water and attack the Britons' chariots, and Vespasian soon led another company across the river at a different point. On the second day, a fresh attack was made by the main Roman body, and the Britons – under pressure from both sides of the water – fell back towards the mouth of the Thames. Here the same process was followed, and again the Britons were caught between Roman forces on both sides of the water. They suffered heavy losses, and soon after Togodumnos was killed in a skirmish.

The Romans waited for some time for the Emperor Claudius himself to land with fresh troops and an elephant corps, and then advanced swiftly on Camulodunum. The great citadel of the Catuvellauni was taken without much difficulty, for Caratacos had decided to vacate the area and to carry on the resistance further west. Having – according to Dio Cassius – 'won over numerous tribes, in some cases by capitulation, in others by force', Claudius soon returned to the Continent, leaving Plautius to complete the conquest. The Roman Senate bestowed the title of 'Britannicus' on the Emperor, ordered a triumphal arch to be constructed for him in Rome and another in Gaul, and decreed that there should be an annual festival to commemorate his victory. Back in Britain, the whole southern half of the island was now on the Roman agenda, and this included – as well as the Belgic peoples – the descendants of the earlier

Celtic settlers who were known as Pritani. Some of these were very strong tribes, whom the Belgae had not yet succeeded in displacing.

Immediately to the north-east of the Belgic Catuvellauni, in the area of the Wash, were the Iceni or Eceni ('people far away'), with their centre at Venta (now Caistor St Edmund). North of the Iceni were the Coritani or Parisi, who controlled a broad coastal area on both sides of the Humber, and whose centre was Ratae (now Leicester). To the east of these were the Brigantes, who were the most powerful people in the whole northern area and who had as centres Eburacon (now York) and Isurium (now Aldborough). To the north of them were the Carvetii ('deer-people'), who had their centre at Luguvalium (now Carlisle); and further north still an apparently related tribe, the Selgovae ('hunters'). To the west of the Brigantes, on the coast of the Irish Sea, were the Setantii (perhaps meaning 'travellers'). All of these groups seem to have been clients of the Brigantes.

In north Wales were the Decantae or Deceangli ('good borderers' or the like); in central Wales the Ordovices ('hammer-fighters'); and in south Wales the Dematae (perhaps 'sheep-herders'), whose centre was Moridunum (now Carmarthen). The Silures (probably an aboriginal people who had been Celticised) had a centre at Venta (Caerwent); and astride the river Severn were the Cornovii ('people of the horned one' – a deity). The Dobunni were in modern Gloucestershire, with a centre at Corinium (Cirencester) – their name has not been explained, unless it be connected with that of their southern neighbours, the Dumnonii. These Dumnonii ('people of the deep', i.e., people far away) were in Devon and Cornwall, with their centre at Isca (now Exeter).

Several of these tribes surrendered to the Romans, the first being the Dobunni of the Severn basin, and soon after the Belgic Atrebates and Trinovantes. Even the long-established tribes of the interior began to waver and submit, including the powerful Iceni, who considered caution the better part of valour. A major factor was the surrender of the Brigantes, who were ruled by Queen Cartimandua and dominated the whole area of northern England. The Romans quickly garrisoned the conquered territories, and within a few years were in complete control of all the eastern region from the Ouse to the Isle of Wight.

In AD 47 the command was handed over to Publius Ostorius Scapula. He followed a policy of coercion, and in the following winter several of the tribes rebelled. They were led by the Iceni, who so far had managed to avoid confrontation with the Romans and whose military

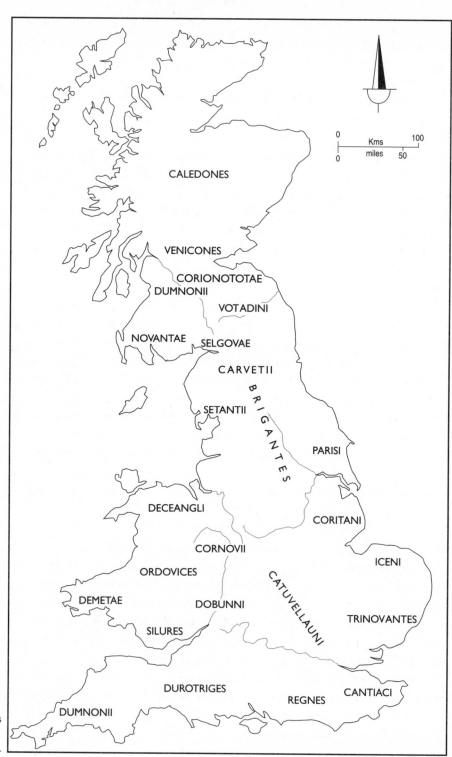

CALEDONES

VENICONES

CORIONOTOTAE
DUMNONII

VOTADINI

NOVANTAE   SELGOVAE

CARVETII

SETANTII

B R I G A N T E S

PARISI

DECEANGLI

CORNOVII

CORITANI

ORDOVICES

ICENI

DEMETAE   DOBUNNI

CATUVELLAUNI

SILURES

TRINOVANTES

DUROTRIGES

CANTIACI

REGNES

DUMNONII

Right:
The major tribes
of Britain in the
first century BC.

strength was therefore undiminished. Although the Roman historian Tacitus states that the rebels 'performed many noble feats' in the ensuing fighting, they were quickly suppressed, and Ostorius then ravaged the western areas, where Caratacos had built up a powerful base among tribes such as the Deceangli, Silures and Ordovices. Being chosen as their war-chief, Caratacos told his supporters that the imminent battle would decide between their freedom or slavery, and he encouraged them greatly by claiming that Julius Caesar himself had been forced to vacate the island. They put up a stubborn fight in the region of Gloucester, holding the Romans back for a long time with missiles, but when the legionaries came to close quarters the Britons – who lacked breastplates and helmets – were no match for them.

In this battle, the family of Caratacos was captured. He himself escaped northwards to the territory of the Brigantes, but Queen Cartimandua soon handed him over to the Romans. He and his family were brought to Rome and paraded as captives there in AD 50. Tacitus says that the other prisoners pleaded for mercy, but not Caratacos. Speaking before the Emperor, he said that he was a king descended from illustrious ancestors and should not be expected to accept slavery. Claudius was so impressed by his demeanour that he granted a pardon to him and his family. It was reported that he wandered about Rome after being set free and, on seeing the size and splendour of the city, exclaimed: 'How can you, who have so many and such fine possessions, covet our poor huts?' Back in Britain, however, the fighting continued, fuelled by the oppression and rapacity of Ostorius and his officers. The Silures raided the Roman garrison in their territory, causing heavy casualties, and then wiped out some Roman cavalry squadrons.

After the death of Ostorius in AD 52, Aulus Didius was appointed in his place, but before he arrived in Britain a whole Roman legion was defeated by the Silures. Didius managed to stabilise the situation, driving the Silures further west and increasing Roman defences in the Severn Valley. In the following years he had to deal with an awkward situation between the Brigantes queen, Cartimandua, and her husband Venutios who was 'pre-eminent in military skill'. This queen had probably succeeded to her office as the leading member of the Brigantes royal family, and her husband was therefore the consort-king. When rivalry developed between them, Cartimandua caused the brother and other relatives of Venutios to be arrested, and as a result many of his tribe supported Venutios in a push against her. The situation deteriorated into civil war, and the Romans intervened on the side of Cartimandua. A legion was sent north to oppose Venutios, but Didius himself was too preoccupied with the Silures in the southwest to involve himself fully. So – after inflicting some setbacks on Venutios – the Romans were content to make an agreement with him which restored Cartimandua to power.

The next Roman governor, Veranius Nepos, boasted that he would make the whole of Britain subject to the new Emperor Nero, but he died within a year and his design was carried forward by his successor, Suetonius Paulinus. This governor brought his forces through north Wales as far as the Irish Sea, causing many refugees to seek shelter on the island of Mona (Anglesey). In the year AD 61, Paulinus decided to attack this island. He brought his infantry over on flat-bottomed vessels, while the cavalry forded or swam across. The defenders resorted to magical postures to frighten and weaken the Romans, and the description given by Tacitus captures the savage drama of what was to follow:

> On the shore stood the opposing army with its dense array of armed warriors, while between the ranks dashed women in black attire like the Furies, with hair dishevelled, waving brands. All around, the druids – lifting up their hands to heaven and pouring forth dreadful imprecations – scared our soldiers by the unfamiliar sight so that, as if paralysed, they stood motionless and exposed to wounds. Then, urged by their general's appeals and encouragements not to quail before a troop of frenzied women, they carried the standards forward, struck down all resistance, and wrapped the foe in the flames of his own brands.

This slaughter was hardly over, however, when news reached Paulinus of a major revolt on the east coast. There the king of the Iceni, Prasutagos, had died, leaving the Roman emperor as his heir in the hope that this would protect his people. The opposite was the result, for his kingdom was plundered by the Roman veterans who had been settled there, the nobles of the Iceni were stripped of their power, and the king's relatives were enslaved. Prasutagos' widow, Boudicca, was flogged, and his two daughters were raped. As the people were evicted from their farms, a temple was erected to the late Emperor Claudius, who had been proclaimed divine, and this temple was regarded as a symbol of the Roman tyranny. The Iceni could take no more, and when Paulinus with his legions was in the west they resorted to rebellion, urging the Trinovantes and others to join them. In the delirious atmosphere, a statue dedicated by the Romans to 'Victory' at Camulodunum fell prostrate, and this was seen by the Britons as a portent of the overthrow of their oppressors. The Roman historian Dio Cassius gives a description of Boudicca:

> In stature she was very tall, in appearance most terrifying, in the glance of her eye most fierce, and her voice was harsh. A great mass of very tawny hair fell to her hips, around her neck was a large gold necklace, and she wore a tunic of varying colours, over which a thick mantle was fastened with a brooch.

Grasping a spear, she spoke to her people, calling them to arms. Dio quotes her speech and – though the actual words which he attributes to her must be speculative – the general drift runs true to character. She complained that the Romans were crushing her people with taxes, and that the Britons should never have allowed them to seize power in the island. They should, she said, have been expelled as their famous Julius Caesar was, and she then made a series of comparisons between the Romans and the Britons.

The Romans, she said, were born into bondage and were extremely protective of themselves, wearing helmets and breastplates and hiding behind palisades and trenches. The Britons, on the other hand, were born free, were so courageous that they fought without preparation and protected only by their shields, and they had such agility and skill that they could conceal themselves in swamps and mountains. The Romans required good food and clothing, whereas the Britons could survive on wild plants and water; the Romans required boats to cross rivers, whereas the Britons swam across naked. In typical warrior fashion, she compared the Romans to 'hares and foxes trying to rule over hounds and wolves', and then proceeded to other satirical comments. The Emperor Nero, she said, was an effeminate fop who played the lyre and tried to beautify himself. The Roman leaders were accustomed to have intercourse with boys, boys moreover who were past their prime! They were slaves to a lyre player, and he was a bad musician at that!

A huge horde of Celtic warriors attacked and took Camulodunum and Verulamium, and then seized all the surrounding countryside, slaughtering about 70,000 Romans, military and civilians alike. Paulinus brought his troops by forced marches through the hostile population to London – which was a Roman trading centre – but, realising that he could not hold it, he withdrew to what he considered a more favourable position, probably at modern St Albans. This, closed in at the rear by a forest, was approached by a narrow defile which opened onto a plain, where the Britons had assembled. Paulinus had about 10,000 soldiers with him, and these were outnumbered several times by the Iceni and their allies.

One Roman report claims that Boudicca had over 200,000 warriors, but that must be a gross exaggeration. With her daughters, she drove in her chariot around tribe after tribe, encouraging them and saying that she was there, not as a noble, 'but as one of the people, avenging my lost freedom, my scourged body, and the outraged chastity of my daughters'. She concluded by telling them that in this battle they must conquer or die. 'This is a woman's resolve – as for the men, they may live and be slaves!' For his part, Paulinus called on his soldiers 'to continue the work of bloodshed and destruction', for after victory 'everything will be in your power!' The Romans advanced silently, while the Britons shouted and chanted battle-songs. Then the two armies joined, and ferocious fighting continued until late in the day, when the Britons retreated, many of them being put to flight and many others slain. The Romans set to slaughtering men, women and children, and the battle ended in a complete rout. Only about 400 Romans fell, compared to almost 80,000 Britons. Boudicca took poison to end her life, and the Romans – soon reinforced from the Continent – brought fire and sword to the tribes who had rebelled and even to those who had wavered. Eventually, news of Paulinus' savagery reached Rome, and he was recalled and replaced by a more merciful governor.

Further rebellions in Gaul

Things were relatively calm for some years, but the extravagance of Nero and the general rapacity of Roman officials led to further increased taxation in Britain and Gaul. In AD 68, an Aquitanian Gaul, Gaius Julius Vindex, called on his people to revolt against Nero, who had 'despoiled the whole Roman world' and whose crimes and buffoonery surpassed all description. Vindex was descended from the kings of his people and, since Gaulish nobles were accepted as Imperial citizens, he was a senator at Rome as well as a general in the Imperial army in Gaul. Dio Cassius describes him as 'powerful in body and of shrewd intellect, skilled in warfare and full of daring'. He now called on the Gauls to 'help themselves and help the Romans, and to liberate the whole world'.

Realising that Vindex's proposals had strong popular support in Rome, the enraged Nero threatened to slaughter all the Gauls who were resident in the city, but Vindex had a strong army under his command in Gaul and he retaliated by sending a letter to the retired Roman general Servius Sulpicius Galba at Cartagena in Spain. Stating that he could provide 100,000 men under arms, Vindex invited Galba to take command of these soldiers and to seize the Imperial office. From this it is clear that Vindex's objective was not to free the Gauls from the Roman yoke, but to ameliorate their circumstances. He gained the tacit support of several Gaulish tribes, including the Aedui, Sequani and Arverni, but others such as the Treveri and Lingones were hostile to him. Nero sent an army against him, under the command of Rufus Gallus, but instead of fighting Rufus held a conference with him at Vesontio (modern Besançon). They agreed to co-operate against Nero, but a large number of Rufus' soldiers who were unaware of the agreement attacked Vindex's army and slew a great number of them. Vindex was so dispirited by the fiasco that he took his own life, but the popular movement which he had started continued to grow and led to the abdication and suicide of Nero that year.

Civil war soon developed between the new Emperor Galba and his army on the Rhine, headed by Aulus Vitellius. Galba was assassinated, and his successor Otho had to deal with the continuing revolt, which gained the support of the Roman legions in northern Gaul and Britain. Although the Treveri and Lingones swore allegiance to Vitellius, most of the Gauls wavered between the two sides, and both groups of Roman armies dealt disdainfully with them. Particularly brutal was the treatment meted out by the rebels to the Helvetii, who withheld their support and as a result thousands of them were massacred or sold into slavery. Such actions, and the fact that Vitellius succeeded in establishing himself as Emperor, caused increasing desperation among the Gauls, and the general situation remained far from predictable.

The group of Boii, who had been settled by Caesar in the Aeduan territory, had established a centre called Gorgobina, and had long been quiescent, but even they became disturbed. In AD 69, a certain Mariccus, described as 'a commoner of the tribe', began to preach rebellion and gathered a force of 8,000 men to challenge the rule of Vitellius. His messianic temperament was expressed in his belief that he was 'a champion of Gaul and a god', and he was gaining significant support among the Aedui until the leaders of that tribe selected a strong force, aided by Roman auxiliaries, to put him down. Mariccus was defeated in battle and taken as a prisoner to Rome, where he was thrown to the wild animals. When the lions refused to devour him, the ordinary people of Rome began to think him invulnerable, until the Emperor personally supervised his execution.

Time was running out for Vitellius himself, however. The legions of the Danube proclaimed Vespasian Emperor in AD 69 and, to foment trouble for Vitellius, he encouraged a revolt by a leader of the Batavi (in present-day Holland), who was called Julius Civilis. This Civilis belonged to the section of his tribe west of the Rhine, who were under Roman sway, and had himself been an officer in the Imperial army. He had good cause to be hostile to Rome, for his brother had been executed on a false charge of rebellion, and he himself had suffered misery in Nero's prisons. His opportunity came soon for, within a few weeks, the corrupt and gluttonous Vitellius had been deposed in Rome and slaughtered in an outbreak of popular fury against him, whereupon Vespasian seized power.

Regardless of the change in Roman politics, Civilis continued his attempts to free the Germanic tribes, and drove the Imperial forces from his territory in the autumn of AD 69. One-eyed like Hannibal and Sertorius, he represented himself as the equal of these two famous generals as an opponent of the Romans. Having taken prisoner some Gauls who were in the Roman army, he sent them back to their tribes with a message urging them to throw off the Roman yoke and to free themselves from the 'wretched slavery' which had been disguised 'under the name of peace'. Seeing his successes, the Gauls were tempted to join Civilis, and when the Treveri and Lingones came over to his side the prospects of a united Gaulish force began to beckon.

Rumours began to spread that the Roman armies were suffering setbacks everywhere and were headed for disaster. Civilis was quick to utilise such rumours, which had for their authority the utterances of a prophetess called Veleda. She belonged to the Bructeri, a German tribe, and lived in seclusion in the Lippe valley, but her title 'Veleda' was in fact a Celtic word meaning 'seeress'. For the Celts themselves, the druids pointed to a recent fire at the Capitol in Rome as a portent of the end of the Empire, and prophesied that the Celts were destined to capture Rome as they had done centuries before. The commander of the Treveri cavalry – called Julius Classicus – was a natural leader, being descended from the kings of his tribe. His boast was that his family 'had given to Rome more enemies than allies'. His own Treveri were to the fore in the revolt, and they were soon joined by the Lingones, Nervii, Aduatuci and others. The

Sequani and the Mediomatrici, however, remained loyal to Rome. They had suffered enough at the hands of Vitellius, and were only too aware of the support which the Treveri and Lingones had given to that tyrant.

For his part, Classicus sent an assassin to dispatch the Roman commander at Novaesium (now Neuss) in Belgae territory, and then he himself entered the Roman camp there and administered an oath to 'the Empire of all Gaul'. Soon after, the Lingones leader, Julius Sabinus, had himself declared the emperor of this new Gaulish state. He claimed to be great-grandson of Julius Caesar through a Gaulish mistress of the great Roman conqueror, but he singularly failed to live up to the military repu-tation of that ancestor. In an ambitious and badly organised attack on the Sequani, his forces were routed. Sabinus faked suicide in a burning house, causing the rumour to be spread that he was dead. With the help of friends, he managed to live in hiding with his wife Eponina, and survived for nine years until eventually they were both captured and slain.

This setback caused the general body of Gauls and Belgae to waver in their support for the rebellion. The Remi – old allies of Rome – were spreading the message throughout Gaul that peace was preferable to freedom, and to settle the matter a conference was held between var-ious tribes. A Treveri leader called Julius Valentinus made a fiery speech to the conference, but he was contradicted by Julius Auspex of the Remi, who warned that the Roman legions were approaching. The result of the conference – Tacitus tells us – was that 'while applauding Valentinus' courage, they followed the advice of Auspex'. The Treveri and Lingones were left alone to continue the war.

A Roman legion from Vindonissa (now Windisch), advanced along the Rhine valley and on the river Nahe it inflicted a stunning defeat on the Treverian troops who were led by Julius Tutor. Next a huge army was sent from Mainz under the command of Petilius Cerialis, and by forced marches this army reached the river Moselle within a few days. Classicus warned Valentinus not to engage the Romans in a pitched battle, but the latter considered it essential to halt the Roman advance and in a pitched battle near Rigodulum (now Riol) the Treverian force led by Valentinus was routed. Valentinus himself was captured, and quickly taken to Rome for execution.

Having taken Trier, the native town of Classicus, Cerialis had the Treveri and Lingones captives assembled before him and he addressed them, harping on the old Caesarian lie that the Romans were merely in Gaul to protect the Gauls from the Germans. Cerialis' army was soon besieged at Trier, however, by the combined forces of Treveri and Batavi, led by Classicus and Civilis respectively. Civilis preferred to prolong the siege, but Tutor argued for a quick attack, and Classicus agreed with this. They attacked by night, routing the Roman cavalry, and were putting the infantry to flight when Cerialis rallied them. The Gauls, thinking that victory was theirs, had begun to squabble over the spoils, when they were counter-attacked by the Romans and scattered. The two Treveri leaders, Classicus and Tutor, survived the debâcle, and they were to the forefront with Civilis until his surrender near the mouth of the Rhine in the late autumn of AD 70.

The days of Celtic Gaul were numbered, and the massive convulsions had taken their toll on traditional beliefs. Even the Arverni, once so proud of their royal traditions and of their predominant role in Gaul, were fabricating a new genealogy for themselves based on the classical lore of Troy. Thus, the poet Lucan in the middle of the first century AD refers disparagingly to 'the Arverni, who dared imagine themselves brothers of the Latins, from their Trojan blood'. Anything of public pride in their origins had to be couched in terms which the Romans would find inoffensive, and this was true also of religious practice. Native deities might be tolerated, but only if disguised in Roman form, a situation which is shown clearly by the numerous 'Jupiter'-columns which were erected by the Gauls in the generations following their conquest by the Romans.

These columns are topped by a horseman, often wielding a solar-disc or a thunderbolt, and overcoming a humanoid monster. The old dualism of light and darkness – as taught by the druids – must be in the background here, and the horseman clearly represents the sun-deity. The identity of the vanquished figure, however, is not only shadowy but sinister as well. If it is in any way a representation of the chthonic powers of the dead, it is a much debased one, and the representation of such a stark contrast – like the columns themselves – owes much to the influence of Roman culture. The builders of the columns were resigned to the final success of Roman power and culture, and so they were content to hide the true identity of their deities behind the guise of Jupiter, Apollo and other Imperial gods.

The conquest of Britain

In Britain, a year later, the Brigantes were again split between Venutios and his wife Cartimandua. Once again the Romans intervened, rescuing the queen, but Venutios survived and assumed complete leadership of the tribe. Now Vespasian sent Petilius Cerialis to Britain to suppress the Brigantes, and within three years Cerialis had achieved this, bringing that whole northern area under his control.

His successor Frontinus subdued the Silures in south Wales and commenced a campaign against the Ordovices in north Wales, and his successor again was the celebrated Cnaius Julius Agricola, who arrived in AD 78. Agricola had served in Britain with both Paulinus and Cerialis, and was a hard-headed and ambitious soldier. He determined immediately to continue the campaign against the Ordovices and, having defeated them, he proceeded to Anglesey and retook it for the Romans without much effort. He reduced the south of Britain to the Pax Romana. He then placed a ring of garrisoned forts around each tribe and began to organise the social life of all the areas on the pattern of Imperial culture, making a special effort to educate the sons of chieftains in Roman manners.

Flushed with success, the Romans began to look further northwards and towards the Celtic groups there. On the modern Scottish-English border, in the east, were the Votadini ('those subject to the father' – a designation which must refer to worship of the ancestor-deity). To their north were the Corionototae ('people of the [fighting] corps'), and north again – around the Firth of Forth, were a group known as Venicones ('tribesmen'). Stretching northwards on the western side from the modern Scottish-English border were, respectively, the Novantae ('energetic ones'), and a branch of the Dumnonii, a larger group of whom – as we have seen – were in Devon and Cornwall.

In AD 81 Agricola led an army northwards, ravaging the country as far as the Tay estuary. His legions were far too strong for the aforesaid Celtic groups, and he encountered no major resistance. He then decided to push on against the tribes called Caledones in the extreme north of Scotland, whom Tacitus described as having 'red hair and large limbs' like the Germans. These and neighbouring tribes were in fact remnants of an earlier pre-Celtic people whom the Romans called by the Latin name Picti ('painted ones'), but their power had been reduced for centuries by Celtic inroads into Britain. By the time of the Roman invasion, their culture and language must have been heavily influenced by Celtic elements, and the designation 'Caledones' itself was Celtic (meaning 'brave people').

In the summer of AD 84, Agricola gathered forces by land and sea for the strike against the far north. Seeing the Roman fleet skirting the shore, the Caledones realised that there was no escape left to them and therefore they determined to fight. They fell upon some of the new Roman fortresses and, as Agricola brought his army against them, they attacked the camp of his Ninth Legion by night. Agricola was warned of this by his scouts and went to relieve the camp, with the result that the Caledones were caught between two Roman forces. They quickly retreated into the marshes and woods to reorganise and – Tacitus says –'to ratify their alliance with sacrificial rites'. Matters were drawing to a conclusion, and in the following summer Agricola brought his army as far as 'Mons Graupius' (in the district of Moray Firth), where the Caledones had established their headquarters. The tribes had assembled a large force there, and they were addressed by the foremost man among their leaders, 'a man of outstanding valour and nobility' called Calgacos. His name was a Celtic one, meaning 'swordsman'.

Tacitus quotes the speech which Calgacos was reported to have made, and it is an impressive one. He started by drawing attention to 'the united force which you are showing today', which would bring 'the dawn of freedom for all of Britain'. The Roman power had so expanded as to threaten even themselves, 'the most distant dwellers on earth, the last of the free'. Condemning the Romans as 'pillagers of the world', he said that 'they give the false name of government to robbery, butchery and plunder – they create desolation and they call it peace'. Unless the Caledones triumphed in battle, they would be robbed of their sustenance, crippled by building roads through forests and marshes under the lash, their women would be defiled and all reduced to slavery. Previously, discord among the tribes had given the Romans the opportunity to control them, but now all would be inspired to regain their freedom. Beyond Agricola's army there was nothing else to fear, for there were only forts without garrisons, colonies of aging veterans, and towns where the population was more than willing to rebel against tyranny.

This speech was greeted 'in barbarian fashion' by his followers with singing and shouting. The Caledonian forces were situated on higher ground, but their front line was on the plain and the others on the rising slopes behind them in series. In front of the whole force, facing the Romans on the plain, were the charioteers, making a great din. The Caledones numbered about 30,000 men, and the Romans somewhat less. Agricola had his auxilaries spread out in the front line, with his cavalry on the flanks, and the legionaries behind. The battle began with an exchange of missiles, with the Caledones showing great skill at parrying the Roman javelins with their huge swords and small shields. Agricola then ordered a charge, and in the hand-to-hand fighting the Caledones were at a disadvantage, for the short swords of the Romans were suitable for cutting and thrusting, whereas the long swords of the Caledones were cumbersome and had no points.

The result was that the Caledonian front line was cut down, and the Romans advanced onto the higher ground. Meanwhile, the Roman cavalry had overthrown the chariots, and they joined in the general melée. The whole Caledonian force soon retreated to nearby woods, but Agricola ordered his men to make a ring around the woods, and the killing continued. Eventually the Caledones took to flight, and they were pursued and slaughtered until nightfall. Next day, the Romans found the whole area deserted, with an eerie silence on the mountain range, and Agricola took his army slowly through all the adjacent territories to over-awe the tribes. He had already sent his fleet around the north of Scotland to show his power to all and sundry, and he was now poised for the total conquest of the island. Luckily for the peoples of Britain, however, the Emperor Domitian was jealous of Agricola's success and had him recalled immediately to Rome.

Independent Celtic Ireland

The historian Tacitus, son-in-law of the Roman commander, states that Agricola lined the side of Britain facing Ireland with fortresses, and that he used to say that Ireland itself could be taken and held by a single legion with a force of auxiliaries. An Irish prince came to Agricola when he was going north in AD 81. This prince had been expelled after a rebellion in his own country, and Agricola kept him in the hope of using him in an invasion of Ireland. There is no indication of the identity of this prince, or to which tribe he belonged, but he probably came from somewhere in the north-east of Ireland.

It is reasonable to assume that the tribal situation in Ireland was particularly strained at this period, due to increasing tension between the Ivernian tribes and the Lagini of the southern midlands. Groups from Britain, escaping from the devastation caused by the Roman legions, would have added to the instability. Such refugee groups tried to gain a foothold at various points on the east coast of Ireland, and then ventured inland in search of new areas to settle. The war against the Brigantes would have caused new sections of that tribe to migrate to Ireland, probably bringing some clients and neighbours with them. These would

Above: Celtic tribes in Ireland in the first century AD.

have included a group of Brigantes called Barreki who settled in the south-eastern corner of Ireland, becoming clients of the Lagini, who were themselves Brigantes in origin. Among the refugees also in all probability were some Parisi, who likewise found patronage with the Lagini, and – more independently – some Setantii who settled in modern County Louth.

The move to Ireland by sections of more northerly tribes would seem to date from the actual campaign of Agricola. Tribesmen of the Votadini seem to have settled in the north-east of Ireland, and a group of Corionototae midway down the east coast where they became known as Coriondi. The most notable of these newcomers belonged to the Dumnonii, some of whom settled in the area of north Dublin. These Dumnonii seem to have managed to form an alliance with the Lagini, agreeing to act as a kind of satellite state of theirs, guarding their borders. The ambitious Lagini had long been trying to extend their influence to beyond the river Shannon, and they used some of the newcomers to this purpose. This would explain how groups of Dumnonii and Parisi came to be settled in areas far to the west. Such refugees wished to get as far away from the Romans as they possibly could, so the likelihood is that the disaffected prince who came to Agricola belonged to one of the longer established groups and that he had fallen out with his fellow tribesmen.

More than likely he was a leading figure in one of the Ivernian tribes. From the fact that Agricola was at that time in the south of Scotland, it is likely that he was seeking assistance against either of the two most powerful Ivernian tribes in the north-east of Ireland, the Uluti ('bearded ones') or the Darinii (devotees of the god Darios – 'he who fertilises'). Archaeological evidence shows that a sacred hilltop site in the modern County Armagh was deliberately destroyed early in the first century BC, and this event would seem to coincide with the takeover of the area by the Uluti. The site was known as Isomnis (later Eamhain, called in English 'Navan Fort'), and the Uluti made it the ritual centre of their kingship. The prince who went to seek Roman aid may therefore have been a refugee from a failed attempt by one of the tribes who had been displaced from the area to regain their possessions.

The Lagini continued to strengthen their position in the middle of Ireland, and were probably already threatening the Ivernian kingdom of Tara at this period, while in the south another group was building up a strong power base. This was the Venii, whose name recalls those of the Veneti and Venelli from the regions now known as Brittany and

Normandy. Given the seafaring abilities of the Veneti, this group would appear the most likely ancestors of the Irish Venii. The Veneti, in Caesar's time, were able to call on auxiliaries from Britain to assist them in war, and this indicates that branches of their tribe had indeed settled there, perhaps in Cornwall. From there it would not be a great step to reach the southern coast of Ireland, and such a journey would have been particularly attractive after Caesar's savage treatment of the Veneti in their homeland.

Struggles continue in Britain

The recall of Agricola to Rome at the end of AD 84 meant that he did not get the opportunity to put his plan for the invasion of Ireland into effect, and even in Britain itself his gains were not secure. Efforts by the Romans to get the Caledonian tribesmen to enlist in their army were unsuccessful, and within some years a new resurgence of these tribesmen took place. They attacked many of Agricola's fortresses, forcing the Romans to abandon them. Then in AD 117 the Brigantes – apparently under the leadership of a king called Arviragos – rebelled and either drove out or massacred the Roman legion which was stationed at York.

The rebellion spread through so much of northern Britain that one contemporary report states that 'the Britons could no longer be held under Roman control'. The Emperor Hadrian arrived a year later, bringing fresh troops, and he soon forced the Brigantes to surrender once more. The Romanisation of southern Britain in language and culture had progressed hand in hand with the building of fortresses and roads and the development of the commercial infrastructure. Now the northern region was open to a similar sea-change, but the Caledonian tribes in the far north were still a major threat. So, with three legions, Hadrian commenced the building of the famous wall – stretching from Bowness to Wallsend – which bears his name and which, with its periodic fortresses, provided a barrier against raids by these tribes. In AD 142, under orders from the Emperor Antoninus, the frontier was doubled with the construction further north of a turf wall along the line of Agricola's old fortresses from the Firth of Forth to the Firth of Clyde.

9

SURVIVAL IN THE WEST

It is difficult to determine the actual number of Celtic-speaking people at the height of their power, and it is well to remember that Greek and Latin sources invariably exaggerated the numbers of Celtic warriors opposing them in battle. Estimates made by modern scholars – based on some references in classical literature and on comparison with later population figures – would indicate that the population of Celtic Gaul fluctuated around the figure of six million, with close on another million people in the territories of the Belgae. At the time of Julius Caesar there probably were almost two million inhabitants in Britain, and close on half a million in Ireland. With regard to the number of Celtic-speaking people in the Iberian Peninsula, in the second century BC these must have easily exceeded a million. A similar number seems to be appropriate to the region of the Alps and northern Italy at that time, while in the broad area along the Danube the number of Celtic or Celticised people may have approached two million. The population of Galatia had risen to a few hundred thousand at the time of their conquest by the Romans.

By the second century AD, however, the rule of Celtic lords and their followers across the great sweep of lands from the North Sea to the Iberian Peninsula and eastwards along the Danube valley stretching into Asia Minor was a thing of the past. The surviving descendants of the Celts in all these areas were being rapidly assimilated to Roman, Germanic and

Greek languages and social structures. Only in the two islands in the extreme north-west did the old tribal life of the Celts survive, and in the greater of these too it was breaking down due to incessant Roman pressure.

Continuing struggle in Britain

Although the barriers and fortifications built by the Romans across the north of Britain were an encumbrance to the semi-Celtic Picts or 'Caledones', these structures did not prevent raiding altogether, and by AD 155 the Romans had begun to withdraw from the Antonine Wall. A decade later Hadrian's Wall was confirmed as the real frontier.

In AD 181 the Caledones stormed the great wall and killed the Roman commander there, causing the Emperor Commodus to send a hardened general, Ulpius Marcellus, against them. He drove the raiders back, but his successor Clodius Septimius Albinus became embroiled in an Imperial power struggle and in AD 197 took the legions across to Gaul to have himself proclaimed Emperor there, in partnership with Septimius Severus, who commanded the legions on the Rhine and Danube. Both of these men had experience of Gaul – Albinus had subdued groups of deserters who had taken to banditry there, while Severus had enriched himself with Gaulish gold when he was the Roman governor at Lyons. Their friendship did not outlast their ambition, however, and when their armies clashed at Lyons in AD 198, Severus emerged victorious, flung the body of his adversary into the Rhône, and proclaimed himself the sole Emperor.

The Caledones, for their part, were emboldened by the departure of the backbone of the Roman army from Britain. They joined with the Maeatae – which seems to have been a general name in use at the time for tribes near Hadrian's Wall such as the Selgovae and Novantae – and began to ravage the area. Dio Cassius states that these tribes had neither towns nor tillage, and that their way of life was confined to herding and hunting. They were used to enduring hunger and cold and various hardships, and they chose their bravest men as rulers. Dio gives the following description of their fighting methods:

> They go into battle in chariots, and they have small swift horses. They also have foot soldiers, who are very swift runners and very firm in standing their ground. As arms they have a shield and short spear, with a bronze apple attached to the end of the spear-shaft, so that

when shaken it clashes and terrifies the enemy. They also have daggers.

The Emperor Severus himself arrived in Britain in AD 208 with a massive army to subdue these tribes, and he advanced northwards. The natives purposely put sheep and cattle in front of the legions, luring them into the swamps, forests and mountains, and attacking them when they were worn out and confused. This stiff guerrilla campaign caused heavy casualties to the Romans – Dio claims that they lost no less than 50,000 men – but Severus continued on his gruelling trek until he pushed the Maeatae and Caledones north as far as Aberdeen.

The Caledones agreed to a treaty and, having secured most of Scotland for the Roman interest, Severus returned to York in AD 210. The Maeatae continued the resistance in the southwest of Scotland, however, and in the following year the Caledones again joined them in arms. Severus ordered his soldiers to invade the territories of these tribes and to slaughter everybody there. Although suffering grievously from gout and from the rebelliousness of his son Antoninus, he prepared to lead a new campaign against them in person, but this was prevented by his death at York in AD 211. Dio Cassius relates a curious story of a discussion between Severus' wife Julia Augusta and the wife of the Caledonian leader Argentocoxos after the treaty of AD 210 was agreed. The Empress joked about the free intercourse of women with men, which was reputedly the Caledonian way, and the other woman replied: 'We fulfil the demands of nature in a far better manner than you Roman women, for we consort openly with the best men, whereas you allow yourselves to be debauched in secret by the vilest men!'

There were other differences too. Whereas the Caledones and Maeatae were much given to plundering and primitive heroism, the ambition of Severus was on a much grander scale, wishing to control the whole world. His attitude to power was well expressed in his final advice to his sons: 'Be harmonious, enrich the soldiers, and scorn all other men.' Although his ruthlessness failed to obtain the Roman objective of the total conquest of Britain, the devastation caused by him in Scotland must have been atrocious. It took the tribes of Caledones and Maeatae – known to the Romans as Picti ('painted ones', i.e. Picts) – several generations to recover. Indeed, many of them must have fled from his legions and taken refuge in Ireland, where the presence of various groups of Cruithni is later attested. This is the Irish version of the word Pritani, the name given to the earlier Celtic inhabitants of Britain who inhabited the northern half of that island. Irish sources, indeed, use the name Cruithni for the Pictish tribes of Scotland, and the same name was given to scattered groups in parts of the north-east and centre of Ireland.

Celtic 'Emperors'

Native Gaul was not yet entirely quiescent. There was some trouble with the Sequani in AD 175, the settling of which caused the celebrated Emperor Marcus Aurelius to take time off from his warring against the Germanic tribes. Some years later, a rebellion in Armorica necessitated the moving of some Roman legions from Britain. The legionaries were under the command of one Artorius Castus, and the rebellion was quelled. Then, after the rough interlude with Albinus and Septimius Severus, the youthful Emperor Alexander Severus had also to busy himself to ensure that the Germanic tribes did not intrude into the region.

He treated the Gauls with strictness, fearing their 'rude and dangerous temperament'. Moreover, in the year AD 235, as he set out on a campaign against the Germans, a druidess did not flinch at making a prediction to him in the Gaulish language to the effect that his demise was near: 'Go,' she said, 'but do not hope for victory, and put no trust in your soldiers!' He was soon after assassinated by his troops in camp near Mayence; and after his death the Gauls had to endure a succession of Roman tyrants, culminating in Gallienus, the son of whom, Saloninus, they assassinated in AD 260. They then proclaimed as their monarch Latienus Postumus, who seems to have been of the Vocontii tribe. A learned man, Postumus was extremely popular in Gaul, but he was a stern commander and was murdered by his soldiers seven years later.

In AD 268, the governor of Gallia Aquitania, Tetricus, assumed power at Bordeaux. He bore the Gaulish pseudonym Esuvius (from the name of the god Esus) and wore the Gaulish trousers (*bracae*). He commanded the Roman forces in both Gaul and Britain and, apparently with Trier as his base, was a pretender to the imperial office from AD 274. Dissatisfied with his unruly army, he wished to be reconciled to the Emperor Aurelian and only half-heartedly took the field against the superior forces of that Emperor at Châlons-sur-Marne. After his defeat in that battle, Aurelian treated him well, restoring him to his position as a Roman Senator.

It is reported that Aurelian consulted druidesses in Gaul, and that they assured him that the Imperial office would remain in his family. This was later borne out in the person of Constantius, but Aurelian himself was slain within a year. The next Emperor, the elderly Claudius Tacitus, was a reformer and under him a letter was sent by the Roman Senate to the council of the Treveri lauding their 'freedom', but he survived for only six months and was succeeded by Probus. The Germanic tribes known as Franks and Alemanni attacked Gaul, but Probus won a resounding victory against them in AD 277 and drove their forces back across the Neckar. He captured a huge amount of booty from them, and recruited thousands of the survivors into his army.

While Probus was campaigning in the East, the Germanic tribes renewed their threat in AD 280. This led to the rebellion of two officers in the Roman army. One of these, the Italian Proculus, a semi-brigand, was supported by the people of Gallia Celtica, and he repulsed the Alemanni. The other officer, Bonosus, had been born in Spain, son of a teacher from Britain and a Gaulish mother. His father died while he was yet a child and, under the guidance of his mother, 'a very brave woman', he rose to the rank of general in the Roman army. Famed for his drinking, he was in charge at Cologne when the Germans burned the Roman galleys on the Rhine, and he seems to have acted in consort with Proculus out of fear of repercussions for having lost the fleet. Proculus was a dissolute and indolent leader and, on the arrival of Probus at the head of a large army including German recruits, he tried to cement an alliance with the Franks. The latter betrayed him, however, and he was defeated and slain by Probus. Though a reluctant rebel, Bonosus was a capable commander. He was defeated by Probus only after a lengthy struggle, whereupon he hanged himself rather than face capture.

One of the sources for these accounts, the fourth-century writer Vopiscus, declares that the Gauls were 'a nation always agitated and desirous of creating either an Emperor or an empire'. He even claimed – incorrectly it would seem – that the greatest of the generals of Aurelian, Julius Saturninus, was a Gaul by birth and that he was distrusted on this account. Saturninus was later proclaimed emperor in Palestine, but was defeated by Probus and slain. It is apparent that the turbulence of the Roman army in Gaul was not entirely due to the ambition of its officers, but that it derived also from the grievances felt by the native population and from the influence of that population on the soldiers.

Probus was acclaimed as the deliverer of Gaul from Germanic attacks, and he effected some improvement in the Gaulish economy by giving farmers there the legal right to cultivate the vine. After a brief but very successful military career, he was overthrown and slain by his own soldiers in Illyricum in AD 282. The army in Raetia then proclaimed as Emperor an officer called Carus, a native of Narbonne in southern Gaul. Carus was very popular with the people of Rome, but died within two years as he crossed the river Tigris on a campaign against the Persians. His two sons attempted to succeed him, but both were soon overthrown. One of them, Numerianus, was held in high regard like his father, but within a year he was murdered by a relative. The other son, Carinus, who had been installed by Carus as governor of Gaul, was of a different character. Irresponsible and dissolute, he was defeated in Dalmatia by Diocletian, who had seized the Imperial Purple, and was killed in AD 286 by a soldier whose wife he had debauched.

In a broader sphere, the triangular struggle for power between Romans, Celts and Germans continued, and the Celts were still the losers. As the third century AD wore on, the Germanic threat to the Roman Empire was recurrent, and on an ever-widening front. The Franks were bursting into northern Gaul, the Burgundians were crossing the Main into eastern Gaul, and the Alemanni were ravaging northern Italy. Then, for the first time, Germanic tribes such as the Franks and Saxons began to raid the coast of Britain. In AD 286, to counter these, a new man was appointed commander of the Roman fleet in the Channel, with instructions to protect the coasts of Gaul and Britain. He belonged to the Menapii, one of the Belgic tribes in north-eastern Gaul, and his name was Carausius. The Latin sources say that he was of humble origin and was at first a seapilot, but that he rose quickly through the ranks of the Roman army. Operating from his headquarters at Gessoriacum (modern Boulogne), Carausius patrolled the Channel and stopped the raids, but suspicion soon fell on him of being in collusion with the pirates and of expropriating some of the loot.

He was condemned to death by the Emperor Maximian, but crossed to Britain and – with the help of the Roman legions there – proclaimed himself ruler of the island. In AD 289 Maximian set out for Britain to suppress him, but the Emperor's fleet was damaged by a storm and scattered by the able seamen of Carausius. Maximian and his fellow Emperor Diocletian had little choice but to leave Carausius to his own devices, and he proclaimed himself the third emperor and had coins struck with his name 'Marcus Aurelius Carausius' on them. The practice of seeking druidic predictions had apparently become fashionable at this time, for Diocletian used to recall how a prophecy had been made to him by a druidess among the Celto-Germanic Tungri to the effect that he would become emperor when he killed a boar. He fulfilled the prophecy later by slaying a leading Roman army officer called Aper ('boar'), which deed was considered the first expression of the cruelty for which he later became infamous.

Meanwhile, fortune had begun to turn against Carausius. In AD 292, the Romans re-took Gessoriacum, confining his power to Britain. As he made preparations to defend his position, Carausius was murdered by his ambitious lieutenant Allectus. Three years later, the new western Emperor Constantius landed in Britain and defeated Allectus, thus restoring the island fully to the Roman fold. Some time afterwards, Constantius returned to the Continent, where in AD 305 he was pro-claimed emperor. In the following year he was back in Britain and, with a view to counteracting raids from the north by the Caledones, he made his headquarters at York, from where in AD 306 he began a campaign into Scotland. His health soon began to fail, however, and he died in the same year at York. His son, Constantine, was proclaimed Emperor there.

It was this Constantine who later made Christianity the official religion of the Empire. The new religion had been gaining converts for some generations – especially among the less powerful elements of the population – and despite persecution had become widespread. It is unclear whether those to whom St Paul preached in Galatia included speakers of Celtic; but through the second and third centuries many Celts, like the other peoples of Asia Minor, were accepting Christianity. Soon, indeed, the inhabitants of Ancyra were so immersed in the new faith as to cause scandal by their bickering over points of doctrine. Christianity was taking root in Gaul and Britain at around the same time, and it spread gradually through the following generations. Several Gaulish and British bishops attended the Council of Arles in AD 314, ten years before the conversion of Constantine.

Ireland and its ambitions

The attacks on the west coast of Britain by Irish raiders, which are first referred to in AD 297, were highly significant. In Ireland itself, power had been fluctuating for some time between the dominant groups, but for information on this we are dependent on the glimpses provided by much later annalistic and legendary sources. There are several indications that the prestigious ritual centre of Tara was seized from the Lugunii or some other Ivernian tribe by the Lagini in the second century AD or there-abouts. The Lagini expropriated the cult of the site, including that of the god Lugus and gave the title Catuveros (meaning 'battle-man') to their own rulers there. They also developed greatly the druidic cult of the deity Vindos, who was associated with the Boyne river, adding motifs to his image from the British cult of the healing-god Nodons which had probably been introduced by newcomers to Ireland under the patronage of the Lagini.

Meanwhile, the group called Venii had come to dominate much of the south of Ireland. The indications are that these claimed descent from an ancestor called Ovogenos (literally 'sheep-conceived'), a type of ram-god appropriate to a people whose chief economic concern was animal husbandry. In the context of military prowess, they liked to apply another specialised pseudonym to themselves, *Ghaisonli or the like ('spear-men') – this was perhaps done in order to compete in propaganda with the Lagini, who used similar names.

At some stage, a strong section of these Venii broke off from the rest and began to move northwards, establishing a kingdom west of the Shannon. These retained the lore of an ancestor called Ovogenos, while their southern kinsmen substituted for it the form Ivogenos ('son of yew'). There may have been a ritual reason for this, as the cult of the yew tree – perhaps borrowed from the Lagini – was known in Ireland at this time, as evidenced from its occurrence in the common personal name Ivocatus ('yew-battler'). At any rate, alteration to their ritual genealogy underlined the division between the two septs. Those who moved north, for their own part, began to use the title Condos ('wise head') for their leaders. Later tradition exemplifies this division by portraying rivalry between the two great groups of Venii, descended respectively from ancestors called Ughan (< Ovogenos) and Eoghan (< Ivogenos), and by developing a legend of them being led in their rivalry by a leader called Conn and by a second Eoghan.

Towards the end of the third century AD, the ambitious northern Venii spread their power into the plain of Meath, where they overthrew the kingship of the Lagini at Tara and took over that whole region. The genealogies written a few centuries later describe a great leader of theirs called 'Tuathal', who warred against other tribes to gain supremacy over them and to secure the kingship of Tara. In the third century AD this name would have been Teutovalos ('tribe-ruler'), and such a personage may well have been the leader who established the power of the sept in that area. The writers of the genealogies furthermore apply the epithet *teachtmhar* to him – this word was no longer understood, but it seems to derive from an ancient Celtic compound meaning 'appropriator of wealth'.

Large-scale raids on the British coast were the work of these 'people of Condos'. Although very strong in the plain of Meath, their expansionist ambitions were being thwarted by the strong kingdom of the Uluti to the north and by the Lagini who, though driven south of the Boyne, were successfully resisting any intrusion into their traditional territory. One way open to the 'Condos-people' to strengthen their position was to accumulate wealth and resources from abroad, and in the process add to their prestige at home, and the easiest way to do this was by raiding the weakly defended areas of western Britain. The initial sorties across the Irish Sea proved successful, and soon these freebooters were rivalling the threat posed by the Picts to Roman Britain. In fact, it would seem that they came to be seen as more typical in the role, for the term used to refer to them, Scotti, was derived from an Irish word meaning 'plunderers'.

Final years of Roman power in Britain
It was in response to these raids from the west and north that Constantine instituted a new command called the Dux Britanniarum ('leader of the Britons'). He also instituted a command called Comes Litori ('protector of the shore') whose function was to defend the eastern and southern coasts against the Saxons. Ultimately, both commands failed in their tasks. The first failure was that of the 'leader of the Britons', who could not prevent the Caledones and Irish from attacking the frontiers in AD 360 and again four years later. The Romans, faced with attacks on Gaul and Raetia by the Germanic Alemanni and on Pannonia by the Sarmations and Quadrians, could not afford to send a large army to the rescue in Britain.

In AD 367, the Caledones overthrew York itself and swarmed southwards, slaying the 'protector of the shore' Nectarides and capturing the 'leader of the Britons', Fullofaudes, in an ambush. A succession of Roman officers were dispatched from the Continent, but to no avail, and finally the Emperor Valentinian saw no alternative but to send a senior Roman commander Theodosius from Gaul. The situation was dire, with the Franks and Saxons ravaging the northern coast of Gaul, but Theodosius nevertheless set out from Boulogne with a strong force of legionaries and auxiliaries and made a quiet crossing to Rutupiae (now

Richborough). The Caledones were divided into two groups, called Dicalydones and Verturiones, and were raiding far to the south. Theodosius encountered advance bands of them near London, and scattered them. He then advanced further north, countering raids by the Irish and the Atecotti. This designation, Atecotti, which in Celtic meant 'ancient people', seems to have referred in general to the Caledones and other Pictish tribes. In AD 368 Theodosius invaded Scotland, ravaged the countryside there, and restored Hadrian's Wall. A Latin poet laudingly referred to how he warmed the north with Pictish blood, and how 'icy Ireland wept for the heaps of dead Scotti'.

Meanwhile, the Saxon attacks were countered on the sea by the Roman galleys, which were kept informed of enemy movements by fleets of scouting skiffs. These skiffs were swift and manageable, with about twenty oars on each side, and were called by the Britons *picati* ('the tardaubed'). They were dyed a sea-green colour for camouflage, and their crew were dressed in clothes of the same colour. The Roman armies on land were continually being reinforced by Germanic and other warriors, who were conscripted after Roman victories on the Continent. All of this meant that a renewed build-up of Roman forces was taking place in Britain, and accordingly the attacks by raiders subsided, but the reinforcements were by no means securely loyal to Rome. Shortly after the success of his campaign, indeed, Theodosius and his Dux Britanniarum, Dulcitius, had to deal with an attempted rebellion within the army led by a Pannonian called Valentinus.

Theodosius was recalled to the Continent soon afterwards, only to be treacherously murdered in AD 376 on the orders of Valens, brother of the Emperor Valentinian, who ruled the eastern part of the Empire. He was succeeded as commander in Britain by Magnus Clemens Maximus, a Spaniard who had married a Briton wife. Maximus had served under Theodosius and seems to have been raised to the office of Dux Britanniarum after Dulcitius. He lost no time in his role as overall commander, continuing the campaign against the Picts and Irish, and in AD 382 he won a decisive victory over them. Having thus stabilised the northern border, the ambitious Maximus began to cast his eyes abroad.

The Roman world had been shaken to its foundations by a crushing victory of the Goths over the eastern Emperor Valens, after which Valens' young nephew Gratian – who ruled in the west – appointed Theodosius, son of the old soldier in Britain, as his colleague. Gratian himself, though an able ruler, was unpopular with the bulk of the

Romans because of his Christianity. Seeing his opportunity, Maximus proclaimed the cult of Jupiter and the old gods, and took his legions with him to Gaul in AD 383 in a bid to obtain the whole Empire for himself. He encountered the official Roman army under Gratian at Paris, and after initial skirmishes that army deserted to him. The unfortunate Gratian fled, and Maximus sent his cavalry commander Andragatius after him. Gratian was seized and murdered as he crossed the bridge at Lyons, after which Maximus set up headquarters at Trier, was baptised a Christian, and ruled as Emperor over Britain, Gaul and Spain.

Gratian's brother, Valentinian II, held out in Italy, and Maximus – biding his time – made a pact with him. Within a few years, however, Maximus found a pretext in Valentinian's authoritative attitude to the Church and in AD 387 he brought a large force of Britons, Gauls and Germans southwards to invade Italy. Valentinian promptly fled to Theodosius in the east, while Maximus prepared for the inevitable final battle. His lieutenant Andragatius sealed off the Alpine passes, but forces loyal to him were defeated in engagements on the Save and the Danube, and Theodosius quickly brought a large army through the eastern Alps in AD 388. Andragatius, not expecting such a rapid overland advance, had withdrawn troops from the Alps and was concentrating instead on assembling a large naval force to prevent a crossing over the Gulf of Venice. Maximus and Andragatius gathered their forces into the town of Aquileia, near Venice, but the army of Theodosius made an onslaught upon them there. They were utterly defeated, and Maximus was captured and beheaded by the son of his old commander. Maximus' own son, Victor, whom he had appointed as co-emperor with himself, was put to death also.

Later Welsh tradition attributes the initial settlements of Britons in the north-west corner of Gaul, Armorica, to Maximus' crossing to the Continent, claiming that many of those who went with him remained in that area. It is indeed likely that the crossing of Maximus, and his brief run of success on the Continent, made the idea of migrating to adjacent parts of Gaul attractive to substantial numbers of Britons. It was nothing new for small communities of them to be settled on the north coast of Gaul, probably as mariners and traders – as early as the first century AD Pliny the Elder refers to a group of 'Britanni' residing at the mouth of the river Somme. Commerce between Britain and Gaul was longstanding, but it accelerated under Roman rule. The crossing of the Channel could be effected in a day, and the principal British imports into Gaul were tin, lead, grain and leather. Diodorus Siculus reports that, having been bought by merchants in the Channel Isles, the tin was carried on horseback on a 30-day journey all the way south to the mouth of the Rhône.

Most of the cross-channel trade in pre-Roman times had been dominated by the fleet of the Veneti, the numerous tribe of Armorica who had strong contacts with south-west Britain. It is likely that large numbers of Veneti had fled to Britain to avoid the vengeance of Julius Caesar during his Gaulish campaign, and the rebuilding of their fortunes in succeeding centuries meant that within the ambit of this tribe much to-ing and fro-ing was taking place between Britain and Gaul. The campaign of Maximus, therefore, would have accelerated a process which was already traditional, and the trend for significant numbers of Britons to settle in Armorica continued despite his defeat. In this way, a Celtic language was brought back to the Continent, possibly mingling with the remains of spoken Gaulish in the area which was to become known as Brittany.

By withdrawing the best soldiers from Britain, Maximus had left that part of the Empire exposed to further attacks, and these soon came. Hadrian's Wall was breached again by the Caledones and – though some legionaries were probably sent back to York and Chester by Theodosius – the pressure intensified. According to the writer Gildas, Britain was for several years 'groaning in a state of shock' as the Irish sea-raiders attacked from the northwest and the Pictish raiders descended overland from the north. As a result of these attacks, the leading citizens of Britain sent letters to Rome imploring help and promising unswerving loyalty. Instability still dogged the Empire, however, and after the death of Theodosius in AD 395 he was succeeded by his young son Honorius. The real power lay with the army general Stilicho, a Vandal by birth, who was married to the first cousin of the boy-emperor Honorius and acted as regent.

Stilicho was an accomplished soldier, and his court-poet Claudian praises him for a campaign in AD 398 in which the sea was cleared of Saxons, the Picts were overwhelmed, and the Irish raiders curbed. Claudian has a metaphorical Britannia speak thus: 'When on the point of death at the hands of neighbouring tribes, I found in Stilicho protection, when the Scotti roused all Ireland and the sea foamed beneath hostile oars.' It is unclear whether Stilicho campaigned in person in Britain or whether the actions were carried out by officers who had been sent there by him. The bout of Irish raiding which was curbed by him or under his command may have been carried out by the powerful king of the 'Condos-people' called Ivocatus, who had the soubriquet

Magumedonos ('slave-ruler'). This was probably in reference to the seizing of captives abroad by him. In later form his name was Eochaidh Muighmheadhón. Even the balking of so eminent a personage, however, had no lasting effect on what had become by now an Irish custom.

Stilicho soon became embroiled in the struggle for power between various Roman factions on the Continent, and insecurity reigned once again in Britain, where the chain of defensive towers constructed along the southern coast gave little confidence that the island could be defended from the Germanic tribes which were by now causing devastation in Gaul. Distrusting the commitment of the authorities on the Continent, the Roman soldiers in Britain proclaimed one of their colleagues, Marcus, as emperor and then killed him when he did not please them. They elected the civilian Gratian as his successor, and killed him also soon afterwards. Finally, in AD 407, they proclaimed as emperor a soldier called Constantine, who seems to have belonged to a British family who had given him that name on account of their devotion to Constantine the Great. The choice of him was greatly helped by the coincidence of the famous name, and by the fact that Constantine the Great had also been proclaimed emperor by the army in Britain 100 years before.

The new pretender, who called himself Constantine III, wasted no time in setting out for Gaul with the bulk of his army. He had initial successes there, spreading his power as far as the Alps, but he was besieged in Valentia by the forces of Sarus, a general who had been despatched against him by Stilicho. One of Constantine's officers, with the Gaulish name Neviogastes, began negotiations with Sarus, but the latter tricked him by swearing oaths of friendship and then treacherously putting him to death. Making no headway, however, Sarus raised the siege, and Constantine was able to secure his western empire. He bestowed the title of Caesar upon his son Constans, and sent him to establish their power in Spain. Constans was accompanied by one of his father's most capable officers, a Briton called Gerontius.

Stilicho himself was put to death in AD 408 after being charged with deliberately weakening the Roman defences against his fellow Vandals. When Alaric, the Visigothic leader, threatened Rome the following year, the Emperor Honorius was in desperate straits. Constantine sent an envoy to him from his headquarters in Arles offering to come to the rescue of Rome with his Gaulish, Spanish and British forces. Knowing, however, that two of his relatives had been seized in Spain by Constans and murdered soon afterwards, Honorius was suspicious and played for time. At the end of AD 409, Constantine decided to replace Gerontius as his commander in Spain but, in anticipation of this, Gerontius rebelled and nominated a certain Maximus as Emperor. Gerontius got substantial support from the army in Spain, and Constantine was greatly weakened as a result.

With scenes unparalleled since the raid on the great city by the Celts 800 years before, Rome was sacked for three days by the Visigoths in the autumn of AD 410. The Emperor Honorius, from his court at Ravenna, decided that it was crucial to the restoration of the Empire to first destroy the pretenders, and so in AD 411 he sent an army to conquer Constantine once and for all. Constantine was indeed under intense pressure, for Gerontius had defeated and slain his son Constans at Vienne and was marching on Arles. On seeing the army of Honorius approach, Gerontius drew off, and soon after was caught in a rebellion of his own troops and committed suicide. When Honorius' army under the general Constantius besieged Arles, Constantine took refuge in a church and was ordained a priest, but he was arrested. While he was being transported as a prisoner to Italy, Honorius sent assassins to kill him, and he was beheaded near the river Mincio.

Britain was by now practically denuded of Imperial troops. With increasing raids by Saxons, Angles and Jutes in the southeast, followed by actual settlements of these Germanic peoples in the area, Roman rule in Britain was finally coming to an end.

Importance of Irish raids

During the war against the pretender Constantine, who made several agreements with the Germanic tribes, Honorius had written to the cities in Britain advising them to act on their own initiative to protect themselves. As a result the Britons themselves organised forces to counteract the Germanic raiders, and in some cases – distrusting Constantine's intentions – even expelled his officials. The Picts had apparently followed the Irish example of raiding by sea, and the raids intensified from these quarters also. The writer Gildas put it colourfully: 'the horrid hordes of Scotti and Picti eagerly emerged from the coracles that carried them across the gulf of the sea'. As 'the barbed spears of their naked enemies got no rest' Britons of various localities were reduced to plundering each other in order to survive, and despair was everywhere among them.

The impetus for going abroad in search of plunder was magnified in Ireland by the ambitions of the dynasty which ruled at Tara, who had been for a while the most powerful group in Ireland and whose wealth and resources were greatly increased by the success of such raiding overseas. There are indications, indeed, that other Irish groups began to follow the example of the 'Condos-people' around this time, and it may be useful to clarify at this point the principal designations by which these were later known in Irish literature. The earliest form of written Irish was in short inscriptions called *ogham*, which date from the fourth to the sixth centuries AD. These are mostly in stone and contain names of individuals, but they tend to reflect early Celtic forms which were becoming increasingly obsolete.

In fact, from the fifth century AD onwards, radical changes were taking place in spoken Celtic. Changes in pronunciation had been effecting both vowels and consonants for a long time, but from the fifth century AD onwards a further series of changes took place in Celtic as spoken in Britain and Ireland. These involved the truncation of final syllables in words and an increasing tendency in Ireland to syncopate unstressed internal syllables. Irish literature, which originated in the sixth century AD, represents the language in this altered state, and such changes explain why the Iverni came to be known as Érainn, the Lugunii as Luighne, the Lagini as Laighin, the Uluti as Ulaidh, and the Venii as Féni. The latter's special designation for themselves became Gaídhil, and their principal groups were now called Connachta and Eoghanacht. Similarly divine names such as Lugus, Vindos and Nodons became Lugh, Fionn and Nuadhu; while other ritual names such as Catuveros, Ivogenos and Condos became Cathaoir, Iughan or Eoghan and Conn respectively.

The Connachta (who had their name from 'Condos', developing into 'Conn') were led at this time by Niall, son of the celebrated Ivocatus (Eochaidh Muighmheadhón). We read that among the slaves taken by this Eochaidh in a raid on Britain was a girl called Caireann. This is an Irish corruption of the Latin name Carina, and the girl became a concubine of Eochaidh and gave birth to Niall. When he grew to manhood, Niall rescued her from servility and demanded recognition for her as a noblewoman. He also managed to succeed his father as leader of the sept. All of this is the subject of a later story which combines memories of the career of Niall with detritus from the rituals of the ancient kings of Tara and with ordinary heroic lore.

In the story, we read that Caireann was resented by Eochaidh's legal wife, who gave her servile tasks to perform, and that her baby was therefore born in the open air. Birds attacked the baby, but the poet Torna took up the child, named it 'Niall' and prophesied its future greatness. Niall was reared by the poet, and when he was of age Torna brought him to Tara. A druid-smith was appointed to compare him with Eochaidh's four legal sons, and he did this by setting fire to a forge where the young men were working. Each of them saved an implement from the fire, but the anvil was saved by Niall who thereby showed his superiority. The five young men then went hunting, and in the wilderness the four legal sons of Niall went to fetch water at a well. They met an extremely ugly hag there, who asked them for a kiss, and they were disgusted and refused. Niall was last to arrive at the well, and he offered not only to kiss her but to lie with her as well. As a result she turned into a beautiful young maiden. 'You are multi-shaped, woman,' said Niall. 'That is true,' said the woman. When Niall enquired who she was, she replied: 'O king of Tara, I am the sovereignty!'

Having thus announced his right to the kingship, the goddess explained to him that sovereignty is loathsome at first, for it must be gained by battles and conflict, but that at last one finds it comely and beautiful. Through this legend of Niall the ambitious Connachta sept asserted their right to kingship through either war or peace. The point of historical truth that survives in the legend is that Niall established his seniority over his brothers and appropriated the rituals of sovereignty to himself. His career proved so successful that, after his death, his descendants as Tara kings gradually laid aside the designation Connachta and for many generations referred to themselves as Uí Néill (literally 'the grandsons of Niall').

Niall is described in early Irish literature as carrying out several great raids on the British coast, and he is said to have been killed on one such raid by a man of the Laighin, whom he had exiled to Britain. This happened in or about the year AD 452. Legendary accounts state that his warriors brought his body home, and when attacked on their way they raised it aloft in the belief that Niall's reputation would weaken the spirit of the enemy. It was apparently on one of these raids into Britain that one Patricius (better known as St Patrick) was captured as a youth and first brought into Ireland. The raid on which he was taken was definitely a large one, for the saint himself states that thousands of people were taken. It is curious to consider that Ireland, the last Celtic country which Christianity reached, was converted not through the power of Rome, but as an indirect result of a predatory campaign carried out by one of the last great Iron Age warriors.

St Patrick was a Romanised Celt from somewhere in the west of Britain, and was sixteen years of age when he was taken to Ireland. Having spent six years as a slave, mostly herding pigs and sheep, he ran away and found passage on a ship to the Continent. Having been ordained to the priesthood he returned again to Ireland and began his famous mission, which seems to have been first directed towards the Ulaidh kingdom in the north and then towards the Tara kingdom ruled over by Niall's son Laeghaire. There were already small groups of Christians in the country, most of them probably being slaves brought from Britain, but Patrick's fearless personality and skilled diplomacy was to make Christianity the central cultural force in the Ireland of the late fifth century AD.

His mission is traditionally dated to between the years AD 432 and AD 461, but scholars are unsure as to the precise dates. The indications are that he had won some influential converts among the Ulaidh, before the kingdom of that sept was overwhelmed by forces led by three sons of Niall in the middle of the fifth century AD. These three sons, Eoghan, Conall and Éanda, set up kingdoms for themselves in the north and west, pushing the Ulaidh and their client peoples into the coastal areas of the northeast. The rapid spread of the Christian religion in Ireland, though it gave rise to a great commitment to learning and asceticism, did not have a profound effect on the struggles for power between the various septs. By this time, there were five loosely marked regions of political power in Ireland, each of these known as a *cúige* ('fifth').

Despite the conquest of its royal centre and of most of its territory by the sons of Niall, the northern 'fifth' of Ireland retained the name Ulaidh. For the kingdom of Tara, ruled over by Laeghaire, a new 'fifth' was carved out and called Midhe ('the middle'). Niall's brother Fiachra took over the lands and overlordship held by the Connachta west of the Shannon, and since this lateral branch kept the old designation of the sept, the western 'fifth' of Ireland came to be known as 'Connachta'. Meanwhile, the Laighin held onto their possessions in the broad area of the southeast, giving their name to that 'fifth'. The huge area of the south-west of Ireland was the 'fifth' known by an ancient name Mumu (meaning 'nurturing-place', later Mumhain), and here the power of the Eoghanacht continued to expand, taking some of the territories held by Érainn groups in that area and bringing others under them as clients.

'England' established by the Anglo-Saxons

With the withdrawal of the Roman legions from Britain, the pressure from the Germanic tribes on the southeast increased, and the raids by the Picts from the north grew intolerable. The sources for this period in Britain are confused and largely unreliable, especially with regard to dating. The most likely sequence of events, however, is that, facing a strong Pictish onslaught and also ravaged by plague, the chief men of Britain called a council in or about the year AD 428. The leading personality in this council seems to have been Vortigern, a king from north Wales who had extended his influence over the south of Britain as far east as Kent. With Vortigern's concurrence, and probably under his direction, the council in their desperation decided on a very risky plan. This was to accept Saxon settlements in Essex, Kent and adjacent areas in return for aid against the Pictish attackers from the north.

The stratagem worked for a while, as the Saxons abided by the agreement and acted as 'foederati' in so far as it gave them the opportunity to build up their forces. A campaign against the Picts was successful, for the historian Bede reports that Vortigern, with his Anglo-Saxon mercenaries, routed their forces in a battle to the north of the river Humber. This put an end to the raids, and for a few years the country was stable and commerce revived. The monk Gildas – writing a century later – refers to the Saxons as 'wolves admitted into the fold', and his description was accurate, for these soon began to demand more for their efforts and then began again to plunder. Soon they had penetrated as far west as Surrey; while their close associates, the Angles, took over large swathes of territory in Suffolk and Norfolk; and another Germanic tribe, the Jutes, took over the Isle of Wight and parts of the Hampshire coast. The situation deteriorated, as the whole of south-eastern Britain came under attacks far worse than before. Towns were devastated, whole communities were slaughtered, and the fire of destruction did not subside until 'it was licking the western ocean with its savage red tongue'.

Gildas states that the Britons sent a letter to Gaul in AD 446 imploring assistance from the Roman Consul Aetius, complaining that 'the barbarians drive us to the sea, the sea drives us back to the barbarians'. The appeal, however, fell on deaf ears and, to add to their woes, a new army of Saxons landed in Kent in AD 449. This army was led by warrior brothers known as Hengist and Horsa, who may already have had experience as mercenaries in Britain. The situation now was one of a war to the death between the native Britons and the Anglo-Saxons.

Vortigern attempted to rally his people, and defeated the invaders at a battle in Kent (probably at Aylesford) in AD 455, in which Horsa was slain. Two years later, however, and again in AD 465 and AD 473, Hengist and his son Aesc inflicted crushing defeats on the Britons and drove them fleeing to the west and north. After the death of Hengist, he was succeeded by Aesc, whose dominance was rivalled for a time by another Saxon leader, Aelle. The latter seems to have landed in England in AD 477, and he quickly established himself in Sussex, massacring the Romano-British defenders of the shore fortress of Anderida (now Pevensey).

Meanwhile, the migrations to Armorica by groups from the south-west of Britain continued. The writer Gildas claimed that Britons, fleeing from the Anglo-Saxons, 'went to lands beyond the sea with great lamentation'. Anglo-Saxon pressure must indeed have caused many Britons to seek refuge in the south-west of the island and, since connections between that area and Armorica were longstanding, it was natural that many of these would continue on and cross the sea. Such a course of flight from aggression might indeed have been established for some generations due to Irish raids on the Cornish peninsula and on south Wales, but the process was now greatly accelerated.

Armorica was a relatively easy place in which to settle, for the native Celtic population had been sujugated by the Romans, and when the imperial forces began to weaken the Armorican towns had been devastated in the fourth century AD by Saxon raids. Furthermore, the latent disaffection among the inhabitants of Roman Gaul had been surfacing periodically in alliances of peasants, slaves and mutinous soldiers, which the Romans called '*Bacaudae*'. In AD 435 such disaffection within much of Gaul found a focus in a rebellion in Armorica led by a certain Tibatto, which was only put down after two years of fighting by the Roman commander in Gaul, Litorius. Tibatto was captured, but he may have escaped again, for he is reported as the leader of another rebellion in AD 442. This time he was killed in the fighting, and after his death Armorica was quiescent – deprived, in effect, of any reasonable prospect of self-defence.

Those Britons settling in Armorica were soon strong enough to dominate local life and to furnish significant armies in the field. In the year AD 468 the Visigothic king Euric was advancing from Spain through southern Gaul, and the western emperor Anthemius in desperation called for aid from 'the Britons'. The contemporaneous writer Jordanes states that 'their king Riothamus came with 12,000 men into the state of the Bituriges by way of the ocean and was welcomed as he disembarked from his ships'. The entry of the forces of this king into the centre of Roman Gaul caused some upset to local lords, and one of these indeed addressed a letter to Riothamus, complaining that his warriors, described as 'noisy, armed and disorderly' were encouraging slaves to take their freedom. The strong likelihood is that Riothamus (Celtic Rigotamos, meaning 'the very kingly man') and his warriors were from the north of Brittany, and that they had sailed down the Atlantic coast to the mouth of the Loire. They probably numbered much less than the quoted 12,000 and, before the Romans could join them, they clashed with a much larger force of Visigoths led by Euric at Bourg-de-Déols. They were routed after a hard-fought battle, and sought refuge among the Burgundians.

In Britain, Vortigern was dead by this time, perhaps killed in internal strife between native Britons. His position of leadership passed to Ambrosius Aurelianus, a man of Roman descent and who belonged to the pro-Roman party which had been sidelined by Vortigern. It is apparent that Ambrosius was regarded as a king in Armorica, and he may indeed have been a native of that region. Some scholars have even considered him to be identical with the Riothamos who fought against the Visigoths. If this identification be correct, he would have returned from Burgundy and taken command in Britain around the year AD 470.

It is reported that the parents of Ambrosius had been slain by the Saxons and, with such an experience, he had every reason to devote himself to a military life. He proved an able leader, and managed to turn the tide of warfare. Under his leadership, or that of his successor, a great victory was gained in or about the year AD 485 at an unidentified place called Mons Badonicus, probably in the vicinity of Bath. Thousands of Saxons were killed in the battle, and the erosion of native Britain was checked for a time. Indeed, facing a counter-attack by the Britons, the Saxons in the south grew uneasy, and there is evidence which suggests that some groups of them returned to the Continent where they were alotted land by the Frankish King Theuderich.

A much later source speaks of twelve battles won by Arthur. This personage was probably historical, though his image was developed out of all recognition in medieval lore. His name, though in Romanised form, was Celtic, meaning 'bear', and had a long martial history among the Romanised Britons, being borne by several distinguished leaders. This particular Arthur appears to have belonged to the northern Britons and to have fought his campaigns in that area. The evidence suggests that he was slain in an internecine battle fought at Camlann (probably Birdoswald, towards the western end of Hadrian's Wall) in or about the year AD 511.

Although their expansion was stalled for the moment by the native resurgence, the overall success of the Anglo-Saxon invasion was undoubted. The whole south-eastern area from the Wash to the Isle of Wight was now dominated by them, and Saxon leaders such as Cerdic and Stuf continued to fight small battles against the Britons until the kingdom of Wessex was established in the year AD 519 or soon after. This kingdom, south-west of the river Thames, penetrated into the heart of Britain, and must have greatly increased the pressure on the Britons in the whole south-western area, causing a sharp increase in the rate of migration from Devon and Cornwall across the sea to Brittany. When the Angles, from their more northern strongholds, began also to press west, the Britons of that area also had good cause for anxiety, and they prepared to face the final onslaught.

Britons, Picts and Irish under pressure

Raiding on Britain by the Irish inevitably developed into settlements. At the same time as the powerful king Niall was involved in his overseas adventures, groups of Laighin were already establishing themselves on parts of the Welsh coast, leaving their name on the Lleyn peninsula. Their presence was reputedly the reason why a Briton leader from south-eastern Scotland, called Cunedda, moved with his eight sons and a considerable force of warriors to Wales. Although this has been linked to the policy of the imperial pretender Maximus, the move seems to have actually been at the instigation of Vortigern, whose strategy to defend Britain from invaders on all sides would have required such allies in the west. The move was successful, for Cunedda drove the Laighin out of north Wales. The warriors led by Cunedda were probably drawn from the Venicones and Votadini of Scotland, and in their new territory they were known as Venedoti. This was the population name preserved by the descendants of Cunedda, who founded the strong kingdom of Gwynedd in that region.

The distribution of Irish inscriptions in the *ogham* alphabet, dating from the fifth and sixth centuries AD, in south Wales, Devon and Cornwall shows that there were extensive Irish settlements in these areas also, and that these continued to operate for some time. Particularly important were settlements made by the Déise in the territory of the Demetae (now Dyfed). These settlers belonged to an extensive Érainn tribe in the south-east of Ireland, and the tradition was that one of their chieftains called Eochaidh Allmhuir had led the migration and was the ancestor of the later Welsh kings of Dyfed. The tribal name Déise meant 'vassals', a reference to the fact that, although holding independent territory (in present County Waterford) they had nominally to accept the overlord-ship of the Eoghanacht. Indeed, emigrants from a branch of the Eoghanacht themselves, the Uí Liatháin, constituted the major part of the Irish settlements in Cornwall.

More northerly settlements in Britain were the work of Ulster septs, particularly the Dál Riada, who were under pressure in east Ulster from the expansion of Connachta power. Groups of Dál Riada established themselves in the Scottish coastal area which came to be known as Oirthear Gaedheal ('eastern realm of the Irish', i.e., Argyll) The main thrust in this extension of the Dál Riada across the sea was carried out by their king Fearghus, son of Erc, around AD 500. Dál Riada power thus spanned the sea, from Antrim to Argyll, and soon their kings took up res-idence on the Scottish side. Tension naturally developed between them-selves and the Picts, and in AD 557 Gabhrán, grandson of Fearghus, was slain in battle against the Pictish king Bruide, son of Maelchú. This Irish foothold in Scotland became increasingly secure, however, and in AD 563 Conall, who had succeeded his uncle Gabhrán as Dál Riada king, granted the small island of Iona, west of Mull off the Argyll coast, to an eminent Irish monk.

The monk's name was Criomhthann, but he was known far and wide by his name in religion Columba. He was in fact a great grandson of Conall Gulban son of the famous Niall, and thus belonged to the northern branch of the Uí Néill. His relative and contemporary, Diarmaid son of Fearghus Cearrbheoil, reigned at Tara and was probably the first king at that site to profess Christianity. After the death of the Dál Riada king Conall in or about AD 574, Aedán son of Gabhrán succeeded to that important kingship, and Aedán was a particularly close friend of the saint. By his social importance, therefore, Columba exemplified the prestige and rapid spread of Christianity in sixth-century AD Ireland, but personally he was also an exceptionally holy and gifted man. From his monastery on Iona he undertook a mission to the Picts, the first in a long series of missions undertaken by Irish clerics in Britain and in Continental Europe. Columba's own mission met with great success, and for the next two centuries the community which he established was the major Christian influence in the whole north of Britain.

The Dál Riada also colonised the Isle of Man, but in a campaign from AD 577 to AD 578 they were overcome there by Baethán, son of Caireall, king of the Dál Fiatach (in present County Down) who were lineal descendants of the old Ulaidh rulers. The rulers of Dál Riada were soon back in possession, however, under their celebrated king Aedán son of Gabhrán. From his headquarters at Dunadd, Aedán took an increasing interest in the affairs of the whole northern region, raiding into the Briton kingdom of Strathclyde and the Pictish lands to the north and east.

Meanwhile, the Anglo-Saxon power continued to spread. Their first kingdom in the north was reportedly established in AD 547 by an Anglian leader called Ida. This was the kingdom of Bernicia in Yorkshire, and brave resistance to Ida's expansionism was put up by the Briton king of the region, Outigern (later known as Eudeyrn). Soon, most of Lincolnshire and Yorkshire was held by a mixed group of the newcomers dominated by Angles, and the kingdom of Deira was added to that of Bernicia. Faced by the common threat to them all, the Britons of the north began to use for themselves the general name Cumbri, which derives from Celtic *combrogii* ('fellow inhabitants'). In its later form, Cymry, the word survived as the term used for themselves by the Welsh.

There were, in fact, different kingdoms among the northern Britons. The strongest of them, ruled by the descendants of the Dumnonii in the basin of the river Clyde, was known as Strad Clud (or Strathclyde) and had as its capital Alt Clud (known to the Irish as Dún Breatan, 'the fortress of the Britons', hence Dumbarton). To their east were the Gododdin, as the ancient Votadini came to be known – their kingdom was called Godeu and had its capital at Din Eidyn (now Edinburgh). The more southerly kingdoms were probably survivals of the powerful Brigantes of old. These were known as Rheged, straddling the modern English-Scotttish border with its capital at Caer Liwelydd (modern Carlisle); and Elfed in Yorkshire, the kingdom which had lost out most to the Angles.

In the latter half of the sixth century AD, the Cumbri forged a military alliance led by Urien, Gwallawg, Rhydderch and Morgant. The first three of these were kings respectively of Rheged, Elfed and Strathclyde; and Morgant may have been king of Godeu. Urien was the principal figure in this alliance, and the fighting continued for several years, first against Ida's son Deodric, whom Urien besieged for three days at Metcaut (now Lindisfarne). It would appear that Urien had pushed the Angles back into that coastal area. This pressure continued on Deodric's successor Hussa, but the British alliance faltered due to rivalry among the leaders, and it is reported that Urien was murdered at the instigation of

Morgant, due to jealousy of his military prowess. The initiative then passed to the Angles, and the kingdom of Elfed succumbed to them soon afterwards, only a remnant of it surviving in the area around Cleveland.

In the south, Cynric succeeded his father Cerdic as king of the West Saxons and won battles against the Britons in AD 552 at Salisbury and in AD 556 at Barbury Hill. After his death in AD 560, Cynric was succeeded by his son Ceawlin. The West Saxon forces under a certain Cuthwulf defeated the Britons at Bedcanford in AD 571, after which the whole area from Buckinghamshire to the upper Thames was overrun. Then Ceawlin himself scored a major victory at Dyrham in AD 577, a battle in which three British kings, Coinmail, Condidan and Farinmail were slain. In yet another battle, at Fethanleag (probably in north-east Oxfordshire) in AD 584, Ceawlin was again successful and seized more territory from the Britons who remained in that area. The towns of Gloucester, Cirencester and Bath soon fell to the West Saxons; and this meant that, although resistance continued, land contact between the Welsh and their fellow Britons in Devon and Cornwall was effectively cut.

Those who had left the turmoil of Britain and settled in Armorica were undergoing trials of their own, due in no small part to internecine warfare. There were three basic, and perhaps distinctive, areas of settlement of these 'Bretons' – the northern region, the south-western region, and the south-eastern region. These corresponded roughly to the ancient Gaulish territories of the Coriosolites, Ossismii and Veneti respectively. It is not known what designations the original Breton settlers used for the three regions, but they later became known as Domnonia, Cornouaille and Bro Weroch.

The earliest ruler of Domnonia was Riwal, who is said to have been the leader of a migration from Britain and to have been allowed to settle there as a subject of Clothair I, king of the Franks in the early sixth century AD. After the death of Riwal, his son and grandson were opposed by Cunomorus of Carhaix who eventually seized the kingship of Domnonia from the surviving heir, Judwal. The kingdom of Cunomorus extended across the Channel, for he held sway over part of Cornwall as well as northern Brittany. He gained a reputation as a power-hungry tyrant. The young Judwal fled to the court of Hildeberht, brother of Clothair, and with the help of that king he later returned to Domnonia and overthrew Cunomorus. The Cornouaille settlement is attributed to Grallon, but he and his early successors are clouded in legend. They probably were descended from some of the earliest migrants from Britain.

The early history of the third region, Bro Weroch, is hardly any clearer, but it was probably the result of an immigration from eastern Wales in the later fifth century AD. The historian Gregory of Tours tells of vicious scheming among the early leaders of this settlement, resulting in the coming to power in AD 577 of Waroc'h, from whom the region got its name. The Frankish rulers claimed power over Brittany and allowed only the title of 'count' rather than 'king' to Breton leaders. Waroc'h, however, soon showed that he resented this overlordship and in the very year of his accession he seized Vannes and made it his headquarters. He continually raided into eastern areas around Nantes and Rennes, and various punitive expeditions sent by the Frankish king Guntram achieved nothing but to increase Breton resentment. Before Waroc'h's death, he nominally submitted to Guntram's general Ebracher, but he soon returned to war and hostilities continued for several generations, with neither side gaining a clear victory.

10

DAWNING OF THE MIDDLE AGES

B y the latter sixth century AD, there were few traces left of the once widespread Celtic culture in Continental Europe. In the west and south Celtic had been replaced by Latin, and in northern and central Europe by Germanic dialects. The rate of decline had, however, varied from place to place.

Disappearance of Celtic

Immediately upon the Roman conquest of each territory, the native language or languages had generally begun to decline there. For instance, the Romans controlled northern Italy even before the second century BC, and had banished the Celts and other peoples from large areas there, so it may be presumed that the Celtic language had largely ceased to be used there by the time of the Emperor Augustus. On the other hand, though most of Iberia had come under Roman control in the second century BC, the conquest was not complete in that region until Augustus' campaign. After this the population of Iberia was anxious to turn over to Latin as quickly as possible, but Celtic and Iberian must have survived for another few generations. In the mountainous region of the northwest, of course, the Basque language was to survive indefinitely, and it is likely that Celtic and Iberian themselves lingered on in remote areas until the third century

AD or even somewhat later.

The rapid overthrow of Gaul by Julius Caesar, and the brutal repression of rebellions under his successors, left the Celtic or 'Gaulish' language in that region in a despised situation. Although the writing of inscriptions in Gaulish continued to the middle of the first century AD, the Roman policy was to extirpate all surviving forms of the native culture, and Gaulish noblemen rushed to take on Roman names and fashions. Schools of Latin were established at Autun, Marseilles, Lyons, Arles, Vienne, Toulouse, Limoges, Reims, Trier and Bordeaux, to which these noblemen sent their sons for education in the new order. Before long, indeed, Gaulish scholars became well known for their rhetorical skills in Latin, thus expressing a respected aspect of their native tradition in a new guise. For example, in the fourth century AD the famous rhetorician Attius Patera was the son of Phoebicius, teacher of rhetoric at Bordeaux – this Phoebicius had been the guardian of a shrine dedicated to the Celtic deity Belenus at Bordeaux and was descended from a druidic family of Armorica.

The region of Gaul was so big, however, and its population so large and scattered, that a complete changeover in language could only be a comparatively slow process. Thus, the Christian bishop of Lyons, St Irenaeus, excused his skill in Greek discourse by saying that he had to 'dwell among Celts, and converse for the most part in a foreign language'. This bishop died, along with many of his Celtic converts, in the persecution of Christians by the Emperor Septimius Severus in 202 AD. The succeeding Emperor, Alexander Severus, was also encouraged to persecution of the Christians by his teacher and legal adviser Ulpian. Ulpian codified and promulgated several laws, which he considered necessary to have translated into Gaulish and other languages spoken within the empire in addition to Latin and Greek. As we have seen, prophecies were given by druidesses in Gaulish to both Alexander Severus and Diocletian in the third century AD.

The evidence for eastern Europe is less direct, but there was a marked decline in the use of Celtic personal names in the second and third centuries AD, and this would indicate that by the end of that period Celtic had ceased to be spoken generally in the eastern Alps and adjacent areas. Remnants of the Volcae tribe in Moravia, of the Norici in Noricum, and of the Scordisci in Pannonia and Dalmatia continued to speak Celtic until the fourth century AD, but after that it may be supposed that Celtic had disappeared entirely from eastern Europe.

In the outpost furthest east, Galatia, the situation was somewhat different. After the overthrow of Celtic power there by the Romans in the second century BC, a degree of autonomy was soon regained due to the diplomacy and opportunism of Galatian leaders, particularly Deïotaros, and the final and complete takeover by the Romans did not occur until the time of Augustus. The original Celtic culture of the Galatians had, of course, become mixed with the indigenous cultures of Asia Minor, but the Celtic language survived. Towards the end of the fourth century AD, St Jerome wrote: 'Although the Galatians, in common with the whole east, speak Greek, their own language is almost identical with that of the Treveri.' He went on to remark that 'through contact with the Greek they have acquired a few corruptions', thus underlying the objective nature of his comments. As well as in Asia Minor, Jerome had spent time at Trier, and it is interesting to note that he had also heard Celtic spoken in that area of north-east Gaul.

Sulpicius Severus, the fifth-century AD biographer of St Martin of Tours, describes a Gaulish cleric excusing his 'rustic speech' and being told by a colleague that he may 'speak rather in Celtic, in Gaulish, if you prefer it'. There is some doubt as to whether this reference is to the actual Celtic language, or to Latin spoken with a Celtic accent, which was regarded as a mark of ignorance by educated Latin speakers. There was, indeed, a strong tendency among speakers of Latin and Greek to regard the Celts as being of low intelligence. This probably originated in a reference made by the third-century BC Greek satirist Callimachus to 'the foolish tribe of the Galati' who attacked Delphi, but it was picked up and applied more generally. St Paul, in his epistle directed to them, chided the 'foolish Galatians', and three centuries later the rhetorician Firmicus Maternus refers to the 'stolid Gauls' and to 'Gaulish stolidity'. This quasi-racist sentiment must have been suggested by Celtic reticence when confronted with the more confident and triumphant Roman culture.

By the end of the sixth century AD, the Celtic language of Gaul seems to have completely disappeared, though it is sometimes claimed that it continued to be spoken among small mountain communities in the north-western Alps until the ninth century AD or even longer. It is much easier to demonstrate other aspects of the question, such as the influence left by Celtic on the pronunciation of the Gaulish dialect of Latin which developed into French. Certain aspects of Spanish pronunciation are similarly attributed to a Celtic substratum. A small number of Celtic words survive in the various languages which have replaced it in different parts of Europe, but much more noticeable is the large number of placenames and river names stretching across Europe from east to west which have their origins in Celtic.

The reintroduction of Celtic from Britain to the greater part of Armorica was, of course, a development contrary to the general trend. If some vestiges of Gaulish lingered on in these surroundings, both dialects would have been mutually comprehensible, but at any rate the British dialect rapidly took root and became predominant. There was one other reintroduction of Celtic to the Continent, though of much shorter duration. This involved a small migration of Britons who, while many of their compatriots were departing for Armorica, ventured even further afield, sailing across the Bay of Biscay and landing on the northern coast of Spain. These were following the path of earlier Christian missionaries who had set out from Britain, and seem to have included laity as well as clergy. They settled in Asturias and eastern Galicia, where their influence was sufficient to gain recognition at the Council of Lugo in AD 567 as a special new diocese called Bretoña. The Iberian Celtic language had, of course, disappeared some generations earlier, but British Celtic probably continued in use among the settlers for two centuries until they were fully absorbed into the Romance-speaking population of the region.

In the far west, the Celtic languages and cultures continued to thrive, but the stage was being set for the political configuration of western Europe as known to modern history.

Huge English gains

After two centuries of fighting and migrations, most of southern Britain had fallen to the Saxon kingdoms, with the exception of parts of the Pennines and Cumbria, Wales and the Dumnonian peninsula.

In the north, the forces of Aethelric, son of Ida and king of Bernicia, were also on the advance. Around the year AD 590 a warrior force was sent against them by a Gododdin king known as 'Mynyddog' ('highlander'), apparently the same person as Morgant. These – drawn from Picts as well as Britons – were defeated at Catterick, being wiped out almost to a man, after which the Bernicians prepared to invade the territory of the Gododdin themselves. When Aethelric's son Aethelfrith succeeded him and began a great push northwards, seizing Northumbria and East Lothian from the Britons, the Dál Riada king Aedán son of Gabhrán, recognised the approaching threat to his own kingdom.

Gathering a substantial army, and drawing in reinforcements from Ulster, he advanced against the invaders in AD 603 and attacked them at Degsastan (probably Dawston in Liddesdale). In the fighting, Aethelfrith's brother, Eanfrith, was slain by Mael Umhai, son of the Tara king from Ireland, but in the end Aethelfrith scored a resounding victory, and Aedán had to flee to his own kingdom with a remnant of his army.

Having overrun Northumbria, Aethelfrith turned west to threaten the strong Briton kingdom of Strathclyde, but he found progress slower in that direction. His greatest success, in fact, was gained in the mid-west of Britain, to which he directed his attention after the weakening of the Mercian kingdom, on his southern border, by internal strife. There, at Chester in or about the year AD 615 he defeated Selyf son of Cynan, king of Powys, in a battle which confirmed the isolation of the northern Britons from their compatriots in Wales. Before this battle, Aethelfrith ordered a large group of monks to be slaughtered because they had prayed for a British victory. The Christian mission to the Saxons, begun by St Augustine of Canterbury, was at that time taking root, but the Bernician king was still a pagan and was not endeared to the Christian religion of the Britons. The Venerable Bede, torn between revulsion at his slaughter of the monks and admiration for him as an Anglo-Saxon champion, described Aethelfrith as surpemely effective against the Britons: 'He made, through exterminating or subjugating the inhabitants, more of their lands tributary to the English or ready for settlement, than any of the leaders before him, or than any of the kings.'

Some years later, Aethelfrith himself was slain in a civil war among the northern Angles, and his enemy Edwin of Deira took command of both kingdoms, Bernicia and Deira. Edwin had converted to Christianity, and it was his ambition to unite all the Anglo-Saxons. He first overthrew the weakened Briton kingdom of Elfed (around modern Leeds) and drove out its king Ceredig. Then, having equipped a fleet, he advanced to the Irish Sea, seizing the Isle of Man for a while and ravaging north Wales. He besieged the king of Gwynedd, Cadwallon, in Ynys Lannog (Priestholm), a little island off Anglesey, but Cadwallon escaped to Ireland and Edwin was deflected from his campaign by an attack on Northumbria made by the Britons of Strathclyde. After some years, Cadwallon returned to Wales and astutely forged an alliance with the accomplished warrior Penda from the Middle Anglian kingdom of Mercia, and with combined forces they defeated and slew Edwin at Hatfield Chase (near Doncaster) in AD 633. Through this alliance,

Cadwallon managed to reopen land contact between the Britons of the north and those of Wales.

After Edwin's death, his kingdom of Deira devolved upon his cousin Osric, while a son of Aethelfrith, Eanfrith, returned from exile among the Dál Riada and Picts and retook the kingdom of Bernicia. Cadwallon ruled Northumbria for a year, ravaging and slaughtering the Anglo-Saxon settlers. In the following summer, he was besieged in a walled town (probably York) by Osric. Cadwallon made a sudden sortie from the town with all his forces, and Osric's army was cut to pieces and he himself killed. Eanfrith then went to Cadwallon to sue for peace, but he was rash enough to go with only twelve warriors as bodyguard and as a result he was seized and killed by the wily Welsh leader. Cadwallon's luck was running out, however. Towards the end of the year Eanfrith's brother Oswald, with a small army attacked his much larger force near Rowley Burn, south of Hexham. In the fighting, Cadwallon was slain and his army was routed.

New geography takes shape

Oswald himself was defeated and slain by Penda of Mercia eight years later, after which Penda – still a pagan – was the most powerful king in England. He had many Celtic allies, including the Gwynedd prince Cadafael, but in AD 654 he was slain in battle with another son of Aethelfrith, Oswiu.

This Oswiu controlled all the north of England, and he and his son and successor, Ecgfrith, took advantage of struggles between the Picts, the Irish of Dál Riada, and the Britons of Strathclyde to extend their dominion. Ecgfrith seized southern Pictish territory, and even gained acceptance as nominal overlord from the Britons of Strathclyde and the Irish of Argyll. In AD 684 he sent an army to Ireland to devastate the Uí Néill territory in the plain of Meath. His purpose in this latter venture may have been to deter the Irish kings from supporting the Argyll Irish, as he planned a new thrust into Scotland. In AD 685 he led an invasion force northwards into Pictish territory. Led by their able king Bruide, son of Beli, the Picts retreated before him, drawing him into a trap, and finally cut his army to pieces at a place called, in Irish, Dún Neachtain or, in English, Nechtansmere (now Forfar).

Ecgfrith was slain, and Bruide followed up his victory by re-taking the land as far as the Northumbrian border, while the Irish of

Argyll and the Britons of Strathclyde heaved a sigh of relief. The successor to Ecgfrith's kingdom in Northumbria was his half-brother Aldfrith, who had strong connections with Ireland. Aldfrith's mother was an Irish princess, Fíona, and he had been educated in the Columbine monastery of Iona, where he was known by the Irish name Flann Fíona. As king of Northumbria, once he had secured the boundaries, he did not pursue a policy of aggression against his neighbours, but devoted more energy to patronising learning. After his death in AD 705, however, his successors did not follow his example but returned to the old ways. The relative stability of Northumbria under Aldfrith's reign was not paralleled in the neighbouring kingdoms, where the struggles between Picts, Irish and Britons continued. Already much weakened by Anglo-Saxon pressure, the Britons were losing ground, and at the turn of the seventh and eighth centuries AD considerable groups of them took up service as mercenaries in the small wars between the various kings in Ireland.

The Pictish king Bruide died in AD 693, but his nation remained intact despite renewed attacks by the Angles of Northumbria. Various Pictish rulers intermarried with the Irish of Argyll, and in AD 731 an ambitious man with an Irish name, Oenghus son of Fearghus, succeeded to their kingship in a bloody civil war. He defeated the Dál Riada in AD 736 and again in AD 741, and then turned his attention to the Strathclyde Britons. In AD 750, however, the Britons inflicted a heavy defeat on his forces, his brother Talorcan being slain along with a large number of Pictish warriors. Six years later, Oenghus made an alliance with the Northumbrian leader Eadberht, and together they laid siege to the headquarters of the northern Britons, the rock bastion of Alt Clud. The siege failed, and Oenghus died five years later, with the subjection of Dál Riada as his one surviving achievement.

The regnal lists of Pictish kings show that for several generations the rulers of this people were heavily influenced by their neighbours the Dál Riada, the Strathclyde Britons, and even the Northumbrian Angles. To take one example, the great Bruide was the son of the Strathclyde king Beli. His mother was a Pictish princess, but her father had been the Angle Eanfrith, who had sojourned in Pictland as a young man and later became king of Northumbria. So Bruide was, in fact, a cousin to his deadly enemy Ecgfrith, whom he defeated at Nechtansmere. His claim to the Pictish kingship rested either on the fact that his mother was Pictish or that he was married to a Pictish wife.

Such a confused situation led Bede to claim a very distinctive system of royal succession for the Picts. Drawing on a fanciful Irish tradition, he claimed that the Picts had been latecomers from the east, and had been directed to the north of Britain by the Irish. 'Having no women with them, these Picts asked the Irish for wives, and they consented to it on the condition that, whenever a doubtful situation arose, they would choose a king from the female royal line rather than from the male royal line.' He goes on to say that 'this custom continues among the Picts to this day'.

This statement has usually been interpreted to imply some kind of matriarchy, but there are examples of Pictish kings succeeding their fathers in the office, though at one remove. The most likely explanation is that kings were chosen from an extended royal family and that female members of the family had a claim to the office, a claim which they expressed through their husbands. This may have been an ancient system among the inhabitants of Britain, even among the Celts, as appears from the situation in the first century AD among the Brigantes. In the case of the Picts of the eighth and ninth centuries AD, with continuous intermarriage among their leaders and princes of the Britons, Irish, and Angles, such a system tended to weaken their political identity.

Further south, the alliance between the Middle Angles of Mercia and the Welsh to their west, as evidenced by the campaigns of Penda and Cadwallon, did not long survive. The descendants of Penda converted to Christianity, but their ambition was not diminished and they upheld their position as the strongest and most influential of all the Anglo-Saxon kingdoms. The most powerful of their rulers was Offa, who succeeded to the kingship in AD 757. His authority was soon recognised throughout most of England, and his importance in international affairs was accepted by the Emperor Charlemagne. That Offa's ambitions extended to Wales are clear from a battle fought by him against the Welsh at Hereford in AD 760, a raid carried out by him into Dyfed in AD 778, and a further expedition into Wales in AD 784. Soon afterwards he commenced the building of a great *vallum* between his Mercian kingdom and Wales. This barrier, known as Clawdd Offa or Offa's Dyke, stretched for over 100km over uneven and even mountainous country, roughly defining the border which has since become traditional between England and Wales. Its objective was obviously to prevent Welsh raiding into his kingdom, but he did not allow himself to be limited by it, and indeed he launched another attack on Dyfed before his death in the year AD 796.

Destiny favoured strong leaders in the north also, where the ambition of Oenghus son of Fearghus, to unite the peoples of Scotland, was to be realised, but in a manner different to what he had intended. Aedh Fionn had ruled the Dál Riada as a subject-king of Oenghus, and in AD 768 he felt emboldened to throw off the Pictish yoke. Advancing on the stronghold of Fortriu (now Strathearn), he met and defeated the Pictish army there, after which he re-established the independence of Dál Riada. Following the death of Aedh Fionn in AD 778, there followed a confused period of shifting power between Dál Riada kings and Pictish kings, several of whom were blood relatives, until the two kingdoms were eventually united. This was done, not without some cynicism, by the Dál Riada king Cionnaedh son of Ailpín. When the Picts were preoccupied with fighting against the Norse invaders, Cionnaedh attacked them in the rear, causing the Pictish kingdom to buckle under pressure from both north and south. After much fighting, and probably also a migration eastwards by a large number of the Dál Riada, Cionnaedh assumed the kingship of all Scotland at the old Pictish royal centre of Scone in AD 842. After that the Pictish language and culture went into rapid decline, being replaced by the Irish.

The future political complexion of Britain was becoming more clearly defined. In the far south-west, the British kingdom of Dyvnaint (Dumnonii) was under serious threat. The river Avon in Somerset was the boundary between Wessex and Dyvnaint until AD 658, when the Britons were defeated by Cenwalh, king of Wessex, at Penselwood. The Britons fled from this battle westwards over the river Parrett, and in AD 682, Cenwalh's successor Centwine drove them beyond the river Taw, 'as far as the sea' in that northern part of the peninsula. In AD 710, near the river Tamar, yet another Wessex king, Ine, inflicted a major defeat on Gereint, king of Dyvnaint, pushing the boundary between Saxons and Britons further still to the west.

The year AD 722 saw some successes for the Britons, particularly a victory over the Saxons at the battle of Hehil, probably near the Camel estuary, but sporadic attacks by the Saxons continued. A prolonged campaign against Dyvnaint was begun in AD 815 by the powerful Wessex king, Ecgbert, who eight years later inflicted a crushing defeat on the Britons at Galford. In AD 838, caught between Norse raiders and Saxon pressure, the Britons decided to join with the former who were preparing a massive raid into Wessex. In a bloody battle fought at Hingston Down near Callington, the combined Norse and British force was routed, following on which the entire west country was subjugated by the Saxons.

Attacks from the North

Although their efforts had not succeeded, by enlisting Norse support the men of Dyvnaint showed political acumen. In fact, the Norse pressure on Britain and Ireland, as well as on adjacent parts of the European land-mass, represented a new and significant development.

One effect of the Norse raiding was that some respite was gained by the Celtic peoples from further English expansion for the next few generations. The raids were followed by settlements, and by the latter ninth century AD there were Norse kingdoms in many places. Most of the north of England was taken over, areas further south were threatened, and even the kingdom of Wessex was ravaged. The continuous, and often confused, struggles between the Celts and the Norsemen on the one hand, and the English and the Norsemen on the other, brought various strong leaders to the fore. The result was a tendency towards internal cohesion among the various peoples, which had long-term consequences in their respective political cultures.

The influence of Alfred of Wessex on subsequent English tradition is best known, but the Celts had comparable figures. Although Cionnaedh son of Ailpín, had benefited indirectly from Norse attacks on Scotland, he proved quite effective at counteracting their expansion southwards into the heart of Scotland, and one of the main reasons for the continuance of his united kingdom was the perceived need for a strong leader who would resist such incursions. His successors as Scottish kings were harder pressed to stave off the incursions, and generally survived by standing idly by or even abetting the Norse attacks. Thus the Pictish stronghold of Fortriu was ravaged in AD 865, and the Briton stronghold of Dumbarton was besieged and destroyed in AD 870. Seven years later, the Scots themselves suffered several defeats at the hands of the Norsemen, who now controlled much of the north of Scotland as well as the Hebrides and the Isle of Man. In time, indeed, a new compound name came to be used for the inhabitants of the Hebrides and the Isle of Man – this was Gall-Ghaeil (an Irish term denoting mixed foreigners and Irish), and among them the Scottish and Manx dialects of Gaelic (i.e. Irish) gradually came to pre-dominate over the Norse language.

The raiders cum settlers were less successful in Wales, where the accession to power in Gwynedd of Rhodri Mawr in AD 844 had dramatic consequences. Anglesey was vital for its cornfields, which supplied grain to most of north Wales, and therefore was of surpreme importance to Rhodri. In or about AD 854, a new group of Norsemen ravaged that area, and to counter this Rhodri built a fleet, with which he defeated the raiders in AD 856 and slew their leader, Holm. Fighting continued, however, and in AD 877 he suffered such setbacks that he had to take refuge in Ireland. He returned to Wales the following year, in an attempt to restore his own kingdom which had been invaded by the English of Mercia, but was slain in battle soon afterwards. In AD 881, his son Anarawd avenged his death by defeating the Mercian army with great slaughter at Cymryd, at the mouth of the river Conway. Although final success eluded him, his career had done much to give confidence to the Welsh and, although rivalry between local **rulers** continued, neither Norsemen nor Saxons could get a proper foothold in Wales for a long time afterwards.

Similar pressure was long being applied on the Continent to the **Bretons**. Throughout the seventh century AD, threats by Frankish rulers to invade the kingdoms of Bro Weroch and Domnonia bore no fruit, and finally in AD 753 the Frankish king, Pépin the Short, marched an army into Brittany and imposed tribute on them. Due to default in the payment of this tribute, however, Pépin's famous son Charlemagne was constrained to send several expeditions against the Bretons, and the continued fighting culminated in a great revolt in AD 818. This was quelled by Louis the Pious and its leader Morvan slain, and a further rebellion led by Wiomarc'h was put down and he too slain in AD 825. Louis the Pious later decided that it would be more politic to appoint a Breton leader loyal to him, and so he set up a chieftain, Nominoë, as duke at Vannes. The arrangement worked for about ten years, but when Louis died in AD 840 Nominoë vacillated in his loyalty. In AD 842, he refused to support Charles the Bald as overlord of Brittany, opting instead for Charles' brother, the Emperor Lothair.

Charles marched against him in AD 845, but after initial successes for Nominoë a treaty was signed which allowed the Breton leader virtual independence. Soon Nominoë had raided Anjou and seized Rennes and Nantes, but he died in AD 851. Charles now sent an army against Nominoë's son Erispoë, but the heir proved as capable as the father and soon after Charles was compelled to cede Rennes and Nantes and even some territory to the south of the Loire to the Bretons. Erispoë was recognised as king of Brittany, but his cousin Salomon plotted against him with the support of Charles the Bald. Norse raids were devastating the coast, and when Erispoë planned an alliance with Charles, Salomon felt outmanoeuvred and rebelled. Erispoë took refuge in a church, but was slain there by his cousin, who then assumed the kingship. Salomon astutely made use of the Norse against Charles, and in AD 867 he forced Charles to concede the territories of Cotentin and Avranches to him. The ambitious Breton king then made an alliance with Charles against the Norsemen, but he had made many enemies and was assassinated in AD 874.

He was succeeded by the leaders of the conspiracy against him – his son-in-law Pascwethen, count of Bro Weroch, and Erispoë's son-in-law Gourvand, count of Rennes. Pascwethen soon enlisted Norse help, but Gourvand successfully defended Rennes against them. The rivalry ended with the deaths of these two nobles, who were succeeded by Gourvand's son Judicaël and Pascwethen's brother Alain, who combined against the Norsemen. Judicaël fell in battle against the invaders, and Alain scored a great victory over them at Questembert in AD 890. This was followed by another victory over the Norsemen by Judicaël's son Bérenger, but the death of Alain in AD 907 opened the way to renewed pillaging and seizure of land by the Norse, which continued for almost three decades.

In Wales, the grandson of Rhodri Mawr, called Hywel Dda ('Hywel the Good'), ruled Seisyllwg in the south from AD 910 or there-abouts and soon after became king of Powys. By a strategic acceptance of the overlordship of the English king, Edward the Elder, in AD 918, he gained security and gradually increased his territory. Edward also became deeply involved in Scotland where – with the conquest of the Picts and the gradual assimilation of the Norsemen – Gaelic power had continued to spread. The Britons of Strathclyde managed to preserve their independence, and towards the end of the ninth century AD even extended their territory southwards to encompass part of Cumberland. The Scottish Gaels, too, under their king, Causaintín III, took some terri-tory in Lothian, leading to a potential clash with Edward. The situation was diffused by a token submission of both Causaintín and the Strathclyde king Dyfnwal to Edward in AD 925.

Edward's son and successor, Athelstan, demanded and got a renewal of the submission two years later, after which he concentrated his efforts on securing the submission of the Welsh leaders. He gained this at Hereford in AD 931, at which Hywel Dda joined with the majority of Welsh leaders to reaffirm his loyalty. Athelstan was considered the most ambitious and ruthless English king yet, and this policy of Hywel was not entirely popular in Wales. A contemporary Welsh poet, indeed, composed an influential work urging its rejection, and calling on Welshmen to join forces with the other Britons, with Gaels, and even with Norsemen, to drive the English back across the North Sea. Hywel, however, was unmoved, and after his cousin Idwal Foel, king of Gwynedd, was slain in battle by the English in AD 942, he moved in and seized that kingdom also. He could then claim to be 'by the grace of God king of all Wales', and he set about bringing a consistent and largely uniform social system in the different areas. Later tradition claimed that Hywel summoned a representative assembly in Y Ty Gwyn (Whitland in Carmarthenshire), at which each cantref (i.e. district) was represented by six men, and that traditional laws were sifted and codified there.

The territory of Dyvnaint (Devon) had been heavily settled by the Saxons of Wessex, and resentment simmered among the native population. Athelstan was well aware of this, and when – after the submission of the Welsh leaders in AD 931 – news reached him of trouble around Exeter, he lost no time in moving south. The Britons, who still made up half the population in that vicinity, had revolted, and Athelstan had sufficient forces to quell any such disturbance. He accordingly expelled the Britons from that area, forcing them to retire behind the river Tamar. Thus the people of Dyvnaint, descendants of the ancient Dumnonii, were being pushed into the far west, where a group of Cornovii had long resided. That area was known from the name of the Cornovii as Kernew, and the English soon occupied it also, calling it Cornwall and settling large numbers of farmers there.

Unease in Scotland at the growing power of Athelstan and at his manner of stressing his overlordship led to renewed hostilities there. In AD 934 Athelstan organised a massive punitive raid on land and sea against the borders of the territory of King Causaintín. The Scots and Britons backed away from conflict, but felt themselves pushed far enough in AD 937 to join an invasion force led by the Norse king of Dublin, Olaf Kvaran. In prolonged fighting in the neighbourhood of Brunanburh (near the Solway), the allied forces were defeated by Athelstan. One result of this defeat was that Strathclyde came under direct English control. Eager to gain Scottish support in his campaign against the Norse kingdom of York, the next English king, Edmund, decided in AD 946 to hand this kingdom over to the Scots, but in AD 971 the Britons of Strathclyde slew the Scots King Cuiléan and regained their independence.

Athelstan had proved himself a deadly enemy to the Celts of Britain, but his influence in Brittany was more benign. There the Norsemen had gained the upper hand, but a grandson of the famous Alain, called Alain Barbetorte, was reared and encouraged by Athelstan at his English court. Alain landed at Dol in AD 936 at the head of a small army of Breton exiles. He won several battles against the Norse, at Dol, St-Brieuc, Plourivo, and Leon; and his wily tactics were so celebrated in Breton tradition that he was referred to as Alan al Louarn ('Alain the Fox'). His most significant victory was at Nantes, after which the Norsemen were cleared from their strong settlements on the Loire. In AD 939 he scored a final great victory over them at Trans, near Cancale. Alain was a close friend of the Frankish king Louis IV, and until his death in AD 952 peace reigned between their two peoples. After this, the predominant position in Brittany reverted to the counts of Rennes, who for well over a century managed to preserve their independence.

In Ireland, too, the Norsemen had initially made many gains. One of their leaders, Turgesius, seized the prestigious centres of Armagh in the north and Clonmacnoise in the mid-west, where his wife set herself up as a pagan priestess on the altar of the celebrated Christian monastery. In AD 845, however, the Uí Néill king Mael Seachnaill seized him and drowned him in the river Shannon. Mael Seachnaill later became high-king (in Irish *ard-rí*, meaning overlord of all the country) and his successor in that office Aedh Fionnliath inflicted a series of crushing defeats on the Norsemen. The latter still held some strong seaports, however, and in AD 919 their king of Dublin, Sigtrygg, defeated and slew the son of Aedh Fionnliath, the high-king Niall Glúndubh, in battle near that city.

The following generations saw shifting alliances between the Norsemen and various Irish septs, but the conquest of further territory by the invaders was finally stopped by Brian Bóraimhe. This celebrated leader belonged to a hitherto unimportant sept called Dál gCais in the present County Clare. By his ambition and ability he took the kingship of Munster from the time-honoured Eoghanacht septs, and in AD 1002 he forced the abdication in his favour of the Uí Néill high-king Mael Seachnaill II. In AD 1014, at Clontarf, just to the north of Dublin, he inflicted a stunning defeat on a Norse force drawn from strongholds in the Orkneys, Caithness, Hebrides and Isle of Man. Unfortunately for the prospect of stability in Ireland, Brian himself was killed in the fighting.

After the death of the Welsh King, Hywel Dda, in AD 950, fighting had broken out again between the rival dynasties in that country, and the Norse raids were renewed and intensified all around the coast. Wales remained a virtual bloodbath for almost a century until Gruffudd, son of Llywelyn, won memorable victories against Norsemen, Mercians and his Welsh rivals from AD 1039 to AD 1055. In AD 1063, however, the

Wessex earl Harold Godwinson (later king of England) savaged Wales with two armies. Gruffudd made a strategic retreat into Snowdonia, but Harold put the price of 300 cattle on Gruffudd's head, which led some of the followers of the great Welsh King to behead 'the man deemed invincible'.

A further alliance between the Scottish Gaels and the Britons of Strathclyde against the English was instanced by the battle of Carham in AD 1016, when Mael Coluim II of the Scots and Owain Foel of the Britons defeated the forces of Uhtred, earl of Northumbria. On the death of Owain two years later, Mael Coluim used the opportunity to have his grandson Donnchadh (known in English as Duncan) appointed as king of Strathclyde. When Donnchadh became king of the Scots as well in AD 1034, the kingdom of Strathclyde was finally at an end, and the British or 'Welsh' language is unlikely to have survived in that northern area for more than a few further generations. By that time, Celtic as a spoken language had died out in all other parts of England, with the notable exception of Cornwall.

By the eleventh century AD, the spectre of a Norse takeover had subsided, but it would return again in the form of the Norsemen who had settled in the north of France and had become known as Normans. When William the Conqueror took England from the Saxons and extended his kingdom in northern France, the stage was set for Norman takeover of all the remaining Celtic lands. After a few centuries of dominance, the Normans themselves succumbed to the resurgent English in Britain and Ireland and to the resurgent French on the Continent, and the subsequent history of the Celtic peoples has focused upon attempts to break free from the control of these two great powers. That history is of course fully documented in accounts of the separate countries.

At the time of the conquest by the Normans of the remaining Celtic lands, the number of people speaking one or other of the Celtic languages would have numbered about two million. This was the highest since the end of the Roman Empire; and the continuing population growth meant that, at its peak in the early nineteenth century, there were over six million speakers of Celtic. The figure, however, represented not much more than a half of the inhabitants of these countries, and the percentage ratio has been in marked decline since then. Today six Celtic languages survive – the Gaelic group comprising Irish, Scots Gaelic and Manx, and the Britonic group comprising Welsh, Breton and Cornish. Four of these are living languages, with unbroken traditions and spoken by considerable numbers of people. The other two ceased to be spoken by actual communities – Cornish in the seventeenth century and Manx in the early twentieth century – but they can be heard as revived languages.

The Celtic tongues remain under threat from commercial and political forces external to them, but there are still well over a million surviving speakers today. The social status of the languages is improving, and there is a growing recognition of their rich cultural heritages. Modern Celts are becoming increasingly aware that they are heirs to one of the major traditions of Europe.

SOURCES AND STUDIES

[As in our text, personal names and placenames are given in the Latin or simplified forms which are usual in English. Where the source is the only known surviving work of a Greek or Latin author, the author's name only is given. In the case of anonymous authors, the standard title of the source is given. References to these texts are based on the standard system in use, e.g. Pliny the Elder 3.6-37, 112-148 indicates main division 3 of that author's work, subdivisions 6 to 37 and 112 to 148. Similarly, Justin 25.2.8-11 indicates division 25 of that author's work, subdivision 2, sub-subdivisions 8 to 11. Alternative numbering systems, where relevant, are given within brackets. For early sources in Celtic languages, the names of modern editors or the titles of modern publications are given. All works of modern scholarship can be identified by the name of the author or authors in the Bibliography]

General lists of the Celtic peoples, and their distribution at various times between 2nd century BC and 2nd century AD, are found in:-

Pliny the Elder, *Naturalis Historiae*, 3.6-37, 112-148 & 4.102-119 & 5.146;

Strabo, *Geographicon*, 3.1-5.1 & 7.1-5 & 12.5;

Julius Caesar, *De Bello Gallico*, 1-7;

Ptolemy, *Geographica Hyphagasis*, 2.2-15 & 3.1, 5-7 & 5.4 & 8.3-8, 17.

Apart from these general references, where theories are advanced concerning the dispositions and fortunes of specific Celtic groups, relevant sources are given below.

Chapter 1

For peoples of ancient Europe, see Dottin (1916).

For tumuli and urn-burials, see Filip, 19-20, 31-50; D. Ellis Evans in *Bulletin of the Board of Celtic Studies 29* (1982), 234; Cunliffe (1997), 42-4, 52-6; Eluère, 13-49; M.J. Green in Price ed, 10-13.

For early Celtic language, see A. Tovar in Schmidt ed, 49-51, 56-61; D. Ellis Evans in *Proceedings of the British Academy 65* (1979), 506-8, 528-36 & in Green (1996), 8-20; H. Wagner in *Transactions of the Philosophical Society* (1969), 202-50; Dottin (1918), 22-35; Lambert, 14-17.

Word 'Celt': Hieronymus of Cardia, from Pausanius 1.3.5; Strabo 4.1.14; Dionysius of Halicarnassus 14.1.3. See Walde/Pokorny, *1*, 436-40; Falk/Torp, 82-4; Holder, *1*, 888-958.

For hill-forts, see Filip, 36-40; Cunliffe (1997), 44, 61-4.

Wine: Diodorus Siculus 5.26.3. See Tierney, 248-9.

For metals, see Filip, 50-8.

For 'Hallstatt' culture, see Filip, 28-47; James, 18-27; Twist, 28-43.

For early Celtic expansion, see Dinan, 10-13, 28-31; Filip, 50-61. See also Hubert (a), 131-88; L. Weisgerber in *Bericht der Römish-Germanischen Kommission 20* (1931), 168-76; Whatmough, 9-85; Birkhan, 85-139.

Burial at Vix: Filip, 39-40.

For origin and archaeology of Cubi, see Hubert (b), 134; S. Delabesse / J. Troadec in Moscati et al, 120; Cunliffe (1997), 65.

For origin of Arverni and other tribes in southern Gaul, see Hubert (a), 253-8 & (b), 134-7; Jullian (1963), 45-51.

For pre-Celtic Indo-Europeans in Spain, see Tovar (1961), 91-111; Savory, 227-38.

Celtic word for iron: Pokorny, 300; Walde/Pokorny, *1*, 4; T.F. O'Rahilly in *Ériu 13* (1942), 119-21; E. Benveniste in *Celtica 3* (1956), 279-83.

For 'La Tène' culture, see Filip, 47-59; James, 29-31; Twist, 44-7.

For Celtic art, see Megaw/Megaw; Duval/Hawkes; Duval/Kruta (1982).

For Celtic wagons and chariots, see Cunliffe (1997), 64-6, 74-5, 99-105 and in Chadwick (1997), 30-2, 42-3.

For kw becoming p among the La Tène Celts, see E. Mac White in *Zeitschrift für celtische Philologie 25* (1956), 12-19; A. Tovar in Schmidt (a) ed, 51-4; D. Ellis Evans in *Proceedings of the British Academy 65* (1979), 516-7; K.H. Schmidt in Neumann/Untermann, 30-5; McCone, 67-8; B. Cunliffe in Chadwick (1997), 44.

For conflict between 'Hallstattian' and 'La Tène' Celts, see Filip, 47-8; M.E. Mariën in Hawkes Festschrift, 214; James, 28-30; Cunliffe (1997), 63-4.

Belovesus and Segovesus: Livy 5.34; Justin 24. See Arbois de Jubainville (1904), 142-4, 163; Dottin (1916), 206.

Migration as a ritual act: Justin 24.4.1-3. See Hubert (b), 119-20; W. Dehn in Duval/Kruta, 15-19.

Lepontii: Pliny the Elder 3.20 (134); cf. Polybius 2.15. See Wissowa et al, Series 1, *12*, 2067-8 ['Lepontii']. For their inscriptions, see Lejeune; Lambert, 20-1; Mallory/Adams, 97, 233-4.

For Senones, Parisii, Sequani and Helvetii, see Hubert (b), 124-5, 132-5.

For partial survival of kw phoneme in northern Gaul, see Schmidt (a), 17.

For Celts in Bohemia, see P. Roualet, A. Haffner, J. Michálek in Moscati et al, 147-54, 155-62, 186-7; Cunliffe (1997), 66-7.

For the terms Galli, Galatae, see Holder, *1*, 1638-1919; E. Zupitza in *Zeitschrift für celtische Philologie 4* (1903), 1-22; Hubert (a), 21-3; Walde/Pokorny, *1*, 539-40, 641; Mallory/Adams, 3; Fleuriot, 56-7; Birkhan, 32-51.

For La Tène Celts on Moselle and Marne, see Cunliffe (1997), 63-5 and in Chadwick (1997), 41-5.

For Belgae, see Wissowa et al, Series 1, *2*, 203-7; C.F.C. Hawkes / G.C. Dunning in *Archaeological Journal 87* (1930-1), 150-335; Hawkes in *Antiquity 42* (1968), 6-16; Whatmough, 668-71; M.E. Mariën in Hawkes Festschrift, 213-41; Wightman (1985), 1-25; Brunaux, 84-5; O. Büschenschütz, C. Wells in Green (1996), 557-63, 603-9.

For origins of Mediomatrici, Treveri, etc, see Wightman (1970), 17-24.

For origin of Aedui, Lingones, etc, see Hubert (b),), 123, 131-2, 134-6.

Iron-mines in Cubi territory: Caesar, *De Bello Gallico*, 7.22.

Ambicatus: Livy 5.34.

For the word 'Biturix', see C.-J. Guyonvarc'h in *Ogam* 13 (1961), 137-42.

For ritual truth of kings, see Dillon, 16-18; Ó hÓgáin (1999), 153-6.

For early Celts in the Iberian Peninsula, see Arbois de Jubainville (1904), 91-110; Bosch-Gimpera; W. Schüle, P. Kalb in Tovar et al, 197-223; Tovar (1961), 56, 77-9, 91; E. Sangmeister in *Madrider Mitteilungen 1* (1960), 89-94; Savory, 239-52; J. de Hoz in MacLennan, 191-207 & in *Zeitschrift für celtische Philologie 45* (1992), 1-19; M. Almagro-Gorbea in Almagro-Gorbea/Zapatero, 121-74; Lenerz-de Wilde (1991) & in Green (1996), 533-47; Cunliffe (1997), 133-41; Birkan, 151-7.

Alcibiades' proposal: Thucydides 6.90.3.

Population explosion: Justin 24.4.1. See Arbois de Jubainville (1902), 220-30, 248.

Himilco: Version by Avienus, *Periplus Massiliensis* - edited in Dinan, 9-27. See also Powell, 21-2; Rankin, 2-8; Tierney, 193.

Ierne, Albion: Avienus, *Periplus Massiliensis*, 108-112, 745-50. See O'Rahilly, 40-2, 385-7; J. Pokorny in Ua Riain, 237-43; Rankin, 2-8; Powell, 21-4; Tierney, 195-6.

For the derivation of 'Albion', see Holder, *1*, 83-5; Wissowa et al, Series 1, *3*, 859-60 ['Britannia']; Rivet/Smith, 39, 247-8.

For the derivation of 'Ierne', see T.F. O'Rahilly in *Ériu 14* (1946), 7-28.

For 'Pritani', see Arbois de Jubainville (1904), 25, 66-7; K. Jackson in Wainwright ed, 158.

Greek interpretation of Ireland as 'sacred isle': Avienus, *Periplus Massiliensis*, 108-9.

For Celts in Britain, see Rivet (1964), 33-59; Birkhan, 386-428.

For 'Eburovices', 'Quariates', see C.-J. Guyonvarc'h in *Ogam 11* (1959), 39-42 and *16*, 428-9.

Fourth-century BC Yorkshire burials: Cunliffe (1991), 77-9, 193-4, 499-504 and (1997), 161-2, 209.

For migrations to Ireland, see E. Mac White in *Zeitschrift für celtische Philologie 25* (1956), 20-4; J. Pokorny in *Celtica 5* (1960), 229-40; F. Mitchell, 120-1, 144-8; Raftery, 26-63; Ó hÓgáin (1999), 36-42.

Hecataeus re Narbon and Nyrax (fragments): Dinan, 8-9. But cf. Duval, 176-7.

Danube: Herodotus 2.33 & 4.49.

For Celtic organisation and society, see Brunaux, 2-8, 49-56.

Descriptions of Celts: Aeschylus - see Dinan, 28-9; Hellanicus - see Dinan, 28-9; Ephorus - see Dinan, 44-5 and Tierney, 270; Aristotle, *Politica* 2.9.7 & 4.17.2; Posidonius in Diodorus 5.32.7; Plato, *Leges* 1.637.

Lack of fear of earthquakes: Aristotle, *Ethica Nicomachea* 3.7.7. See also Herodotus 1.27.30; Livy 40.58.

Celts and aquatic disaster: Strabo 7.2,1; Pseudo-Aristotle, *Ethica Eudemia* 3.1.25; Stobaeus,

Florilegium, 3.7.39; Ammianus Marcellinus 15.9. See also Duval, 189, 193, 307.

Fondness for war: Xenophon, *Hellenica VII*, 1.20, 31; Strabo 4.4.2 (195).

Appearance and clothing: Diodorus 5.28, 30-1; Strabo 4.4.2; Dio Cassius 7.3; Caesar, *De Bello Gallico* 2.30; Dionysius of Halicarnassus 14.12. For archaeological evidence of Celtic dress, see Filip, 34.

Virgil reference: *Aeneidos*, 8.658-60.

Eating and drinking: Athenaeus 4.36, 40 (151-2, 154); Diodorus 5.26, 28.

Duelling and fighting: Athenaeus 4.40 (154); Silius Italicus 16.537; Strabo 3.4.18; Plutarch, *Sertorios*, 14.4; Valerius Maximus 2.6.11.

Carrion-crows: Silius Italicus 3.340-3; Aelianus, *Natura Animali* 10.22. See also note to Chapter 2 on battle-raveness.

Social disposition: Caesar, *De Bello Gallico*, 6.23.9 & 6.11.2-5; Strabo 6.4.2.

Selection of war-leader: Strabo 4.4.1.

Brigandage: Caesar, *op cit*, 6.23.5-9. For young men's societies in European antiquity, see Wikander. This Celtic tradition survived in Ireland, where in early Christian times it was known as *fianas*.

Pytheas re sun: in Geminius, *Elementorum Astronomiae* V.22. Cf. also Strabo 2.1.18.

Otherworld island: Plutarch, *Moralia*, 419, 941. See Graves 2, 132-5, 140-1; Ó hÓgáin (1999), 55-9.

Timaeus reference: in Diodorus 4.56.

Timagenes references: Ammianus 15.9.4, 8.

For Celts as dominant class among indigenous peoples, see Hubert (a), 27-32.

Artemidorus' reference to island: cited in Strabo 4.4.6.

Island in Loire: Strabo 4.4.6.

Senae: Pomponius Mela, *De Chorographia*, 3.48. For the river in Ireland, see O'Rahilly, 4-5.

Druids: Strabo, 4.4.4; Diodorus 5.31. For other Classical references to the druids, see Kendrick, 73-106, 212-221. See also Walde/Pokorny, 1, 293-4, 804-6; Piggott, 20-75; Le Rouz/Guyonvarc'h, 125-216; M.J. Enright in Ní Chatháin/Richter, 219-27.

Druidesses: Tacitus, *Historiae*, 4.61, 65 & 5.22, 24 & *Germania*, 8; Dio Cassius 67.12.5; Lampridius, *Severus Alexander* [in *Historia Augusta*], 60; Vopiscus, *Aurelianus*, 44 & *Numerianus*, 14 [in *Historia Augusta*]. See Chadwick, 78-82.

For goddesses, see Holder, *1*, 1239, 1273-4 and *2*, 468-70; Dinan, 62-3; Green (1986), 72-102; Vries; Olmsted (1994).

For river and well worship, see MacCulloch, 181-97; Green (1986), 138-66 & (1995), 89-116; Brunaux, 89-97.

For gods, see Caesar, op cit, 6.18.1. See also Walde/Pokorny, *1*, 772-3; Eliade 7, 198-200; E.

Windisch in *Irische Texte 1*, 463; C.-J. Guyonvarc'h in *Ogam 11* (1959), 284-5 and *12*, 49; Green (1986); Vries; Olmsted (1994).

Foundation of Marseilles: Justin 43.3-5.

Ritual story of Marseilles: Athenaeus 13.36 (576 - citing Aristotle); also in Justin 43.3. See Zwicker (1934), 2-3, 95; Koch/Carey, 32-3.

Influence of Marseilles on Celts: Justin 43.4.1.

Sacred groves: Pliny the Elder 16.44(107); Lucan, *Pharsalia*, 1.450-8; Dio Cassius 62.6. See Chadwick (1966), 13-4; C.-J. Guyonvarc'h in *Ogam 12* (1960), 188-93; Piggott, 54-7; Le Roux/Guyonvarc'h, 217-31; Brunaux, 7-41, 116-9.

Worship of oak: Maximus of Tyre, 2.8.

For tree worship in general among Celts, see MacCulloch, 198-207; Ó hÓgáin (1990), 77, 178 & (1999), 70-1, 228.

Nicander's testimony: Tertullian, *De Anima*, 57.10.

Druidic teaching on afterlife: Strabo 4.4.4; Pomponius Mela, *De Chorographia*, 3.19; Valerius Maximus 2.6.10; Caesar, *De Bello Gallico*, 6.14; Diodorus 5.28.

Praise-poets: Athenaeus 6.49 (246); Diodorus 5.31. See also Dottin (1915), 146-9; D. Ward in *Journal of Indo-European Studies 1* (1973), 127-44; Ó hÓgáin (1990), 364-9.

Chapter 2
Wine: Livy, 5.33; Pliny the Elder 12.1(5) & 14.13-14(87-8) & 17.35(211). See Cunliffe (1997), 69.

Clusium story: Livy 5.33; Dionysius of Halicarnassus 1.41 & 13.10-11; Dio Cassius 7.1-4.

Invasions of Italy: Livy 5.33-35; Polybius 2.17-18; Diodorus 14.113.1-7; Appian, *Celtica*, 2 (fragment). See O.-H. Frey in Green (1996), 515-8.

Catumandus' dream: Justin 43.5.

For Insubres settlement, see Cunliffe (1997), 70-2; for their name, see Belloguet, 405.

For Salluvii, Libui, and other intruders, see Hubert (b), 18-19.

Capture of Melpum: Pliny the Elder 3.17(125).

Native peoples in Apennines: Polybius 2.16.

Description of Celtic intruders: Polybius 2.17. See O.-H. Frey in Green (1996), 519-32.

Sack of Rome: Polybius 2.18; Livy 5.35-39 [placing these events some years earlier, in 390 BC]; Dio Cassius 7.1-7; Florus 1.7 (1.13); Dionysus of Halicarnassus 13.7-9, 12; Diodorus 14.114-7; Appian, *Celtica*, 2-3 (fragments).

Celtic drunkenness: Dio Cassius (Zonaras) 7.23.

For Veneti, see Wissowa et al, Series 2, *8A*, 705-84; Arbois de Jubainville (1904), 118- 20; Mallory/Adams, 620-1.

Story of Camillus and Celts: Livy 5.49; Plutarch, Camillos, 29; Dionysus of Halicarnassus 13.6 & 14.9; Frontinus, *Strategematon*, 2.6.1 & 3.13.1; Appian, *Celtica*, 1.1 & 4-9 (fragments). For the unhistorical nature of these accounts, see Dumézil, 54-61, 112-8.

Accounts of other early wars with Romans: Livy 6.42 & 7.1-15, 22-26; Florus 1.7 (1.13); Dionysius of Halicarnassus 13.6 & 14.8-10 & 15.1; Dio Cassius 7.24; Diodorus 14.5-7; Appian, *Celtica*, 1.1-2 (fragment); Frontinus, *Strategematon*, 2.4.5. For the dubious nature of these accounts, see Arbois de Jubainville (1904), 148-9.

The Gallica road: Frontinus, *Strategematon*, 2.6.1.

Manlius Torquatus: Livy 7.9-10; Dio Cassius (Zonaras) 7.24.

Marcus Valerius: Livy 7.26; Dio Cassius (Zonaras) 7.25; Dionysius of Halicarnassus 15.1; Appian, *Celtica*, 10 (fragment).

Single combat before battle: Diodorus 5.29. See also Jackson (1964), 30-1.

For battle-raveness, see W .M. Hennessy in *Revue Celtique 1* (1870), 32-5; Ross, 282-5, 313-8; Ó hÓgáin (1990), 307-9, 439. See also note to Chapter 1 re carrion-crows.

For Irish references to withdrawing after death of leader, see Jackson (1938), 73; Knott, 45-6; Binchy, 17.

War of 299-297 BC: Polybius 2.19.

War of 296-283 BC: Livy 10.16-30; Polybius 2.19-20; Frontinus, *Strategematon*, 1.8.3 & 2.1.8; Appian, *Celtica*, 11 (fragment).

Slaughter of Senones: Dionysus of Halicarnassus 19.13; Appian, *Celtica*, 11 (fragment).

Chapter 3
Augury from birds: Justin 24.4.

Celtic tribes in eastern Europe: Strabo 7. 2; Hecataeus (fragment) - Dinan, 8-9. See also Arbois de Jubainville (1904), 123-30; Hubert (b), 57-66; Heavey, 2-4; Szabó, 10-28; Mócsy, 2-7; Rankin,14-20.

Wars against Illyrians and Pannonians: Polyaenus 7.42; Justin 24.4 & 32.3; Diodorus 22.9, 18; Pausanius 10.23.

Illyrians tricked: Theopompus (fragment) - see Dinan, 46-9; Athenaeus 10.60.

Philip's assassination: Diodorus 16.94; Justin 9.6.

Celtic ambassadors to Alexander: Strabo 7.3.8; Arrian, *Anabasis*, I.4.6 & 7.15.4; Diodorus 17.113.2. See also Dinan, 88-93; Hubert (b), 33-5.

Molistomos and Cassander: Appian, *Illyrica*, 4; Diodorus 20.19. See Wissowa et al, Series 1, 2, 2593 ['Autariatai']; Hubert (b), 35, 38.

Cambaules: Pausanius 10.19.

For names of Boii and Volcae, see Lambert, 34-5, 44, 58.

Kings buy peace from Celts: Justin 24.4, apparently quoting Hieronymus of Cardia, who lived in the fourth-third century BC - see Dinan, 92-3, 132-3.

Ptolemaeus Ceraunus: Justin 24.4-5; Pausanius 1.16 & 10.19; Polybius 9.35; Diodorus 22.3-4; Eusebius of Caesarea, *Chronicoi Canones*, 1 [*Asianorum et Syrorum reges*, 7]. See also Lemprière, 571, 615-6.

For pseudonym 'Thunderbolt', see Holder, *1*, 374-84; O'Rahilly (1946), 43-71.

Sosthenes: Justin 24.5-6; Eusebius of Caesarea, *Chronicoi Canones*, 1.236.

Identity of Brennos: Strabo V.1.12-3 states he 'is said by some to have been a Prausan, but neither am I able to state in regard to the Prausans where on earth they lived formerly'. Callimachus, *Galatea*, refers to Brennos leading his army from 'the western sea' to attack Greece. See also Holder, *1*, 520-4; C.-J. Guyonvarc'h in *Ogam 19* (1967), 268.

Brennos' trick to instill confidence: Polyaenus, *Strategematon*, 7.35, 45.

Great raid on Macedonia and Greece and failed attack on Delphi: Polybius 2.20; Pausanius 1.4 & 10.19-23; Justin 24.4-8 & 26.2.6; Livy 38.16; Memnon, **14**; Diodorus 22.8-9; Dio Cassius 7.3; Cicero, *De Divinatione* 1.37. See Heavey, 6-21; Ellis (1997), 76-90.

'Trimarcisia': Pausanius 10.19. See also Livy 44.26.3-4.

Suicide of Brennos and succession of Acichorios: Pausanius 10.23; Justin 24.8.11; Diodorus 22.9.2-3. See Dinan, 130-1.

Soteria: Diodorus 22.3-5; Justin 24.4; Pausanius 1.4 & 10.5-13. See Rankin, 97-100; Cunliffe (1997), 82.

Celts in Thrace: Polybius 4.46; Justin 32.3.6; Trogus Pompeius cited in 'prologue' to Justin 25; Livy 38.16; Stephen of Byzantium s.v. 'Tylis'. See Wissowa et al, Series 2, *6*, 433-5; Pârvan, 110-5; Hubert (b), 42-61; Danov, 368-75 and in *Studia Celtica 10-11* (1975-6), 29-39; Hoddinott, 62-3; O.H. Frey / M. Szabó in Moscati, 478-84; S. Mitchell, *1*, 13-4.

Tribute from Byzantines: Polybius 4.46; Athenaeus 6.23-5 (233-4). See Rankin, 188.

For ancient references to Boii, Volcae, and other Celtic tribes in the east, see the relevant entries in Wissowa et al and in Holder. See also Filip, 61-74; Whatmough, 1156-62, 1214.

For Boii and Volcae power in the east, see Alföldy, 39; Mócsy, 60-3.

For Celtic influence in southern Poland, see Wozniak.

For Celts towards the Black Sea, see Arbois de Jubainville (1904), 166; Pârvan, 112-3, 110-5; Hubert (b), 44-5; Michael Treister in *Antiquity 67* (1993), 789-804; M.B. Shchukin in *Oxford Journal of Archaeology 14* (1995), 201-27; Ellis (1997), 59-60.

Attack on Olbia: Dittenberger (1915-24), *1*, 737-43 [no 495].

Sea of Azov, Plutarch, *Marios*, 18. See also Pausanius 1.35.5.

Scordisci: Athenaeus 6.25 (234); Pliny the Elder 3.25(147); Strabo 7.5.12; Ptolemy, 11.15. See also Wissowa et al, Series 2, *2A*, 831-5; Wilkes (1969), 171-2; Mócsy, 5-12; Wilkes (1992), 77-84; Todorovic (1968) & (1974); B. Jovanovíc in Duval/Kruta, 179-87; B. Jovanovic / P. Popovic in Moscati, 337-47.

For Danubian coinage, see Allen/Nash, 45-53.

Partial Celticisation of Iapodes: Strabo 7.5.4; Dionysius of Halicarnassus, fragment 16. See Hubert (b), 59; Wilkes (1969), 159.

For Celtic influence in Hungarian Plain, see Szabó.

Taurisci: Pliny the Elder 3.19(131) & 3.25(148); Strabo 4.6.12. See Wissowa et al, Series 2, *5A*, 1-14; Alföldy, 25-7; Cunliffe (1997), 220-1; D. Bozic in Moscati, 471-7.

Norici: Pliny the Elder 3.19(131) & 3.24 (146); Sempronius Asellio - fragment in Peter, *1*, 183. See also Wissowa et al, Series 1, *17*, 963-77; Arbois de Jubainville (1902), 194-6; Alföldy, 14-35; Cunliffe (1997), 217-8.

Galati raids and settlements in Asia Minor: Justin 25.2.8-11; Memnon 1-2, 14, 16, 19-20; Strabo 12-13; Pausanius 1.4 & 10.22-23, 30, 32; Polybius 4.46; Livy 38.16; Strabo 12.3.9 & 12.5.1 & 13.1.27; Zosimus 2.37.1; Stephanus of Byzantium ('Auríai', 'Aukura'). See Arbois de Jubainville (1902), 84; Holder, *1*, 1522-1620; Stähelin, 6-10; Hubert (b), 45-6; Heavey, 22-7; Magie, 5-6, 730-2; Rankin, 192; S. Mitchell, *1*, 14-20; Birkhan, 139-148.

Antigonus Gonatas and Celts: Justin 25.1-3 & 26.2; Livy 28.16; Trogus Pompeius cited in 'prologue' to Justin 26; Pausanius 10.23.8; Diodorus 22.5.2, 9, 11; Diogenes Laertius 2.141-2; Polyaenus 4.6.17; Appian, *Syriaca*, 65. See Hubert (b), 41-2; S. Mitchell, *1*, 13-5.

Pyrrhus and Celtic mercenaries: Pausanius 1.13.2; Plutarch, *Pyrros*, 26; Justin 25.3; Diodorus 22.11.

Celts desecrate tombs in Macedonia: Plutarch, *Pyrros*, 26; Diodorus 22.12.

Organisation of the Galati: Pliny the Elder 5.42(146); Strabo 12.5.1-4; Franzius, 73 [no. 4010]; Dittenberger (1905), *1*, 453-4 [nos 275-6] & 2, 208-9 [no 537]. See Stähelin, 39-50, 105-6; Hubert (b), 48-51; Heavey, 51-68; Magie, 731-2; S. Mitchell, *1*, 27-9, 42-58.

Defeat by Antiochus I: Simonides of Magnesia cited in Suidas; Lucian, *Zeuxis*, 8-11; Appian, *Syriaca*, 65; Eusebius of Caesarea, *Chronicoi Canones*, 1 [*Asianorum et Syrorum reges, 3*]. See Stähelin, 12-13, Hubert (b), 46; Heavey, 30-3; Magie, 5-8, 94-5, 731; S. Mitchell, *1*, 18-9.

Defeat of Seleucus II: Justin 27.2 & 41.4.7; Athenaeus 13 (593e); Polyaenus 4.9.6; Plutarch, *Moralia*, 489; Eusebius of Caesarea, *Chronicoi Canones*, 1. 251. See S. Mitchell, *1*, 20.

Depredations and 'Galatica': Livy 38.16.10-14 & 38.47.11; Dittenberger (1905), *2*, 518-22 [no 765]; Pausanius 1.4.5 & 10.22.4, 30.9, 32.4-5; Memnon, 14, 16; Jerome, *Adversus Jovinianum*, 1.41; Parthenius, *Narrationes Amatoriae*, 8; *Anthologia Palatina* 7.492. See Hubert (b), 47; Heavey, 22-34; Magie, 6-7, 95, 138, 730-3, 829-30; Rankin, 189; S. Mitchell, *1*, 16-9.

Defeat by Philetaros: Roussel, 100 [no 1105]. See Magie, 4-6, 729, 732.

Defeat by Attalus: Justin 27; Polybius 18.41; Livy 33.21.3 & 38.16-17; Pausanius 1.4.5 & 1.8.2 & 1.25.2 & 10.15, 30-32; Strabo 12.5.1 & 13.4.2; Polyaenus 4.20. See Hubert (b), 45-9; Stähelin, 19-39; Heavey, 40-50; Magie, 7-9, 734-9; S. Mitchell, *1*, 21-2; Ellis (1997), 132-40.

Trick with gold on battlefield: Frontinus, *Strategematon*, 2.13.1.

Trogmi and Tolistoboii named from leaders: Strabo 12.5.1.

For central shrines, see Hubert (b), 232-3; Byrne, 58.

Phylarchus' account of great feast: Athenaeus 4.33-4 (150).

Phrygian mother-goddess cult: Strabo 12.5.3. See Akurgal, 178-9, 277-8, 283-7.

For Galati and slaves, see S. Mitchell, *1*, 30, 46-7.

For Galati as mercenaries, see Heavey, 36-9, 71-81.

Celtic mercenaries in Syria: Polybius 4.48 & 5.53, 79 & 30.25.

Celtic mercenaries in Egypt: Pausanius 1.7.2; Callimachus, *Eis Delon*, 184-6; Dittenberger (1905), *2*, 498-9 [no 757]. See Hubert (b), 51.

Battle of Rafah: Polybius 5.82-86.

Celtic mercenaries in Pergamon: Polybius 5.77-78, 111; Memnon 24.

Massacre by Prusias: Polybius 5.111.

For attack on Apollonia, see C. Danov in *Studia Celtica 10-11* (1975-6), 36.

Cavaros: Polybius 4.46-52 & 8.22.

Chapter 4
Fighting tactics of mercenaries in Peloponnesian War: Xenophon, *Hellenica*, 7.1; Diodorus 15.70.1.

Drunkenness: Plato, *Leges*, 1.637.

Celts in Iberia: Posidonius in Strabo 3.1-4, 12-15 and in Diodorus 5.33-34; Pliny the Elder 3.1-3(8-30). See Holder, *1*, 959-75; Wissowa et al, Series 1, *3*, 1886-93; Arbois de Jubainville (1904), 109-16; Hubert (b), 75-81; Cunliffe (1997), 141-4; Birkhan, 158-63.

Celtiberians and Greeks: Ephorus, cited in Strabo 4.4.6. See also Avienus 4.689-91.

For Volcae on northern side of Pyrenees, see V. Kruta in Schmidt/Ködderitzch, 46-7.

Minerals in Iberia: Pliny the Elder 3.3(30) & 4.20(112).

Original expedition into Peninsula of Celtiberi and Berones: Strabo 3.4.5, 12.

Celtici and Turduli: Strabo 3.3.5. For Celtici, see also Wissowa et al, Series 1, *3*, 1892-3.

Admixture of Celts and Iberians: Diodorus 5.33.1; Lucan 4.9-10; Strabo 3.2.15 & 3.4.13.

River Areva: Pliny the Elder 3.3(27).

Arevaci = Celtiberi: Strabo 3.4.13; Pliny the Elder 3.3(19). See also Wissowa et al, Series 1, *2*, 400, 682. Town of Vacca: Isidorus 9.2.107. For Vaccaei in general, see Wissowa et al, Series 2, *7*, 2034-8.

Co-operative agriculture among the Vaccaei: Diodorus 5.34.3-4.

Artabri and Celtici: Strabo 3.3.5; Pomponius Mela, *De Chorographia*, 3.13; but Pliny the Elder 4.20(111) & 4.22(114) regarded 'Artabri' as a corruption. See also M. Alberro in *Anuario Brigantino 22* (1999), 60.

For connections through eastern Pyrenees, see Savory, 253-4; J. de Hoz in *Zeitschrift für celtische Philologie 45* (1992), 4; M. Lenerz-de Wilde in Green (1996), 550.

For possible Volcae connection, see Mócsy, 61-3.

Volciani: Livy 21.19.

Oretani Germani: Pliny the Elder 3.3(25). For the name Oretani, see Meid (1994), 34; and for the name Germani see J. Pokorny in *Zeitschrift für celtsiche Philologie 21* (1938), 103-7; C.F.C. Hawkes in *Celticum 12* (1965), 1-7.

Placename Belgida: Orosius 5.23.11. This may be a mistake for Segeda, in the territory of the Belli.

Name 'Moenicaptos': Livy 24.42. See also Arbois de Jubainville (1904), 115-6.

Language and culture of Celtici: Pliny the Elder 3.1(13).

Posidonius account: Diodorus 5.33-34; Strabo 3.4.14-18.

Celtiberians expert horsemen and swordsmen: Polybius [fragments number 95-96].

Unnamed god: Strabo 3.4.16.

For Lugus in Celtiberian inscriptions, see Meid (1994), 30-7; J. de Hoz in *Zeitschrift für celtische Philologie 45* (1992), 26-8.

For Deivoréks in inscription, see Meid (1994), 38-44.

For religion among Celtiberians, see Birkhan, 162-3; Simón (1998) & in Amagro-Gorbea/Zapatero, 477-512.

Celtiberian mercenaries with Carthaginians: Diodorus 11.15.

Celtiberian mercenaries in Sicily and Epirus: Diodorus 16.73.3 & 20.11.1, 64.2 & 23.21.1; Polybius 2.5-7; Frontinus, *Strategematon*, 3.16.2-3; Diodorus 23.8.3.

Revolt of mercenaries in Carthage: Polybius 1.66-88; Diodorus 25.2-8.

Hamilcar Barca and Celtiberians: Polybius 2.1; Livy 21.1-2; Diodorus 25.9-10 (Oretani referred to as 'Orissi'); Appian, *Iberica*, 1 (4-5); Cornelius Nepos 22.4 (where Hamilcar's death is attributed to the Vettones).

Hasdrubal builds Carthaginian power in Spain: Polybius 2.13; Livy 21.2; Diodorus 25.12.

For coinage in Cisalpine Gaul, see Allen/Nash, 42-5.

Great war in Italy between Celts and Romans: Polybius 2.21-35; Plutarch, *Marcellos*, 3-8; Diodorus 25.13; Florus 1.20 (2.4); Frontinus, *Strategematon*, 4.5.4; Valerius Maximus 3.2.5; Ausonius, *Technopaegnion*, 10.83; Eutropius 2.6; Propertius 4.10.39-45.

For sacred nudity in war, see Henry, 33-8; S. Mitchell, *1*, 45.

Assassination of Hasdrubal: Livy 21.2; Polybius 2.36; Diodorus 25.12; Appian, *Annibaica*, 1 (2). See Arbois de Jubainville (1904), 188-90.

Imilce: Livy 24.41.7; Silius Italicus 3.97-9.

Hannibal and Spain: Polybius 3.8, 13-17, 33-5; Livy 21.5-15; Diodorus 25.15.

Roman envoys rejected by Celts: Livy 21.19-20.

Hannibal negotiates with Celts: Polybius 3.34; Livy 21.23-24.

Boii and Insubres rebel in Italy: Polybius 3.40; Livy 21.25-26.

Boii delegation to Hannibal: Livy 21.29.

Hannibal in Gaul: Polybius 3.36-46; Livy 21.26-32.

Hannibal crosses the Alps: Polybius 3.47-55; Livy 21.32-37; Appian, *Annibaica*, 1 (4).

Hannibal in Italy: Polybius 3.56-111; Livy 21-30; Diodorus 26.1-17; Appian, *Annibaica*, 2-9 (5-61).

Hannibal and single combat of Celtic prisoners: Polybius 3.62; Livy 21.42-43.

Hannibal in disguise from Celts: Polybius 3.78; Livy 22.1; Appian, *Annibaica*, 2 (6).

Flaminius killed by Celt: Polybius 3.84; Livy 22.6.

Gauls and Celtiberians at Battle of Cannae: Polybius 3.113-5; Livy 22.46; Appian, *Annibaica*, 4 (20-3).

Boii ambush Roman army: Polybius 3.118; Livy 23.24.

Head-cult among the Celts: Diodorus 5.29.

Celtiberi defeat Hasdrubal: Livy 22.21.

Abilyx: Polybius 3.97-99; Livy 22.22.

Moenicaptos and Vismaros: Livy 24.42.

Celtiberian mercenaries with Romans: Livy 24.48.

Hasdrubal's bribe: Livy 25.32-33.

Indibilis and Mandonius: Polybius 9.11 & 10.18, 35-40 & 11.25-33; Livy 22.21 & 25.34 & 26.49 & 27.17-19 & 28.24-25, 34 & 29.1-3; Appian, *Iberica*, 8 (37-9); Diodorus 26.22.

Single combat between Corbis and Orsua: Livy 28.21.

Capture of Cartagena: Livy 26.41-46.

Release by young Scipio of prisoners and hostages: Livy 26.47-50.

Hasdrubal in Italy: Livy 27.39-49.

Defeat of Hanno: Livy 28.1-2.

Celtiberian force arrive in Carthage and massacred by Scipio: Polybius 14. 7, 11-16; Livy 30.7-8.

Battle of Zama: Polybius 15.5-15; Livy 30.29-35.

Chapter 5

For 'Casses' as tribal gods, see Holder, *1*, 824-5; Wissowa et al, Series 1, 3, 1654.; Hubert (b), 125-6.

For Belgae in northern Gaul and Britain, see O'Rahilly, 456-9; Cunliffe (1991), 108-10, 545.

Aremorici connected with Belgae: Strabo 4.4.1; Ausonius, *Technopaegnion*, 10, 83. See Jullian, *2*, 488; Hubert (b), 101-2, 130; Chadwick (1969), 29-31; C.-J. Guyonvarc'h in *Ogam* 20 (1970), 352-6.

For shift of power from Bituriges to Aedui, see Jullian (1920), *2*, 543-52.

Carnutes at 'centre of Gaul': Caesar, *De Bello Gallico*, 6.13.

For 3rd-2nd century BC Ireland, see O'Rahilly, 2-57, 92-146, 391-4; H. Wagner in *Zeitschrift für celtische Philologie 42* (1987), 14-20; A. Mac an Bhaird in *Ainm 5* (1991-1993), 1-20; Ó hÓgáin (1999), 36-42, 159-65.

For Tara as ritual site, see Bhreathnach, 27-34, 220-66.

Italian war of 200-197 BC: Livy 31.2, 10, 21 & 32.28-31.

War of 196 BC: Livy 33.36-37.

War of 194-3 BC: Livy 34.46-47 & 35.11.

War of 191 BC: Livy 36.38-40.

Murder of Boii nobleman: Livy 39.42.

Roman consolidation in north Italy: Livy 36.39 & 39.54 & 40.17, 53 & 41.1-5; Pliny the Elder 3.19(131). See also Arbois de Jubainville (1904), 182-4.

'Gallia Togata': Dio Cassius 46.55.5.

Cenomani disarmed: Diodorus 29.14; Livy 38.42 & 39.3.

Celts in Roman army: Livy 41.1.8 & 41.3.5 & 41.5.

Ligurian and Celtic uprising 175 BC: Livy 41.19.2-4.

Conquest of Galati by Romans: Polybius 21.33-46; Livy 38.12-27, 45-48. See Stähelin, 50-61; Heavey, 81-92; S. Mitchell, *1*, 23-5.

Ortagio and wife: Polybius 22.21; Plutarch, *Moralia*, 258 (=MV 22); Livy 38.24; Valerius Maximus 6.1.2; Florus 1.27 (2.11).

Eastern wars of 181-165BC: Polybius 3.3.6 & 22.8.5 & 23.1.4 & 24.14-15 & 25.2 & 29.22 & 30.1-3, 19, 28; Livy 39.46.9 & 40. 57-8 & 42.41-44.42 & 44.26-7 & 45.19, 34; Polyaenus 4.8.1; Memnon 19; Strabo 13; Justin 31-34; Diodorus 30.19, 21.3 & 31.14. See Heavey, 93-101; Magie, 22-3, 766-7.

Galati slaughter prisoners: Diodorus 31.12-3.

Galatian dependence on Rome: Polybius 30.28, 30 & 31.1-2, 8, 15, 32 & 32.1; Livy 45.44; Diodorus 31.7, 14. See Stähelin, 61-85; Magie, 26, 770-1; S. Mitchell, *1*, 25-6.

Roman slave-raid and gold-rush in Balkans: Livy 43.5; Polybius - cited in Strabo 4.6.12. See Alföldy, 31-5; Cunliffe (1997), 220-1.

Catmelos and Balanos: Livy 41.1.8, 3.5 & 43.14.1 & 44.14.

Venetia, Histria, Macedonia and Illyricum conquered by Romans: Livy 41.27 & 41.11 & 44.26-7 & 45.16.

Turdetani rebellion: Strabo 3.2.15; Livy 33.19, 25, 43-44.

Cato's campaign: Livy 34.8-21; Plutarch, *Caton*, 10-11; Appian, *Iberica*, 8 (39-41).

Battle of Toletum: Livy 35.7.

War of 181 BC: Livy 35.7 & 40.30-33, 39-40; Orosius 4.20.16.

Battle of Manlian Pass: Livy 40.35-40.

War of 179 BC: Livy 40.47-50; Frontinus, *Strategematon*, 2.5.3 & 4.7.33.

Policy of Gracchus: Appian, *Iberica*, 8 (43); Strabo 3.4; Diodorus 11.29.26 & 31.39.1; Livy 40.50 & 41.7 & (summary) 41.

Rebellion of 174 BC: Livy 41.26.

Salendicos: Florus 1.33 (2.17).

For date change, see Wissowa et al, Series 1, 7, 268 ('Fulvius'); Curchin, 34, 195.

'Fiery war': Polybius 35.1 (fragment).

War against Nobilior: Livy (summary) 47; Appian, *Iberica*, 9 (44-7); Diodorus 31.39-41. See Schulten (1933), 41-8.

Policy of Marcellus: Polybius 35.2-4 (fragment); Appian, *Iberica*, 9 (48-50).

Lucullus and Galba in Spain: Appian, *Iberica*, 10-11 (51-60); Suetonius, *Galba*, 3; Valerius Maximus 9.6.2; Orosius 4.21.10.

Massacre of Lusitani: Appian, *Iberica*, 9 (52). See Curchin, 35, 195.

Viriatos: Appian, *Iberica*, 11-12 (61-74); Dio Cassius 22; Florus 1.33 (2.17); Eutropius 4.16; Valerius Maximus 6.4; Livy (summary) 53-54; Velleius 2.1; Strabo 3.4.5; Frontinus, *Strategematon*, 2.5.7 & 2.13.4 & 3.10.6 & 3.11.4 & 4.5.22; Diodorus 33.1, 21; Orosius 5.4. See also Lemprière, 719.

Funeral of Viriatos: Appian, *Iberica*, 12 (75).

Surrender of Tautalos: Diodorus 33.1.4; Appian, *Iberica*, 12 (75).

Mancinus: Appian, *Iberica*, 13 (80-3); Cicero, *De oratore*, 1.40; Livy (summary) 54-56; Plutarch, *Tiberios Gracchos*, 5; Velleius 2.1; Diodorus 33.24-7; Orosius 5.4.20. See also Lemprière, 382.

Scipio's campaign: Appian, *Iberica*, 14 (81-3); Obsequens 26; Livy (summary) 56.

Siege of Numantia: Appian, *Iberica*, 14-15 (84-98); Valerius Maximus 2.7.1; Livy (summary) 59; Orosius 5.7-7; Florus 1.34 (2.18); Eutropius 4.17, 19; Diodorus 34-35.4. See Schulten (1914).

Chapter 6

For Gaulish inscriptions, see Dottin (1918), 35-173; Lambert, 81-183. A celebrated calendar inscribed on bronze and dating to the 1st century BC was found at Coligny in the French department of Ain - see Olmsted (1992).

For Gaulish coinage, see Allen/Nash, 53-60, 68-82.

For gradual change in political system of Gaul, see Brunaux, 49-56.

Marseilles and Romans: Polybius 33.8-10; Livy (summary) 60; Strabo 4.1.5; Florus 1.37 (3.2); Diodorus 34.23. See Jullian 3, 7-37; Hubert (b), 144.

Generosity of Lovernios: Athenaeus 4.37 (152); Strabo 4.2.3.

War of Romans against Salluvii, Allobroges and Arverni: Livy (summary) 60-61; Strabo 4.1.11 & 4.2.3; Valerius Maximus 9.6; Velleius, 1.15 & 2.10; Florus 1.37 (3.2); Diodorus 34-35.23; Jerome, *Chronicon* [sub 127-121 BC]; Orosius 5.13-14; Apollodorus 4 (fragment); Appian, *Celtica*, 1.2 & 12 (fragments); Eutropius 4.22-23; Obsequens (fragment). See Hirschfeld et al, *1*, 53; Jullian, *3*, 14-19; Duval, 232.

Ahenobarbus on elephant: Suetonius, *Nero*, 2.1.

Contoniatus: Diodorus 34-35.36.

Tribe commits suicide: Orosius 5.14.

Cimbri and Celts: Strabo 7.2.2.

Scordisci at war with Romans: Livy 40.57 & 41.19 & summaries of 54, 56, 63, 65; Florus 1.39 (3.4); Diodorus 34-35.30ab; Eutropius, 4.10-11 & 5.4; Frontinus, *Strategematon*, 3.10.7; Obsequens 16; Ammianus 27.4.3-10.

Galatea story: Diodorus (citing Timaeus from the 3rd century BC) 5.24; Silius Italicus 3.417; Appian, *Illyrica*, 1-2; Ammianus 15.

War of Cimbri and Teutones against Romans: Livy (summary) 67-68; Plutarch, *Marios*, 11-27; Florus 1.38 (3.3); Strabo 5.1.8 & 5.2.14; Appian, *Celtica*, 13-14 (fragments); Livy 63 (summary); Diodorus 34-35:37.1; Velleius 2.12; Orosius 5.16. See Hubert (b), 103-111.

For the names Teutoboduos and Boiorix, see Arbois de Jubainville (1904), 213. For Boiorix, see also Livy (summary) 67.

Victory of Nitiobroges: Livy (summary) 65; Caesar, *De Bello Gallico* 1.7; Orosius 5.15. See Duval, 229-30.

Capture of Copillos: Plutarch, *Sullas*, 4.1.

Tectosages and treasure: Cicero, *De oratore*, 2.18.124 & *De natura deorum*, 3.30 (74); Diodorus 14.93.5; Justin 32.3.9-12; Strabo 4.1.13-4; Aulus Gellius 3.9.7; Dio Cassius 27[90]; Valerius Maximus 4.7.3 & 6.9.13; Livy (summary) 67; Orosius 5.15; Hirschfeld et al, XII, 626.

For bad luck of Caepio, see also Wissowa et al, Series 2, *2A*, 1785-6.

Connections between Asia Minor and south-east Gaul: Dittenberger, *3*, 116-9 [no 591]; Strabo 4.1.13. See Hubert (b), 187-8; S. Mitchell, *1*, 22-3, 58.

Salluvii rebellion: Livy (summary) 73.

Overthrow of Scordisci: Florus 1.39 (3.4); Appian, *Illyrica*, 1 (5); Orosius 5.23. See also Wissowa et al, Series 1, *4*, 1484 & *17*, 976-7 & Series 2, *2A*, 834-5.

Celts with Spartacus: Livy (summary) 97; Caesar, *De Bello Gallico* 1.40; Florus 2.8 (3.20); Appian, *Emphylion*, 1.116-120; Plutarch, *Crassos*, 8-11; Sallust, *Historiae*, 3.6; Frontinus, *Strategematon*, 2.4.7 & 2.5.34; Orosius 5.24.

Sertorius: Plutarch, *Sertorios*; Florus 2.10 (3.22); Orosius 5.23; Livy 91 (fragments); Exuperantius, *De Marii*. See Curchin, 42-6.

Galati and the Pessinus temple: Dittenberger (1905), *1*, 482-90 [no 315]. See S. Mitchell, *1*, 26, 48-50.

Story of Camma: Plutarch, *Moralia*, 257, 768; Polyaenus 8.39. See Koch/Carey, 34-6.

Galati in Roman army: Appian, *Mithridateios*, 2-3 (11-19) & 11 (78); Memnon 44; Plutarch, *Lucullos*, 14.1 & 28.2. See S. Mitchell, *1*, 29-31.

Mithradates and Galati: Appian, *Mithridateios*, 2 (11) & 3 (17) & 6 (41) & 7 (46) & 10 (68) & 17 (118); Justin 38.4; Memnon, 29-36; Plutarch, *Moralia*, 259 (M V 23); Strabo 12.3.1.

Mithradates and other Celts: Appian, *Mithridateios*, 10 (68) & 16 (109, 112) & 17 (116); Justin 38.4.

Bitocos: Livy (summary) 102.; Appian, *Mithridateios* 16 (111); Dio Cassius 37.10-14.

Deïotaros against Mithradates: Appian, *Mithridateios*, 11 (75); Strabo 12.13.1; Livy (summary) 94; Cicero, *Philippica*, 11.33-4; Orosius 6.2.18. See also Stähelin, 85-8; Magie, 222-94, 1176; Ellis (1997), 183-92.

Mithradates almost captured: Memnon 44; Plutarch, *Lucullos*, 28.2; Appian, *Mithridateios*, 82. See Heavey, 104; S. Mitchell, *1*, 31.

Ariovistus and Celts: Caesar, *De Bello Gallico*, 1.30-31, 47, 53.

Catugnatos: Dio Cassius 37.47-48 & 39.65.1; Livy 103 (summary); Cicero, *De Provinciis Consularibus*, 32.

Conspiracy of Catalina: Cicero, *Pro M Fonteio*; Sallust, *Catalina*; Suetonius, *Julius Caesar*, 14-17; Plutarch, *Caisar*, 7-8 & *Cicero*, 18; Florus 2.12 (4.1).

Anecdote of Caesar in Alps: Plutarch, *Caisar*, 11.

Caesar's campaign against Celtic tribes in Spain: Plutarch, *Caisar*, 11-12; Suetonius, *Julius Caesar*, 18, 34, 54; Dio Cassius 37.52-3.

Boerebistas and defeat of the Boii: Strabo 5.1.6 & 7.1.5 & 7.3.11 & 7.5.2; Pliny the Elder 3.24(146); Caesar, *De Bello Gallico*, 1.5; Jornandes, *Getica*, 11.67; 'Prologue' to Trogus Pompeius 32.10. See Jullian (1920-6), 3, 149-52; Hubert (b), 115; Alföldy, 39-41; Mócsy, 18-21; Z. Wozniak in Duval/Kruta, 213-8; Cunliffe (1997), 222-3, 314.

Chapter 7

War of Helvetii: Caesar, *De Bello Gallico* [henceforth referred to as BG] 1.1-29; Plutarch, *Caisar* [henceforth referred to as *Caisar*), 18; Dio Cassius 38.31-33; Appian, *Celtica*, 1.3 & 15 (fragments).

Caesar's war with Ariovistus: BG 1.30-54; *Caisar* 19; Florus 1.45 (3.10); Dio Cassius 38.34-50; Appian, *Celtica*, 1.3 & 16-17 (fragments); Frontinus, *Strategematon*, 2.1.16. See Hans Diller in Rasmussen ed, 189-207.

Diviciacos of the Suessiones: BG 2.4.7. See Cunliffe (1991), 110.

For tribes descended from Moselle Celts, see M.E. Mariën in Hawkes Festschrift, 214-20.

War of Belgae: BG 2.1-33; *Caisar* 20; Dio Cassius 39.1-5; Appian, *Celtica*, 1.4 (fragment).

Origin of Aduatuci: BG 2.29; Tacitus, *Germania*, 2.

Rebellion in Alps: BG 3.1-6.

Strength of Veneti: BG 3.13; Strabo 4.4.1. See Chadwick (1969), 34-58; Fleuriot, 14-15, 19-22.

War in north-west Gaul: BG 3.7-19; Florus 1.45 (3.10); Dio Cassius 39.40-43; Frontinus, *Strategematon*, 3.17.7. See P. Emmanuelli in *Annales de Bretagne 63* (1956), 55-87; Chadwick (1969), 89-98.

War in south-west Gaul: BG 3.20-27.

Caesar's campaign in north-east Gaul and Germany: BG 3.28-29 & 4.1-19; *Caisar* 22-23; Appian, *Celtica*, 1.4-5 & 18 (fragments).

Invasions of Britain by Caesar: BG 4.20-38 & 5.1-23; *Caisar* 23; Florus 1.45 (3.10); Dio Cassius 39.50-53 & 40.1-3; Appian, *Celtica*, 1.5 & 19 (fragments).

For tradition that Cassivellaunos had defeated Caesar, see Bromwich, 301-2.

Dumnorix: BG 1.3, 9, 17-20 & 5.6-7.

Rebellion of Indutiomaros, Ambiorix, and Acco: BG 5.24-58 & 6.1-8, 29-44; *Caisar* 24; Florus 1.45 (3.10); Dio Cassius 40.4-11; Frontinus, *Strategematon*, 2.5.20.

For Ambiorix, see Otto Seel in Rasmussen ed, 279-338.

Rebellion of Vercingetorix: BG 7.1-90; *Caisar* 25-27; Dio Cassius 40.31-44 & 41.1-3 & 43.19.4, 22.2; Florus 1.45 (3.10); Appian, *Celtica*, 21 (fragment).

Resistance by Gutuator, Commios, and Correos: Aulus Hirtius, *De Bello Gallico*, 8.1-23; Dio Cassius 40.42-43.

Commios' trick with ships: Frontinus, *Strategematon*, 2.3.11.

Devastation of Eburones and Treveri: Aulus Hirtius, op cit, 8.24-25.

For the word 'gutuater', see Chadwick, 38-9; Le Roux/Guyonvarc'h, 444.

End of the war: Aulus Hirtius, op cit, 8.26-49; Frontinus, *Strategematon*, 3.7.2.

For critique of Caesar's account of the war, see Goudineau.

Figures for the destruction: Plutarch, *Pompeios*, 67.6; Appian, *Celtica*, 1.2 (fragment).

Chapter 8
Deïotaros as king of Galatia: Aulus Hirtius, *De Bello Alexandrino*, 34-41, 65-78; Dio Cassius 41.63 & 42.46-49 & 47.24, 28 & 48.33; Appian, *Mithridateios*, 17 (114); Eutropius 6.14.1; Cicero, *Pro rege Deiotaro* - also *De Divinatione*, 1.26 & 2.20, 76-78 & *Philippica*, 2, 11 & *Brutus*, 21 & *Epistolarum* ad *Atticum*, 5, 11, 14-15 & *Epistolarum ad Familiares*, 8-9, 11, 15 & *De Haruspicum Responsis*, 13; Tacitus, *Dialogus de Oratoribus*, 21; Strabo 12.3.13 & 12.5.1-3 & 13.4.3; Plutarch, *Moralia*, 258 (= MV 21). See also Stähelin, 88-97; Heavey, 103-10; Magie, 389-433, 1235-8, 1259-67, 1275-7; S. Mitchell, *1*, 28, 31-7; Ellis (1997), 192-228.

For burial of Deïotaros Philopator, see Magie, 1235, 1266-7; Akurgal, 283; S. Mitchell, *1*, 55-7. Compare Strabo 12. 5.2.

Successors of Deïotaros: Appian, *Emphylion*, 5.75; Strabo 12.5.1 & 12.6.1; Plutarch, *Antonios*, 61-63; Dio Cassius 49.32 & 50.13 & 53.26; Eutropius 7.10. See Stähelin, 97-100; Heavey, 110-2; Magie, 433-53, 1282-6, 1291, 1303-4; S. Mitchell, *1*, 37-41; Ellis (1997), 228-35.

Death of Amyntas: Strabo 12.6.5. See Magie, 1303.

Romans take over Galatia: Dio Cassius 50.13 & 51.7 & 53.26. See Hubert (b), 88-9; Magie, 453-9, 1291, 1304-11; Akurgal, 284-6; S. Mitchell, *1*, 70-9; Ellis (1997), 142-70.

Dyteutus, son of Adiatorix: Strabo 12.3.35 & 12.8.9.

Celtic mercenaries in Judaea: Josephus, *Ioudaichos archaiologias*, 15.7.3 & 17.8.3.

Defeat of Alpine and Danubian Celts: Augustus, *Res Gestae*, 26.2-3; Dio Cassius 49.34-38 & 50.28 & 54.20-22, 31-32; Florus 2.25-7 (4.12); Appian, *Illyrica*, 4 (16) & 5 (29); Velleius 2.39, 90; Strabo 4.6.3-9; Horatius Flaccus, *Odes*, 4.4. See Wissowa et al, Series 1, *17*, 975-8; Alföldy, 52-6; Mócsy, 31-40; J. Untermann in Neumann/Untermann, 46-50.

Salluvii and tribute from Brutus: Strabo 4.6.7 (205).

Cottius and his kingdom: Strabo 4.1.3; Suetonius, *Tiberius*, 37.3; Dio Cassius 60.24.4; Dessau, *1*, 25 [no 94]; Tacitus, *Annales*, 15.32; Pliny the Elder 3.20(135). See Wissowa et al, Series 1, *10*, 576-7; Pauli, 33.

Monument and defeat of forty-five tribes: Pliny the Elder 3.20(133-7); Hirschfeld et al, *5*, 7817. See Pauli, 32-7.

For Romanisation of the Danube region, see Hubert (b), 155-7; Filip, 68, 74; Salmon, 107-10; Alföldy, 132-42; Mócsy, 40-71; Szabó (1971), 61-72 & in Moscati et al, 515-8; Cunliffe (1997), 249-50.

For Romanisation of the Alps, see Pauli, 33-48.

Gaulish disturbances 44-27 BC: Dio Cassius 46.50.4 & 51.20.5 & 51.21.6; see Hubert (b), 149; Whatmough, 57.

Roman campaign in Spain: Augustus, *Res Gestae*, 26.2; Dio Cassius 51.20.5 & 53. 22-9 & 54.4-5, 11, 20; Suetonius, *Augustus*, 20-21, 26, 29, 81; Strabo 3.4.18; Florus 2.33 (4.12); Plutarch, *Moralia*, 322C; Orosius 6.21; Crinagoras 9.419. See David Magie in *Classical Philology 15* (1920), 323-39; R. Syme in Cook et al, 342-5; Schulten (1942); Keay, 44-6; Curchin, 52-3.

Romanisation of the Iberian Peninsula: Strabo 3.2.15. See W.V. Harris in Astin et al, 138-42; Keay, 47-71; J. Untermann in Neumann/Untermann, 1-17; Curchin; Alarcão.

For administrative division of Gaul, see Whatmough, 20-4.

Census of 29 BC: Livy (summary) 134; Dio Cassius 53.22.

Licinus: Dio Cassius 54.21; Seneca, *Ad Lucilium*, 20.119-20; Persius, *Saturae*, 2.35-36.

For Romanisation of Gaul, see King, 63-88; Wightman (1970) & (1985); Rivet (1988); C. Goudineau in Moscata et al, 509-13; Woolf.

Census and expropriation of autumn cult: Dio Cassius 54.32; Livy (summary), 139; Suetonius, *Claudius*, 2; Velleius 2.121.1; Jerome, *Chronicon* [sub 25 BC]. See Hirschfeld et al, *2*, 35-8 [no 1668].

Rebellions of Florus and Sacrovir: Tacitus, *Annales,* 3.40-46; Velleius 2.129.3. See Wightman (1985), 64-5.

Persecution of druidry: Pliny the Elder 29.12(52-54) & 30.4(13); Suetonius, *Claudius,* 25; Pomponius Mela, *De Chorographia,* 3.18; Aurelius Victor, *De Caesaribus,* 4.2. See Chadwick (1966), 70-8.

For Celtic tribes in Britain see Cunliffe (1991), 130-98; Rivet/Smith.

For trade across the Channel, see Cunliffe (1991), 438-43.

Heavy Roman duties: Strabo 4.5.3.

For coinage in Britain, see D.F. Allen in Duval/Hawkes, 265-82; Arsdell; Cunliffe (1991), 110-29.

Invasion of Britain by Claudius: Dio Cassius 60.19-23; Suetonius, *Claudius,* 17, 24 and *Vespasianus,* 4. See Dudley/Webster (1965); Ireland, 44-50.

Rebellion of Iceni and resistance of Caratacos: Tacitus, *Annales,* 12.31-39; Dio Cassius 61.33.3. See Ireland, 51-7.

Rule of Didius: Tacitus, *Annales,* 12.40.

Nepos' boast and Paulinus' attack on Anglesey: ibid, 14.29-30.

War of Boudicca: ibid, 14.31-38 and *Agricola,* 15-16; Dio Cassius 62.1-12. See Dudley/Webster (1962).

Rebellion of Vindex: Plutarch, *Galbas,* 4-6; Dio Cassius 63.22-26; Suetonius, *Nero,* 40-47 & *Galba,* 9-12; Philostratus, *Apollonios,* 5.10.1-2.

Persecution of Helvetii: Tacitus, *Historiae,* 1.67-70.

Rebellion of Mariccus: Tacitus, *Historiae,* 2.61.

General rebellion of 69-70 AD: Tacitus, *Historiae,* 4.12-5.24; Frontinus, *Stratagematon,* 4.3.14. See Wightman (1985), 66-9.

Arverni and 'Trojan origin': Lucan, *Pharsalia,* 1.427-8. See Hubert (a), 26-7.

For Jupiter-columns: see Wightman (1970), 215-25; Green (1986), 61-8.

Brigantes war of 71 AD: Tacitus, *Historiae,* 3.45 and *Agricola,* 17; Statius, *Silvae,* 5.142-9. See Ireland, 73-83.

Agricola's campaign in Britain: Tacitus, *Agricola;* Dio Cassius 66.20.1-3.

For Pictish tribes, see Henderson, 15-19; 29-31; Wainwright, 1-53.

Plan for invasion of Ireland: Tacitus, *Agricola,* 24. Referred to also in Juvenal 2.160.

For Celtic refugees from Britain to Ireland, see Seán de Búrca in *Studia Celtica 1* (1966), 128-37.

For the strong groups in Ireland, see Ó hÓgáin (1999), 153-83.

For survival of Veneti in Armorica, see Chadwick (1969), 95-100.

For the Venii > Féni, see A. Mac an Bhaird in *Ainm 5* (1991-3), 9 [re Ptolemy 2.2.6]; D. O'Brien in *Ériu 11* (1932), 182-3; Liam Ó Buachalla in *Journal of the Cork Historical and Archaeological Society 49* (1944), 25-9.

For people of Gaulish descent in Ireland, see K. Meyer in *Ériu 4* (1910), 208.

Arviragos and Brigantes: Juvenal 4.127 & 14.196; Spartianus, *De Vita Hadriani*, 11 [in *Historia Augusta* - henceforth referred to as HA]. See Frere, 105-11.

Hadrian's Wall and Antonine Wall: Spartianus, *De Vita Hadriani*, 5.1-2 & 11.2 [in HA]; Capitolinus, *Antoninus Pius*, 5.4 [in HA]. See Collingwood/Myres, 120-160; Winbolt, 24-30; Salway, 173-95; Frere, 105-25; Ireland, 87-92.

Chapter 9

For population numbers, see Lot, 56-8; McEvedy/Jones, 41-72, 86-114; Alföldy, 3-4; Fleuriot, 22-4; Wightman (1985), 32-3; Fowler, 32-6; Frere, 6, 301-2, 324; Birkhan, 160-1, 183-90, 305-6, 997-8.

For the large-scale Romanisation of Britain, see Winbolt; Jackson (1953), 97-112; Rivet (1964); Frere, 295-325; Millett.

Marcus Aurelius and the Sequani: Capitolinus, *Marci Antononi Philosophi*, 22.1 [in HA]; Aurelius Victor, *De Caesaribus*, 16.3.

Artorius Castus and Armorican rebellion: Mommsen et al, 303 [no 1919], 2131 [no 12791]; Dessau, *1*, 548 [no 2770]. See Fleuriot, 19, 47-8.

Campaign of Commodus: Dio Cassius 72.8-9 & 77.12; Lampridius, *Commodus Antoninus*, 6, 8, 13 [in HA]. See Frere, 147-53.

Septimius Severus: Dio Cassius (summary) 77.10-16; Herodian 2-4; Spartianus, *Severus*, 3, 18-19, 22-23 [in HA]; Orosius 7.17. See Frere, 154-80.

For Cruithni in Ireland, see O'Rahilly, 34-5, 341-84; O'Brien, 41, 153-4, 195, 375; K. Meyer in *Zeitschrift für celtische Philologie 8* (1912), 313; Anderson, 79-81; Ó hÓgáin (1990), 361-2.

Albinus: Spartianus, *Severus*, 10-11 & Capitolinus, *Vita Clodii Albini*, 5, 7-10, 12 [in HA]; Aurelius Victor, *De Caesaribus*, 20.8-9; Dio Cassius 74.3.2 & 75.5-7; Herodian 3; Jerome, *Chronicon* [sub 205 BC].

Alexander Severus: Lampridius, *Alexander Severus*, 59-61 [in HA]; Aurelius Victor, *De Caesaribus*, 24.2.

Saloninus, Postumus: Pollio, *Tyranni Triginta*, 3 [in HA]; Aurelius Victor, *De Caesaribus*, 33.1-3, 8-14.

Tetricus and Aurelian: Pollio, *Tyranni Triginta*, 24 & Vopiscus, *Divus Claudius*, 32, 34, 39, 44 [in HA]; Eutropius 9.10-13; Aurelius Victor, *De Caesaribus*, 35.3-4.

Aurelian and druidesses: Vopiscus, *Divus Aurelianus*, 44 [in HA].

Proculus, Bonosus, and Probus in Gaul: Vopiscus, *Firmus* etc, 13-15, 18 [in HA]; Eutropius 9.17; Aurelius Victor, *De Caesaribus*, 37.3; Jerome, *Chronicon* [280 BC].

Saturninus: Vopiscus, *Firmus* etc, 7, 9 [in HA]; Zosimus 1.66.1.

Carus and sons: Vopiscus, *Carus etc* [in HA]; Eutropius 9.18-19; Aurelius Victor, *De Caesaribus*, 38.2 & 39.12; Eusebius of Caesarea, *Chronicoi Canones*, 2.150.

Carausius: Eutropius 9.14, 21-22; Aurelius Victor, *De Caesaribus*, 39.20-21, 39-42; *Panegyrici Latini Veteres*, 8(5).12; Bede, *Historia*, 1.6. See Chadwick (1969), 126-32; Malcolm Todd, 207-11; Ireland, 124-33.

Druidess and Diocletian: Vopiscus, *Carus etc*, 14-15 [i.e. *HA*].

Raids on Britain by Germanic peoples: Ammianus 26.4.5; Libanius, *Oratio*, 18.82-3.

Constantius, Constantine and Constans: Aurelius Victor, *De Caesaribus*, 39.41-42 & 40.1-4; Eutropius 9.21-22 & 10.1-2; *Panegyrici Latini Veteres* 8(5) & 6(7); Libanius, *Oratio 59*, 139-41, Ammianus 20.1; Zosimus 2. See Collingwood/Myres, 277-83; Malcolm Todd, 211-32; Frere, 198-9, 331-6; Ireland, 124-35.

Early Christianity in Galatia: Paul, *Galatas Epistola*. See Burton, xxi-xliv; Fitzmyer/Brown, 236-7; Magie, 703, 1565; S. Mitchell, *2*, 62-71, 91-5; Ellis (1997), 248-54.

Early Christians in Gaul and Britain: Irenaeus, *Pros Haireseis*, 1.10.2 & 1.13.7 & 3.4.2; Eusebius of Caesarea, *Ecclesiastice Historia*, 5.1-4; Tertullian, *Adversus Iudaeos*, 7.22; Origen, *Ezekiel: Homilia 4*; Sulpicius Severus, *Chronica*, 2.32.1; Gregory of Tours, *Historiae Francorum*, 1.28. See Griffe, 15-200; Thomas, 35-60; Branigan, 269-73; de Paor, 8-22, 53-6; Ireland, 204-14.

Raiding by the Irish c 297 AD: *Panegyrici Latini Veteres* 8 (5).20. See Ireland, 124-5.

For the words *Catuveros, *Ivogenos, *Ovogenos see K Meyer in *Sitzundsberichte der Königlich Preussischen Akadamie der Wissenschaften 3* (1913), 45; O.S. Bergin in *Ériu 11* (1932), 142 & *12* (1938), 224-5; J. Pokorny in *Celtica 3* (1956), 306-8; McManus, 102-3; McCone, 25, 131.

For Vindos and Nodons, see Ó hÓgáin (1999), 118-27, 136-7.

For the title *Condos, see O'Rahilly, 281-3, 514-5.

Ughain (also Úghaine) and Eoghan as mythical ancestors: O'Brien, 513, 618-9.

For the words *Ghaisonli, *Teutovalos, see Seán de Búrca in *Studia Celtica 1* ((1966), 134-5; O'Rahilly, 169-70.

For stories of Conn, Eoghan, and Tuathal Teachtmhar, see Ó hÓgáin (1990), 116-9, 182-3, 409-10.

Raids by Picts and Irish 360-382 AD: Ammianus 20.1 & 26.4.5 & 27.8; Claudian & Pacatus, *Panegyrici; Chronica Gallica* [AD 382]. See Ireland, 149-52, 155.

Theodosius: Zosimus 4.12, 35; Ammianus 27.8 & 28.3. See Frere, 247-8, 340-8.

Skiffs: *Epitoma Rei Militaris* 4.37. See Ireland, 154.

Magnus Maximus: Orosius 7.34.9-10, 35.3-4; Zosimus 4.35, 37; Theodoret 1.5; Prosper Tiro, *Chronicon: Gratiani*, 4; Sozomenus 7.13; Ambrose 2.40; Pacatus, *Vettonius*, 12; *Chronica Gallica* [452 AD]; Gildas, 14-15. See Collingwood/Myres, 286-94; Bromwich, 451-4; Ireland, 155-8; Snyder, 12-14, 93-8, 397.

Maximus associated with settlement in Armorica: Nennius 27; Geoffrey of Monmouth, *Historia*, 5.14. See Chadwick (1969), 163-5.

Britanni in northern Gaul: Pliny the Elder 4. 17 (106).

Commerce and travel between Britain and Gaul: Julius Caesar, *De Bello Gallico*, 3.8 & 4.20; Pliny the Elder 34.164; Diodorus Siculus 5.22; Libanius 18.82-3; Ammianus Marcellinus

18.2.3. See Fleuriot, 13-19; Ireland, 124-5, 145-6, 218-28; G. Le Duc in Black/Gillies/Ó Maolalaigh, 133-51.

Stilicho and Irish raids: Claudian, *De Bello Gothico*, 404-418 & *De Consulatu Stilichonis*, 2.247-255 & *In Eutropium*, 1.391-3. See Malcolm Todd, 236-7; Ireland, 159-61.

For Eochu Muighmheadhón, see O'Rahilly, 216-7; O'Brien, 147, 615; Byrne, 74-6, 280, 298.

Tower-defences in south of Britain: Gildas 18.

The pretender Constantine: Orosius 7.40.4, 7.42.1-4; Sozomenus 9.11-14; Zosimus 5-6; Frigeridus 2.9; Procopius 3.2.31; *Chronica Gallica* [408 AD]. See Ireland, 162-4; Snyder, 19-24.

Misery of Britons: Gildas 19-26.

For Ogham inscriptions see Macalister; McManus.

For changes in spoken Celtic, see Jackson (1953); McCone (1996) and in Ó Fiannachta Festschrift, 61-219.

Niall: *Ériu 4* (1910), 91-111; *Otia Merseiana 2* (1900), 75-6, 84-92. See O'Rahilly, 209-34; Byrne, 70-86; Mac Niocaill, 9-16; Ó hÓgáin (1999), 165-6, 184-5.

For war between Connachta and Ulaidh, see Dillon/Chadwick, 85-6; Byrne, 71-4.

For St Patrick, see Bieler; Conneely.

Vortigern: Gildas, 23; Bede, *Historia*, 1.15; Nennius 31-49, 66; Geoffrey of Monmouth, *Historia*, 6.6-8.2 See Alcock, 33-4, 102-9; Snyder, 102-6.

Letter to Aetius: Gildas 20. See Alcock, 107-8, Snyder, 44, 279-81.

Saxon settlements in south-east Britain: Gildas 23-5; Bede, *Historia*, 1.15; Anglo-Saxon Chronicle [sub 449-491 AD].

Britons in Armorica: Gildas 25; Procopius, *De Bello Gothico*, 4.19. See also Gougaud (1932), 104-9; Dillon/Chadwick 115-21; Jackson (1953), 11-23; Gouvril, 44-71; Chadwick (1969), 162-206; Fleuriot, 110-219; Ellis (1993), 101-5; Snyder, 67-8.

For derivation of Breton language, see D. Ellis Evans in *Proceedings of the British Academy 65* (1979), 525-6. See also Fleuriot, 50-109; G. Le Duc in Black/Gillies/ Ó Maolalaigh, 145-7.

For weakening of Gallo-Roman Armorica, see Chadwick (1969), 124-61.

Tibatto's rebellion: *Chronica Gallica* [435, 437 AD]; Jornandes, *Getica*, 36.191.

Riothamos: Jordanes, *Getica*, 45.237-8; Sidonius, *Epistolae*, 1.7.5 & 3.9.1-2; Gregory of Tours, *Historiae Francorum*, 2.18, 25. See Chadwick (1969), 195-7; Snyder, 82-3, 296-7.

Ambrosius Aurelianus: Gildas 25; Bede, *Historia*, 1.16; Nennius 31, 40-2, 48, 66; Geoffrey of Monmouth, *Historia*, 6.8 & 8.2-14. See Alcock, 26-9, 105.

For identification of Riothamos with Ambrosius, see Fleuriot, 170-6, 299-300.

Arthur: Nennius 50; *Annales Cambriae* - ed in *Y Cymmrodor 9* (1888), 141-83 [sub 518, 539 AD]; Aneirin, *Y Gododdin* (in Koch, 22). See K. Malone in *Modern Philology 22* (1925), 367-74; Chambers, 1-19, 233-82; R. Bromwich, 274-7 & in *Studia Celtica 10-11* (1975-6), 163-81; Alcock, 80-8, 358-64.

Wessex against Britons: Anglo-Saxon Chronicle [sub 495-527 AD].

Irish in north Wales and Cunedda: Nennius 14, 62. See Bromwich, 312-3; Dillon/Chadwick, 112-5; Byrne, 134-5; Frere, 373-4; Alcock, 124-9; Snyder, 267.

For Ogham in Wales and south-west Britain, see McManus, 61-4, 171.

Irish in south Wales: *De causis Torche na nDéisi* - ed K. Meyer in *Ériu 3* (1907), 135-42; *Sanas Cormaic* - ed in *Anecdota from Irish Manuscripts 4* (1912), 75. See V. Hull in *Zeitschrift für celtische Philologie 27* (1958-9), 31, 51; Byrne, 182-4; Tomás Ó Cathasaigh in *Éigse 20* (1984), 1-33; Alcock, 123-4.

Dál Riada in Scotland: Bede, *Historia*, 1.1; *Annála Thighearnaigh* - ed in *Revue Celtique 17* (1896), 116-263 [sub 501, 506 AD]; *Senchus Fer nAlban* (in Bannerman, 41-7). See MacNeill, 194-7; Anderson/Anderson, 1-5; Dillon/Chadwick, 104-7; Bannerman, 68-80, 108-56; Anderson 243, 301; Broun, 69-73.

Bruide defeats Gabhrán: *Annála Uladh* (in Hennessy) [557 AD].

St Columba: Adomnán, *Vita Columbae*; Bede 3.4. See Gougaud (1932), 133-7; Richter, 48-88.

For Diarmaid as 'high-king' of Ireland, see Byrne, 87-105; Ó hÓgáin (1990), 158-61.

For Irish Christian missionaries abroad from the sixth to the ninth centuries, see Gougaud (1932), 129-84 and (1939); Richter, 89-134.

Baethán: *Annála Uladh* [580, 586 AD]. See Anderson/Anderson, 87-8; Byrne, 109-11; Bannerman, 2-4; Anderson, 149-50.

Aedán: Adomnán, *Vita Columbae*, 1.8-9 & 3.5; *Annála Uladh* [575, 579, 582, 589, 605 AD]. See Anderson/Anderson, 86-97, 125; Bromwich, 264-6; Henderson, 47-51; Dillon/Chadwick, 105-7; Bannerman, 80-90; Anderson, 145-9.

West Saxon advances: Anglo-Saxon Chronicle [sub 552, 571, 584, 597, 614 AD].

Northern Britons: Nennius 63. See K. Jackson in *Antiquity 29* (1955), 77-88 & in O'Donnell Lectures 1963, 60-9; Dillon/Chadwick, 107-12.

For designation *combrogii > Cymry* , see Lloyd, *1*, 164; Jackson (1953), 445, 652-3; Fleuriot, 55.

Outigirn: Nennius 62; Bartrum, 188; Bede, *Historia*, 5.24. See Colingwood/Myres, 420-2; Stenton, 75-6; Williams, xi-xiii.

Urien: *Canu Taliesin* (ed Williams); Nennius 62-3; Bartrum, 216. See Lloyd, 164-7, Bromwich, 516-20; Williams, xxxvi-lv.

For Morgant, see Bromwich, 465-7.

For other northern Briton leaders, see Bromwich, 375-7, 430-3, 504-5; Williams, lv-lix.

For early kingdoms of Domnonia and Cornouaille, see Cleuziou, 64-6; Chadwick (1969), 220-5; Delumeau, 71-3.

For placenames Cornouaille, Bro Weroch, see Jackson (1967), 241-2, 271.

Rivalry in Bro Weroch: Gregory of Tours, *Historiae Francorum*, 4.4, 20.

Waroc'h: Gregory of Tours, *Historiae Francorum*, 5.16, 26 & 9.18, 24 & 10.9, 11. See Cleuziou,

62-4; Chadwick (1969), 226-30; Delumeau, 73-5; Ellis (1993), 105-6.

Chapter 10

Celtic in Gaul: Irenaeus, *Pros Haireseis*, 1.3 (preface); Ulpian, cited in Justinian, *Digesta*, 32.11; Lampridius, *Severus Alexander* 60.6 [in *Historia Augusta*]; Sulpicius Severus, *Dialogi*, 1.27.1-4. See Hubert (b), 274-5; D. Ellis Evans in *Bulletin of the Board of Celtic Studies 16* (1955), 174-81; Fleuriot, 55-9.

For Celtic in north Italy, see D. Ellis Evans in *Bulletin of the Board of Celtic Studies 16* (1955), 518-20; C. de Simone in Neumann/Untermann, 66-7, 70-1.

For Celtic in Iberian Peninsula, see J. Untermann in Neumann/Untermann, 5-14.

Latin schools in Gaul: Suetonius, *De Grammaticis, 3*; Ausonius, *Commemoratio professorum Burdigalensium*, 4-6, 10; Jerome, *Epistolae*, 120 (preface); Pacatus, *Theodosius*, 29; Sidonius Apollinaris, *Epistolae*, 5.10. See Chadwick (1955), 21-35.

Celtic 'stupidity': Callimachus, *Eis Delon*, 184; Paul, *Galatas Epistola*, 3.1; Sidonius Apollinaris, *Ad Ecdicium*; Firmicus Maternus, *Mathesis* 1.2.3-4.

For rapid decline of Celtic in eastern Europe, see Szabó, 29-31; Alföldy, 134-40, 232-41; Mócsy, 61-9, 259-63; D. Ellis Evans in *Bulletin of the Board of Celtic Studies 16* (1955), 520-3.

For possible survivals of Celtic there in fourth century AD, see Filip, 73; Wilkes (1969), 157-9, 171-2, 283.

Celtic in Galatia: Lucian, *Alexander*, 51; Pausanius 10.36.1; Jerome, *Commentarii - Epistola ad Galatas* 2.3. See also L. Weisgerber in Geffcken Festschrift, 151-75; G. Neumann in Neumann/Untermann, 176-8; Heavey, 65-8; Duval (1971), 673; S. Mitchell, *1*, 50-1, 175-6; K.H. Schmidt in A. Ó Corráin, 13-28.

For death of Continental Celtic, see Whatmough, 70-3; D. Ellis Evans in *Proceedings of the British Academy 65* (1979), 501, 524-6; K.H. Schmidt in Neumann/Untermann, 35-60; Lambert, 10-11, 81.

For possible survival of spoken Celtic until the 9th century in the Alps, see J.U. Hubschmied in *Vox Romanica 3* (1938), 48-155. Criticism of this view in Whatmough, 1158; D. Ellis Evans in *Bulletin of the Board of Celtic Studies 16* (1955), 179-80.

For influence of Celtic on French and Spanish languages, see D. Ellis Evans in *Proceedings of the British Academy 65* (1979), 526-8.

For British diocese in Asturias-Galicia, see Gougaud (1932), 105; Ellis (1993), 100-1.

Battle of Catterick: Aneirin, *Y Gododdin* (ed Koch, 2-129). See also K. Jackson in O'Donnell Lectures 1963, 69-70; Koch, xiii-xlii.

Kingdom of Elfed taken: Nennius, 63. See Lloyd, 1, 183.

Battle of Degsastan: Bede, *Historia*, 1.34; Anglo-Saxon Chronicle [603 AD], *Annála Uladh* [sub 599 AD]. See Anderson/Anderson, 123; Byrne, 111, 259.

Battle of Chester: Bede, *Historia*, 2.2; *Annales Cambriae* [613 AD]; Anglo-Saxon Chronicle [sub

605 A.D.]. See Anderson/Anderson, 140-2; Lloyd, 1, 179-81; Bromwich, 163-5; Stenton, 77-8; N.K. Chadwick in Jackson et al (1963), 167-85.

Cadwallon: Bede, *Historia*, 2.20-3 & 3.1; Adomnán, *Vita Columbae*, 1.1; Anglo-Saxon Chronicle [633 AD]; Nennius 64; *Annála Thighearnaigh* [sub 630 AD]; Geoffrey of Monmouth, *Historia*, 11.12-12.13. See Anderson/Anderson, 154-8; Lloyd, 1, 184-8; Bromwich, 293-6; Stenton, 80-1.

For expansion by Oswiu and Ecgfrith, see Stenton, 83-8; Henderson, 52-6.

Raid on Ireland and battle of Nechtansmere: Bede, *Historia*, 4.26; *Annála Uladh* [685 AD]; Anglo-Saxon Chronicle [684-5 AD]; Nennius, 65. See F.I. Wainwright in *Antiquity 22* (1948), 82-97; Henderson, 54-9; Anderson/Anderson, 191-5; Richter 98-9.

For continuing fighting between Picts, Irish, and Britons, see Henderson, 48-55.

For Britons as mercenaries in Ireland, see MacNeill, 202-3.

Aldfrith of Northumbria: Bede, *Historia* 4.26 & *Vita Sancti Cuthberti*, 24; V.E. Hull in *Speculum 4* (1929), 95-102; C. Ireland in *Celtica 22* (1992), 64-78. See Stenton, 88-90; Henry, 217-8; Richter, 94-7.

Pictish king Oenghus: Skene (1886), 305; *Annála Uladh* [728-9, 733, 735, 738, 740, 749, 760 AD]. See Henderson, 60-6; Dillon/Chadwick, 145-6; Anderson, 249, 307.

For Bruide's relatives, see Stanton, 87; Henderson, 55; Anderson, 171-3; Anderson/Anderson, 193.

Pictish 'matriarchy': Bede, *Historia*, 1.1. See J. Fraser in Loomis Festschrift, 407-12; Stenton, 86-8; F.T. Wainwright in Wainwright, 25-8; Henderson, 31-3; Dillon/Chadwick, 99-104.

Offa's battles against Welsh: *Annales Cambriae* [778, 784, 796 AD].

For Offa's dyke, see Lloyd, 1, 195-202; Stenton, 211-3.

Battle in Fortriu: *Annála Uladh* [sub 767 AD].

For struggle between Dál Riada and Picts, see Henderson, 93-6.

Cionnaedh: Skene (1867), 8, 151, 209 & (1886), 306; *Annála Uladh* [sub 857, 861 AD]. See Anderson/Anderson, 267-72, 287-91; Henderson, 96-103; Dillon/Chadwick, 146-7; Anderson, 266-7, 304; Hudson, 37-47.

For language of Picts, see K. Jackson in Wainwright, 129-66.

Collapse of Cornwall: Anglo-Saxon Chronicle [sub 658, 682, 710, 753, 755-6, 813, 823, 835 AD]; *Annales Cambriae* [722 AD]; Chronicle of Ethelwerd [sub 836 AD]. See Stenton, 233, 337; Wakelin, 53-9; Ellis (1974), 25-7.

For Norsemen in Scotland, see Skene (1886), 302-432.

For Norsemen on the Isle of Man, see Moore, 82-138.

For Rhodri Mawr, see Lloyd, 1, 323-8.

Breton affairs: Annals of Saint-Bertin [846-7, 851, 856, 863 AD]. See Villemarqué, 112-9; Cleuziou, 69-100; Chadwick (1969), 230-4; Delumeau, 75-85, 156-9; Ellis (1993), 106-7.

For Hywel Dda, see Lloyd, *1*, 333-43.

Poet encourages unity against English: *Armes Prydein* (ed Williams 1972).

Rebellion at Exeter: William of Malmesbury, *Gesta Regum*, 2.6. See Wakelin, 59-61.

For Cornovii in Cornwall, see Rivet/Smith, 325.

For extension of Strathclyde, see K. Jackson in O'Donnell Lectures, 72; Koch, xxxiii.

For Scottish affairs in tenth century, see Skene (1886), 349-83; Hudson, 64-107.

For battle of Brunanburh, see Skene (1886), 352-60; Smyth, 30-88; Hudson, 76-81.

For Britons slaying Cuiléan, see Hudson, 92-3.

Alain Barbetorte: Nantes Chronicle; Charter of Sainte-Croix, Abbey of Quimperlé [931, 936 AD]. See Villemarqué, 120-2; Cleuziou, 101-6; Chadwick (1969), 234; Delumeau, 87-92.

For Norse in Ireland, see D. Ó Corráin, 80-110.

Brian Bóraimhe: *Cogadh Gaedheal re Gallaibh* (ed. J.H. Todd); *Brennu-Njáls Saga*, 154-7 (ed Sveinsson). See Goedheer; D. Ó Corráin, 120-31.

For Gruffudd, see Loyd, 2, 358-71.

For end of Strathclyde kingdom, see Skene (1886), 361-3; Dickinson/Donaldson/Milne, 28-30; O'Donnell Lectures, 71-84; Anderson/Anderson, 449, 576-7; Hudson, 117-23.

For surviving Celtic languages and their cultures, see the various contributions in Price ed.

BIBLIOGRAPHY

Most of the Greek and Latin texts are edited with translation in the Loeb Classical Library series. Many of these texts are also published in translation in the Penguin Classics series. The following is a list of other edited material and of analytical works referred to in the Sources and Studies:

Akurgal, Ekrem, *Ancient Civilizations and Ruins of Turkey* (Istanbul, 1978)

Alarcão, Jorge de, *Portugal Romano* (Lisbon, 1974)

Alcock, Leslie, *Arthur's Britain* (Middlesex, 1973)

Alföldy, Géza, *Noricum* (London, 1974)

Allen, Derek F. / Nash, Daphne, *The Coins of the Ancient Celts* (Edinburgh, 1980)

Almagro-Gorbea, M. / Zapatero, G., eds, *Los Celtas: Hispania y Europa* (Madrid, 1993)

Anderson, A. / Anderson, M., *Early Sources of Scottish History, 1* (Stamford, 1990)

Anderson, Marjorie O., *Kings and Kingship in Early Scotland* (Edinburgh, 1973)

Arbois de Jubainville, H. d', *Sur l'Histoire des Celtes* (Paris, 1902)

         Les Celtes (Paris, 1904)

Arsdell, Robert D. van, *Celtic Coinage of Britain* (London, 1989)

Astin, A.E. et al, *The Cambridge Ancient History, 8* (Cambridge, 1989 - new ed)

Bannerman, John, *Studies in the History of Dalriada* (Edinburgh, 1974)

Bartrum, P.C., *Early Welsh Genealogical Tracts* (Cardiff, 1966)

Belloguet, Roget Bon de, *Glossaire Gaulois* (Paris, 1872)

Bhreathnach, Edel, *Tara: a Select Bibliography* (Dublin, 1995)

Bieler, Ludwig, *The Patrician Texts in the Book of Armagh* (Dublin, 1979)

Binchy, Daniel A., *Celtic and Anglo-Saxon Kingship* (Oxford, 1970)

Birkhan, Helmut, *Kelten: Versuch einer Gesamtdarstellung ihrer Kultur* (Vienna, 1997)

Black, R. / Gillies, W. / Ó Maolalaigh, R. eds, *Celtic Connections, 1* (East Linton, 1999)

Bosch-Gimpera, P., *Two Celtic Waves in Spain* (London, 1939)

Branigan, Keith, *Roman Britain: Life in an Imperial Province* (London, 1980)

Bromwich, Rachel, *Trioedd Ynys Prydein* (Cardiff, 1961)

Broun, Dauvit, *The Irish Identity of the Kingdom of the Scots* (Woodbridge, 1999)

Brunaux, Jean Louis, *The Celtic Gauls* (London, 1988)

Burton, Ernest de Witt, *The Epistle to the Galatians* (Edinburgh, 1921)

Byrne, Francis John, *Irish Kings and High-Kings* (New York, 1973)

Chadwick, Nora K., *Poetry and Letters in Early Christian Gaul* (London, 1955)

         The Druids (Cardiff, 1966)

         Early Brittany (Cardiff, 1969)

         The Celts [foreword by Barry Cunliffe] (London, 1997)

Chambers, E. K., *Arthur of Britain* (London, 1966)

Cleuziou, Alain, Raison du, *La Bretagne* (Saint-Brieuc, 1914)

Collingwood, R.G. / Myres, J.N.L., *Roman Britain and the English Settlements* (Oxford, 1937)

Conneely, Daniel, *The Letters of St Patrick* (Maynooth, 1993)

Cook, S.A., etc *The Cambridge Ancient History, 10* (Cambridge, 1934)

Cunliffe, Barry, *Iron Age Communities in Britain* (London, 1991)

         The Ancient Celts (Oxford, 1997)

Curchin, Leonard A., *Roman Spain: Conquest and Assimilation* (London, 1991)

Danov, Christo M., *Altthrakien* (Berlin, 1976)

de Paor, Liam, *Saint Patrick's World* (Dublin, 1993)

Delumeau, Jean, *Documents de l'Histoire de la Bretagne* (Toulouse, 1971)

Dessau, Hermannus, *Inscriptiones Latinae Selectae 1-3* (Berlin, 1962)

Dickinson, W.C. / Donaldson, G. / Milne, I.A., *A Source Book of Scottish History, 1* (London, 1958)

Dillon, Myles, *Celt and Hindu* (Dublin, 1973)

Dillon, Myles / Chadwick, Nora, *The Celtic Realms* (London, 1973)

Dinan, William, *Monumenta Historica Celtica* (London, 1911)

Dittenberger, Wilhelm, *Orientis Graeci Inscriptiones Selectae* (Leipzig, 1905)

       Sylloge Inscriptionum Graecarum, 1-4 (Leipzig, 1915-24)

Dottin, Georges, *Manuel de l'Antiquité Celtique* (Paris, 1915)

       Anciens Peuples de l'Europe (Paris, 1916)

       La Langue Gauloise (Paris, 1918)

Drinkwater, J.F., *Roman Gaul* (Beckenham, 1983

Dudley, Donald R. / Webster, Graham, *The Rebellion of Boudicca* (London, 1962)

       The Roman Conquest of Britain (London, 1965)

Dumézil Georges, *Camillus: Indo-European Religion as Roman History* (Berkeley, 1980)

Duval, Paul-Marie, *La Gaule jusqu'au Milieu du Ve Siècle* (Paris, 1971)

Duval, Paul-Marie / Hawkes, Christopher, eds, *Celtic Art in Ancient Europe* (London, 1976)

Duval, Paul-Marie / Kruta, Venceslas, eds, *Les Mouvements Celtiques* (Paris, 1979)

       L'Art Celtique de la Période d'Expansion (Geneva, 1982)

Eliade, Mircea, ed., *The Encyclopaedia of Religion 1-16* (New York, 1987)

Ellis, P. Berresford, *The Cornish Language and its Literature* (London, 1974)

       Celt and Saxon (London, 1993)

       Celt and Greek (London, 1997)

Eluère, Christiane, *The Celts, First Masters of Europe* (London, 1993)

Falk Hjalmar / Torp, Alf, *Wortschatz der germanischen Spracheinheit* (Göttingen, 1979)

Filip, Jan, *Celtic Civilisation and its Heritage* (Prague, 1977)

Fitzmyer, Joseph A. / Brown, Raymond E., *The Jerome Biblical Commentary, 2* (London, 1969)

Fowler, P.J., *The Farming of Prehistoric Britain* (Cambridge, 1983)

Fleuriot, Léon, *Les Origines de la Bretagne* (Paris, 1982)

Franzius, Ionnes, *Corpus Inscriptionum Graecarum, 3* (Berlin, 1853)

Frere, Sheppard, *Britannia: a History of Roman Britain* (London, 1987)

Geffcken Festschrift, *Natalicium Johannes Geffcken* (Heidelberg, 1931)

Goedheer, A.J., *Irish and Norse Traditions about the Battle of Clontarf* (Haarlem, 1938)

Gougaud, Louis, *Christianity in Celtic Lands* (London, 1932)

       Cinnirí Gaedhealacha na Críostaidheachta (Dublin, 1939)

Goudineau, Christian, *César et la Gaule* (Paris, 1990)

Gourvil, Francis, *Langue et Littérature Bretonnes* (Paris, 1960)

Graves, Robert, *The Greek Myths 1-2* (Middlesex, 1960)

Green, Miranda, *The Gods of the Celts* (Gloucester, 1986)

       ed, *The Celtic World* (London, 1996)

Griffe, Élie, *La Gaule Chrétienne a l'Époque Romaine, 1* (Paris, 1964)

Hawkes Festschrift = John Boardman / M.A. Brown / T.G.E. Powell, eds, *The European Community in Later Prehistory* [for C.F.C. Hawkes] (London, 1971)

Heavey, Margaret M., *The Galatians* [MA Thesis, University College Galway, 1928]

Henderson, Isabel, *The Picts* (London, 1967)

Hennessy, William M., *Annála Uladh: The Annals of Ulster, 1* (London, 1887)

Henry, P.L., *Saoithiúlacht na Sean-Ghaeilge* (Dublin, 1978)

Hirschfeld, Heinrich O. / Zangemeister, Carl / Domaszewski, Alfred von, et al, *Corpus Inscriptionum Latinarum, XII-XIII, 1-2* (Berlin, 1873-1933)

Hoddinott, R.F., *The Thracians* (London, 1981)

Holder, Alfred, *Alt-Celtischer Sprachschatz 1-3* (Leipzig, 1896)

Hubert, Henri, (a) =*The Rise of the Celts* (London, 1934)

       (b) =*The Greatness and Decline of the Celts* (London, 1934)

Hudson, Benjamin T., *Kings of Celtic Scotland* (Connecticut, 1994)

Ireland, S., *Roman Britain: a Sourcebook* (London, 1996)

Jackson, Kenneth H., *Cath Maighe Léna* (Dublin, 1938)

       Language and History in Early Britain (Edinburgh, 1953)

       The Oldest Irish Tradition (Cambridge, 1964)

       A Historical Phonology of Breton (Dublin, 1967)

Jackson, Kenneth H., et al, *Celt and Saxon* (Cambridge, 1963)

James, Simon, *Exploring the World of the Celts* (London, 1993)

Jullian, Camille, *Histoire de la Gaule 1-3* (Paris, 1920)

       Vercingétorix (Paris, 1963)

Keay, S.J., *Roman Spain* (London, 1988)

Kendrick, T.D., *The Druids* (London, 1927)

King, Anthony, *Roman Gaul and Germany* (London, 1990)

Knott, Eleanor, *Togail Bruidne Da Derga* (Dublin, 1936)

Koch, John T., *The Gododdin of Aneirin* (Cardiff, 1997)

Koch, John T. / Carey, John, *The Celtic Heroic Age* (Massachusetts, 1997)

Kruta, Venceslas, *The Celts of the West* (London, 1985)

Lambert, Pierre-Yves, *La Langue Gauloise* (Paris, 1994)

Le Roux, Francoise / Guyonvarc'h, Christian-J., *Les Druides* (Ouest-France, 1986)

Lejeune, Michel, *Lepontica* (Paris, 1971)

Lemprière, John, *Classical Dictionary* (London, 1984 ed)

Lenerz-de Wilde, M., *Iberia Celtica* (Stuttgart, 1991)

Lloyd, John Edward, *A History of Wales 1-2* (London, 1939)

Loomis Festschrift, *Medieval Studies in Memory of Gertrude Schoepperle Loomis* (Paris, 1927)

Lot, Ferdinand, *La Gaule* (ed. Paul-Marie Duval - Verviers, 1967)

Mac Niocaill, Gearóid, *Ireland before the Vikings* (Dublin, 1972)

Macalister, R A S, *Corpus Inscriptionum Insularum Celticarum 1-2* (Dublin, 1945-9)

MacCulloch, J.A., *The Religion of the Ancient Celts* (London, 1911)

MacLennan, Gordon W., *Proceedings of the First North American Congess of Celtic Studies* (Ottawa, 1988)

MacNeill, Eoin, *Phases of Irish History* (Dublin, 1919)

Magie, David, *Roman Rule in Asia Minor, I-II* (Princetown, 1950)

Mallory, J.P. / Adams, D.Q,. *Encyclopedia of Indo-European Culture* (London, 1997)

McCone, Kim, *Ancient and Medieval Celtic Sound Change* (Maynooth, 1996)

McEvedy, Colin / Jones, Richard, *Atlas of World Population History* (Middlesex, 1978)

Megaw, Ruth & Vincent, *Celtic Art* (London, 1989)

Meid, Wolfgang, *Gaulish Inscriptions* (Budapest, 1992)

    Celtiberian Inscriptions (Budapest, 1994)

Millett, Martin, *The Romanization of Britain* (Cambridge, 1990)

Mitchell, Frank, *The Irish Landscape* (Dublin, 1986)

Mitchell, Stephen, *Anatolia, 1-2* (Oxford, 1993)

Mócsy, András, *Pannonia and Upper Moesia* (London, 1974)

Mommsen, Theodorus / Hirschfeld, Heinrich O/ Domaszewski, Alfred von,

    Corpus Inscriptionum Latinarum, III (Berlin, 1873-1902)

Moore, A.W., *A History of the Isle of Man, 1* (London, 1900)

Moscati, Sabatino, co-ordinating ed., *The Celts* (Milan, 1991)

Neumann, Günther / Untermann, Jürgen, eds, *Die Sprachen im römischen Reich de Kaiserzeit*

    (Köln, 1980)

Ní Chatháin, Próinséas / Richter, Michael, eds, *Ireland and Europe in the early Middle Ages*

    (Stuttgart, 1996)

O'Donnell Lectures = *Angles and Britons* (Cardiff, 1963)

Ó Corráin, Ailbhe, ed, *Proceedings of the Fifth Symposium of Societas Celtologica Nordica*

    (Uppsala, 2001)

Ó Corráin, Donncha, *Ireland before the Normans* (Dublin, 1972)

Ó Fiannachta Festschrift = *Stair na Gaeilge* [for Pádraig Ó Fiannachta] (Maynooth, 1994)

Ó hÓgáin, Dáithí, *Myth, Legend and Romance* (London, 1990)

    The Sacred Isle (Cork, 1999)

Olmsted, Garrett S., *The Gaulish Calendar* (Bonn, 1992)

    The Gods of the Celts and the Indo-Europeans (Budapest, 1994)

O'Rahilly, Thomas F., *Early Irish History and Mythology* (Dublin, 1946)

Pârvan, Vasile, *Dacia* (Cambridge, 1928)

Pauli, Ludwig, *The Alps: Archaeology and Early History* (London, 1984)

Peter, Hermann, *Historicorum Romanorum Reliquiae, I* (Leipzig, 1870)

Piggott, Stuart, *The Druids* (London, 1968)

Planta, Peter C., *Das alte Raetien Staatlich und Kulturhistorisch Dargestellt* (Berlin, 1872)

Pokorny, Julius, *Indogermanisches Etymologisches Wörterbuch* (Bern, 1959)

Powell, T.G.E., *The Celts* (London, 1958)

Price, Glanville, ed, *The Celtic Connection* (London, 1992)

Raftery, Barry, *Pagan Celtic Ireland* (London, 1994)

Ramm, Herman, *The Parisi* (London, 1978)

Rankin, David, *Celts and the Classical World* (London, 1987)

Rasmussen, Detlef, *Caesar* (Darmstadt, 1967)

Richter, Michael, *Ireland and her Neighbours in the Seventh Century* (New York, 1999)

Rivet, A.L.F., *Town and Country in Roman Britain* (London, 1964)

    Gallia Narbonensis (London, 1988)

Rivet, A.L.F. / Smith, Colin, *The Place-Names of Roman Britain* (London, 1979)

Ross, Anne, *Pagan Celtic Britain* (London, 1967)

Roussel, Petrus, *Inscriptiones Graecae, XI, Fasc 4* (Berlin, 1914)

Salmon, Edward T., *A History of the Roman World* (London, 1968)

Salway, Peter, *Roman Britain* (Oxford, 1981)

Savory, H.N., *Spain and Portugal: The Prehistory of the Iberian Peninsula* (London, 1968)

Schmidt, Karl H., (a) = *Die festlandkeltischen Sprachen* (Innsbruck, 1977)
       (b) = ed, *Indogermanisch und Keltisch* (Wiesbaden, 1977)
Schmidt, K.H. / Ködderitzch, R., eds, *History and Culture of the Celts* (Heidelberg, 1986)
Schulten, Adolf, *Die Keltiberer und ihre Kriege mit Rom* (Munich, 1914)
        Geschichte von Numantia (Munich, 1933)
        Los Cantabros y Astures y su guerra con Roma (Madrid, 1942)
Simón, Francisco Marco, *Die Religion im keltischen Hispanien* (Budapest, 1998)
Skene, W.F., *Chronicles of the Picts and Scots* (Edinburgh, 1867)
        Celtic Scotland, 1 (Edinburgh, 1886)
Smyth, Alfred P, *Scandinavian York and Dublin, 2* (Dublin, 1979)
Snyder, Christopher A., *An Age of Tyrants* (Pennsylvania, 1998)
Stähelin, Felix, *Geschichte der kleinasiatischen Galater* (Leipzig, 1907)
Stenton, F.M., *Anglo-Saxon England* (Oxford, 1947)
Sveinsson, Einar Ó, *Brennu-Njáls Saga* (Reykjávik, 1954)
Szabó, Miklós, *The Celtic Heritage in Hungary* (Budapest, 1971)
Thomas, Charles, *Christianity in Roman Britain* (London, 1981)
Tierney, J.J., 'The Celtic Ethnography of Posidonius' in *Proceedings of the Royal Irish Academy*
        60 C5 (1960), 189-275
Todd, James H., *The War of the Gaedhil with the Gaill* (Dublin, 1967)
Todd, Malcolm, *Roman Britain* (London, 1981)
Todorovic, Jovan, *Kelti na tlu Beograda* (Belgrade, 1968)
        Skordisci (Novi Sad, 1974)
Tovar, Antonio, *The Ancient Languages of Spain and Portugal* (New York, 1961)
Tovar, A. / Faust, M. / Fischer, F. / Koch, Michael, *Actas del II Coloquio sobre Lenguas y*
        Culturas Prerromanas de la Peninsula Iberica (Salamanca, 1979)
Twist, Clint, *Atlas of the Celts* (London, 2001)
Ua Riain, Eoin, *Féil-sgríbhinn Eoin Mhic Néill* (Dublin, 1940)
Villemarqué, Hesart de la, *Barzaz-Breiz* (Paris, 1903)
Vries, Jan de, *Keltische Religion* (Stuttgart, 1961)
Wainwright, F.T., ed. *The Problem of the Picts* (Edinburgh, 1955)
Wakelin, Martyn F., *Language and History of Cornwall* (Leicester, 1975)
Walde, A. / Pokorny, J., *Vergleichendes Wörterbuch der Indogermanischen Sprachen 1 -2* (Berlin,
        1927-1930)
Whatmough, Joshua, *The Dialects of Ancient Gaul* (Harvard, 1970)
Wightman, Edith M., *Roman Trier and the Treveri* (London, 1970)
        Gallia Belgica (London, 1985)
Wikander, Stig, *Der arische Männerbund* (Lund, 1938)
Wilkes, John J., *Dalmatia* (London, 1969)
        The Illyrians (Oxford, 1992)
Williams, Ifor, *The Poems of Taliesin* (Dublin, 1968)
        Armes Prydein (Dublin, 1972)
Winbolt, Samuel E., *Britain under the Romans* (Middlesex, 1945)
Wissowa, Georg / Kroll, Wilhelm / Witter, Kurt, *Paulys Real-Encyclopädie der Classischen
Altertumswissenschaft* (Stuttgart, 1894-1937) – Series 1 [A-R], Series 2 [S-Z]
Woolf, Greg, *Becoming Roman: the Origins of Provincial Civilization in Gaul* (Cambridge, 1998)
Wozniak, Zenon, *Osadnictwo celtyckie w Polsce* (Wroclaw, 1970)

INDEX